W9-AFN-881

MAO'S GREAT FAMINE

The Age of Openness: China before Mao

Exotic Commodities: Modern Objects and Everyday Life in China

Narcotic Culture: A History of Drugs in China

Crime, Punishment and the Prison in Modern China

Imperfect Conceptions: Eugenics in China

Sex, Culture and Modernity in China

The Discourse of Race in Modern China

MAO'S GREAT FAMINE

THE HISTORY OF CHINA'S MOST DEVASTATING CATASTROPHE, 1958–1962

FRANK DIKÖTTER

Walker & Co.
New York

Published by Walker Publishing Company, Inc., New York

All papers used by Walker & Company are natural, recyclable products made
from wood grown in well-managed forests. The manufacturing processes
conform to the environmental regulations of the country of origin.

LIBRARY OF CONGRESS CATALOGING-IN-PUBLICATION DATA.

Dikötter, Frank.
Mao's great famine : the history of China's most devastating
catastrophe, 1958–1962 / Frank Dikötter.
p. cm.
Includes bibliographical references and index.
ISBN 978-0-8027-7768-3
1. Famines—China. 2. Food supply—China. 3. China—
Economic policy—1949–1976. I. Title.
HC430.F3D55 2010
951.05'5—dc22
2010013141

Visit Walker & Company's Web site at www.walkerbooks.com

First U.S. edition 2010

1 3 5 7 9 10 8 6 4 2

Typeset by Hewer Text UK Ltd, Edinburgh
Printed in the United States of America by Worldcolor Fairfield

'Revolution is not a dinner party.'

Mao Zedong

CONTENTS

Preface

Between 1958 and 1962, China descended into hell. Mao Zedong, Chairman of the Chinese Communist Party, threw his country into a frenzy with the Great Leap Forward, an attempt to catch up with and overtake Britain in less than fifteen years. By unleashing China's greatest asset, a labour force that was counted in the hundreds of millions, Mao thought that he could catapult his country past its competitors. Instead of following the Soviet model of development, which leaned heavily towards industry alone, China would 'walk on two legs': the peasant masses were mobilised to transform both agriculture and industry at the same time, converting a backward economy into a modern communist society of plenty for all. In the pursuit of a utopian paradise, everything was collectivised, as villagers were herded together in giant communes which heralded the advent of communism. People in the countryside were robbed of their work, their homes, their land, their belongings and their livelihood. Food, distributed by the spoonful in collective canteens according to merit, became a weapon to force people to follow the party's every dictate. Irrigation campaigns forced up to half the villagers to work for weeks on end on giant water-conservancy projects, often far from home, without adequate food and rest. The experiment ended in the greatest catastrophe the country had ever known, destroying tens of millions of lives.

Unlike comparable disasters, for instance those that took place under Pol Pot, Adolf Hitler or Joseph Stalin, the true dimensions of what happened during the Great Leap Forward remain little known. This is because access to the party archives has long been restricted to all but the most trusted historians backed up with party credentials. But a new archive law has recently opened up vast quantities of archival material to professional historians, fundamentally changing the way one can study the Maoist era. This book is based on well over a thousand archival documents, collected over several years in dozens of party archives, from the Ministry of Foreign Affairs in Beijing and large provincial collections in Hebei, Shandong, Gansu, Hubei, Hunan, Zhejiang, Sichuan, Guizhou, Yunnan and Guangdong to smaller but equally invaluable collections in cities and counties all over China. The material includes secret reports from the Public Security Bureau, detailed minutes of top party meetings, unexpurgated versions of important leadership speeches, surveys of working conditions in the countryside, investigations into cases of mass murder, confessions of leaders responsible for the deaths of millions of people, inquiries compiled by special teams sent in to discover the extent of the catastrophe in the last stages of the Great Leap Forward, general reports on peasant resistance during the collectivisation campaign, secret opinion surveys, letters of complaint written by ordinary people and much more.

What comes out of this massive and detailed dossier transforms our understanding of the Great Leap Forward. When it comes to the overall death toll, for instance, researchers so far have had to extrapolate from official population statistics, including the census figures of 1953, 1964 and 1982. Their estimates range from 15 to 32 million excess deaths. But the public security reports compiled at the time, as well as the voluminous secret reports collated by party committees in the last months of the Great Leap Forward, show how inadequate these calculations are, pointing instead at a catastrophe of a much greater magnitude: this book shows that at least 45 million people died unnecessarily between 1958 and 1962.

The term 'famine', or even 'Great Famine', is often used to describe these four to five years of the Maoist era, but the term fails to capture the many ways in which people died under radical collectivisation. The blithe use of the term 'famine' also lends support to the widespread view that these deaths were the unintended consequence of half-baked and poorly executed economic programmes. Mass killings are not usually associated with Mao and the Great Leap Forward, and China continues to benefit from a more favourable comparison with the devastation usually associated with Cambodia or the Soviet Union. But as the fresh evidence presented in this book demonstrates, coercion, terror and systematic violence were the foundation of the Great Leap Forward. Thanks to the often meticulous reports compiled by the party itself, we can infer that between 1958 and 1962 by a rough approximation 6 to 8 per cent of the victims were tortured to death or summarily killed – amounting to at least 2.5 million people. Other victims were deliberately deprived of food and starved to death. Many more vanished because they were too old, weak or sick to work – and hence unable to earn their keep. People were killed selectively because they were rich, because they dragged their feet, because they spoke out or simply because they were not liked, for whatever reason, by the man who wielded the ladle in the canteen. Countless people were killed indirectly through neglect, as local cadres were under pressure to focus on figures rather than on people, making sure they fulfilled the targets they were handed by the top planners.

A vision of promised abundance not only motivated one of the most deadly mass killings of human history, but also inflicted unprecedented damage on agriculture, trade, industry and transportation. Pots, pans and tools were thrown into backyard furnaces to increase the country's steel output, which was seen as one of the magic markers of progress. Livestock declined precipitously, not only because animals were slaughtered for the export market but also because they succumbed en masse to disease and hunger – despite extravagant schemes for giant piggeries that would bring meat to every table. Waste developed because raw resources and supplies were poorly allocated, and because factory bosses deliberately bent the rules to increase output. As everyone cut corners in the relentless pursuit of higher output, factories spewed out inferior goods that accumulated uncollected by railway sidings. Corruption seeped into the fabric of life, tainting everything from soy sauce to hydraulic dams. The transportation system creaked to a halt before collapsing altogether, unable to cope with the demands created by a command economy. Goods worth hundreds of millions of yuan accumulated in canteens, dormitories and even on the streets, a lot of the stock simply rotting or rusting away. It would have been difficult to design a more wasteful system, one in which grain was left uncollected by dusty roads in the countryside as people foraged for roots or ate mud.

The book also documents how the attempt to leap into communism resulted in the greatest demolition of property in human history – by far outstripping any of the Second World War bombing campaigns. Up to 40 per cent of all housing was turned into rubble, as homes were pulled down to create fertiliser, to build canteens, to relocate villagers, to straighten roads, to make room for a better future or simply to punish their occupants. The natural world did not escape unscathed either. We will never know the full extent of forest coverage lost during the Great Leap Forward, but a prolonged and intense attack on nature claimed up to half of all trees in some provinces. The rivers and waterways suffered too: throughout the country dams and canals, built by hundreds of millions of farmers at great human and economic cost, were for the greatest part rendered useless or even dangerous, resulting in landslides, river silting, soil salinisation and devastating inundations.

The significance of the book thus is by no means confined to the famine. What it chronicles, often in harrowing detail, is the near collapse of a social and economic system on which Mao had staked his prestige. As the catastrophe unfolded, the Chairman lashed out at his critics to maintain his position as the indispensable leader of the party. After the famine came to an end, however, new factional alignments appeared that were strongly opposed to the Chairman: to stay in power he had to turn the country upside down with the Cultural Revolution. The pivotal event in the history of the People's Republic of China was the Great Leap Forward. Any attempt to understand what happened in communist China must start by placing it squarely at the very centre of the entire Maoist period. In a far more general way, as the modern world struggles to find a balance between freedom and regulation, the catastrophe unleashed at the time stands as a reminder of how profoundly misplaced is the idea of state planning as an antidote to chaos.

———

The book introduces fresh evidence about the dynamics of power in a one-party state. The politics behind the Great Leap Forward has been studied by political scientists on the basis of official statements, semi-official documents or Red Guard material released during the Cultural Revolution, but none of these censored sources reveals what happened behind closed doors. The full picture of what was said and done in the corridors of power will be known only once the Central Party Archives in Beijing open their doors to researchers, and this is unlikely to happen in the near future. But the minutes of many key meetings can be found in provincial archives, since local leaders often attended the most important party gatherings and had to be kept informed of developments in Beijing. The archives throw a very different light on the leadership: as some of the top-secret meetings come to light, we see the vicious backstabbing and bullying tactics that took place among party leaders in all their rawness. The portrait that emerges of Mao himself is hardly flattering, and is far removed from the public image he so carefully cultivated: rambling in his speeches, obsessed with his own role in history, often dwelling on past slights, a master at using his emotions to browbeat his way through a meeting, and, above all, insensitive to human loss.

We know that Mao was the key architect of the Great Leap Forward, and thus bears the main responsibility for the catastrophe that followed.[1] He had to work hard to push through his vision, bargaining, cajoling, goading, occasionally tormenting or persecuting his colleagues. Unlike Stalin, he did not drag his rivals into a dungeon to have them executed, but he did have the power to remove them from office, terminating their careers – and the many privileges which came with a top position in the party. The campaign to overtake Britain started with Chairman Mao, and it ended when he grudgingly allowed his colleagues to return to a more gradual approach in economic planning a few years later. But he would never have been able to prevail if Liu Shaoqi and Zhou Enlai, the next two most powerful party leaders, had acted against him. They, in turn, whipped up support from other senior colleagues, as chains of interests and alliances extended all the way down to the village – as is documented here for the first time. Ferocious purges were carried out, as lacklustre cadres were replaced with hard, unscrupulous men who trimmed their sails to benefit from the radical winds blowing from Beijing.

But most of all this book brings together two dimensions of the catastrophe that have so far been studied in isolation. We must link up what happened in the corridors of Zhongnanhai, the compound which served as the headquarters of the party in Beijing, with the everyday experiences of ordinary people. With the exception of a few village studies based on interviews, there is simply no social history of the Maoist era, let alone of the famine.[2] And just as the fresh evidence from the archives shows how responsibility for the catastrophe extended far beyond Mao, the profuse documentation which the party compiled on every aspect of daily life under its rule dispels the common notion of the people as mere victims. Despite the vision of social order the regime projected at home and abroad, the party never managed to impose its grand design, encountering a degree of covert opposition and subversion that would have been unheard of in any country with an elected government. In contrast to the image of a strictly disciplined communist society in which errors at the top cause the entire machinery to grind to a halt, the portrait that emerges from archives and interviews is one of a society in disintegration, leaving people to resort to whatever means were available to survive. So destructive was radical collectivisation that at every level the population tried to circumvent, undermine or exploit the master plan, secretly giving full scope to the profit motive that the party tried to eliminate. As famine spread, the very survival of an ordinary person came increasingly to depend on the ability to lie, charm, hide, steal, cheat, pilfer, forage, smuggle, trick, manipulate or otherwise outwit the state. As Robert Service points out, in the Soviet Union these phenomena were not so much the grit that stopped the machinery as the oil that prevented the system from coming to a complete standstill.[3] A 'perfect' communist state could not provide enough incentives for people to collaborate, and without some degree of accommodation of the profit motive it would have destroyed itself. No communist regime would have managed to stay in power for so long without constant infringements of the party line.

Survival depended on disobedience, but the many strategies of survival devised by people at all levels, from farmers hiding the grain to local cadres cooking the account books, also tended to prolong the life of the regime. They became a part of the system. Obfuscation was the communist way of life. People lied to survive, and as a consequence information was distorted all the way up to the Chairman. The planned economy required huge inputs of accurate data, yet at every level targets were distorted, figures were inflated and policies which clashed with local interests were ignored. As with the profit motive, individual initiative and critical thought had to be constantly suppressed, and a permanent state of siege developed.

Some historians might interpret these acts of survival as evidence of 'resistance', or 'weapons of the weak' pitting 'peasants' against 'the state'. But techniques of survival extended from one end of the social spectrum to the other. Just about everybody, from top to bottom, stole during the famine, so much so that if these were acts of 'resistance' the party would have collapsed at a very early stage. It may be tempting to glorify what appears at first sight to be a morally appealing culture of resistance by ordinary people, but when food was finite, one individual's gain was all too often another's loss. When farmers hid the grain, the workers outside the village died of hunger. When a factory employee added sand to the flour, somebody down the line was chewing grit. To romanticise what were often utterly desperate ways of surviving is to see the world in black and white, when in reality collectivisation forced everybody, at one point or another, to make grim moral compromises. Routine degradations thus went hand in hand with mass destruction. Primo Levi, in his memoir of Auschwitz, notes that survivors are rarely heroes: when somebody places himself above others in a world dominated by the law of survival, his sense of morality changes. In *The Drowned and the Saved* Levi called it the grey zone, showing how inmates determined to survive had to stray from their moral values in order to obtain an extra ration. He tried not to judge but to explain, unwrapping layer by layer the operation of the concentration camps. Understanding the complexity of human behaviour in times of catastrophe is one of the aims of this book as well, and the party archives allow us for the first time to get closer to the difficult choices people made half a century ago – whether in the corridors of power or inside the hut of a starving family far away from the capital.

———

The first two parts of the book explain how and why the Great Leap Forward unfolded, identifying the key turning points and charting the ways in which the lives of millions were shaped by decisions taken by a select few at the top. Part 3 looks at the scale of destruction, from agriculture, industry, trade and housing to the natural environment. Part 4 shows how the grand plan was transformed by the everyday strategies of survival by ordinary people to produce something that nobody intended and few could quite recognise. In the cities workers stole, dragged their feet or actively sabotaged the command economy, while in the countryside farmers resorted to a whole repertoire of acts of survival, ranging from eating the grain straight from the fields to taking to the road in search of a better life elsewhere. Others robbed granaries, set fire to party offices, assaulted freight trains and, occasionally, organised armed rebellions against the regime. But the ability of people to survive was very much limited by their position in an elaborate social hierarchy which pitted the party against the people. And some of these people were more vulnerable than others: Part 5 looks at the lives of children, women and the elderly. Finally, Part 6 traces the many ways in which people died, from accidents, disease, torture, murder and suicide to starvation. An Essay on the Sources at the end of the book explains the nature of the archival evidence in more detail.

Chronology

1949:

The Chinese Communist Party conquers the mainland and establishes the People's Republic of China on 1 October. Generalissimo Chiang Kai-shek, the leader of the defeated Guomindang, takes refuge on the island of Taiwan. In December Mao leaves for Moscow to pursue a strategic alliance with the Soviet Union and seek help from Stalin.

October 1950:

China enters the Korean War.

March 1953:

Stalin dies.

Autumn 1955–spring 1956:

Mao, displeased with the slow pace of economic development, pushes for the accelerated collectivisation of the countryside and for huge increases in the production of grain, cotton, coal and steel. His 'Socialist High Tide', also referred to by some historians as the 'Little Leap Forward', produces industrial shortages and famine in parts of the countryside. Zhou Enlai and other economic planners urge a slower pace of collectivisation in the spring of 1956.

February 1956:

Khrushchev denounces Stalin and the cult of personality in a secret speech in Moscow. Criticism of Stalin's disastrous campaign of collectivisation strengthens the position of those opposed to the Socialist High Tide in China. Mao perceives deStalinisation as a challenge to his own authority.

Autumn 1956:

A reference to 'Mao Zedong Thought' is removed from the party constitution, the principle of collective leadership is lauded and the cult of personality is decried. The Socialist High Tide is halted.

October 1956:

Encouraged by deStalinisation, people in Hungary revolt against their own government, forcing Soviet forces to invade the country, crush all opposition and install a new regime with Moscow's backing.

Winter 1956–spring 1957:

Mao, against the wishes of most of his colleagues, encourages a more open political climate with the 'Hundred Flowers' campaign to secure the support of scientists and intellectuals in developing the economy and avoid the social unrest that led to the Soviet invasion of Hungary.

Summer 1957:

The campaign backfires as a mounting barrage of criticism questions the very right of the party to rule. Mao turns around and accuses these critical voices of being 'bad elements' bent on destroying the party. He puts Deng Xiaoping in charge of an anti-rightist campaign, which persecutes half a million people – many of them students and intellectuals deported to remote areas to do hard labour. The party finds unity behind its Chairman.

November 1957:

Mao visits Moscow. Impressed by the Soviet sputnik, the first satellite launched into orbit, he declares that the 'East wind prevails over the west wind.' In response to Khrushchev's announcement that the Soviet Union will outstrip the United States in economic production in fifteen years, he declares that China will overtake Britain in the same period.

Winter 1957–spring 1958:

In a series of party conferences Mao attacks Zhou Enlai and other senior leaders who opposed his economic policy. He promotes his own vision of mass mobilisation and accelerated collectivisation of the countryside, demanding increased agricultural and industrial targets. The slogan 'going all out, aiming high, and achieving more, faster and more economical results' becomes the party line.

Winter 1957–summer 1958:

A campaign of repression targets hundreds of thousands of party members critical of economic policy. Several provincial party leaders are purged and replaced by close followers of Mao. Opposition from within the party is silenced.

Winter 1957–spring 1958:

A massive water-conservancy campaign is launched, marking the start of the 'Great Leap Forward' for hundreds of millions of ordinary villagers compelled to work for weeks on end on remote projects, often without sufficient rest and food.

Summer 1958:

Khrushchev visits Beijing, but tensions appear as Mao decides to shell several islands in the Taiwan Strait without first consulting his Soviet ally, triggering an international crisis with the United States. Moscow is forced to take sides by throwing its weight behind Beijing, proclaiming that an attack on the People's Republic of China would be considered an attack on the Soviet Union.

Summer 1958:

The mass mobilisation of villagers around huge water projects requires much larger administrative units in the countryside, leading to the amalgamation of farm collectives into gigantic people's communes of up to 20,000 households. Everyday life in the communes is run along military lines. Almost everything, including land and labour, is collectivised. Communal dining replaces private kitchens, while children are left in the care of boarding kindergartens. A work-point system is used to calculate rewards, while even money is abolished in some communes. Backyard furnaces are used to melt all sorts of metal objects in order to contribute to the party's escalating steel target. Famine conditions appear in many parts of the country.

November 1958–February 1959:

Mao turns against local cadres who produce inflated targets and promise an imminent transition to communism. He tries to rein in some of the worst abuses of the Great Leap Forward, but continues to push forward with collectivisation. He announces that mistakes made by the party are only 'one finger out of ten'. In order to meet foreign obligations and feed the cities, food procurements in the countryside increase sharply. The famine spreads.

March 1959:

At a Shanghai conference Mao launches a withering attack on senior party members and presses for even higher procurement targets in the countryside, up to a third of all grain, despite widespread famine.

July 1959:

At the Lushan conference Mao denounces Peng Dehuai and other leaders as an 'anti-party clique' for criticising the Great Leap Forward.

Summer 1959–summer 1960:

A campaign of repression is launched against party members who expressed critical views similar to Peng Dehuai and his allies. Tens of millions of villagers die of starvation, disease or torture.

July 1960:

Soviet advisers are withdrawn from China by Khrushchev. Zhou Enlai and Li Fuchun move the trade structure away from the Soviet Union towards the West.

October 1960:

A report on mass starvation in Xinyang, Henan, is handed over to Mao by Li Fuchun.

November 1960:

An emergency directive is issued allowing villagers to keep private plots, engage in sideline occupations, rest for eight hours a day and restore local markets, among other measures designed to weaken the power of the communes over villagers.

Winter 1960–1:

Investigation teams spread over the countryside, bringing to light the full dimensions of the catastrophe. Large quantities of food are imported from the West.

Spring 1961:

Inspection tours by leading party members result in a further retreat from the Great Leap Forward. Liu Shaoqi places the blame for the famine on the shoulders of the party but absolves Mao of all responsibility.

Summer 1961:

The consequences of the Great Leap Forward are discussed at a series of party meetings.

January 1962:

At an enlarged party gathering of thousands of cadres in Beijing, Liu Shaoqi describes the famine as a man-made disaster. Support for Mao wanes. The famine abates, but continues to claim lives in parts of the countryside until the end of 1962.

1966:

Mao launches the Cultural Revolution.

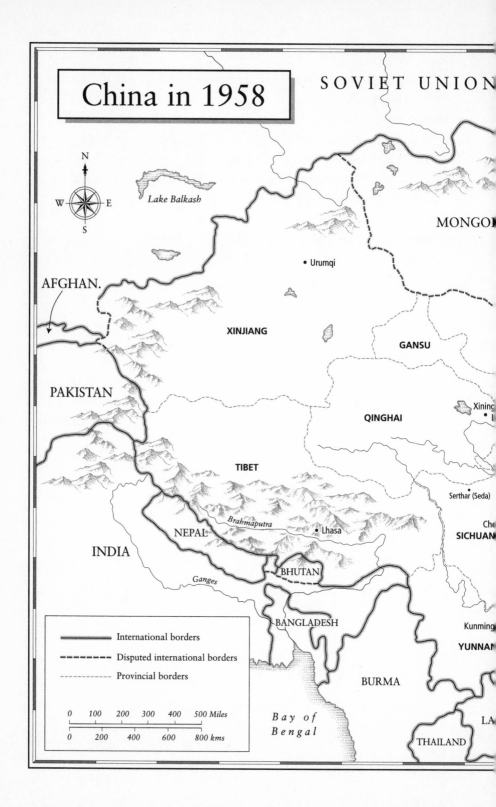

China in 1958

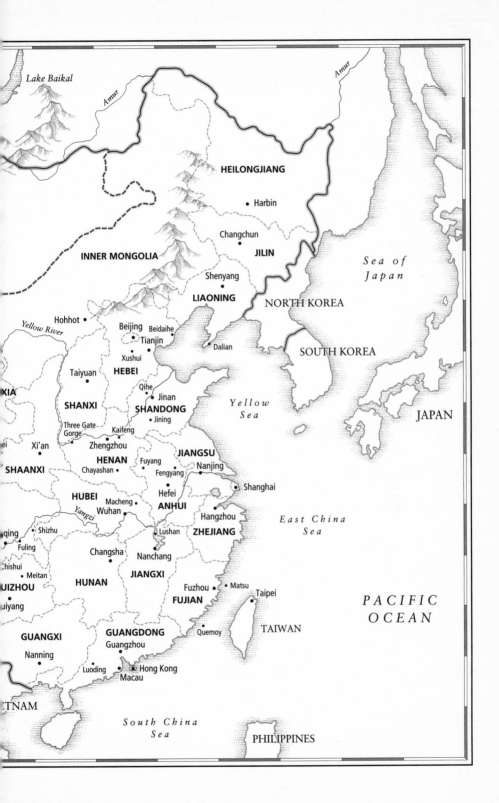

PART ONE

The Pursuit of Utopia

I

Two Rivals

Stalin's death in 1953 was Mao's liberation. For more than thirty years Mao had had to play supplicant to the leader of the communist world. From the age of twenty-seven, when he was handed his first cash payment of 200 yuan by a Soviet agent to cover the cost of travelling to the founding meeting of the Chinese Communist Party in Shanghai, Mao's life was transformed by Russian funds. He had no qualms about taking the money, and used the Moscow link to lead a ragged band of guerrilla fighters to ultimate power – but not without endless reprimands from Moscow, expulsions from office and battles over party policy with Soviet advisers. Stalin constantly forced Mao back into the arms of his sworn enemy Generalissimo Chiang Kai-shek, the leader of the nationalist Guomindang that ruled much of China. Stalin placed little faith in Mao and his peasant soldiers, and openly favoured Chiang, even after the Guomindang had presided over a bloody massacre of communists in Shanghai in 1927. For the best part of a decade Chiang's troops relentlessly hounded an embattled Mao, forcing the communists to find refuge on a mountain base and then to traverse some 12,500 kilometres towards the north in a retreat later known as the Long March. When Chiang was kidnapped in Xi'an in 1936, Stalin promptly sent a telegram ordering Mao to release his hostage unharmed. After Japan had invaded China a year later, Stalin demanded that Mao again form a United Front with his arch enemy Chiang, sending planes, arms and advisers to the Guomindang regime. All Mao got during the Second World War was a planeload of propaganda leaflets.

Instead of confronting the Japanese, Mao strengthened his forces in northern China. At the war's end in 1945 Stalin, always the hard pragmatist, signed a treaty of alliance with the Guomindang, diminishing the prospects of support for the communists in the event of a civil war. Soon after Japan's surrender, full-scale war between the communists and the nationalists resumed. Stalin, again, stayed on the sidelines, even warning Mao to beware the United States, which had sided with Chiang Kai-shek, now recognised as a world leader in the Allies' defeat of Japan. Mao ignored his advice. The communists eventually gained the upper hand. When they reached the capital, Nanjing, the Soviet Union was one of the few foreign countries to permit its ambassador to flee alongside the Guomindang.

Even when victory seemed inevitable, Stalin continued to keep Mao at arm's length. Everything about him seemed suspicious to the Soviet leader. What kind of communist was afraid of workers, Stalin wondered repeatedly, as Mao stopped his army outside Shanghai for weeks on end, unwilling to take on the task of feeding the city? Mao was a peasant, a caveman Marxist, Stalin determined after reading translations of the Chinese leader's writings, which he dismissed as 'feudal'. That there was a rebellious and stubborn streak in Mao was clear; his victory over Chiang Kai-shek, forced to retreat all the way to Taiwan, would have been difficult to explain otherwise. But pride and independence were precisely what troubled Stalin so deeply, prone as he was to seeing enemies everywhere: could this be another Tito, the Yugoslav leader who had been cast out of the communist family for his dissidence against Moscow? Tito was bad enough, and Stalin did not relish the prospect of a regime that had come to power without his help running a sprawling empire right on his border. Stalin trusted no one, least of all a potential rival who in all probability harboured a long list of grievances.

Mao, indeed, never forgot a snub and deeply resented the way he had been treated by Stalin, but he had no one else to turn to for support. The communist regime desperately needed international recognition as well as economic help in rebuilding the war-torn country. Mao declared a policy of 'leaning to one side', swallowing his pride and seeking a rapprochement with the Soviet Union.

Several requests to meet Stalin were rebuffed. Then, in December 1949, Mao was finally asked to come to Moscow. But rather than being welcomed as the leader of a great revolution that had brought a quarter of humanity into the communist orbit, he was given the cold shoulder, treated as one guest among many other delegates who had travelled to Moscow to celebrate Stalin's seventieth birthday. After a brief meeting Mao was whisked off to a dacha outside the capital and left to wait in isolation for several weeks for a formal audience. With every passing day he was made to learn his humble place in a communist brotherhood which revolved entirely around the Soviet dictator. When Mao and Stalin met at last, all he got was $300 million in military aid divided over five years. For this paltry sum Mao had to throw in major territorial concessions, privileges that harked back to the unequal treaties in the nineteenth century: Soviet control of Lüshun (Port Arthur) and of the Chinese Eastern Railway in Manchuria was guaranteed until the mid-1950s. Rights to mineral deposits in Xinjiang, China's westernmost province, also had to be conceded. But Mao did obtain a treaty providing for mutual protection in the event of aggression by Japan or its allies, in particular the United States.

Even before Mao and Stalin had signed the Alliance and Friendship Treaty, Kim Il-sung, the communist guerrilla fighter who seized control of the north of Korea after his country's division in 1948, had been contemplating the reunification of the peninsula by military force. Mao supported North Korea, seeing in Kim a communist ally against the United States. The Korean War broke out in June 1950, but it prompted American intervention in defence of the south. Faced with overwhelming air power and tank battalions, an embattled Kim was pushed back all the way to the Sino-North Korean border. Worried that the Americans might cross the Yalu River and attack China, Mao dispatched volunteers to fight in Korea, having been promised air cover by Stalin. A ferocious war followed, the casualties on the Chinese side all the higher as the planes that Stalin had pledged came only sparingly. When the conflict reached a bloody stalemate, Stalin repeatedly obstructed negotiations to bring it to an end. Peace was not in his strategic interests. To add insult to injury, Stalin also demanded payment from China for the Soviet military equipment he had sent to Korea. His death in March 1953 brought about a rapid armistice.

For thirty years Mao had suffered humiliation at the hands of Stalin, willingly subordinating himself to Moscow out of sheer strategic necessity. The Korean War had made him even more resentful of the Soviet Union's patronage, a feeling widely shared by his fellow leaders who likewise craved a sense of equality in their country's dealings with Moscow.

The Korean War also deepened Mao's hold over his colleagues. The Chairman had led the party to victory in 1949. Korea, too, was his personal glory, as he had pushed for intervention when other leaders in the party had wavered. He was the man who had fought the United States to a stalemate – albeit at a huge cost to his own soldiers. He now towered above his peers. Mao, like Stalin, was incapable of seeing anybody as an equal, and, like Stalin, the Chairman had no doubt about his own role in history. He was sure of his own genius and infallibility.

After Stalin's death Mao finally saw a chance to secure independence from the Kremlin and claim leadership of the socialist camp. The Chairman naturally assumed that he was the leading light of communism, which was about to crush capitalism, making him the historical pivot around which the universe revolved. Had he not led his men to victory, bringing a second October Revolution to a quarter of the world? Stalin could not even claim to have presided over the Bolshevik revolution; still less could Nikita Khrushchev, the man who soon took charge in Moscow.

Coarse, erratic and impulsive, Khrushchev was viewed by many who knew him as an oaf limited in both ability and ambition. It was precisely this reputation which had allowed him to survive under Stalin, who treated him with an affectionate condescension that saved him from the fate of far more impressive colleagues who blundered in their dealings with the dictator. 'My little Marx!' Stalin once mockingly called him, gently tapping his pipe against Khrushchev's forehead and joking, 'It's hollow!'[1] Khrushchev was Stalin's pet. But he was as paranoid as Stalin, and underneath deceptive clumsiness was a cunning and hugely ambitious man.

Khrushchev was scathing of Stalin's handling of Mao, and resolved to outdo his former master by putting relations with Beijing on a new footing. He would be Mao's benevolent tutor, steering the peasant rebel towards a more enlightened form of Marxism. Khrushchev also played the role of beneficent patron, presiding over a massive transfer of technology as hundreds of factories and plants were financed with Soviet aid. Advisers in every domain, from atomic energy to mechanical engineering, were sent to China, while some 10,000 Chinese students were trained in the Soviet

Union in the first years following Stalin's death. But instead of showing gratitude, leaders in Beijing saw this largesse as their due, seeking to extract ever greater amounts of economic and military support through a mixture of bargaining, begging and cajoling. Khrushchev gave in. Having over-played his hand, he had to bully his colleagues in Moscow into accepting an aid package that far outstripped what the Soviet Union could afford.

Khrushchev went out on a limb to satisfy Beijing, and he expected a lot in return. Mao instead treated him with contempt, locking the man into the role of the boorish, immature upstart from which he had been so keen to escape. The key turning point came in 1956, when Khrushchev denounced the crimes of his former master in a secret report delivered at a party congress – without consulting Mao. The Chairman praised this speech, as he sensed that it would weaken Moscow's authority within the communist bloc. But he would never forgive Khrushchev, as he also saw deStalinisation as a challenge to his own authority, accustomed as he was to interpreting the world with himself at its centre. To diminish Stalin was to undermine Mao, who constantly compared himself to the Soviet dicta-tor, despite bearing a long list of grievances against him. Mao also thought that he alone occupied a moral position lofty enough to impart judgement on Stalin's mistakes and achievements. An attack on Stalin, furthermore, could only play into the hands of the Americans.

Above all, the move against Stalin implied that criticism of Mao was also permissible. Khrushchev's secret speech gave ammunition to those who feared the Chairman's growing power and wanted a return to collective leadership. At the Eighth Party Congress in Beijing in September 1956, a reference to 'Mao Zedong Thought' was removed from the party consti-tution, the principle of collective leadership was lauded and the cult of personality was decried. Constrained by Khrushchev's secret report, Mao had little choice but to go along with these measures, to which he contrib-uted himself in the months prior to the congress.[2] But the Chairman felt slighted and did not hide his anger in private.[3]

Mao encountered another setback when his economic policy, known as the 'Socialist High Tide', was halted in late 1956, at the second plenum of the party congress. A year earlier an impatient Mao, displeased with the slow pace of economic development, had repeatedly criticised those who favoured a more cautious tempo as 'women with bound feet'. He prophesied a leap in agricultural output brought about by the accelerated collectivisation of the countryside, and in January 1956 called for unrealistic increases in the production of grain, cotton, coal and steel. The Socialist High Tide – later referred to by some historians as the 'Little Leap Forward' – rapidly ran into trouble.[4] Industrial production in the cities suffered from all sorts of shortages and bottlenecks, as the required funds and raw materials for increased output were unavailable. In the countryside, collectivisation was met with widespread resistance as farmers slaughtered their animals and hid the grain. Famine appeared in some provinces by the spring of 1956. Trying to control the damage created by the shock tactics of their Chairman, premier Zhou Enlai and economic planner Chen Yun called for an end to 'rash advance' (*maojin*) and tried to reduce the size of collective farms, revert to a limited free market and allow greater scope for private production in the countryside. Frustrated, Mao saw this as a personal challenge. Atop a June 1956 editorial of the *People's Daily* criticising the Socialist High Tide for 'attempting to do all things overnight', forwarded to him for his attention, Mao angrily scrawled, 'I will not read this.' Later he wondered, 'Why should I read something that abuses me?'[5] His position was furthered weakened because Khrushchev, in his secret speech, had highlighted the failure of Stalin's agricultural policies, which included collectivisation of the countryside. Criticism of Stalin looked like an unintended assessment of Mao's drive towards collectivisation. The Eighth Party Congress scrapped the Socialist High Tide.

More humiliation followed after Mao, despite major reservations from other party leaders, encouraged open criticism of the party in the Hundred Flowers campaign launched in April 1957. His hope was that, by calling on ordinary people to voice their opinions, a small number of rightists and counter-revolutionaries would be uncovered. This would prevent the havoc created by deStalinisation in Hungary, where a nationwide revolt against the communist party in October 1956 had forced Soviet forces to invade the country, brutally crush all opposition and install a new government with Moscow's backing. In China, Mao explained to his reluctant colleagues, the party would break up any opposition into many small 'Hungarian incidents', all to be dealt with separately.[6] A more open climate, he surmised, would also help secure the support of scientists and intellectuals in developing the economy. The Chairman badly miscalculated, as the mounting barrage of criticism he had produced questioned not only the very right of the party to rule, but also his own leadership. His response was to accuse these critics of being 'bad elements' bent on destroying the party. He put Deng Xiaoping in charge of the anti-rightist campaign, which was carried out with extraordinary vehemence, targeting half a million people – many of them students and intellectuals deported to remote areas to do hard labour. Mao struggled to regain control, and the whole affair was a huge embarrassment, but his strategy was partly successful in that it created the conditions in which he could assert his own pre-eminence. Assailed from all sides, its right to rule having been called into question, the party found unity behind its Chairman.

The collapse of the Hundred Flowers campaign in June 1957 also confirmed the Chairman's suspicion that 'rightist conservatism' was the major ideological enemy, and that rightist inertia was behind the current economic stagnation. He wanted to revive the policies of the Socialist High Tide, which had been discredited by an outpouring of criticism from the very experts he had tried to court. If so many of the intellectuals who had the professional skills and scientific knowledge to help with economic development were disaffected, it would be politically unwise to base the country's future on their expertise. This view was shared by Liu Shaoqi, the party's second-in-command, and he rallied behind the Chairman in pushing for higher targets in rural production.[7] In October 1957, with support from Liu, Mao had the slogan which crystallised his vision reinstated: 'Greater, Faster, Better and More Economical'. He also managed to replace the term 'rash advance' (*maojin*), with its connotations of reckless hurling forward, with 'leap forward' (*yuejin*): in the midst of a ferocious anti-rightist campaign, few party leaders dared to oppose it. Mao was having his way, and he was ready to challenge Khrushchev.

2

The Bidding Starts

On 4 October 1957 a shiny steel sphere the size of a beach ball hurtled through the sky, reached its orbit and then started circling the globe at about 29,000 kilometres per hour, emitting signals that radio operators around the world picked up. Taking the United States completely by surprise, the Soviet Union had successfully launched the world's first earth satellite, opening a new chapter in the space race that was met with both awe and fear. To hurl an 84-kilo satellite into orbit, observers noted, a rocket engine as powerful as an intercontinental ballistic missile was required, which meant that the Russians could also launch atomic bombs that would reach the United States. A month later a much heavier satellite whirled overhead, carrying the first living creature to travel around the earth through space: dressed in a custom-made space suit, a little dog called Laika made history as the passenger in *Sputnik II*.

In a bold move, Khrushchev inaugurated an era of missile diplomacy, backed up by ceaseless propaganda from Moscow about successful experiments with intercontinental ballistic missiles. The second satellite launch was designed to coincide with the fortieth anniversary of the October Revolution, to be celebrated in Red Square in the presence of thousands of communist party leaders invited from all over the world.

Yet, despite the triumph of the satellite launches, Khrushchev was in a vulnerable position. Less than half a year earlier he had barely survived an attempted coup against him by Stalinist hardliners Molotov, Malenkov and Kaganovich. Marshal Zhukov, a Second World War hero who had led the final assault on Germany and captured Berlin, used army transport planes to rush key allies to Moscow in defence of his boss. But Zhukov commanded an army, and could just as well throw his tanks against

Khrushchev. Ever fearful of a military coup, the Soviet leader manoeu-
vred to have Zhukov deposed in early November. Justifying the purge of
Molotov, Malenkov and Kaganovich, now referred to as an 'anti-party
group', was one thing, but how could he explain the removal of the most
decorated Soviet general to his foreign guests, who were already trauma-
tised by his secret speech and the Hungarian revolt? Josip Tito, the fiercely
independent leader of Yugoslavia who refused to take orders from the
Soviet Union, was another potential source of opposition that could mar
the anniversary. In mid-October he objected to a Soviet draft declaration
to be published at the Moscow meeting of party leaders and declined to
attend the event.

Khrushchev found a key ally in Mao, despite their differences on foreign
policy and ideology. Mao, in turn, had good reason to help his rival. He had
badgered the Soviet leader repeatedly for assistance in acquiring nuclear
weapons. Ever since the United States had started to provide military
support for Taiwan, and after the Americans introduced tactical nuclear
missiles in March 1955, Mao had been set on having the bomb. Now, on
the eve of the international summit, Khrushchev shored up support by
signing a secret agreement with China on 15 October, providing for the
delivery of a Soviet atom bomb by 1959.[1]

Mao was ebullient. He knew that his moment had come. Khrushchev
depended on him, and lavished the Chairman and his entourage with
attention. Two Tu-104s were sent to fly the Chinese delegation to Moscow.
The Soviet leader, flanked by some of the most senior party bosses, warmly
greeted Mao at Vnukovo airport and personally escorted him to his quarters. China was the only delegation out of all sixty-four attending the
conference to be housed in the Great Kremlin Palace.

Mao was put up in Empress Catherine's private quarters, which were
upholstered in damask and the ceiling painted with foliate volutes. The
entire west wing was extravagantly furnished, with tall columns topped
by bronze capitals, walls draped in water silk or panelled in walnut, gilded
stucco on vaults and thick carpets throughout. Mao seemed oblivious to it
all and used his own chamber pot.[2]

On 7 November came the public climax of the anniversary gala: as Mao
stood next to Khrushchev on top of the Lenin mausoleum to review the

four-hour parade through Red Square, the Soviet armed forces showed off their new weapons. People waved Chinese flags and shouted 'Long live Mao and China!'

Despite all the privileges accorded Mao, he enjoyed carping about his hosts. He disparaged the food and was scornful of Russian culture, condescending to other party delegates and aloof with Khrushchev. 'Look at how differently they're treating us now,' he quipped to his doctor with a smile of disdain. 'Even in this communist land, they know who is powerful and who is weak. What snobs!'[3]

But he delivered the crucial support on which Khrushchev counted. On 14 November, in front of all party delegates, he pronounced: 'We are so many people here, with so many parties, we must have a head . . . If the Soviet Union is not the head, then who is? Should we do it by alphabetical order? Albania? Vietnam with comrade Ho Chi Minh? Another country? China does not qualify to be the head, we do not have enough experience. We know about revolution, but not about socialist construction. Demographically we are a huge country, but economically we are small.'[4]

But if Mao gave his showpiece pledge of allegiance, he had also come to Moscow to show that he, rather than Khrushchev, was the true senior eminence of the communist camp. He missed few opportunities to diminish the Soviet leader, even telling him to his face that he had a bad temper which offended people.[5] Two days later, on 18 November, came the moment he had been anticipating. Brushing aside the conference protocol with an impromptu speech, Mao addressed the delegates from his seat, invoking his poor health for his refusal to stand up. As Khrushchev later recollected in his memoirs, Mao thought himself a cut above the rest.[6] In a long and rambling monologue, the Chairman turned to Khrushchev, offering him advice as if speaking to a pupil: 'No matter who, everyone needs support . . . There is a Chinese saying that while there is beauty in a lotus it needs the support of its green leaves. You, comrade Khrushchev, even though you are a lotus, you too need to be supported by leaves.' As if this was not cryptic enough, Mao then declared that the showdown between Khrushchev and the Stalinist hardliners in June 1957 had been a 'struggle between two lines: one was erroneous and the other relatively correct'. Was this to be understood as faint praise or as a veiled barb? It was certainly lost on the translator, who muttered something vague about 'two different groups' in which one 'tendency led by Khrushchev won the day'. What exactly Mao said, the Yugoslav ambassador later recollected, 'nobody except the Chinese knew', but it produced a deathly silence.[7] Further embarrassing his host, Mao then went on to describe Molotov, one of the chief plotters of the June coup, as 'an old comrade with a long history of struggle'.[8]

The core of Mao's speech was more frightening to his Russian hosts. 'There are two winds in the world, an east wind and a west wind. We have a saying in China that if the east wind does not prevail over the west wind, then the west wind prevails over the east wind. I think that the key point of the international situation right now is that the east wind prevails over the west wind, that is to say that the forces of socialism have become overwhelmingly superior to the forces of capitalism.'

Mao continued with a review of the changing balance of power between the two camps, and then shocked party delegates with his musings about an impending world war.[9] 'Let us imagine how many people would die if war breaks out. There are 2.7 billion people in the world, and a third could be lost. If it is a little higher it could be half . . . I say that if the worst came to the worst and one-half dies, there will still be one-half left, but imperialism would be erased and the whole world would become socialist. After a few years there would be 2.7 billion people again.'[10] The United States was nothing but a 'paper tiger', Mao continued, seemingly immune to the loss of life he was contemplating. He was bluffing, on this occasion and on others like it, but the point of all the sabre-rattling was to show that he, not Khrushchev, was a more determined revolutionary.

Mao not only totted up population figures for his audience. For some time, he had been carefully following Khrushchev's push for a decentralisation of the economy and his undermining of desk-bound bureaucrats in Moscow in order to transfer power instead to new economic regional councils supervised by his own local henchmen. Khrushchev had crisscrossed the countryside lecturing peasants on how to increase agricultural yields: 'You must plant potatoes in square clusters. You must grow cabbage as my grandmother did.'[11] He was scathing about economists with fancy pedigrees who were 'arithmetically' correct but failed to understand what the Soviet people were capable of: 'Let the ideologists of the capitalist world go on prattling for too long a time. Let the comrade economists blush. Sometimes man must exceed his own strength by making a sudden spurt.'[12] And that sudden spurt, created by freeing the farmers from the dead hand of the Stalinist state, would create such abundance that even the United States would be overtaken economically: when 'people come to know their own strength, they create miracles'. In May 1957 Khrushchev had crowed that within the next few years the Soviet Union would catch up with the United States in per-capita production of meat, milk and butter.[13] Now, in Moscow, in front of foreign party delegates, Khrushchev proclaimed the success of his economic drive in his keynote address to celebrate the October Anniversary: 'Comrades, the calculations of our planners show that, within the next fifteen years, the Soviet Union will be able not only to catch up with but also to surpass the present volume of output of important products in the USA.'[14]

Mao wasted no time. He publicly took up the challenge and immediately announced that China would outstrip Britain – then still considered a major industrial power – within fifteen years: 'This year our country has 5.2 million tonnes of steel, and after five years we can have 10 to 15 million tonnes; after a further five years 20 to 25 million tonnes, then add five more years and we will have 30 to 40 million tonnes. Maybe I am bragging here, and maybe when we have another international meeting in future you will criticise me for being subjective, but I speak on the strength of considerable evidence . . . Comrade Khrushchev tells us that the Soviet Union will overtake the United States in fifteen years. I can tell you that in fifteen years we may well catch up with or overtake Britain.'[15] The Great Leap Forward had begun.

3

Purging the Ranks

In Moscow, Khrushchev had provided Mao with the ammunition to charge ahead. Not only had the sputnik demonstrated the ability of the relatively backward Soviet Union to take a lead over an economically advanced nation like the United States, but Soviet planners themselves were preparing a major economic drive similar to the Socialist High Tide the Chairman had been forced to abandon.

Back in Beijing, less than two weeks after his return from the Soviet Union, Mao secured the backing of senior vice-chairman Liu Shaoqi for a leap forward. A frugal and taciturn man, tall but slightly stooped with greying hair, Liu had dedicated his career to the party line, regularly toiling away through the night. He also saw himself as the Chairman's successor, a position he believed would come to him as a reward for years of hard and selfless work. A few months earlier Mao himself had indicated his intention of stepping down from the post of head of state, and may even have privately assured Liu that he supported him in his role as heir apparent.[1] Liu embraced Mao's vision: 'In fifteen years, the Soviet Union can catch up with and surpass the United States in the output of the most important industrial and agricultural products. In the same period of time, we ought to catch up with and overtake Britain in the output of iron, steel and other major industrial products.'[2] Before the end of the year press articles heralding great advances in water conservancy, grain production and steel output appeared all over the country. On New Year's day in 1958 the *People's Daily* published an editorial approved by Liu Shaoqi which captured the leader's vision: 'Go All Out and Aim High'.[3]

Li Fuchun, a bookish man with a self-effacing air who as head of the State Planning Commission regularly sent blueprints as thick as a telephone book to each province, detailing how much of each product should be produced, also lent his support to Mao. A fellow Hunanese and childhood acquaintance of the Chairman, a veteran of the Long March, Li was the first among the economic planners to jump on to the bandwagon of the Great Leap Forward, whether out of fear, conviction or ambition. He joined Liu Shaoqi in praising Mao's bold vision.[4]

Under the drumbeat of propaganda, and goaded and coaxed by Mao in private meetings and party conferences, provincial leaders threw their weight behind his go-all-out campaign, promising higher targets in a whole range of economic activities. At a small gathering of party bosses in Hangzhou in early January 1958, Ke Qingshi, a tall man with a bouffant haircut who was mayor of Shanghai and lived in genuine awe of the Chairman, enthused about the 'new high tide in socialist construction', proposing that the country 'ride the wind and break the waves' by relying on the great masses.[5] Surrounded by supporters, and energised by Ke Qingshi, Mao was no longer able to contain the anger pent up over several years, exploding in the face of Bo Yibo, one of the chief economic planners who had resisted his vision. Bo was a veteran revolutionary, but one of his concerns was to keep a balanced budget. 'I will not listen to that stuff of yours!' Mao yelled. 'What are you talking about? For the past few years I have stopped reading the budgets, but you just force me to sign off on them anyway.' Then he turned to Zhou Enlai: 'The preface to my book *The Socialist Upsurge in the Countryside* has had a tremendous influence on the entire country. Is that a "cult of personality" or "idolatry"? Regardless, newspapers and magazines all over the country have reprinted it, and it's had a huge impact. So now I have really become the "arch criminal of rash advance!" '[6] The moment had come to crack the whip and herd the planners on to the road to utopia.

———

Situated in the extreme south of the country, Nanning is known as the 'green city' because of its lush, subtropical climate, mild enough for sweet peach, betel nut and palm trees to thrive all the year round. With citrus trees in blossom and a balmy temperature of 25 degrees Celsius in the middle of January, the setting should have provided some relief for party leaders coming from wintry Beijing, but the atmosphere was tense. As Zhang Zhongliang, the zealous leader of Gansu province, enthused, 'From start to finish the Chairman criticised rightist conservative thinking!'[7] Mao set the tone on the opening day of the meeting: 'Don't mention this term "opposition to rash advance" again, all right? This is a political problem. Any opposition would lead to disappointment, and 600 million discouraged people would be a disaster.'[8]

Over several days Mao repeatedly lost his temper as he badgered the planners, accusing them of 'pouring cold water on the enthusiasm of the people' and holding back the country. Those guilty of opposing 'rash advance' were a mere 'fifty metres away from the rightists'. Wu Lengxi, editor of the *People's Daily* which had published the critical editorial on 20 June 1956, was at the very top of the list of leaders summoned by Mao. The Chairman's verdict: 'Vulgar Marxism, vulgar dialectics. The article seems to be anti-leftist as well as anti-rightist, but in fact it is not anti-rightist at all but exclusively anti-leftist. It is sharply pointed against me.'[9]

Huge pressure was applied to the assembled leaders, and even for hardened men accustomed to the rigours of party life the stress was soon to prove too much. Huang Jing, chairman of a commission responsible for technological development and former husband of Mao's wife, collapsed after the Chairman took him to task. Lying in bed, staring at the ceiling and mumbling incomprehensibly, he gave the doctor a bewildered look, begging for forgiveness: 'Save me, save me!' Put on a plane for medical treatment, he fell to his knees to kowtow before Li Fuchun, who was accompanying him to Guangzhou. Placed in a military hospital, he jumped through a window and broke a leg. He died in November 1958 aged forty-seven.[10]

But the real target for Mao's ire was Zhou Enlai. On 16 January Mao brandished in front of the premier a copy of Ke Qingshi's 'The New Shanghai Rides the Wind and Breaks the Waves, Accelerating the Construction of Socialism'. 'Well, Enlai, you are the premier, do you think you could write anything as good?' he asked scornfully. 'I couldn't,' the premier muttered, straining to absorb the attack. Then, after the ritual of public humiliation, came the blow: 'Aren't you opposed to "rash advance"? Well, I am opposed to opposition to "rash advance"!'[11] A number of leftist party leaders joined the fray. Ke Qingshi and Li Jingquan, the radical leader of Sichuan, tore into the premier.[12] Three days later Zhou made a lengthy speech of self-criticism, taking full responsibility for the reversal in 1956, admitting that it was the result of 'rightist conservative thinking' and accepting that he had deviated from the Chairman's guiding policy. Mao's notion that mistakes made by the party should not be overemphasised, being only 'one finger out of ten', was enshrined in the meeting's manifesto, thus marginalising those who had attacked the Little Leap Forward.[13]

Zhou Enlai, whose suave, soft-spoken, slightly effeminate manners made him the ideal choice as China's foreign emissary, had a talent for landing right side up. He could be all modesty and humility when required. Before the communist victory the nationalists used to call him Budaoweng, the Chinese name for the weighted toy tumbler that always lands upright.[14] Early in his career as a revolutionary, Zhou had resolved never to challenge Mao. His decision was made after both had clashed in an incident that had left Mao seething with resentment. At a conference in 1932, critics of guerrilla warfare had ripped into Mao and handed command over the battlefront to Zhou instead. The result was a disaster, as a few years later nationalist troops mauled the Red Army, forcing the communists on the Long March away from their base areas. In 1943, as Zhou realised that Mao's authority had become supreme, he proclaimed his undying support to the Chairman: 'The direction and leadership of Mao Zedong', he declared, 'is the direction of the Chinese Communist Party!' But Mao did not let him off the hook so easily. Zhou's loyalty was tested in a series of self-criticism meetings in which he had to admit to his political crimes, labelling himself a 'political swindler' who lacked principles. It was a gruelling experience in self-abasement, but one from which Zhou emerged as the Chairman's faithful assistant. From here onwards an uneasy and paradoxical alliance developed. Mao had to keep Zhou at bay as a potential contender for power; on the other hand he needed him to run the show. Mao lacked interest in matters of daily routine and organisational detail, and he was often abrasive with other people. Zhou was a first-rate administrator with a knack for organisation, a smooth operator skilled at forging party unity. As one biographer puts it, Mao 'had to draw

Zhou close even as he raised the whip, and sometimes lashed the man he could not live without'.[15]

———————

The whipping did not stop at Nanning. Two months later, in Chengdu, the final days of a party gathering were devoted to rectification seminars. But first Mao spewed disdain on the blind faith with which the planners had been following Stalin's economic path: a heavy emphasis on large industrial complexes, a sprawling apparatus of bureaucrats and a chronically underdeveloped countryside. As early as November 1956 he had lambasted some of his colleagues for 'uncritically thinking that everything in the Soviet Union is perfect, that even their farts are fragrant'.[16] Creative thinking was needed to find China's own path to communism, rather than rigid adherence to Soviet methods, now frozen into socialist dogma. China should 'walk on two legs', simultaneously developing industry and agriculture, tackling heavy as well as light industry. And Mao, as the leader on that road, now demanded full allegiance. 'What is wrong with worship? The truth is in our hands, why should we not worship it? . . . Each group must worship its leader, it cannot but worship its leader,' Mao explained; this was the 'correct cult of personality'.[17] The message was immediately picked up by Ke Qingshi, who quivered enthusiastically: 'We must have blind faith in the Chairman! We must obey the Chairman with total abandon!'[18]

Having consecrated his own cult of personality, Mao handed over the proceedings to Liu Shaoqi, his political crony. While virtually all the participants offered self-criticisms, the situation must have been agonising for Zhou. Both men were intensely competitive, and Liu may have seen Zhou as a threat to his prospects of taking over from the Chairman.[19] That day Liu outdid Zhou in adulation of the leader: 'Over the years I have felt Chairman Mao's superiority. I am unable to keep up with his thought. Chairman Mao has a remarkable knowledge, especially of Chinese history, which no one else in the party can reach. [He] has practical experience, especially in combining Marxist theory and Chinese reality. Chairman Mao's superiority in these aspects is something we should admire and try to learn from.'[20] Zhou, for his part, felt intense pressure to appease the

Chairman, who had stripped him of his authority in economic planning after Nanning. Again, he submitted a long confession about his errors, but his offerings failed to impress Mao.

In May, at a formal party gathering of over 1,300 people, Zhou Enlai and the party's economics tsar Chen Yun were summoned to prepare yet another self-examination. No longer knowing what would satisfy Mao, Zhou spent days in self-imposed isolation, struggling to find the right turn of phrase. After a telephone conversation with Chen Yun, who was in a similar predicament, he sank into such dejection that his mind simply went blank. All he could do was mumble a few words followed by long silences as he stared at his secretary. That evening late at night his wife found him sitting slumped at his desk. Trying to help, the secretary pencilled in a passage about Zhou and Mao having 'shared the boat through many storms'. When Zhou later pored over the document, he angrily rebuked the secretary, tears welling in his eyes, accusing the man of knowing too little about party history.[21] In the end Zhou grovelled, lavishing praise on the Chairman in front of the assembled party leaders and telling the audience that Mao was the 'personification of truth' and that mistakes occurred only when the party became divorced from his great leadership. A few days after this display, Zhou handed Mao a personal letter promising to study his writings earnestly and to follow all his directives. The Chairman was finally satisfied. He declared Zhou and the others to be good comrades. Zhou had saved his job.

During these first months of the Great Leap Forward, Zhou was repeatedly humiliated and demeaned, but he never withdrew his support, choosing instead quietly to accept the Chairman's blistering outburst in Nanning. Zhou Enlai did not have the power to overthrow his master, but he did have the planners behind him, and he could have stepped back – at the cost of his career. But he had learned to accept humiliation at the hands of the Chairman as a way of staying in power, albeit in his colleague's shadow. Zhou was loyal to Mao, and as a result the many skills of the servant went to abet his master.[22] Mao Zedong was the visionary, Zhou Enlai the midwife who transformed nightmares into reality. Always on probation, he would work tirelessly at the Great Leap Forward to prove himself.

As Zhou Enlai was debased in a spectacle of power and humiliation, other top economic officials quickly fell in line. Li Fuchun, chair of the State Planning Commission, never had to resort to self-criticism, having broken ranks with the other planners by rallying round Mao's slogans in December 1957. Chen Yun made several self-critical statements. Li Xiannian, minister of finance, and Bo Yibo, chair of the State Economic Commission, both opponents of the Little Leap Forward in 1956, now realised that they could not resist the tide. None dared to disagree. Li Fuchun and Li Xiannian were enlisted in the secretariat, the inner core of the party, after they had proclaimed their allegiance to Mao.

To increase the political pressure on the top echelon, the Chairman also presided over a shift in power from the centre to the provinces. Nanning was the first in a series of impromptu conferences called by Mao, who strictly controlled the list of participants, set the agendas and dominated the proceedings, allowing him to cajole his followers towards the Great Leap Forward. He brought the secretariat to the provinces, rather than summon the provinces to come to the more formal sessions of established bodies like the State Council in Beijing.[23] By so doing he tapped into a deep current of dissatisfaction among provincial leaders. Tao Lujia, first secretary of Shanxi, spoke for many local cadres when he expressed his impatience with the country's widespread poverty.[24] Mao's vision of a China which was 'poor and blank' resonated with idealists who believed in the party's capacity to catapult the country ahead of its rivals. 'When you are poor you are inclined to be revolutionary. Blank paper is ideal for writing.'[25] Radical provincial leaders lapped up their leader's vision. Wu Zhipu, leader of Henan, heralded a 'continuous revolution' to crush rightist opponents and leap forward. Zeng Xisheng, long-term veteran of the People's Liberation Army and leader of Anhui, provided the slogan 'Battle Hard for Three Years to Change the Face of China'. But most of all, having witnessed the ritual abasement of their superiors on their own turf, the provinces were encouraged to launch their own witch-hunts, as a wind of persecution blew through the country.

Mao could be cryptic, leaving his colleagues guessing at the nature of his message, but this time there was plenty of pressure from Beijing concerning the right direction. To make sure that the purges against rightist elements were carried out thoroughly, Mao sent his bull terrier Deng Xiaoping to a series of regional meetings. Instructions were clear. In Gansu, Deng explained, the struggle against vice-governors Sun Diancai, Chen Chengyi and Liang Dajun had to be unequivocal.[26] Gansu boss Zhang Zhongliang wasted no time, and a few weeks later he announced that an anti-party clique had been uncovered inside the party provincial committee. Coincidentally, its leaders were Sun Diancai, Chen Chengyi and Liang Dajun: they were accused of denying the achievements of the Socialist High Tide in 1956, attacking the party, denigrating socialism and promoting capitalism – among other heinous crimes.[27]

These were powerful leaders toppled with the support of Beijing. The purges, however, were carried out at all levels of the party, silencing most critical voices. Few dared to oppose the party line. In parts of Gansu, a poor province near the deserts of Inner Mongolia, any critical comment about grain procurement or excessive quotas simply became unthinkable. The message to party members concerned about the crop was blunt: 'You should consider carefully whether or not you are rightists.'[28] In Lanzhou University, located in the capital city of Gansu, up to half of all students were given a white flag, the sign of a politically conservative laggard. Some had a note pinned on their back: 'Your father is a white flag.' Others were beaten. Those who took a neutral stand were denounced as reactionaries.[29] The purge continued for as long as Zhang Zhongliang remained in power. By March 1960, some 190,000 people had been denounced and humiliated in public meetings, and 40,000 cadres were expelled from the party, including 150 top provincial officials.[30]

Similar purges took place throughout the country, as radical leaders seized the opportunity to get rid of their more timorous rivals. From December 1957 onwards, the southern province of Yunnan was in the grip of an anti-rightist purge that reached from party seniors down to village cadres. In April 1958 the tough local boss Xie Fuzhi, a short man with a double chin, announced the overthrow of the leaders of an 'anti-party clique': Zheng Dun and Wang Jing, the heads of the Organisation Department, were guilty of 'localism', 'revisionism', advocating capitalism, attempting to overthrow the party's leadership and opposing the socialist revolution.[31] By the summer of 1958 the inquisition had resulted in the removal of some 2,000 party members. One in fifteen top leaders were fired, including more than 150 powerful cadres working at the county level or higher up in one of the province's dozen administrative regions. A further 9,000 party members were labelled as rightists as the campaign unfolded.[32]

'Anti-party' cliques were uncovered almost everywhere. Mao prodded the provincial leaders on. 'Better me than you as dictator,' he declared in March 1958, invoking words from Lenin. 'It's similar in the provinces: is it going to be Jiang Hua or Sha Wenhan as dictator?'[33] In Zhejiang Sha Wenhan was hounded by Jiang Hua, and similar battles took place in Guangdong, Inner Mongolia, Xinjiang, Gansu, Qinghai, Anhui, Liaoning, Hebei and Yunnan, among other provinces.[34] In Henan, one of the provinces that would be most affected by famine, a moderate leader called Pan Fusheng was swept aside by Wu Zhipu, a zealous follower of Mao. Pan had painted a grim picture of collectivisation during the Socialist High Tide. 'The peasants . . . are the same as beasts of burden today. Yellow oxen are tied up in the house and human beings are harnessed in the field. Girls and women pull ploughs and harrows, with their wombs hanging out. Co-operation is transformed into the exploitation of human strength.'[35] Here, it seemed, was a blatant case of a retreat to capitalism, and all of Pan's followers were hunted down, dividing party and village. Scarecrows with slogans appeared along dusty roadsides, reading 'Down with Pan Fusheng' or 'Down with Wu Zhipu'. Most local cadres could see which way the wind was blowing, and fell in line behind Wu Zhipu.[36]

But, however great the pressure, there were always choices to be made. When Mao toured Jiangsu and asked the local leader whether they were fighting the rightists, Jiang Weiqing gathered up his courage and told the Chairman that if there were any bad elements he would have to be counted as their leader. The party should get rid of him first. Mao laughed: 'You don't fear being cut in pieces for pulling the emperor off his horse! Well, just leave it then . . .'[37] As a result, fewer cadres were denounced in Jiangsu than elsewhere.

But rare were those who had the conviction, the courage or the inclination to swim against the tide. The purges percolated down the ranks of the party. Just as Mao imposed his will in Beijing, local overlords laid down the law in their own provinces, denouncing any opposition as 'conservative rightism'. And just as provincial capitals had their hegemons, county leaders and their cronies used the purge to eliminate their rivals. They turned a blind eye on local bullies. On the ground, a world far removed from the utopia envisaged on paper started to emerge.

An early warning sign came in the summer of 1958, as a report circulating among the top brass showed how violence had become the norm during the anti-rightist campaign in Fengxian county, just south of Shanghai. A hundred people committed suicide, many others being worked to death in the fields. Wang Wenzhong, county leader, set the example with a motto that compared 'the masses' to dogs intimidated only by the sight of a stick in a cadre's hands. Thousands of villagers were accused of being 'landlords' or 'counter-revolutionaries' in public meetings that punctuated daily life for months on end. Many were routinely beaten, tied up and tortured, some being carried away to special labour camps set up throughout the county.[38]

Fengxian was a dire warning of the darkness to come. At the top, however, floating far above the ground, faith in the ability of the people to change heaven and earth was boundless. In December 1957 Chen Zhengren, one of Mao's most trusted colleagues, attacked the conservatism of 'rightists' who hampered the enthusiasm of the masses in the water-conservancy campaign. This was the rallying cry of the Great Leap Forward.[39]

4

Bugle Call

A muddy river runs through the heart of China, flowing some 5,500 kilo-metres from the barren mountains in Qinghai to empty in the Bohai Sea, the innermost gulf of the Yellow Sea near Beijing. The upper reaches of the river flow through mountain valleys where the water is clear, but after a series of steep cliffs and gorges it meanders through the dusty loess plateau, picking up the soft, silty sediment left behind over time by wind storms. As mud and sand are further discharged into the river, it turns into a dirty ochre colour. The loess is deposited in the slower sections downstream, caus-ing the river bed to rise. By the time it passes the ancient city of Kaifeng, the river bed runs ten metres above the surrounding fields. When the banks burst, the flat, northern plain is easily inundated, turning the river into one of the most perilous natural hazards on record. Kaifeng itself was flooded, abandoned and rebuilt several times. Ditches and embankments were tradi-tionally used as flood defences but they had little effect, the river carrying an estimated 1.6 billion tonnes of silt annually. 'When the Yellow River flows clear', in Chinese, is the equivalent of the expression 'when pigs fly'.

Another traditional saying heralds the advent of a miraculous leader: 'When a great man emerges, the Yellow River will run clear.' Could Chairman Mao tame the river that flooded so often that it had earned the name 'China's sorrow'? Early propaganda posters showed him sitting pensively on a rock overlooking the river, perhaps pondering ways to clear the water.[1] In 1952, when these photos were taken, Mao had toured the river and uttered a single, somewhat cryptic line: 'Work on the Yellow River must be carried out well.'[2] Heated debates about the scheme ensued among engi-neers while Mao remained on the sidelines, and a faction in favour of a large dam finally prevailed. Soviet experts, themselves enamoured with gigantic projects, surveyed the lower reach and identified the Three Gate Gorge in Henan as a suitable site. A design for a dam setting the normal pool water at 360 metres was delivered in April 1956, meaning that close to a million people would have to be relocated as some 220,000 hectares of land would be submerged. The project was officially launched in April 1957, despite the reservations of several hydraulic engineers. Huang Wanli, an American-trained geologist who had visited every major dam in the United States, argued that dire consequences would follow from the attempt to clear the river of sediment. Blocking dirt and loess behind a giant dam would limit the reservoir's lifespan and eventually lead to disaster. Then Mao intervened. 'What is this trash?' was the angry headline of his editorial published in June 1957 by the *People's Daily*. The article listed a series of charges against Huang, alleging, among other things, that he had attacked the Chairman, harmed the party, propagated bourgeois democracy and admired foreign cultures.[3] All criticism of the Three Gate Gorge Dam was brushed aside.

By the end of 1958 the Yellow River was blocked. Some 6 million square metres of earth had been moved in a pharaonic enterprise involving the labour of tens of thousands of villagers. A year later the dam was ready. The water was clear. But the initial design had provided for several outlets and tubes, allowing accumulated sediment to be flushed through the dam. These had been blocked by reinforced concrete in the haste to complete the project on schedule. Within a year the sediment started inching upstream, raising the waters and threatening to flood the industrial centre of Xi'an. Extensive rebuilding was required to purge the sediment, which in turn caused a drop in the pool level. With a lower waterline the 150,000 kilo-watt turbines, installed at great cost, became completely useless and had to be removed to another site. The water was no longer clear. By 1961 the amount of silt carried by the Yellow River had doubled, Zhou Enlai himself admitted. Up to 95 per cent of a section of the Yellow River west of Zhengzhou consisted of mud.[4] A few years later the area was so silted up that foreigners were banned from visiting the dam.[5]

––––––––––

The term 'Great Leap Forward' was first used in the context of the water-conservancy drive launched towards the end of 1957. Determined to overtake Britain in fifteen years, Mao saw a key to rapid industrialisation in the substitution of labour for capital. The masses were the country's real wealth, and they should be mobilised during the slack winter season, before the spring ploughing, to transform the countryside. If water could be diverted to irrigate the thin topsoil of the many impoverished villages strewn across the arid north, if floods could be contained with giant dykes and reservoirs in the subtropical south, the yield of grain would jump. All over China tens of millions of farmers joined irrigation projects: collectively, so the propaganda went, they could accomplish in a matter of months what their forefathers had done in thousands of years. Some 30 million people were recruited in October 1957. By January one in six people was digging earth in China. More than 580 million cubic metres of rocks and soil were moved before the end of the year.[6] Henan, where the Three Gate Gorge Dam was being built, took the lead, as local boss Wu Zhipu ruthlessly pushed the labour force into grandiose projects designed to impress Beijing. In the region bordering Henan and Anhui, centre of an ambitious 'Harness the Huai River' campaign which would unfold for several decades, more than a hundred dams and reservoirs were built between 1957 and 1959.[7]

In a country in the grip of gigantism, massive irrigation schemes appeared everywhere, although the leadership gave special emphasis to the north-west. Critical voices were few and far between. Mao distrusted intellectuals, and in the summer of 1957 persecuted hundreds of thousands of those who had dared to voice a critical opinion during the Hundred Flowers. But as we have seen in the previous chapter, the purge of party leaders in the anti-rightist campaign from late 1957 onwards was even more effective in removing opposition to the Great Leap Forward.

In Gansu province, for instance, senior leaders such as Sun Diancai and Liang Dajun were denounced as the heads of an 'anti-party' clique and expelled in February 1958. One of the accusations levelled against them was that they had expressed doubts about the speed and extent of the water-conservancy movement: for every 50,000 hectares of irrigated land, they had claimed, a hundred villagers paid with their lives. Their removal from power allowed local boss Zhang Zhongliang to take the lead and respond to the call from Beijing. Some 3.4 million farmers, close to 70 per cent of the Gansu workforce, were deployed on irrigation projects that cut across one of the country's most arid provinces. Many of the villagers were made to build small dams and reservoirs, but these were not enough to satisfy the leadership. Zhang Zhongliang had a more daring vision of the future, one in which a large water highway would tunnel through snow-capped mountains and span deep valleys to provide water to the central and western regions of the province. The Tao River, quite literally, would 'move up the mountains', as it was diverted up the hills before flowing 900 kilometres from the Jiudian Gorges to Qingyang.[8] As clean drinking water would be brought to parched villages across the province, Gansu would be turned into a giant park as lush and green as the Summer Palace in Beijing.[9]

Work started in June 1958, and attracted support from the country's leadership. In September 1958 Marshal Zhu De used his calligraphy to signal the momentous nature of the project. The inscription read: 'Raising the Tao River up the mountains is a pioneering undertaking by the people of Gansu in transforming nature.'[10] But the project was bedevilled by problems from the start. Soil erosion caused frequent landslides, reservoirs filled with silt, rivers turned to mud.[11] Villagers enlisted on the project had to dig caves in the mountains for shelter in the freezing cold of winter, foraging for herbs to supplement a meagre diet of grain.[12] By the summer of 1961 work came to a halt, and in March 1962 the project was abandoned altogether. Total irrigated surface: zero hectares. Cost to the state: 150 million yuan. Number of work days: 600,000. Cost to the people: inestimable. At its peak some 160,000 people had been made to work on the project, and most of these were villagers diverted away from agricultural work. At least 2,400 died, some in accidents, but many more as a result of a brutal regime which forced workers to slave day and night in order to reach ever higher targets.[13] Such was the frenzy with which cadres pushed villagers that Tongwei, an impoverished county in the mountains situated at the heart of the project, would have one of the highest death rates in the country: slow starvation and widespread physical punishment changed this desolate place into a site of horror.

Targets in water conservancy were measured by the number of tonnes of earth a province could move. This magic number – entirely unrelated to the actual usefulness of the projects being undertaken – was then compared nationwide in a spirit of emulation which determined the political clout of a province. Liu Derun, deputy director of the Office of Water Conservancy established specifically to supervise the campaign, later recalled that 'Our daily work consisted of making phone calls to the provinces inquiring about the number of projects they were building, how many people were involved, and how much earth they had moved. With hindsight, some of the data and figures we gathered were obvious exaggerations, but no one back then had the energy to check them out.'[14]

In this campaign the tone was set by Beijing, and in the capital Mao made sure that everybody got involved. Some thirty kilometres north of Beijing, in a serene and sparsely populated valley, defended from the northern winds by several hills, many of the Ming emperors and their wives lay buried in their underground mausoleums. Protected by statues of elephants, camels, horses, unicorns and other mythical beasts, which in turn were followed by human sculptures in a funeral cortège, these emperors were now accused of having built vast palaces for themselves while their subjects were exposed to the torrents rushing down from the bare slopes of the mountains. In January 1958 the soldiers of the People's Liberation Army started work on a reservoir near the tombs. By damming a river in the valley, a regular supply of water would help the people. Shock troops were provided by the army. Work proceeded around the clock, manpower being furnished by factories and institutions from the capital, while the press and the radio brought constant coverage to the public.

The Ming Tombs Reservoir was to be the flagship of the Great Leap Forward, an example to be emulated by the rest of the country. Soon tens of thousands of 'volunteers' from the capital joined the effort, including students, cadres and even foreign diplomats. Work went on in all weathers and proceeded at night by the light of torches, lanterns and pressure lamps. Hardly any machinery was used: the people who turned up were given picks, shovels, baskets and poles to dump the rubble in railway wagons, which were shuttled to the dam where it was ground into gravel. Hewn stone was lifted by block and tackle. Then, on 25 May 1958, Mao appeared in front of the crowds and posed for the photographers with a bamboo pole slung across his shoulders, two buckets filled with earth dangling from the pole.[15] The photos appeared on the front page of every newspaper, galvanising a nation.

Jan Rowinski, a young student from Poland, participated in the building of this reservoir. He and other volunteers were given a pole with two baskets which they filled with rubble, working their way around the track with straw hats for protection against the summer sun. The workers were divided into units of ten with an overseer who reported to a group of a hundred, who in turn answered to the next man up the chain of command. Everybody slept in tents put up by the military or in peasant huts, with banners proclaiming that 'Three Years of Hard Work is Ten Thousand Years of Happiness'. Rowinski was quick to realise that the emperors, denounced for exploiting the common people, had probably used similar tactics to build the Great Wall, the Imperial Canal and the Ming Tombs – fusing tens of thousands of labourers armed with nothing but a bamboo pole into a docile but efficient workforce.[16]

Mikhail Klochko, a foreign adviser who had volunteered to help, was also sceptical, noting that the few spadefuls of earth he had shovelled around had little propaganda value, although it did provide a welcome opportunity for hundreds of workers to take a few minutes' rest as they gathered around and gawked at the foreigner digging. Most of the work was disorganised, and a few hundred men with excavators and lorries would have done a more efficient job than the thousands of workers compelled to participate, all having to be transported, billeted and fed for weeks on end.[17]

The haste with which the project was executed resulted in major miscalculations, and in April 1958 leaks appeared in the reservoir. A Polish expert on soil solidification was flown in from Gdansk to freeze the ground, preventing the water from escaping. At long last, the dam was formally opened with a brass band and officiating dignitaries praising Mao and paying tribute to the voluntary workers.[18] As the reservoir was built in the wrong location, it dried up and was abandoned after a few years.

———

Work at the Ming Tombs may have been an exciting event for some foreign students, but most people dreaded the back-breaking work. Mao himself started perspiring after half an hour of digging in the sun, his face turning bright red. 'So little effort and already I'm dripping with sweat,' he said, before retiring to the command tent for some rest.[19] His immediate entourage – secretaries, bodyguards and private doctor – were also sent to the reservoir by Mao. 'Just work until you are exhausted. If you really can't stand it, just let me know.' Group One, as they were known, remained a privileged elite, sleeping on quilts on the floor of a classroom when everybody else spent the night on reed mats outdoors. They were also spared the scorching heat of early summer, being assigned a night shift by the general in charge. Li Zhisui, Mao's personal doctor, was healthy and still young at thirty-eight years of age, but the digging and carrying was the most arduous work he had ever done in his life. After two weeks he was exhausted, aching in every limb and trembling with cold at night; every reserve of energy in his body had been used up. Nobody in Group One wanted to continue, not even the strong bodyguards, but who would want to be labelled a backward element by suggesting that they quit? Mercifully, they were ordered back to Zhongnanhai.[20]

But outside the capital the pressure was much greater, and villagers were the ones who bore the brunt of the campaign: they were not called off after a mere two weeks of work to return to the luxuries of an elite cadre lifestyle. They were marched off in groups to construction sites far away from home and family, made to perform exhausting labour all day long for months on end, sometimes throughout the night without any rest, poorly fed and barely clothed, and exposed to the elements, come snow, rain or heat.

Yunnan provides a good example of what happened far away from the glare of publicity. Some villages in the subtropical province started work on reservoirs in the winter of 1957–8, but the local party boss was unimpressed. In early January 1958 Xie Fuzhi, the man who a few months later so ruthlessly purged his colleagues in the anti-rightist movement, complained loudly that far too many farmers were laggards who failed to perform their collective duties in the slack winter months. Eight hours of work a day was a strict minimum for every adult, while the amount of food consumed by workers on irrigation projects should be curtailed.[21] Then, on 15 January, the *People's Daily* listed Yunnan as one of the worst performers in the water-conservancy campaign.[22] Determined to catch up, Xie called an emergency meeting the following day. Up to half the workforce in the province should join the movement, he commanded, and villagers were to work for up to ten hours a day, through the night if necessary. Shirkers should be punished, and targets should be met at any cost. Cadres who failed to comply would be sacked.[23] Coming in the midst of an unfolding anti-rightist campaign which had already stripped thousands of local cadres of their jobs, this was no idle threat. Results followed promptly. On 19 January the *People's Daily* reported that Yunnan, singled out only a few days earlier, now had 2.5 million people, a third of the workforce, moving earth.[24] Emboldened, Xie Fuzhi declared that the province would be completely irrigated within three years.[25]

The cost of success was high. In Chuxiong, near a highland lake as large as a sea, farmers enrolled on irrigation projects were routinely cursed and beaten. Villagers were tied up for stealing a few vegetables, others who failed to work hard enough were stabbed with knives by cadres trying to impose a ruthless work regime. A makeshift labour camp took care of recalcitrant elements. Party leaders higher up the chain of command were aware of these practices. In April 1958 a team was sent by the Yunnan provincial party committee to investigate the county. Hopeful rumours began to circulate among the villagers, one courageous individual trying to muster support for a collective grievance about insufficient food and long working hours. He was denounced as a 'reactionary' and a 'saboteur' in the final report sent to Xie Fuzhi.[26]

Some 130 kilometres to the east of the provincial capital Kunming, in the midst of a primeval forest with craggy mountains shaped out of sand and stone by erosion, Luliang county had been savaged by the provincial party committee for giving in to 'farmers' rightist demands' for grain in 1957. The new leader Chen Shengnian rigidly adhered to the party line, organising military squads who patrolled the village streets with leather whips, making sure that even sick villagers went out to work in the fields.[27] The first cases of death by starvation appeared in February 1958. By June oedema, or water retention, was widespread and a thousand villagers died of hunger, most of whom had worked on the Xichong reservoir. Oedema happens when fluids accumulate in the feet, ankles and legs or beneath the skin in other parts of the body. In developed countries it can be caused by mild changes in behaviour, for instance by eating too much salt or standing a lot when the weather is warm. In poor countries, however, it is caused by lack of protein and is seen as a symptom of malnutrition; it is sometimes called famine oedema. In Luliang medical teams were dispatched on several occasions to investigate these cases, but in the midst of the anti-rightist campaign none had the courage to identify oedema as a condition generally caused by hunger – as was well known in a country with a long record of famine. Some doctors even wondered whether it might be a contagious disease and prescribed antibiotics instead of bed rest and food.[28] At first the bodies of the dead were buried in coffins, but after a few months they were simply covered in mats and dumped in the ditches and ponds near construction sites.[29]

Yunnan was no exception. All over China farmers were being driven to the edge of starvation on gigantic irrigation schemes, pushed hard by cadres afraid of being labelled rightists. Having spent half an hour shovelling gravel himself, Mao was in a good position to see the human cost of the irrigation campaign. In March 1958, as he listened to a report by Jiang Weiqing on irrigation in Jiangsu, he mused that 'Wu Zhipu claims he can move 30 billion cubic metres; I think 30,000 people will die. Zeng Xisheng has said that he will move 20 billion cubic metres, and I think that 20,000 people will die. Weiqing only promises 600 million cubic metres, maybe nobody will die.'[30] Mass mobilisation on water-conservancy schemes continued unabated for several years, claiming the lives of hundreds of thousands of exhausted villagers already weakened by hunger. In a chilling precursor of Cambodia under the Khmer Rouge, villagers in Qingshui, Gansu, called these projects the 'killing fields'.[31]

Launching Sputniks

Charts with rising targets, beautifully drafted with colour-coded diagrams, made a stark contrast with the killing fields. As targets rocketed skywards in every conceivable domain, from grain output and steel production to the number of wells dug in the countryside, a dark chasm appeared between a world of slogans and the reality on the ground. Behind the pressure which produced this gap was the hand of Mao. In informal exchanges he needled and goaded local bosses to commit to ever higher production targets.

Zhou Xiaozhou, the cautious leader of Mao's native Hunan, was one of the first to be harangued in November 1957. 'Why can't Hunan increase its agricultural production?' Mao asked, on a visit to the provincial capital Changsha. 'Why do the Hunan peasants still plant only one crop of rice a year?' After Zhou explained that the weather permitted only a single crop a year, Mao pointed out that Zhejiang was on the same latitude as Hunan and planted two crops of rice. 'You are not even studying other experiences. That's the trouble,' Mao continued.

'We will study the matter, then,' Zhou responded meekly.

'What do you mean study?' Mao demanded. 'You won't get anywhere with your study. You can go now,' he added, dismissing the party leader. He opened a book and began to read.

A humiliated Zhou then promised: 'We'll try to start two plantings right away.' Mao ignored him.[1]

A few months later, when Zhou's representative met the Chairman in Beijing, Mao lavished praise on Henan instead. Henan produced half the country's wheat: 'What do you think of that?' Then he shared his disappointment with Hunan. Luxembourg had a population of 300,000 but produced 3 million tonnes of steel a year. Now how many people were there in Hunan?[2]

Mao also sent close allies to hammer home the message. Just as Deng Xiaoping was his trusted lieutenant in the campaign against rightists, Tan Zhenlin was a zealot put in charge of agriculture. A short man topped by a bush of dense hair with thick glasses and trout lips, he was a close follower of Mao and an ally of Ke Qingshi, the rising star of Shanghai. He was described by a former colleague as a sarcastic man who was ruthlessly 'mission-oriented'.[3] His advice to colleagues who were summoned by the Chairman was to proffer instant self-criticism, whether or not they were at fault.[4] Tan spent many months touring the country, whipping up the pressure behind the Great Leap Forward. He was unimpressed with what he saw in Hunan, a province he considered a laggard.[5] As he threatened to denounce it as politically backward, a reluctant Zhou Xiaozhou started inflating the crop figures.[6]

Outside the corridors of power where one-to-one encounters took place, the telephone was used to keep up the pressure. In a country the size of China, it allowed a leader to stay in touch with his subordinates regardless of physical distance. In the frenzy to produce more steel, for instance, Xie Fuzhi would phone around Yunnan to impress on county secretaries the danger of falling behind neighbours Guangxi and Guizhou.[7] The party secretary, in turn, was regularly given updates by the Ministry of Metallurgy. On 4 September 1958, for instance, the latest results were phoned in by Beijing.[8] Then on 6 September a speech by Mao was transmitted in a telephone conference, followed by a talk on steel targets by Bo Yibo on 8 September, by Peng Zhen on 11 September, and by Wang Heshou on 16 September. In the meantime, countless other conferences on agriculture, industry and collectivisation were given by telephone from the capital.[9] How often the phone was used we do not know, but at the height of the campaign one local cadre in a commune in Guangdong estimated that some ninety telephone conferences took place in a single season in 1960 to ensure close planting (sowing seeds more densely in the hope that the crop would increase – also known as close cropping).[10]

Pressure was also maintained through the ad-hoc party gatherings called by Mao, who dominated the agenda to promote new ideological themes and escalate production targets.[11] Bo Yibo – one of the planners taken to task by Mao for opposing a surge in output – contributed in no small measure to the frenzy by replacing a single set of national targets with a system of dual planning at the Nanning meeting in January 1958. To this Mao added a third set. It worked as follows: the centre was to have one set of targets that had to be achieved, while the second plan was merely expected to be accomplished. This second plan was handed over to the provinces and became their first set of targets which had to be reached at all cost. The provinces were then asked to have a second plan reflecting what they expected to be accomplished, making for three sets in total. The system percolated downwards to the counties, in effect adding a fourth set of production plans. As the national targets were ceaselessly revised upwards at party meetings, the whole system of defined and desired targets created an orgy of inflation all the way down to the village, resulting in a great leap in targets.[12]

A process of emulation further added to the political tension. Mao not only denigrated timorous colleagues and praised the more radical ones in full view of their subordinates, he was also inclined to compare everything and everyone with something else to heighten a competitive spirit. Hunan was juxtaposed to Luxembourg in steel production, China was stacked up against Britain when it came to industrial output, Gansu was set against Henan in the irrigation drive. This, too, was enshrined in the directives Mao distributed to party leaders at Nanning: to boost its competitive spirit the whole nation was to engage in comparison. Regular reviews in endless meetings at all levels bestowed three categories of designation on provinces, cities, counties, communes, factories and even individuals, all on the basis of their achievements. A 'red flag' was granted to those judged to be advanced, a 'grey flag' was given to those considered mediocre, and a 'white flag' was punishment for the backward. Handed out during meetings after work, these symbolic designations, sometimes drawn on a blackboard next to a unit's name, had the power to confer shame in a society in which even the slightest lack of political enthusiasm could cause somebody to be labelled a rightist. The whole country became a universe of norms, quotas and targets from which escape was all but impossible, as loudspeakers blasted slogans, cadres checked and appraised work, and

committees endlessly ranked and rated the world around them. And classi-
fication of individual performance would increasingly determine the kind
of treatment meted out – down to the ladle of gruel in the canteen in
times of hunger. Mao was clear: 'Compare: how should we compare? What
we call "comparison" [*bi*] is really "compulsion" [*bi*].'[13] A county official
recalled the experience thus:

> That year, we pooled all our able hands together to work on water
> well drilling, leaving spring farming unattended. The prefecture party
> committee held a *pingbi* [assessment and comparison] meeting at which
> we received a 'red flag' for well drilling and a 'white flag' for spring
> farming. I went back to the county party committee to report this and
> got blasted by the party secretary: 'how could you have left with a red
> flag but come back with a white flag!' I realised then that the problem
> was very serious. I myself could be picked as a 'white flag'. Thus I had
> to leave my sobbing wife who was due to give birth soon and my dying
> sister who was infected with tetanus to go back to the work site in the
> mountains.[14]

Soon all of China was in the grip of target fever, as fantastic figures for
agricultural and industrial output competed for attention. These claims
were trundled out at party meetings and publicised by a powerful propaganda machine, covering the leaders behind the latest record in glory. The
numbers were stratospheric, and achieving a new high was called 'launching a sputnik' – in honour of the first satellite hurled into space by the
socialist camp the previous year. To 'launch a sputnik', to 'join the party
in combat', to 'work hard for a few days and nights' were ways of getting a
red flag. In Chayashan, Henan, soon to become the country's first people's
commune (known as the 'Sputnik Commune'), a goal of 4,200 kilos of
wheat per hectare was set in February 1958. As 6,000 activists roamed the
countryside with a river of banners, posters, leaflets and slogans, targets
were cranked up. By the end of the year an entirely fictitious level of 37.5
tonnes per hectare was promised.[15]

Many of these records were achieved on 'sputnik fields', high-yield experimental plots touted by local cadres keen on setting new records. These were generally limited to a small strip of land in any one collective farm, but the plots acted as showcases for new agricultural techniques that found a much wider application. Increasing the yield encouraged a scramble for fertiliser. Every conceivable kind of nutrient was thrown on to the fields, from weed dragged from the sea and garbage salvaged from refuse heaps to soot scraped from chimneys. Animal and human waste was carried to the fields by endless rows of people, sometimes until deep into the night. Where excrement was traditionally viewed as a dirty and polluting substance by the many minority people who lived along the outer reaches of the empire, outdoor toilets were built for the first time, the party riding roughshod over local sensibilities. Collecting it became a task assigned to punishment teams.[16] Human waste extended to hair, and in some Guangdong villages women were forced to shave their heads to contribute fertiliser or face a ban from the canteen.[17]

But most of the time buildings made of mud and straw were torn down to provide nutrients for the soil. Walls of buildings where animals had lived and especially where they had urinated, such as stables, could provide useful fertiliser. At first old walls and abandoned huts were destroyed, but as the campaign gained momentum entire rows of houses were systematically razed to the ground, the mud bricks shattered and strewn across the fields. In Macheng, nestled against the south of the Dabie mountain range in Hubei, thousands of houses were demolished to collect fertiliser. In January 1958 the model county was exalted by Wang Renzhong, party secretary of the province, for reaching a rice yield of six tonnes per hectare: 'Let Us Learn from Macheng!' the *People's Daily* declared rapturously. Once it had been praised by Mao for its experimental plots, Macheng became a shrine. In the following months it attracted half a million cadres, including Zhou Enlai, foreign minister Chen Yi and Li Xiannian. By August a new record was achieved with a yield of 277 tonnes of rice per hectare: 'The Era of Miracles!' the propaganda machine proclaimed.[18]

On the ground the pressure was unremitting, wild boasts and false figures vying for attention. In one Macheng commune the head of the Women's Federation took the lead by moving out of her house and allowing it to be turned into fertiliser: within two days 300 houses, fifty cattle pens and hundreds of chicken coops had been pulled down. By the end of the year some 50,000 buildings had been destroyed.[19] Trying to outdo one another, other communes throughout the country followed suit. In Dashi, Guangdong, a commune that also attracted nationwide attention with its 'Twenty-five-Tonne Grain University' and 'Five-Thousand-Kilo Field', local cadres pulverised half of all houses in Xi'er.[20] Other organic matter found its way into the fields: in parts of Jiangsu province, the land was covered in white sugar.[21]

Deep ploughing was another revolutionary recipe meant to free the farmers from the capricious soil. The deeper the planting, the stronger the roots and the taller the stalk, or so ran the logic behind this experiment. 'Use human waves, and turn every field over,' commanded Mao.[22] If shovelling gravel on irrigation projects was tough, deep tilling to a depth ranging from forty centimetres to more than a metre – sometimes three metres – was totally exhausting. Where tools were lacking, ranks of farmers dug furrows by hand, sometimes throughout the night by the light of fire torches. Goaded by cadres eager to achieve a coveted red flag, villagers now and then burrowed through the earth to bedrock, destroying the topsoil. By September 1958 some 8 million hectares had been tilled to a depth of about thirty centimetres, but the leadership still demanded more, all of it at least sixty centimetres deep.[23]

This was followed by heavy concentrations of seed in the search for higher yields. Initially these half-baked experiments were carried out on artificial plots, but they spread to the fields in the following years under the watchful eyes of radical cadres. In Diaofang, Guangdong, up to 600 kilos of seed were sown per hectare in barren, mountainous areas in the middle of the famine in 1960.[24] Elsewhere in the province farmers were conscripted to sow more than 250 kilos of kernels on a single hectare: by the end of the season the yield per hectare turned out to be a paltry 525 kilos of peanuts.[25]

Close cropping was the cornerstone of innovative tilling. Seeds too, it seemed, showed a revolutionary spirit, those belonging to the same class sharing light and nutrients in a spurt of equality. Explained Chairman Mao: 'With company they grow easily, when they grow together they will be more comfortable.'[26] More often than not, villagers were instructed to transplant rice shoots from adjacent strips on to the experimental plot, squeezing the clumps closely together. Villagers, of course, knew better: they had tilled the land for generations, and knew how to care for a precious resource on which their livelihoods depended. Many were incredulous, some trying to reason with the cadres: 'You plant the seedlings too closely, there is not enough breathing space between them, and then you add ten tonnes of fertiliser per field. It will suffocate them to death.' But advice was ignored: 'It's a new technique, you don't understand!'[27]

Most villagers, having witnessed a series of anti-rightist campaigns since 1957, were too wily ever to object in public. Every survivor who was interviewed for this book told a similar story: 'We knew about the situation, but no one dared to say anything. If you said anything, they would beat you up. What could we do?'[28] Another explained: 'Whatever the government said, we had to follow. If I said something wrong, if what I said was against the general line, then I would be labelled as a rightist. No one dared to say anything.'[29] What happened in a village in Quxian county, Zhejiang, provides a good example: large cauldrons of gruel were set up in the fields, and nobody was allowed to leave, be they pregnant mothers who needed to feed their children or elderly people wishing to take a rest. People had to slog throughout the night, since cadres had blocked off all exits back to the village. Those who objected to close planting were beaten by party activists. One stubborn old man who somehow failed to show enough enthusiasm was yanked by his hair and pushed face down into the ditch. Then the villagers were ordered to pull out the seedlings and start all over again.[30]

Visits were carefully stage-managed. In Macheng, villagers were warned never to say a bad word about the Great Leap Forward in front of visitors. As provincial leader Wang Renzhong inspected the fields, he saw farmers tucking into mounds of rice, carefully laid out for his visit.[31] In Xushui, Zhang Guozhong, a military man, ruthlessly ensured that the image presented to the outside world was flawless: undesirable elements disappeared into an elaborate labour-camp system, extending from the county down to every commune, brigade and production team. In order to 'stimulate production', laggards were paraded before being locked up, some 7,000 people being rounded up between 1958 and 1960.[32] In

Luoding, Guangdong, inspection committees visiting Liantan commune in late 1958 were welcomed by a posse of young girls, expensive perfumes, white towels and a lavish banquet with sixteen dishes. Dozens of farmers worked for days on end to carve a huge slogan praising the communes into the mountainside.[33] Li Zhisui, who accompanied Mao on his visits, was told that farmers had been ordered to transplant rice plants along the Chairman's route to give the impression of a bumper harvest. The doctor commented that 'All of China was a stage, all the people performers in an extravaganza for Mao.'[34] But in reality a dictatorship never has one dictator only, as many people become willing to scramble for power over the next person above them. The country was full of local hegemons, each trying to deceive the next one up into believing that their achievements were genuine.

Mao was delighted. As reports came in from all over the country about new records in cotton, rice, wheat or peanut production, he started wondering what to do with all the surplus food. On 4 August 1958 in Xushui, flanked by Zhang Guozhong, surrounded by journalists, plodding through the fields in straw hat and cotton shoes, he beamed: 'How are you going to eat so much grain? What are you going to do with the surplus?'

'We can exchange it for machinery,' Zhang responded after a pause for thought.

'But you are not the only one to have a surplus, others too have too much grain! Nobody will want your grain!' Mao shot back with a benevolent smile.

'We can make spirits out of taro,' suggested another cadre.

'But every county will make spirits! How many tonnes of spirits do we need?' Mao mused. 'With so much grain, in future you should plant less, work half time and spend the rest of your time on culture and leisurely pursuits, open schools and a university, don't you think? . . . You should eat more. Even five meals a day is fine!'[35]

At long last, China had found a way out of grinding poverty, solving the problem of hunger and producing more food than the people could possibly eat. As reports came in from all over the country pointing at a bumper harvest twice the size of the previous year, other leaders joined in the chorus. Tan Zhenlin, in charge of agriculture, toured the provinces to galvanise the local leadership. He shared Mao's vision of a communist cornucopia in which farmers dined on delicacies like swallows' nests, wore silk, satin and fox furs, and lived in skyscrapers with piped water and television. Every county would have an airport.[36] Tan even explained how China had managed to leave the Soviet Union in the dust: 'Some comrades will wonder how we manage to be so fast, since the Soviet Union is still practising socialism instead of communism. The difference is that we have a "continuous revolution". The Soviet Union doesn't have one, or follows it loosely . . . Communisation *is* the communist revolution!'[37] Chen Yi, on the other hand, opined that since enough grain could be stored over the next couple of years, farmers should then stop growing crops for two seasons and devote their time instead to building villas with all modern amenities.[38] Local leaders were just as enthusiastic. In January 1959 the State Council had to put a stop to the deluge of people, letters and gifts sent by communes to Beijing to testify to new records set in agriculture. The Chairman was inundated.[39]

6

Let the Shelling Begin

The remains of Laika, the stray dog catapulted into orbit days before the celebration marking the October Revolution, were burned up as *Sputnik II* disintegrated on re-entering the atmosphere in April 1958. As the space coffin circled the earth, the world below it changed. Fired by the missile gap the Russians had exposed, President Eisenhower sent ballistic missiles to Great Britain, Italy and Turkey. Khrushchev responded with submarines carrying nuclear missiles. But, for his threat to be credible, a submarine base in the Pacific Ocean was needed, which in turn required a radio transmitter station. Moscow approached Beijing with a proposal to build long-wave radio stations on the Chinese coast, suggesting that they might serve a joint submarine fleet.

On 22 July Soviet ambassador Pavel Yudin sounded out the Chairman with a proposal. Mao flew into a rage. During a stormy meeting, he attacked the hapless ambassador, claiming, 'You just don't trust the Chinese, you only trust the Russians. Russians are superior beings, and the Chinese are inferior, careless people, that's why you came up with this proposal. You want joint ownership, you want everything as joint ownership, our army, navy, air force, industry, agriculture, culture, education: how about it? Why don't we hand over our thousands of kilometres of coastline to you, we will just maintain a guerrilla force. You have a few atomic bombs and now you want to control everything, you want to rent and lease. Why else would you come up with this proposal?' Khrushchev, Mao continued, behaved towards China like a cat playing with a mouse.[1]

The outburst came like a bolt out of the blue to the Russians: seeing conspiracies everywhere, Mao was convinced that the proposal for a joint fleet was a manoeuvre by Khrushchev to renege on a promise made a year earlier to deliver an atom bomb, and no amount of explaining could allay Mao's suspicions.[2]

On 31 July Khrushchev flew to Beijing to save the situation. But whereas lavish hospitality had welcomed Mao in Moscow seven months earlier, the Soviet leader was met with a cool reception at the airport. 'No red carpet, no guards of honour, and no hugs,' recalled interpreter Li Yueran, just a stony-faced team including Mao Zedong, Liu Shaoqi, Zhou Enlai and Deng Xiaoping.[3] Khrushchev was relegated to lodgings without air-conditioning up in the hills far out of Beijing. Moving his bed to the terrace to escape the stifling heat, that night he was devoured by swarms of mosquitoes.[4]

Immediately after Khrushchev's arrival a long and humiliating meeting was held at Zhongnanhai. The Soviet leader was forced to explain Yudin's démarche at great length, and took pains to defuse a visibly irritated Mao. Impatient, Mao at one point jumped out of his chair to wave a finger in Khrushchev's face: 'I asked you what a common fleet is, you still didn't answer me!'

Khrushchev became flushed and strained to stay calm.[5] 'Do you really think that we are red imperialists?' he asked in exasperation, to which Mao retorted that 'there was a man who went by the name of Stalin' who had turned Xinjiang and Manchuria into semi-colonies. After more squabbling about real or perceived slights, the idea of a joint fleet was finally abandoned.[6]

More humiliation followed next day, as Mao, clad only in a bathrobe and slippers, received Khrushchev by the side of his swimming pool in Zhongnanhai. Mao realised that Khrushchev did not know how to swim, and put the Soviet leader on the defensive. After spluttering about with a bulky lifebelt in the shallow end, Khrushchev ended up crawling out of the pool and floundered on the edge, clumsily dangling his legs in the water while Mao swam back and forth, showing off different strokes to his guest before turning on to his back and floating comfortably in the water.[7] All the while, interpreters scurried about at the side of the pool trying to catch the meaning of the Chairman's political musings. Later Mao explained to his doctor that this had been his way of 'sticking a needle up Khrushchev's arse'.[8]

Mao had started a bidding war with Khrushchev in Moscow half a year earlier. Now, treading water as his host sat defeated by the side of the pool, the Chairman talked about the success of the Great Leap Forward. 'We have so much rice that we no longer know what to do with it,' he bragged, echoing what Liu Shaoqi had told Khrushchev a few days earlier at the airport when reviewing the country's economy: 'What we worry about now is not so much lack of food, but rather what to do with the grain surplus.'[9] A baffled Khrushchev diplomatically replied that he was unable to help Mao with his predicament. 'We all work hard yet never manage to build up a good reserve,' Khrushchev thought. 'China is hungry but now he tells me there is too much rice!'[10]

Over the years Mao had taken the measure of Khrushchev. Now he bossed him around, dismissing the need for a submarine base and brushing aside a request for a radio station. The Soviet delegation went home empty-handed. But this was not the end of it, as Mao was determined to take the initiative in world affairs. A few weeks later, on 23 August, without advance warning to Moscow, Mao gave the order to start shelling the offshore islands of Quemoy and Matsu in the Taiwan Strait, controlled by Chiang Kai-shek, triggering an international crisis. The United States responded by reinforcing its naval units and arming a hundred jet fighters in Taiwan with air-to-air missiles. On 8 September Moscow was forced to take sides by throwing its weight behind Beijing, proclaiming that an attack on the People's Republic of China would be considered an attack on the Soviet Union.[11] Mao was jubilant. He had forced Khrushchev to extend the protective mantle of nuclear power to China while at the same time wrecking Moscow's bid to reduce tensions with Washington. As he put it to his doctor, 'The islands are two batons that keep Khrushchev and Eisenhower dancing, scurrying this way and that. Don't you see how wonderful they are?'[12]

But the real reason for the bombing of the islands had nothing to do with international relations. Mao wanted to create a heightened sense of tension to promote collectivisation: 'A tense situation helps to mobilise people, in particular those who are backward, those middle-of-the-roaders . . . The people's communes should organise militias. Everyone in our country is a soldier.'[13] The Taiwan Strait crisis provided the final rationale for the entire militarisation of the country. An East German studying in China at the time called it 'Kasernenkommunismus', or communism of the barracks, and it found its expression in the people's communes.[14]

7

The People's Commune

A day after the meeting with Khrushchev by the swimming pool, Li Zhisui was summoned by Mao. At three o'clock in the morning, the Chairman wanted an English lesson from the doctor. Later, over breakfast, a relaxed Mao handed him a report about the creation of a people's commune in his model province, Henan. 'This is an extraordinary event,' Mao said excitedly about the fusion of smaller agricultural co-operatives into a giant collective. 'This term "people's commune" is great.'[1] Could this be the bridge to communism that Stalin had never found?

Soon after the water-conservancy campaign had kicked off in the autumn of 1957, collective farms had started to merge into much larger entities, in particular in regions where large inputs of manpower were required. One of the largest collectives appeared in Chayashan, Henan, where some 9,400 households were fused into a giant administrative unit. But the inspiration behind the people's communes can be traced back to Xushui county.

Located a hundred kilometres south of Beijing in the dry and dusty countryside of North China, marked by harsh winters, spring floods and an alkaline soil that hardly yielded enough grain for villagers to survive on, Xushui, a small county of some 300,000 people, quickly came to the attention of the Chairman. Its local leader Zhang Guozhong approached the irrigation projects like a field campaign. Conscripting a workforce of 100,000 men, he divided farmers along military lines into battalions, companies and platoons. He cut off links with the villages and had the troops live in the open, sleeping in makeshift barracks and eating in collective canteens.

Zhang's approach was highly effective and attracted the attention of the leadership in Beijing in September 1957.[2] Tan Zhenlin, for one, was bowled over: 'Xushui county', he exclaimed in February 1958, 'has created a new experience in water conservancy!' By collectivising the villagers into disciplined units responding to the call with military precision, Zhang had simultaneously solved the problem of labour and that of capital. Where other counties faced labour shortages as the men abandoned the fields to work on irrigation schemes, he deployed his troops in a continuous revolution, tackling one project after another, one wave coming in as another crested. The key terms were 'militarisation' (*junshihua*), 'combatisation' (*zhandouhua*) and 'disciplinisation' (*jilühua*). Each brigade was handed responsibility for seven hectares from which an annual yield of fifty tonnes was mandated. 'Two or three years of hard work will transform our natural environment,' explained Zhang. 'A mere two seasons and a Great Leap Forward appears!' enthused Tan.[3] Mao read the reports and added his comment: 'the experience of Xushui should be widely promoted'.[4]

A few weeks later the *People's Daily* hailed Xushui, identifying the militarisation of the workforce as the key to success.[5] Then, in a short article in *Red Flag* published on 1 July 1958, Chen Boda, the Chairman's ghost-writer, envisaged farmers armed as militia, all welded into giant communes: 'a nation in arms is absolutely vital'.[6] In a spurt of publicity, Mao toured the country, visiting Hebei, Shandong and Henan, praising the way in which farmers were regimented into battalions and platoons, and lauding the canteens, nurseries and retirement homes which freed women from domestic burdens to propel them to the front line. 'The people's commune is great!' he proclaimed. China was on a mobilisation footing, as local cadres throughout the country scrambled over the summer to fuse collective farms into people's communes, bringing together up to 20,000 households into basic administrative units. By the end of 1958 the whole of the countryside was collectivised into some 26,000 communes.

———

At the leadership's annual retreat by the beach resort of Beidaihe, where large, luxurious bungalows overlooked the Bohai Sea, Mao believed he stood on the verge of a millennial breakthrough. On 23 August 1958, as the heavy bombardment of Quemoy was about to start, he poured scorn on the rigid system of material incentives devised by Stalin. 'With a surplus of grain we can implement the supply system . . . The socialism we are building right now nurtures the sprouts of communism.' The people's commune was the golden bridge to communism, bringing free food to all: 'If we can provide food without cost, that would be a great transformation. I guess that in about ten years' time commodities will be abundant, moral standards will be high. We can start communism with food, clothes and housing. Collective canteens, free food, that's communism!'[7]

Zhang Guozhong, lionised over the summer at party conferences in Beijing, responded to Mao's prompting, and confidently predicted the arrival of communism by 1963.[8] On 1 September the *People's Daily* declared that in the not too distant future Xushui Commune would carry its members into a paradise where each could take according to his needs.[9] In the midst of a nationwide euphoria, Liu Shaoqi visited the commune a week later. He had promised communism earlier than anybody else, telling workers at an electricity plant in July that 'China will soon enter communism; it won't take long, many of you can already see it.' Overtaking Britain, he added, was no longer a matter of a decade: two or three years would suffice.[10] Now, having seen the communes, he pushed for a supply system in which meals, clothes, shelter, medical care and all other essential aspects of everyday life were provided without pay by the commune.[11] By the end of the month Fanxian county, Shandong, at a giant meeting of thousands of party activists, solemnly pledged to pass the bridge to communism by 1960. Mao was ecstatic. 'This document is really good, it is a poem, and it looks as if it can be done!'[12]

The people's communes satisfied a growing demand on the part of local cadres for labour, as they strained to accomplish ever more onerous tasks in the Great Leap Forward. On the ground, however, villagers were less enthusiastic. As everyday life came to be organised along military lines, villagers were 'footsoldiers' who had to 'fight battles' on the 'front line' in 'battalions' and 'platoons', while 'shock brigades' might 'stage a march' in 'mobile warfare'. A revolutionary's appointed position in society was a 'sentry post', while a group of people working on a large project was a 'great army'.[13]

Martial terms were matched by military organisation. 'Everyone a soldier,' Mao had proclaimed, and the formation of popular militias helped to regiment the rest of society into people's communes: 'In the past in our army there was no such thing as a salary, or a Sunday, or eight hours of work a day. Rank and file, we were all the same. A real spirit of communism comes when you raise a giant people's army . . . We need to revive military traditions.' He explained: 'Military communism in the Soviet Union was based on grain procurements; we have twenty-two years of military traditions, and the supply system is behind our military communism.'[14]

'Ballistic missiles and atom bombs will never scare the Chinese people,' bellowed the People's Daily as shells hit Quemoy, the nation rising as one man, ready to do battle against the forces of imperialism: 250 million men and women were to be transformed into a sea of soldiers.[15] By October 30 million militiamen in Sichuan spent two hours in military training in the evening. In Shandong 25 million fighting men were the 'main army' on the 'front line' of steel and grain production. In Yingnan county alone, 70,000 of these drilled men took charge of half a million villagers in the battle to deep-plough. In Heilongjiang, out in northern Manchuria, there were 6 million militiamen, as martial habits were instilled into nine out of ten young men.[16] Tan Zhenlin raved about the militia, prescribing that each adult should learn how to use a gun and fire thirty bullets a year.[17] In reality few carried guns. Many merely went through the motions, training half-heartedly by the fields with a few old-fashioned rifles after work. But a small proportion practised with live ammunition and were trained as shock troops.[18] They would turn out to be crucial in enforcing discipline, not only during the frenzy to establish communes, but throughout the years of famine that lay ahead.

The militia movement and a small corps of trained fighters brought military organisation to every commune. All over China farmers were roused from sleep at dawn at the sound of the bugle and filed into the canteen for a quick bowl of watery rice gruel. Whistles were blown to gather the workforce, which moved in military step to the fields, carrying banners and flags to the sound of marching songs. Loudspeakers sometimes blasted exhortations to work harder, or occasionally played revolutionary music. Party activists, local cadres and the militia enforced discipline, sometimes punishing underachievers with beatings. At the end of the day, villagers returned to their living quarters, assigned according to each person's work shift. Meetings followed in the evening to evaluate each worker's performance and review the local tactics.

Labour was appropriated by the communes, men and women being at the command of team leaders, more often than not without adequate compensation. Explained party secretary Zhang Xianli in Macheng: 'Now that we have communes, with the exception of a chamber pot, everything is collective, even human beings.' This was understood by poor farmer Lin Shengqi to mean: 'You do whatever you are told to do by a cadre.'[19] Wages, as a consequence, were virtually abolished. Members of a production team, working under the supervision of a squad leader, were credited with points instead, calculated according to a complex system based on the average performance of the team as a whole, the job carried out and the age and gender of each worker. At the end of the year, the net income of each team was distributed among members 'according to need', and the surplus was in principle divided according to the work points that each had accumulated. In practice a surplus hardly ever existed, as the state came in and took the lot. Work points, moreover, devalued rapidly during the Great Leap Forward. In Jiangning county, just outside Nanjing, one work day was equivalent to 1.05 yuan in 1957. A year later it was worth no more than 28 cents. By 1959, its value had declined to a mere 16 cents. Locals referred to the point system as 'beating a drum with a cucumber': the harder you beat the less you heard, as all incentives to work had been removed.[20]

Some never got paid at all. Chen Yuquan, a sturdy young man interviewed in February 1961 in Xiangtan county, Hunan, recalled that he had made a total of 4.50 yuan in 1958, with which he bought a pair of trousers. The following year, having been dispatched to a coal mine where no record of work was kept, he did not receive anything.[21] Some communes did away with money altogether. In Longchuan county, Guangdong, villagers who sold their pigs were handed credit notes instead of cash, prompting people to slaughter and eat the animals themselves.[22] But in many cases villagers had to borrow from the commune, entering a form of bonded labour. Li Yeye, who had to feed his chronically ill wife and five children by carrying manure all day long, never had any cash: 'People like us had no money, we were constantly in debt. We had to pay back our debt to the commune.'[23] Feng Dabai, a barber from northern Sichuan who looked after a family of nine during the famine, had to borrow so much food that he was still paying off his debt fifty years later.[24]

In the most radical communes, private plots, heavy tools and livestock all had to be turned over to the collective. In many cases people were allowed to keep nothing but the bare essentials. As Li Jingquan, the leader of Sichuan, put it: 'Even shit has to be collectivised!'[25] In response villagers tried to salvage as much of their property as possible. They slaughtered livestock, hid grain and sold assets. At the very start of the movement, Hu Yongming, a farmer from the humid, hilly north-east of Guangdong, killed four chickens, followed on day two by three ducks. Then came three female dogs, the puppies being slaughtered next. Finally the cat was eaten.[26] Many did the same, as farmers devoured poultry and livestock. Throughout the villages of Guangdong, chicken and ducks were eaten first, followed by hogs and cows. Local officials, keen on numbers, thought that the consumption of pork and vegetables alone increased by some 60 per cent with the advent of the communes, as locals consumed the produce of their private plots in fear of collectivisation.[27] A common saying in Guangdong was 'What you eat is yours, what you don't is anyone's.'[28]

A similar scenario followed in the cities, although attempts to impose urban communes were generally abandoned until a few years later. In the first few weeks of October 1958 over half a million yuan was withdrawn from the bank in one single district in Guangzhou.[29] In Wuhan there was a run on the bank, a fifth of all savings having been cashed within two days of the foundation of the East commune.[30] Some workers in small enterprises even sold the sewing machines on which they relied for their livelihoods, others tearing up the floorboards of their homes for timber, to be sold as fuel.[31] Afraid that their savings would be confiscated, once parsimonious people started to indulge in conspicuous consumption. Ordinary workers bought expensive brands of cigarettes and other luxury goods; some even splurged on extravagant banquets.[32] Rumours fired collective fears: it was said that in some villages each person was allowed only a blanket, everything else being communal: 'even clothes have numbers'.[33]

In the drive to increase production and meet ever higher targets, homes were also confiscated: the commune, after all, needed bricks for the canteens, dormitories, nurseries and retirement homes planned on paper. In Macheng, as we have seen, houses were initially pulled down for fertiliser, a trend made worse by the advent of the people's communes. Throughout the county villagers started sharing houses, some families ending up in makeshift sheds. Recalcitrant farmers were told that 'no grain rations will be issued to those who do not move out'. In some villages a grandiose vision of modernity justified the elimination of old houses. In Guishan commune, thirty dwellings were pulled down to make way for a utopian plan in which paved streets and skyscrapers would replace the mud huts lining dusty lanes. Not a single new house was built, and some families ended up living in pigsties or abandoned temples, with rain leaking through the roof and wind blowing though porous walls built of mud and straw. 'Destroying my home is even worse than digging up my ancestor's gravestone,' one villager cried. But few dared to complain. Most quietly stood by, sometimes in tears, as the local leader walked past without uttering a word, simply lifting his finger to mark out a house for destruction.[34] In Dianjiang county, Sichuan, a team of eleven people went around torching hundreds of straw huts. 'Destroy Straw Huts in an Evening, Erect Residential Areas in Three Days, Build Communism in a Hundred Days' was the leading slogan. Some villages were emptied altogether, although somehow nobody quite managed to get beyond the destruction phase of the plan.[35] Houses were also pulled down specifically to separate men from women in the great drive to regiment the countryside. In Jingning, Gansu, some 10,000 dwellings were pulverised during the Great Leap Forward on the order of provincial boss Zhang Zhongliang. Most of the displaced people ended up not in dormitories as envisaged by model communes but living on the streets, destitute.[36]

Except for the most deprived villagers, most people did not like the canteens, if only because sprawling collectives run on a shoestring could hardly cater to individual whims, tastes and diets. Some people had to walk for many kilometres to reach the collective facilities. In Hunan over two-thirds of all villagers were opposed to communal eating, according to the head of the province, Zhou Xiaozhou.[37] Across the country cadres had to apply pressure to get the villagers into the canteens. In Macheng they used a simple but effective approach by simply cutting off grain supplies to the village. But families who had hoarded their own provisions still failed to turn up. They were denounced as 'rich peasants' intent on 'sabotaging the people's communes'. The militia then stepped in, patrolling the streets and fining families who had smoke escaping from the chimney. The final step was house-to-house confiscation of food and utensils.[38]

Once they sat down, villagers tucked in with a vengeance, all the keener as the new facilities had been set up with funds, food and furniture taken from the village. In one commune in Macheng, some 10,000 pieces of furniture, 3,000 hogs and 57,000 kilos of grain as well as countless trees, chopped down from private plots for fuel, went into the canteens.[39] Their labour exploited, their possessions confiscated and their homes demolished, villagers were presented with an opportunity to share in their leaders' vision. Communism was around the corner, and the state would provide. 'To each according to his needs' was taken literally, and for as long as they could get away with it people ate as much as they could. For about two months, in many villages throughout the country, people 'stretched their bellies', following Mao's directive at Xushui: 'You should eat more. Even five meals a day is fine!' Especially in regions where crops other than food were grown – for instance cotton – restraint was less pronounced, as the grain was provided by the state. Workers stuffed themselves, some being scolded for lack of appetite. Leftover rice was poured down the toilet by the bucketload. In some teams people held competitions to see who could eat the most, children being reduced to tears for failing to keep up. Others took Mao at his word, 'launching a sputnik' by having five meals a day. Food that would have fed a village for half a week vanished in a day.[40] In Jiangning county, Jiangsu, some villagers gobbled down a kilo of rice in a sitting. Extravagance in consumption was even greater in the cities, some 50 kilos of rice ending up in the gutter on a single day in late 1958 in a Nanjing workshop. Steamed dough buns blocked the toilets:

one punctilious inspector noted that the rice on the bottom of a sewage vat was thirty centimetres thick. In some factories workers wolfed down up to twenty bowls of rice a day; the leftovers were fed to the pigs.[41] The feast did not last.

8

Steel Fever

Stalin had financed industry at the expense of agriculture, as punishing procurements drained the countryside of all wealth. In search of an alternative to the Soviet model, Mao instead wanted to bring industry to the village. Industrial output in the people's communes could be raised immediately by relying on inexpensive innovations and indigenous techniques which did not require large amounts of investment, leading to an instant jump in productivity. This, in turn, would galvanise the villagers to achieve even greater economic targets: here was the key to industrialising a backward countryside without big foreign investment. Bourgeois specialists were excoriated as conservative rightists, while the earthbound wisdom of simple peasants was hailed instead. In Yunnan party boss Xie Fuzhi openly scoffed at geological measurements and technological surveys recommended by Russian experts, relying instead on the wisdom of the masses in building dams and reservoirs.[1] Intuitive knowledge and native ingenuity, rather than foreign expertise, would introduce cheap and effective innovations that would propel the villages of China past the Soviet Union. The countryside was to be mechanised through simple devices, developed by ordinary farmers in research institutes. 'The humble are the cleverest, the privileged are the dumbest,' Mao wrote on a report showing how workers had managed to build a tractor by themselves.[2] Or, as Xie Fuzhi claimed, repeating words of wisdom from the Chairman, 'We are supernatural. Maybe we are supernaturals of the second order. Maybe on another planet there are people who are brighter than we are, in which case we are of the second order, but if we are brighter than they are then we are supernaturals of the first order.'[3]

Model workers peopled party propaganda. He Ding, a poor farmer from Henan who never had a day of schooling in his life, devised a system of wooden earth-carriers moving on overhead cables with an automatic dump-and-return mechanism which reduced the amount of labour needed to build a reservoir by eight times.[4] Wooden conveyor belts, wooden threshing machines and wooden rice-planting machines, all were hailed as everyman miracles. In Shaanxi province, villagers even trotted out native cars and locomotives: every part was made of wood.[5] Most of these were innocent enough, but the waste could reach huge proportions. In Diaofang commune, Guangdong, some 22,000 beams, trusses and floorboards were torn out of people's homes overnight in a movement to mechanise the commune. The carts produced were so ramshackle that they fell to pieces the moment anyone tried to use one.[6]

But the real benchmark was steel. Here was material worthy to stand for socialism – hard, shiny, industrial, modern and working class. 'Stalin' stood for a man of steel willing to smash all the enemies of revolution to smithereens. Smoking factory stacks, whirring machine tools, the hooting of factory whistles, towering blast furnaces glowing a deep red with fire: these were the consecrated images of a socialist modernity. Alexei Gastev, the worker poet, wrote, 'We grow out of iron,' as man coalesced with iron in a fusion announcing a world in which machine became man and man was a machine. Steel was the sacred ingredient in the alchemy of socialism. The amount of steel produced was a magic figure recited with religious fervour in socialist countries. Steel output magically distilled all the complex dimensions of human activity into a single, precise figure that indicated where a country stood on the scale of evolution. Mao may not have been an expert on industry, but he seemed able to rattle off the steel output of virtually every country at the drop of a hat. He was possessed by steel, and overtaking Britain increasingly meant outstripping its annual steel production. Steel was the prime mover in the escalation of targets, and he pushed hard to have its output increased. It was 5.35 million tonnes in 1957. The target for 1958 was set at 6.2 million in February 1958, which was increased to 8.5 million tonnes in May, until Mao decided in June that 10.7 million tonnes could be produced. This changed to 12 million tonnes in September. As he juggled with the numbers he became convinced that by the end of 1960, China would catch up with the Soviet Union, the United States being overtaken in 1962 when an output of 100 million tonnes would be achieved. Then China would pull away, reaching 150 million tonnes in a few years. Seven hundred million tonnes of steel would be produced by 1975, leaving Britain trailing far behind.[7]

Mao was encouraged in his ravings by some of his close colleagues. Li Fuchun, for one, pronounced that China could develop at a speed unprecedented in human history thanks to the superiority of the socialist system: Britain could be outstripped in a mere seven years. Then he presented an extravagant plan seeking to overtake Britain in iron, steel and other industrial commodities in less than three years.[8] In early June 1958, as Mao lounged by the swimming pool and asked minister of metallurgy Wang Heshou if steel production could be doubled, the minister replied, 'No problem!'[9] Ke Qingshi bragged that East China alone could produce 8 million tonnes.[10] Provincial leaders such as Wang Renzhong, Tao Zhu, Xie Fuzhi, Wu Zhipu and Li Jingquan all made extravagant pledges about steel production, indulging the Chairman in his visionary whims.

The key to success was small furnaces operated by villagers in every backyard of the people's communes. Built of sand, stone, fire clay or bricks, they were relatively simple affairs allowing every villager to be mobilised in the effort to overtake Britain. A typical backyard furnace was some three or four metres high with a wooden platform at the top, supported by beams. A sloping ramp provided access to the furnace, farmers scuttling up and down with sacks of coke, ore and flux on their backs or baskets slung on long poles. Air was blown through the bottom, the molten iron and slag being released through tap holes. Based on traditional blast methods, some may well have worked, but many were a sham, forced on the communes by cadres in the grip of steel fever.

The drive reached a climax in the late summer of 1958. Chen Yun, the party planner who had fallen into disgrace earlier in the year, was put in charge of the movement, and worked hard to redeem himself. On 21 August he transmitted orders from Mao that not a tonne below target would be tolerated, failure to fulfil the plan resulting in punishments ranging from a warning to expulsion from the party.[11] To maintain momentum Mao visited Wuhan in September to inaugurate a giant iron and steel combine built with Soviet help, watching the molten iron from the first firing come out of the furnace. That same day Beijing dispatched a team of 1,500 party activists to spread out over the country, whipping up support for the steel drive.[12] Then 29 September was designated as the day to achieve an even higher target in celebration of National Day. Two weeks ahead of the event, minister of metallurgy Wang Heshou in a telephone conference asked provincial leaders to rise to the challenge. They in turn galvanised county representatives by phone the following day.[13]

In Yunnan, Xie Fuzhi ordered everyone to become a soldier in the campaign, announcing a day-and-night assault for two weeks to increase production.[14] Party activists fanned out in the morning, some leaving well before sunrise to reach remote villages in good time. In Dehong county, 200,000 villagers were thrown into the campaign, as the sky shone crimson with the glow cast by thousands of brick furnaces. Villagers dispersed into the forests in search of fuel, others collected coal, sometimes digging with pick, spade and hands in the open country. In the frenzy to achieve targets, accidents were frequent. Trees were randomly felled, keeling over on villagers; explosive devices used by inexperienced workers to open up mines also claimed lives.[15] Xie Fuzhi phoned regularly to check the latest results.[16] He, in turn, was egged on by Bo Yibo, who transmitted a new target of 12 million tonnes, boasting that 40 million workers operated some 500,000 furnaces all over the country.[17] On National Day Bo announced that October should be the leap month for steel production, and another bout of madness followed. In Yunnan, the number of people involved in the movement jumped from 3 to 4 million, as a special 'high production' week was announced to set another record. 'The eyes of the world are fixed on China,' exclaimed Xie Fuzhi, as the country had to achieve the target it had trumpeted or face a humiliating climbdown.[18]

With pressure all the way from the top, villagers had little choice but to participate in the campaign. In the Qujing region, Yunnan, floorboards were torn up, and chickens were slaughtered so that their feathers could be used to feed the flames or make bellows. Squads of party activists moved from door to door to collect scrap iron, often confiscating household implements and farming tools. Those who failed to show enough enthusiasm were verbally abused, pushed around or even tied up and paraded. Critical reports written by party inspectors at the time talk about fear and intimidation. Coming in the wake of a year of relentless campaigns, one following on the heels of the last – irrigation schemes, fertiliser campaign, deep ploughing, close cropping, the onslaught of the people's communes – the mere mention of the slogan 'launching a satellite' was enough to instil dread, as it augured another 'bitter war' or 'night battle' in which nobody would be allowed any sleep for days on end. Some tried to slip away and sleep in the cold and wet forest in order to get a few hours of rest, looking from a distance at the furnaces glowing like fireflies in the night. They were cold and poorly fed: local cadres tried to lower the cost of making steel, thus inflating the figures, by skimping on provisions, which were now entirely in their hands thanks to the advent of collective canteens.[19]

China was dipped into a sea of fire. Everywhere furnaces were red hot, although the human dramas which played out during the campaign were different in each village. In Yunnan some farmers were forced to go without adequate food or rest and were worked to death near the furnaces in the rush to complete the production target.[20] In other hamlets across the country people got away with a small gift of a pot or a pan. But two new dimensions were added to the theatre of violence, nipping in the bud any suspected insubordination. First, cadres could now count on the militia established within the people's communes to force through their orders. In Macheng, for instance, militiamen would come to a village and conscript people for work on the furnaces for days on end. One man who left work early was paraded through the streets with a dunce's cap inscribed: 'I am a deserter.'[21] Second, as all the food was now in the hands of the communes, cadres could use rations as a form of reward or punishment. Refusal to work – or any sign of slacking – was punished with a ration cut or deprivation of food altogether. Women who stayed home at night in Macheng to look after their children were banned from the canteen.[22] As Zhang Aihua, who lived through the famine in Anhui, later explained: 'You did as you were told, otherwise the boss gave you no food: his hand held the ladle.'[23] The grip cadres had over the food supply was reinforced even further as everywhere pots and pans were routinely taken away.

In the cities too the campaign was tough on ordinary people. In Nanjing one furnace alone set a record of 8.8 tonnes in a single day, but the fires had to be fed constantly and some teams went so hungry that they fainted by the smelters. Despite huge pressure, still people protested. Wang Manxiao simply refused to work more than eight hours a day. When challenged by a party secretary, Wang was defiant, asking point-blank, 'What are you going to do about it?' Others openly doubted that backyard furnaces would help to overtake Britain in steel production. Close to half of all the workers in some teams were described as 'backward', meaning that they shirked hard work.[24]

In the end, the leadership got its record, although much of it was slag, unwashed ore or mere statistical invention. Iron ingots from rural communes accumulated everywhere, too small and brittle to be used in modern rolling mills. According to a report from the Ministry of Metallurgy itself, in many provinces not even a third of the iron produced by backyard furnaces was usable. And the price tag was exorbitant. One tonne of iron from a backyard furnace was estimated to cost 300 to 350 yuan, twice the amount needed by a modern furnace, to which had to be added four tonnes of coal, three tonnes of iron ore and thirty to fifty working days.[25] The total losses from the iron-and-steel drive in 1958 were later estimated by the Bureau for Statistics at 5 billion yuan – not including damage to buildings, forests, mines and people.[26]

When Mikhail Klochko, a foreign adviser who had grown up in the Ukraine with its undulating and irregular fields, travelled to southern China in the autumn of 1958 he was taken aback by the bare, yellow patches of earth divided into narrow terraces: these were the fabled rice paddies, but hardly a single human being could be seen.[27]

Where were the farmers? Many were mobilised by the militia on backyard furnaces, some were deployed on large irrigation schemes, and others had left the village in search of work in the many factories chasing after ever higher targets. In total more than 15 million farmers moved to the city in 1958, lured by the prospect of a better life.[28] In Yunnan the number of industrial workers jumped from 124,000 in 1957 to 775,000, meaning that over half a million people were taken out of the country-side.[29] One-third of the entire workforce in the province was sent to work on water-conservancy projects at some point or another that year.[30] To put it differently, out of the 70,000 working adults in rural Jinning, Yunnan, 20,000 were deployed on irrigation schemes, 10,000 on build-ing a railway, 10,000 in local factories, leaving only 30,000 to produce food.[31] But the figures masked another shift in patterns of work: as most of the men left the village, women had to work in the fields. Many had almost no experience in maintaining complex rice paddies, planting the seedlings unevenly and allowing weeds to invade the fields. In Yongren county a fifth of the crop rotted as a consequence.[32]

Up to a third of the time devoted to agriculture was lost,[33] but Mao and his colleagues believed that innovations such as deep ploughing and close cropping amply compensated for this shortfall. On the other hand, in the 'continuous revolution' hailed by the leadership, farmers were deployed along military lines, moving from the industrial field in the slack season back to the agricultural front during the harvest. As Xie Fuzhi put it, 'a continuous revolution means ceaselessly coming up with new tasks'.[34] But even as all available sources of manpower were mobilised in the harvest-ing campaign, from office clerks, students and teachers, factory workers and city dwellers to the armed forces, the situation on the ground was chaotic. Many of the farming tools had been destroyed in the iron and steel campaign, labour was still diverted to building dams, and communal granaries in the people's communes were poorly managed. In Liantan, the model commune where a slogan praising the Great Leap Forward had been chiselled in the mountains to welcome an inspection team, several thousand farmers were conscripted to deep-plough seven hectares during the autumn harvest; as nobody was available to collect the crop, some 500 tonnes of grain were abandoned in the fields.[35]

But deliveries of grain to the state had to be made according to yields that local cadres had officially declared. The actual grain output for 1958 was just over 200 million tonnes, but on the basis of all the claims made about bumper crops the leadership estimated that it was close to 410 million tonnes. Punitive extractions based on entirely fictitious figures could only create fear and anger in the villages. The stage was set for a war on the people in which requisitions would plunge the country into the worst famine recorded in human history. Tan Zhenlin was blunt, addressing some of the leaders of South China in October 1958: 'You need to fight against the peasants . . . There is something ideologically wrong with you if you are afraid of coercion.'[36]

PART TWO

THROUGH THE VALLEY OF DEATH

9

Warning Signs

People died of hunger even before the people's communes were introduced. As early as March 1958, at a party conference on grain, a number of delegates voiced their concern about food shortages as the farmers were taken from the fields to work on irrigation projects. Telltale signs of famine were gangs of people shuffling along dusty roads begging for food, leaving behind empty villages. Li Xiannian, minister of finance, swept these reservations aside and pressed ahead with grain targets.[1]

By the end of April hunger and want had spread across the country. In Guangxi one person in six was without food or money, and villagers died of hunger in parts of the province. In Shandong some 670,000 were starving, while 1.3 million were destitute in Anhui. In Hunan one in every ten farmers was out of grain for more than a month. Even in subtropical Guangdong close to a million people were hungry, the situation being particularly bad in Huiyang and Zhanjiang, where children were sold by starving villagers. In Hebei grain shortages were such that tens of thousands roamed the countryside in search of food; children were sold in Cangxian, Baoding and Handan. From the devastated villages 14,000 beggars made it to Tianjin, where they were put up in temporary shelters. In Gansu many villagers were reduced to eating tree bark; hundreds died of hunger.[2]

This was spring famine, and it could be explained as a temporary aberration, but in parts of the country hunger got worse over the summer. Such was the case in Luliang, Yunnan. We saw in an earlier chapter how as early as February 1958 forced labour on irrigation campaigns resulted in cases of starvation. But famine was not restricted to villagers conscripted to work on dams and reservoirs. In the township of Chahua, to take but one example, one in six villagers died between January and August 1958, amounting to a total of 1,610 people. Some were beaten to death, although most died of hunger and disease.[3] The county boss Chen Shengnian had been brought in to replace a party official purged for having been soft on grain requisitions in 1957. Chen encouraged the use of violence to impose strict discipline. Two out of three cadres in Chahua routinely resorted to corporal punishment, depriving villagers who were too weak to work of the right to eat.[4]

The problem was not confined to Luliang alone. Throughout the Qujing region in Yunnan people died of hunger. In Luliang some 13,000 were reported to have perished: thousands were also starving in Lunan, Luoping, Fuyuan, Shizong and other counties.[5] In Luxi county the local party committee inflated the crop as early as 1957, proclaiming that each farmer had some 300 kilos of grain a year when only half of that amount was available. After May 1958, starvation claimed some 12,000 lives, equivalent to one in every fourteen people. In some hamlets a fifth of all villagers were buried.[6]

How many died in the Qujing region is difficult to assess, but hidden in the archives is a set of population statistics which throw some light on the issue. They show that 82,000 people died in 1958, or 3.1 per cent of the population. The number of births declined dramatically, from 106,000 in 1957 to 59,000 in 1958. In the province as a whole, the death rate stood at 2.2 per cent, more than double the national average of 1 per cent for 1957.[7] Xie Fuzhi, the party boss in Yunnan, thought long and hard about Luliang and finally decided to report the losses to Mao in November 1958. The Chairman liked the report. Here, it seemed, was somebody he could rely on to tell him the truth. A year later Xie was promoted to head the Ministry of Security in Beijing. As to the deaths, Mao considered them to be a 'valuable lesson'.[8]

Another 'lesson' came from Xushui, a shrine of the Great Leap Forward where Mao had enjoined farmers to have five meals a day to get rid of the grain surplus. Behind the splendid façade of Xushui, Zhang Guozhong ran an elaborate labour camp which held 1.5 per cent of the local population, from recalcitrant farmers to party secretaries who failed to toe the line. Punishment inside the camp was brutal, ranging from flogging to naked exposure to the cold in the midst of winter. One hundred and twenty-four people died as a result; others were maimed or crippled for life. Outside the camp some 7,000 people were tied up, beaten, spat upon, paraded, forced to kneel or deprived of food, resulting in another 212 deaths.[9] Li Jiangsheng, the apparently affable head of the Dasigezhuang Brigade who had welcomed Mao and many other visitors to his showcase village, regularly beat farmers, some being hung up to freeze to death during the winter.[10] Despite all the violence, the crop yield was nowhere near what Zhang had promised. When Zhou Enlai passed through Hebei in December 1958, he was approached by a humbled Zhang, who confided that Xushui had produced only 3,750 kilos per hectare, a far cry from the fifteen tonnes he had boasted over the summer. Xushui, in effect, was starving. Zhou promised to help.[11]

Much, but not all, of this came to light in a report written in October 1958 by the Office of Confidential Affairs at Mao's behest. Mao circulated the document to others in the central committee, writing at the bottom that 'these kinds of problems may not be restricted to one commune alone'.[12] But as Zhang Guozhong fell from grace, the Chairman embraced the county of Anguo, eighty kilometres south of Xushui, as a model instead. After listening to reports about farmers producing 2,300 kilos of grain a year each, he contemplated the output of Hebei province soaring from a mere 10 million tonnes in 1957 to 50 million by 1959.[13] When Hebei boss Liu Zihou warned Mao that some of these figures might be inflated, the Chairman brushed off these concerns and airily stated that errors were inevitable.[14]

Mao received numerous reports about hunger, disease and abuse from every corner of the country, whether personal letters mailed by courageous individuals, unsolicited complaints from local cadres or investigations undertaken on his behalf by security personnel or private secretaries. Xushui and Luliang are two telling examples; others will be invoked elsewhere in this book, while many more remain buried in the Central Archives in Beijing, closed to all but a few researchers hand-picked by the party.

By the end of 1958 Mao did make a few gestures to appease concern about widespread abuse on the ground. In the comments he circulated about the Luliang report, he accepted that the living conditions of villagers had been neglected at the expense of increased output. But to him Luliang was merely a 'lesson' that somehow magically 'immunised' the rest of the country against similar mistakes. In the case of Xushui, Mao simply switched his allegiance to the next county down the road willing to outdo others in extravagant production claims. As we will see in Chapter 11, Mao did slow down the pace of the Great Leap Forward between November 1958 and June 1959, but he was unwavering in his pursuit of utopia. The Great Leap Forward was a military campaign fought for a communist paradise in which future plenty for all would largely compensate for the present suffering of a few. Every war had its casualties, some battles would inevitably be lost, and a few ferocious clashes might exact a tragic toll that could have been avoided with the benefit of hindsight, but the campaign had to press on. As foreign minister Chen Yi put it in November 1958, addressing some of the human tragedies on the ground, 'casualties have indeed appeared among workers, but it is not enough to stop us in our tracks. This is a price we have to pay, it's nothing to be afraid of. Who knows how many people have been sacrificed on the battlefields and in the prisons [for the revolutionary cause]? Now we have a few cases of illness and death: it's nothing!'[15] Other leaders ignored the famine altogether. In Sichuan, in the grip of a terrible hunger in the winter of 1958–9, radical leader Li Jingquan enthused about the communes, noting that some villagers in Sichuan ate more meat than Mao Zedong, gaining several kilos in weight: 'Now what do you think of the communes? Is it a bad thing that people get fat?'[16]

For a party attuned to decades of guerrilla warfare, having survived the Long March after five campaigns of annihilation by the Guomindang in 1935, constant harassment from the Japanese army in the Second World War and a vicious civil war with massive casualties, a few losses were to be expected. Communism would not be achieved overnight. The year 1958 had been a blitzkrieg, an unremitting assault on several fronts at once. The generals in command recognised that the footsoldiers needed some rest: 1959 was to be spent conducting more conventional guerrilla warfare. This meant, in a nutshell, that none of the key decisions about the Great Leap Forward was reversed.

Economics dictated that the pressure should be kept up in the early months of 1959. While Mao was concerned about cooling off the frenzy with which collectivisation had been pushed through, he was never given any reason to doubt that there had been an upsurge in agricultural production. In a joint report that was sent to him, the top economic planners Li Xiannian, Li Fuchun and Bo Yibo confirmed that 'when it comes to grain, cotton and edible oils, output has increased hugely compared to last year as a result of a Great Leap Forward in agricultural production, and we only need to carry out our work and earnestly resolve any problems that may arise in order to get ahead'.[17]

According to the planners, the biggest problem was that the countryside was not sending enough food to the cities. The amount of grain procured for the urban population, which had swollen to some 110 million people, had increased by a quarter in the second half of 1958, reaching a total of 15 million tonnes.[18] But it was not enough. In December Peng Zhen, the bald and vigorous mayor of Beijing, rang the alarm bell, followed by central planner Li Fuchun. Nanning and Wuhan, he noted, had no more than a few weeks of reserves, while Beijing, Shanghai, Tianjin and the province of Liaoning had procured barely enough to last for another two months. At least 725,000 tonnes should have been stored in December, but a mere quarter of that amount had actually been delivered, with large shortages from provinces such as Hubei and Shanxi. All three cities, as well as Liaoning, were placed under special protection, and provinces that declared a surplus – Sichuan, Henan, Anhui, Shandong and Gansu – were required to transfer an extra total of 415,000 tonnes. Insufficient grain was not the only problem, as many cities did not get enough meat to last for more than a day or two, with provinces such as Gansu and Hunan remitting a mere fraction of the hogs required. Vegetables, fish and sugar were also tight.[19]

Not only were cities given a privileged status, but exports were granted top priority too. As we shall see next, China spent vast amounts of money buying foreign equipment in 1958. Then, in the euphoria of the autumn harvest, more orders were placed for 1959. As the bills were coming in, the reputation of the country hinged on its ability to meet foreign commitments. From the end of 1958 onwards, Zhou Enlai, with the support of his colleagues and the backing of the Chairman, relentlessly pressed the countryside into fulfilling ever greater procurements for the export market. To ensure that the cities were fed and foreign contracts were honoured, no retreat on the ground was possible.

Shopping Spree

If the glittering path to communism was to be found in mobilising the masses, large quantities of industrial equipment and advanced technology were nonetheless required to help China transform itself from an agricultural country into an industrial giant. From the moment Mao returned from Moscow, where he had boasted that China would overtake Britain in fifteen years, Beijing started buying liberally from its foreign friends. Steel mills, cement kilns, glass factories, power stations, oil refineries: entire plants and equipment for heavy industry were purchased. Cranes, lorries, generators, motors, pumps, compressors, harvesters and combines, all were imported in unprecedented quantities. Deliveries of metal-cutting machine tools (not including complete factories) rose from 187 units in 1957 to 772 in 1958, planting and sowing machines from 429 units to 2,241, tractors from 67 units to 2,657, lorries from 212 units to 19,860.[1] Supplies of rolled ferrous metals, aluminium and other raw materials jumped, while the amount of transportation and communications equipment was also revised sharply upwards.

Most of this came from the Soviet Union, on which China had depended for economic and military help since May 1951, when the United Nations had imposed an embargo on strategic imports. Trade restrictions had been enforced after the United States had branded China an aggressor state in the Korean War. In the 1950s China signed a series of agreements with Moscow for the construction of more than 150 turnkey projects, to be built and handed over in a ready-to-use condition. In January 1958, in order to propel the Great Leap Forward, a further contract provided for an expansion of economic and military assistance. In August 1958 another forty-seven complete sets of equipment for industrial plants, to be built with Soviet technical aid, were agreed upon – in addition to some 200 already signed up to in earlier years. In February 1959 another agreement further widened economic and scientific co-operation, including thirty-one additional large industrial plants: this brought the number of industrial enterprises, factory shops and other plants to be installed to about 300.[2]

Table 1: **Imports from the Soviet Union, with Major Commodity Groups and Items (million rubles)**

	1957	1958	1959	1960	1961	1962
China's imports from Soviet Union (total)	556	576	881	761	262	190
Trade	183	292	370	301	183	140
Petrol and petroleum products	(80)	(81)	(104)	(99)	(107)	(71)
Equipment for plants	245	174	310	283	55	9
Military equipment	121	78	79	72	12	11
New technology	7	31	122	104	12	30

Source: Ministry of Foreign Affairs, Beijing, 6 Sept. 1963, 109-3321-2, pp. 66–7 and 88–9; although rates varied constantly, 1 ruble was roughly equivalent to 2.22 yuan and US$1.1. Figures may not add up perfectly because of rounding.

Beijing also pressed Moscow for early delivery. In March 1958 military veteran Zhu De enjoined the Russians to hasten the completion of the two steel combines at Baotou and Wuhan.[3] A similar plea was made to S. F. Antonov, the Russian chargé d'affaires in Beijing, by one of Zhou Enlai's personal envoys in July.[4] Such was the pressure of the Great Leap Forward that entire branches of Soviet industry had to reorganise their production system in order to meet urgent demands and mounting orders for a whole array of commodities, often for delivery ahead of schedule.[5] Imports from the Soviet Union rose by an astounding 70 per cent in 1958 and 1959, as shown in Table 1. Where imports were 556 million rubles in 1957, by 1959 they stood at 881 million, of which some two-thirds consisted of machinery and equipment. China also relied on the Soviet Union for large imports of iron, steel and petrol. While Beijing depended on Moscow for half its oil, machine parts and heavy industrial equipment, a large proportion also came from other countries in the socialist bloc, East Germany in particular. In 1958 Walter Ulbricht agreed to build sugar refineries, cement factories, power plants and glassworks, sharply increasing the level of exports to China.[6] Imports from East Germany climbed to 120 million rubles, an amount which was followed by a further 100 million in 1959.[7]

But it was not merely the volume of imports which underwent drastic change during the Great Leap Forward. In pursuit of the best equipment to power its way to communism, Beijing dramatically changed the structure of foreign trade with an overture to Western Europe, made possible by a gradual collapse of the embargo imposed by the United States. Washington was unable to maintain pressure on its allies, as Britain was keen to enter China's huge market and vigorously campaigned to eliminate the system of export controls from 1956 onwards. Purchases from Britain doubled from £12 million in 1957 to £27 million in 1958 and £24 million in 1959, while West German imports soared from DM 200 million in 1957 to DM 682 million in 1958 and DM 540 million in 1959.[8]

All of these imports were industrial in nature, but Mao was also dogged in his pursuit of the most advanced military equipment. Starting in 1957 the leadership in Beijing focused on extracting from Moscow as much military equipment and 'new technology' as possible. Zhou Enlai wrote to Khrushchev in June 1958 requesting aid in building a modern navy. Two months later, during the shelling of the offshore islands of Quemoy and Matsu in the Taiwan Strait, he asked for the latest technology in aerial surveillance. In May 1959 a purchase order was submitted to the Russians for strategic material related to 'defence and aviation equipment'. A reminder followed in September 1959, with Zhou Enlai pointing out that Beijing planned to spend a total of 165 million rubles in 1960 on Soviet military equipment.[9] Just how much Beijing spent has remained something of a mystery, since the published statistics perused by foreign observers did not include 'invisible' items such as military supplies. However, archives from the Ministry of Foreign Affairs now provide a clear overview of imports from Moscow of both 'special goods', meaning military equipment, and 'new technology': as Table 1 shows, these two groups ballooned to over 200 million rubles in 1959, representing close to a quarter of China's imports from the Soviet Union.

China also had to discharge its debtor's obligations towards the Soviet Union. The amount lent by Moscow to Beijing between 1950 and 1962 stood at 1,407 million rubles.[10] Even before China dramatically increased loan repayments after the rift with the Soviet Union in the summer of 1960, the debt-service instalments must have amounted to more than 200 million rubles a year. China's limited foreign currency and gold reserves meant that both debt and actual imports had to be paid for in kind through exports, straining its limited resources. The basic trade pattern was the exchange of credit, capital goods and raw materials for rare minerals, manufactured goods and foodstuffs. Pork, for example, was bartered for cables, soybeans for aluminium, grain for steel rolls. Since the amount of rare metals such as antimony, tin and tungsten was limited, Beijing's shopping spree meant that more foodstuffs had to be extracted from the countryside to pay the bill (see Table 2). Over half of all exports to the Soviet Union consisted of agricultural commodities, ranging from fibres, tobacco, grain, soybeans, fresh fruit and edible oils to tinned meat. The value of the rice exported to Moscow alone trebled from 1957 to 1959, as Tables 2 and 3 indicate. The brunt of the imports, in other words, fell on the farmers.

Table 2: Exports to the Soviet Union: Major Commodity Groups (million rubles)

	1957	1958	1959	1960	1961	1962
China's exports to Soviet Union (total)	672	809	1006	737	483	441
Industry and mining	223	234	218	183	140	116
Farm and sideline processed products	227	346	460	386	304	296
Farm and sideline products	223	229	328	168	40	30

Source: Ministry of Foreign Affairs, Beijing, 6 Sept. 1963, 109-3321-2, pp. 66–8; figures may not add up perfectly because of rounding.

Table 3: Exports of Grain and Edible Oils to the Soviet Union (thousand tonnes and million rubles)

	1957		1958		1959		1960		1961	
	value	weight	value	weight	value	weight	value	weight	value	weight
Grain	77	806	100	934	147	1418	66	640	1.2	12
Rice	(25)	(201)	(54)	(437)	(88)	(784)	(33)	(285)	(0.2)	(1.8)
Soybeans	(49)	(570)	(45)	(489)	(59)	(634)	(33)	(355)	(0.9)	(10.4)
Edible oils	24	57	23	72	28	78	15	41	0.4	0.4

Source: Ministry of Foreign Affairs, Beijing, 6 Sept. 1963, 109-3321-2, pp. 70–1; figures may not add up perfectly because of rounding and selection of commodities.

Who was the architect of foreign trade in China? In a planned economy imports and exports were normally controlled by annual trade agreements, as the increase in external trade was designed to match the projected growth of the economy. There was thus a direct relationship between the rate of capital investment, the volume of foreign trade and the size of the harvests. The overall economic plan, agreed by the central leadership, determined the volume and structure of imports, which in turn set the level of exports from the country. Trade plans were prepared by the Ministry of Foreign Affairs, which then delegated the import and export to corporations dealing in a defined range of agricultural and industrial products.[11]

In the bureaucratic maze of communist China premier Zhou Enlai retained overall supervision of foreign trade. He was keen on enhanced economic relations with the rest of the world, not only the Soviet Union but also countries outside the communist bloc. Economic development, according to Zhou, could be achieved only with adequate capital, technology and expertise, all of which had to come from abroad. A close ally of Zhou Enlai, foreign trade minister Ye Jizhuang was also in favour of dramatically increased exports, which could be used to pay for imported machinery and industrial plants. But in 1957 Zhou reined in the enthusiasm of his delegate, sounding a cautious retreat in foreign trade. In October 1957 Ye had to explain to a foreign trade delegation that the population had suffered from the volume of food exports, in particular edible oils, which had led to serious shortages. Zhou Enlai had decided that the volume of trade with all countries would have to be cut in 1958.[12]

Zhou Enlai's gradual approach in economic planning jarred with Mao's vision of a bold Great Leap Forward. As we have seen, Mao angrily swept aside the reservations voiced by the premier, silencing his opponents at the Nanning conference in January 1958. Instead he leaned towards Zhu De. A military veteran of legendary reputation, Marshal Zhu De had joined forces with Mao back in 1928. Both came to rely on each other, Zhu providing military skills while Mao excelled at party politics. A wily politician himself, Zhu De knew how to lend support to the Chairman's vision of a jump forward into communism. In October 1957, he had already suggested that 'we must fight to expand exports and imports, so that we can gradually become a large importer and large exporter'. A few weeks later he argued that 'if we want to build socialism, we need to import technology, equipment, steel, and other necessary materials'.[13]

'Larger imports and larger exports', an idealistic policy that ran rough-shod over the actual capacity of the country to export foodstuffs and materials, became a major catchphrase in 1958. It suited Mao, who could show off the success of his policies on the international stage. Once he had asserted his authority over his colleagues and silenced those who were critical of the Great Leap Forward, few leaders thought it wise to argue in favour of financial discipline. As the projected output of industry and agriculture was ceaselessly revised upwards, so the quantity of imports rose. In other words a tightening of foreign trade was feasible only once Mao recognised the failure of the Great Leap Forward. Politics was in command, and an overshoot in imports was seen not as a sign of budgetary indiscipline, but as an indication of boundless faith in the power of the masses to transform the economy. The purpose of spending on capital goods imported from abroad was to create the capacity to produce machinery and manufactured goods, catapulting the economy into a dramatically higher level of indus-trial development which would ultimately free China from its economic dependence on the Soviet Union.

Mao had few opponents at home. Abroad, in the Soviet bloc, leaders may have harboured doubts about the Great Leap Forward, but increased quantities of foodstuffs shipped from China suited them well. Khrushchev, after all, was shifting the emphasis in the Soviet economy away from heavy industry towards the needs of consumers, and defiantly promising to over-take the USA in per-capita production of meat, milk and butter. In East Germany Ulbricht was desperate to stop the flow of people who voted with their feet by escaping to West Germany. He, too, made extravagant claims, announcing at the Fifth Party Congress in 1958 that a socialist society was in the making, as the per-capita quantity of consumer goods would soon 'catch up and overtake' that of West Germany, a process envisaged to be completed by 1961.[14] In the meantime, he collectivised the countryside, causing severe food shortages which only increased reliance on imports from China. East German leaders may have had doubts about the size of the 1958 crop in China, but they were keen on more foodstuffs.[15] Not only did rice become a staple food in East Germany during the Great Leap Forward, but the margarine industry depended on imports of edible oils from China. Trade delegates pushed hard for greater imports of animal fodder, tobacco and peanuts.[16] Such was the pressure that in June 1959 a Chinese trade representative was forced to explain that the fodder exported for pigs in Germany was needed to feed people in China.[17]

China not only exported more to its Soviet-bloc allies, but also started dumping products in Asia and Africa. At the fortieth anniversary of the October Revolution in Moscow, Khrushchev had triumphantly declared his intention to catch up with the United States in the production of farm products. He also announced a trade offensive. 'We declare war on you in the peaceful field of trade,' he threatened, starting a worldwide economic initiative designed to cripple US foreign trade and lure the economies of developing nations into the Soviet embrace. Russia sold tin, zinc and soybean products at prices nobody could match, and delivered lorries, cars and machinery in the Middle East at less than production cost – often with loans offering low interest rates and preferential repayment terms.[18] In a planned economy which subordinated economics to politics, the Soviet Union could overpay for raw materials, ignore market prices and sustain heavy losses to win influence around the globe.

China was goaded into its own trade war, dumping goods as if they were all surplus to internal demand in the age of plenty brought about by the Great Leap Forward. Bicycles, sewing machines, thermos flasks, canned pork, fountain pens: all sorts of goods were sold below cost to demonstrate that the country was ahead of the Soviet Union in the race for true communism. In the British colony of Hong Kong, raincoats made in China sold for 40 per cent less than in Guangzhou.[19] Leather shoes went for US$1.50 per pair, frozen quail for 8 cents each, violins for US$5.[20]

But the main enemy in the economic war against imperialism was Japan, and China did its best to undercut its rival in soybean oil, cement, structural steel and window glass. Most of all, clothes became the battle-field where communist supremacy had to be asserted, as products from grey sheeting to cotton prints flooded the market. The cost of exporting goods below economic cost was enormous for a country living on the edge. In 1957 some 8.7 million bolts of cloth were exported for more than US$50 million. In the first nine months of 1958 alone 9.2 million bolts found their way on to the international market, bringing in a mere US$47 million, or 12 per cent less. By the end of the year, as poor farmers in the countryside were facing a winter without cotton-padded clothes, some 14 million bolts had been sold abroad below cost.[21] All that was done in order for China to be able to claim the title of the world's third largest exporter of cloth – instead of being fifth. As Ye Jizhuang acknowledged at a party conference on foreign trade at the end of 1958, flooding the market with goods below cost had been a disaster, as more had been sold than before but for far less revenue: 'we really hurt ourselves, we frightened our friends and we awakened our enemies'.[22]

'I hear that in the Ministry of Foreign Trade some people sign contracts in a very casual way. Who allowed you to export that much?' Zhou Enlai enquired, distancing himself from the scheme.

'We thought that we had a big cotton crop and would not encounter any problems so we did not ask for permission,' interjected Ma Yimin, an administrator from the Ministry of Foreign Trade.[23]

But neither the cotton crop nor the grain crop, nor, for that matter, industrial output, was anywhere near what had been pledged during the Great Leap Forward. China had a yawning trade deficit. Promised deliveries to socialist allies were not met. Only a third of an agreed 2,000 tonnes of frozen poultry had been handed over to East Germany in 1958, and Walter Ulbricht demanded the rest in time for Christmas. East Germany was owed some 5 to 7 million rubles, Hungary 1.3 million, Czechoslovakia 1.1 million, and all of them requested compensation in the shape of rice, peanuts or animal hides. Zhou agreed to free up an extra 15,000 tonnes of rice and 2,000 tonnes of peanuts for Hungary and Czechoslovakia. He also brushed aside Zhu De's policy of 'large imports, large exports'. Noting a shortfall of 400 million yuan in exports to the socialist bloc for 1958, he declared that 'we are against large imports and large exports, as foreign trade must be measured'.[24]

How should the shortfall be addressed? Zhou Enlai was the first to state in November 1958 that 'I would rather that we don't eat or eat less and consume less, as long as we honour contracts signed with foreigners.'[25] 'To take goods without anything in return is not in the style of socialism,' he added a few weeks later.[26] Deng Xiaoping chimed in: if everybody could just save a few eggs, a pound of meat, a pound of oil and six kilos of grain the entire export problem would simply vanish.[27] Li

Xiannian, Li Fuchun and Bo Yibo agreed: 'In order to construct socialism and build a better future, people will agree to eat a little less if we
explain the reasons.'[28]

In order to honour foreign obligations, exports for 1959 were substantially increased from 6.5 to 7.9 billion yuan, while imports grew only 3 per
cent to 6.3 billion.[29] Grain earmarked for foreign markets, for instance,
was doubled to 4 million tonnes.[30] Some readers may think that this was
merely a few percentages of the total grain output, but in a poor country
a few million tonnes made the difference between life and death. As Wang
Renzhong bitterly pointed out in 1961, when the country was groping for
a way out of the famine, Hubei province (of which he was leader) received
200,000 tonnes from Beijing to fight mass starvation in 1959, but the state
exported more than 4 million tonnes the same year.[31]

The responsibility for reaching export targets was passed on to provincial leaders, each region being given a proportion of the national target.
But in the winter of 1958–9 provincial bosses were confronted with growing shortfalls. By January 1959 a mere 80,000 tonnes of grain for export
had been procured nationwide. The following month Hubei refused to
provide more than 23,000 out of a planned 48,000, while Li Jingquan
agreed to come up with two-thirds of Sichuan's quota, making up the rest
in a variety of inferior grains. In Anhui Zeng Xisheng approved the delivery of only 5,000 out of a planned 23,500 tonnes. Fujian handed over
nothing.[32] In other export commodities too, most provinces met only half
of their export quota, and regions such as Guizhou, Gansu and Qinghai
slipped to below a third of their obligations.[33]

Complaints about non-delivery reached Beijing: hospitals and kindergartens in Leningrad, for instance, were out of rice in the middle of the
winter.[34] As the issue of foreign trade slipped out of control, it was discussed
at a party meeting in Shanghai in March–April 1959. Mao stepped in
and recommended vegetarianism as a solution: 'We should save on clothing and food to guarantee exports, otherwise if 650 million people start
eating a little more our export surplus will all be eaten up. Horses, cows,
sheep, chicken, dogs, pigs: six of the farm animals don't eat meat, and
aren't they all still alive? Some people don't eat meat either, old Xu didn't
eat meat and he lived till he was eighty. I heard that Huang Yanpei didn't

eat meat, he too lived to eighty. Can we pass a resolution that nobody should eat meat, and that all of it should be exported?'[35] Having heard the Chairman's command, Peng Zhen, the mayor of Beijing, was willing to go even further, suggesting that the consumption of grain be cut as well in order to increase exports. Zhou Enlai, now emboldened, suggested that 'we should not eat any pork for three months so that we can guarantee meat exports'.[36] Besides meat, the use of edible oil was also curtailed. On 24 May 1959 an order was issued to all provinces: in the interests of the export market and the construction of socialism, no more edible oil should be sold in the countryside.[37]

But as the pressure to deliver increased, another problem appeared. Local units started cutting corners in order to meet their targets, leading to falling standards in the quality of exports. The Soviet Union lodged repeated complaints about the quality of meat, which was often contaminated by bacteria. Up to a third of the pork tins were rusty.[38] Grievances were filed about other goods as well: some 46,000 shoes sent to the Soviet Union had defects, paper exported to Hong Kong was unusable, batteries bought by Iraq were leaking, while the Swiss found that a fifth of the shipped coal consisted of stones. West Germany discovered salmonella in 500 tonnes of eggs, and in Morocco a third of all pumpkin seeds bought from the People's Republic were infested with insects.[39] The cost of replacing tainted merchandise delivered in 1959 amounted to 200 or 300 million yuan, while China also acquired a bad reputation abroad which would prove difficult to shake.[40]

Still unable to overcome the growing trade deficit, Beijing undertook emergency measures in October 1959. The State Council directed that all commodities which could be reduced or eliminated from domestic consumption be squeezed, while any remaining shortfalls should be replaced by other obtainable goods.[41] To back up the readjustment, a special Export Office was established to monitor both the quality and the quantity of all export commodities.[42] Trade agreements were made on a calendar basis, and the new arrangements were part of an end-of-year drive to ensure the completion of export targets. This meant that pressure was added just as the country was entering winter. The amount of pork, for instance, was below quota, and in November a campaign was organised to procure an extra 9 million pigs before the end of the year.[43]

As 1959 came to an end, ruthless extraction meant that 7.9 billion yuan had been exported, in line with Zhou Enlai's target. Grain and edible oil reached 1.7 billion yuan. Of the 4.2 million tonnes of grain exported that year, 1.42 went to the Soviet Union, a million to Eastern Europe and close to 1.6 million to 'capitalist countries'.[44] But despite all these efforts it was simply not enough. The trade deficit with Eastern Europe in 1958 and with the Soviet Union in 1959 alone amounted to 300 million yuan.[45] Tensions would come to a boil in the summer of 1960.

Dizzy with Success

Mao had nudged, cajoled and bullied his colleagues into the Great Leap Forward, launching the country into a race to catch up with more developed countries through breakneck industrialisation and collectivisation of the countryside. Leaders who had been wary about the pace of economic development had been publicly degraded and humiliated, while on the ground those critical of the Leap had been swept away in a swirl of terror. Then, as the frenzy to come up with higher yields snowballed out of control and evidence about the damage on the ground accumulated, Mao turned around and started blaming everybody else for the disruptions that his campaign had created. A shrewd politician with an instinct for self-preservation honed by decades of political purges, he not only deflected the responsibility for the chaos on to the local party officials as well as his close colleagues, but also managed to portray himself as the benign leader concerned about the welfare of his subjects. During the process, which lasted from November 1958 to June 1959, the pressure temporarily abated, although the reprieve would turn out to be short-lived.

Misinformation proliferated in the political order entrenched by Mao. The Chairman was no fool, understanding all too well that the one-party system he had contributed to building could generate false reports and inflated statistics. In all communist regimes elaborate monitoring mechanisms existed to sidestep the official bureaucracy. Supreme leaders in particular had every interest in finding out about the problems which lower party officials preferred to keep to themselves, as failure to stay in touch could lead to a coup. Control organs supervised the formal workings of government bodies and party leaders, carrying out checks on finance, appointments, procedures and reporting. The state security, besides its usual tasks of preventing crime, running prisons and keeping the country safe, regularly surveyed popular opinion and gauged the extent of social discontent. In that capacity the minister of the Public Security Bureau was vital to Mao, and it is not surprising that he appointed Xie Fuzhi to the job in 1959: here, after all, was a leader who could be relied upon to tell the Chairman the truth. At all levels of the party machinery, confidential reports were regularly issued on a whole range of topics, although of course these too could be biased. These, in turn, could be bypassed by sending trusted officials on fact-finding missions. This is what Mao did in October 1958, also taking to the road himself to tackle the problems of the people's communes directly with leading cadres in the provinces. As evidence about statistical inflation mounted, he became increasingly worried. In Wuchang, confronted with a critical report in which his close ally Wang Renzhong showed that his province could produce 11 million tonnes of grain at most, instead of a projected 30 million tonnes, his confidence was dealt a blow and he became dejected.[1]

A lifeline was provided by Zhao Ziyang, the secretary of Guangdong province. In a report to his boss Tao Zhu, he revealed in January 1959 that many of the communes had hidden grain and hoarded cash. In a single county some 35,000 tonnes were uncovered.[2] Following up this clue, Zhao launched an anti-hiding campaign which turned up over a million tonnes of grain.[3] Tao Zhu praised the report and sent it to Mao.[4] Then came news from Anhui, under the leadership of radical Zeng Xisheng: 'The issue of so-called grain shortages in the countryside has nothing to do with lack of grain, nor is it linked to excessive state procurements: it is an ideological problem, in particular among local cadres.' The report went on to explain that team leaders on the ground had four apprehensions: namely, that the communes would not provide them with sufficient grain, that other teams might purposely fail to pull their weight and hide a part of the harvest, that excess grain might be confiscated in the case of a spring famine, and that heavier quotas would follow if they fully declared their true grain output.[5] Mao immediately circulated these reports, commenting that 'The problem of brigade leaders who hide grain and secretly divide it up is very serious. It worries the people and has an effect on the communist morality of local cadres, the spring crop, the enthusiasm for the Great Leap Forward in 1959 and the consolidation of the people's communes. The problem is widespread throughout the country and must be solved at once!'[6]

Mao took on the pose of a benevolent sage-king protective of the welfare of his subjects. The wind of communism had blown over the country-side, he explained. As overzealous cadres had taken collectivisation too far, randomly appropriating assets and labour in the name of the people's communes, the villagers had started to hide the grain. In March 1959 Mao even spoke with admiration for the strategies that the farmers adopted in evading grain procurements, threatening that he might join them if the party did not change its ways.[7] 'I now support conservatism. I stand on the side of right deviation. I am against egalitarianism and left adventur-ism. I now represent 500 million peasants and 10 million local cadres. It is essential to be right opportunists, we must persist with right opportunism. If you don't all join me in going to the right, then I will be a rightist on my own, and alone will face expulsion from the party!'[8] Only Mao could have used the label 'rightist', which would have spelled political death for anybody else, so flippantly, as he postured as the lonely hero daring to speak truth to power. As to the local cadres whom he blamed for the excesses, 5 per cent should be purged. 'No need to shoot every one of them.'[9] A few months later Mao quietly increased the quota to 10 per cent.[10]

Mao also took his colleagues to task. The emperor, it seemed, had been misled by his close advisers: there was a bumper crop, but nothing like the fantastic claims made earlier in the campaign. Mao confronted the party bosses, repeatedly pouring scorn on outlandish predictions and demanding that projections for economic output be scaled back to more realistic levels. When a cautious Bo Yibo failed to cut back on industrial projects in March 1959, Mao was full of disdain. 'What kind of people are running our indus-try: the spoilt sons of a rich family! What we need in industry right now is a Qin emperor type. You people in industry are too soft, always talking about justice and virtue, so much so that as a result you accomplish nothing.'[11]

Particular blame was reserved for the close cronies who had so faithfully implemented his wishes. In front of the assembled leaders in Shanghai in April, Mao recollected: 'When I convened a small meeting at the Beidaihe conference in August nobody objected when we discussed the targets for 1959. At the time I was mainly busy with the shelling of Quemoy.

The question of the people's communes was not really mine, it was Tan Zhenlin who was in charge – I just wrote a few lines.' About the resolution taken on the people's communes he had the following thoughts: 'That was somebody else's idea, not mine. I had a look at it but I didn't understand it, I just had a faint impression that communes are good.' Contributing to inflated targets were incomprehensible documents: 'We should forbid all these incomprehensible documents from leaving the room. You are university students, professors, great Confucian minds, I am merely an ordinary student, so you should write in plain language.' And in case anybody had any doubts about his leadership, he warned his colleagues: 'Some comrades still have not acknowledged that I am the leader . . . Many people hate me, in particular [defence minister] Peng Dehuai, he hates me to death . . . My policy with Peng Dehuai is as follows: if you don't attack me, I won't attack you, but if you attack me I for sure will attack you.' Then Mao launched into a rambling tirade in which every party leader who had disagreed with him in the past was mentioned by name, including Liu Shaoqi, Zhou Enlai, Chen Yun, Zhu De, Lin Biao, Peng Dehuai, Liu Bocheng, Chen Yi, even Ren Bishi, who had long since passed away. Every leader present was named, with the exception of Deng Xiaoping.[12] The point of the outburst was to show that Mao had been right all along, while those who had opposed him at one point or another in the party's past had all been wrong. Standing on the side of history, Mao was accountable to no one.

And no one was left in any doubt about the overall correctness of his line and the primacy of success. Mao never missed a chance to laud the Great Leap Forward: 'No matter how many problems we have, in the final analysis it does not amount to more than one finger out of ten.'[13] To mistake a tenth for the whole was an error. Even to think that a campaign of such a momentous nature could have been launched without making a single mistake was an error. To doubt the Great Leap Forward was an error, and to stand by and watch from a critical distance was an error.[14] Mao could not be swayed from his overall strategy.

———

In the first half of 1959 close cropping and deep ploughing continued unabated, irrigation schemes proceeded apace and collectivisation went

ahead. In a moment of retrenchment following an all-out drive to collec-
tivise the countryside, Stalin had allowed farmers to leave the collective
farms after he published an article entitled 'Dizzy with Success' in 1930.
Unlike his former patron, Mao did very little about the people's communes.
He merely indicated that the brigade should be the basic accounting unit
rather than the commune. Historians have interpreted this period as one
of 'retreat' or 'cooling off', but this was simply not the case. Deng Xiaoping
made this clear to the lieutenants on the battlefield in February 1959: 'We
need to warm up, not cool down.'[15]

Requisitions from the countryside to feed the cities and satisfy foreign
clients were drastically increased precisely during this period. In the top-
secret minutes distributed only to participants of a meeting held in the
Jinjiang Hotel in Shanghai on 25 March, Mao ordered that a third of all
grain be procured, far above previous rates: 'If you don't go above a third,
people won't rebel.' Regions that failed to fulfil their procurement quotas
should be reported: 'This is not ruthless, it's realistic.' The country had a
bumper harvest, and cadres should study the example of Henan in raising
procurements: 'he who strikes first prevails, he who strikes last fails'. Mao
made an extra 16,000 lorries available to carry out the task. As to meat, he
praised the decision taken by Hebei and Shandong to ban the consumption in the countryside for a period of three months: 'this is good, why can
the whole country not do the same?' Edible oils should be extracted to the
maximum. He brushed aside an interjection by a colleague suggesting that
the state should guarantee eight metres of cloth per person a year: 'Who
has ordered that?' And as we saw in the last chapter, Mao also reversed the
priority given to the local market. Exports trumped local needs and had to
be guaranteed: 'we should eat less'. A firm (*zhuajin*) and ruthless (*zhuahen*)
approach was warranted in times of war when confronting practical problems. 'When there is not enough to eat people starve to death. It is better
to let half of the people die so that the other half can eat their fill.'[16]

Mao's word was the law. But what was the meaning of some of his
more obscure pronouncements, for instance 'he who strikes first prevails,
he who strikes last fails'? Tan Zhenlin, put in charge of agriculture by the
party's secretariat, clarified this in June 1959 in a telephone conference
on procurements. He explained that the grain should be taken before the

farmers could eat it: speed was of the essence, as each side tried to get to the crop first. 'But this saying of "he who strikes first prevails" should be used only by county and regional party secretaries; if it were used below that level it could easily lead to misunderstandings.'[17] Wang Renzhong, the man who had told Mao how cadres had inflated the crop figures, had the following recommendation: 'We will try peaceful means before we resort to force. If they still fail to comply with the state's unified planning, then we will apply the necessary measures, from a formal warning to dismissal or even removal from the party.'[18]

Signs of famine had appeared in 1958. In the first half of 1959 starvation became widespread, as villagers were hit by increased procurements ordered by the state. Even a zealot like Tan Zhenlin estimated that as early as January some 5 million people were suffering from famine oedema, 70,000 having starved to death. Zhou Enlai put the latter figure at 120,000. Both men were far below the mark, but had little incentive to investigate further.[19] Mao was aware of the famine but downplayed it by circulating reports showing that villagers in distressed regions were getting enough food, up to half a kilo a day in model province Henan.[20] On the ground local cadres were unsure how to respond, bewildered by the shifting and contradictory signals emerging from Beijing. At the top the leadership was taken aback by Mao's outburst in Shanghai: it was an omen of things to come.

12

The End of Truth

A vast mountain range runs across the north of Jiangxi province with summits and craggy peaks rising 1,500 metres above sea level. Mount Lushan itself is an area of sedimentary rocks and limestone out of which gullies, gorges, caves and rock formations have been carved by water and wind, giving it a wild and rugged character much admired by visitors. Forests of fir, pine, camphor and cypress, clinging to cliffs and crevices, compete with waterfalls for attention, while temples and pagodas offer views as far as the sand dunes on the shores of the Boyang Lake down in the Yangzi valley. A temperate climate gives much-needed respite during the stifling heat of summer. Before the revolution Europeans also trekked to the region during the winter months to toboggan and ski. An English missionary first bought the Guling valley in 1895, and over the following decades several hundred bungalows, built of soft granite hauled up from the valley, turned Lushan into a sanatorium and summer residence for foreigners. Chiang Kai-shek, leader of the ruling Guomindang, acquired an attractive villa where he and his wife spent many summers in the 1930s. Mao reserved the place for himself, making sure that the name of Meilu Villa, carved into a stone by the Generalissimo himself, was preserved.

The Chairman opened the Lushan meeting on 2 July 1959. Party leaders referred to the gathering as a 'meeting of immortals'. Immortals lived far above mere humans, seated on the clouds of heaven, playfully gliding through the mist, unencumbered by earthly restraints. Mao wanted his colleagues to feel free to talk about any topic they wanted, and he had in mind eighteen initial points for discussion. But he had overheard critical comments made by defence minister Peng Dehuai that very day and added a nineteenth point to his agenda: party unity.[1] He set the tone by praising the achievements of the Great Leap Forward and lauding the enthusiasm and energy of the Chinese people.

One way for Mao to find out what party leaders thought about the Leap was to have them discuss problems in small groups divided geographically: each reviewed issues specific to their own regional area for a week, while the Chairman retained overall oversight by being the only one to be given a daily report about each group's meetings. Despite his suspicion that Peng Dehuai might be up to something, Mao seemed at first in good spirits, full of plans to visit the rock caves, Buddhist temples and many Confucian landmarks for which Lushan was so famous. The local leadership also organised evening entertainment with music and dance troupes performing in a former Catholic church, which was invariably followed by dancing parties at which Mao found himself surrounded by several young nurses. Mao would entertain them in his room, tightly protected by special security.[2]

Mao did not intervene, but was briefed by the reports submitted by reliable provincial bosses on how each group approached the question of the Great Leap Forward. Many of the conference participants believed that the Lushan gathering would push further for economic reform, as problems with the Great Leap Forward had already been discussed at previous meetings and some measures had been taken to tackle a situation sliding out of control. As the days went by, the absence of any intervention by the Chairman and the intimacy of a small group setting lured some leaders into talking more and more openly about starvation, bogus production figures and cadre abuses in the countryside. Peng Dehuai, assigned to the north-west group, was outspoken, on several occasions blaming Mao for the direction of the Great Leap Forward: 'We all have a share of responsibility, including Mao Zedong. The steel target of 10.7 million tonnes was set by Chairman Mao, so how could he escape responsibility?'[3] But silence from the Chairman was not approval, and Mao was becoming increasingly upset as the limits within which he thought discussion would take place were being ignored and some leaders started focusing not only on the failures of collectivisation but also on his personal role in them.

Mao spoke again on 10 July, convening a meeting of the regional leaders and arguing that the achievements of the past year far exceeded the failures.

He used the metaphor consecrated at the Nanning meeting in January 1958: 'Doesn't everybody have ten fingers? We can count nine of those fingers as achievements, and only one as a failure.' The party could resolve its problems, but only through unity and shared ideology. The general line, he said, was completely correct. Liu Shaoqi chimed in by explaining that the few problems that had appeared were the result of a lack of experience: was there not always a tuition fee to be paid for valuable lessons? Zhou Enlai added that the party was quick in discovering problems and expert in solving them. The Chairman concluded: 'The situation in general is excellent. There are many problems, but our future is bright!'[4]

Silence followed Mao's speech. But not everybody was willing to fall in line. Defence minister Peng Dehuai was well known for being stubborn. When Peng had gone back to his home in Xiangtan, Hunan, the same region where Mao had grown up, he found abuse and suffering everywhere, from farmers forced to practise close cropping to cadres tearing down houses in the iron and steel campaign. Visiting a retirement home and a kindergarten, he saw nothing but misery, the children in rags and the elderly crouched on bamboo mats in the freezing winter. Even after his visit he continued receiving letters from his home town about widespread starvation.[5] Peng felt strongly about what he had witnessed in the countryside, and had high hopes of addressing the failures of the Great Leap in Lushan. He now feared that the meeting would turn into a mere formality in which out of deference to Mao the subject of the famine would be skirted.[6] None of the leaders, he believed, had the courage to speak out: Liu Shaoqi had just become head of state, Zhou Enlai and Chen Yun had been silenced a year earlier, Zhu De had few critical ideas, Marshal Lin Biao was in poor health and had a limited understanding of the problems, while Deng Xiaoping was reluctant to voice any criticism.[7] He decided to write to Mao instead, dropping off a long letter at his lodging as the Chairman was asleep on 14 July.

With the body of a bull and the face of a bulldog, a stout man with a shaven head, Peng Dehuai was known for being a leader who did not hesitate to speak his mind openly to Mao.[8] Mao and Peng went back to the early days of guerrilla fighting in Jinggangshan, but had clashed on several occasions, notably during the Korean War when an incensed Peng had stormed past a guard into Mao's bedroom to confront the Chairman about military strategy. The Chairman disliked the old marshal intensely.

Peng's letter of opinion started like a memorial: 'I am a simple man and indeed I am crude and lack tact. For this reason, whether this letter is of value or not is for you to decide. Please correct me wherever I am wrong.' Peng was careful to give due praise to the accomplishments of the Great Leap Forward, as agricultural and industrial production had soared while the backyard furnaces had brought new technical skills to the peasants. Peng even predicted that Britain would be overtaken in a mere four years. Whatever problems had appeared, he wrote, were due to a poor understanding of the Chairman's ideas. In the second part of his letter Peng insisted that the party could learn from the mistakes of the Great Leap Forward: these included considerable waste of natural resources and manpower, inflated production claims and leftist tendencies.

His letter was balanced and prudent, all the more so in light of what was to come in the following days, yet it managed to incense Mao. Peng's mention of 'petty-bourgeois fanaticism leading to leftist errors' had touched a raw nerve in the Chairman. Just as offensive was an ironic statement according to which 'dealing with economic construction does not come quite as easily as bombing Quemoy or dealing with Tibet'.[9]

According to his doctor, Mao did not sleep all night. Two days later he called a politburo standing committee in his villa, receiving the leaders in a bathrobe and slippers.[10] Rightists elements outside the party had attacked the Great Leap Forward, Mao explained, and now people from within the ranks were undermining the movement as well, claiming that it had done more harm than good. Peng Dehuai was one such person, and his letter was to be distributed to all 150 participants at the Lushan meeting for discussion in small groups. He then asked Liu Shaoqi and Zhou Enlai to call in reinforcements from Beijing: Peng Zhen, Chen Yi, Huang Kecheng and others were to join the meeting as soon as possible.[11]

Most senior cadres by now understood how serious the situation had become and spoke out against Peng. Zhang Zhongliang, the Gansu leader, claimed that the successes in his province illustrated the wisdom of the Great Leap Forward. Tao Zhu, Wang Renzhong and Chen Zhengren, all of whom had a stake in the Leap, also agreed.[12] But several did not. Huang Kecheng, army chief of staff, arriving the following day from Beijing, unexpectedly spoke in favour of Peng Dehuai. As Huang would admit in the weeks to come, he had been unable to sleep because of the scale of starvation in the countryside.[13] Tan Zhenlin, who could always be counted on, exploded: 'Have you eaten dog meat [meaning, are you hot in the head]? Are you suffering from fever? All this nonsense! You should know that we asked you to come to Lushan to help us out.'[14] Others wavered too. Zhou Xiaozhou, the first party secretary of Hunan province, praised the letter, although he agreed that it contained a few barbs. The turning point was a bombshell dropped by Zhang Wentian in a stunning attack on Mao and the Great Leap Forward on 21 July.

Zhang Wentian had defied Mao's leadership in the early 1930s as a member of the opposing faction, but later rallied to the Chairman's cause. As vice-minister of foreign affairs he carried considerable weight, and Mao could only see his support of Peng as an alliance between the Ministry of Defence and the Ministry of Foreign Affairs.[15] Zhang spoke for several hours on 21 July, despite frequent heckling from Mao's supporters. Contrary to established party rituals, he brushed aside the achievements in a short opening paragraph and stormed straight into a close examination of the problems caused by the Great Leap Forward. Targets were far too high, claims about the crop were bogus, and as a consequence people were dying of hunger. The cost of the backyard furnaces was 5 billion yuan, to say nothing of a crop lost because peasants were too busy smelting iron to collect the harvest from the fields. Zhang denounced slogans such as 'Let All the People Smelt Steel' as absurd. Stoppages in production were frequent. Foreigners complained about the low quality of products made in China, damaging the country's reputation. Most of all, the Great Leap Forward had made no difference in the countryside: 'Our country is "poor and blank", and the socialist system gives us the conditions to change this rapidly, but we are still "poor and blank".' Mao encouraged leaders to pull the emperor off his horse, Zhang conceded, yet nobody dared to speak out for fear of losing his head. In conclusion, he inverted Mao's metaphor of ten fingers: 'The shortcomings outweigh the achievements by a factor of nine to one.'[16]

Mao must have wondered whether this was a concerted attack on his leadership. Peng Dehuai commanded the army, Zhou Xiaozhou headed a province, Zhang Wentian was in foreign affairs. Could there be more opponents hiding in the background? Peng had been assigned to the north-west group on account of his experience of Gansu province, which he had toured in the previous months, and both Peng and Zhang repeatedly discussed the problems that had appeared in that part of the country.[17] As the Lushan meeting was unfolding, a coup took place in Gansu province. After Zhang Zhongliang, the man in charge of Gansu, had left Lanzhou to attend the Lushan meeting, the provincial party committee was swayed by his rival Huo Weide. On 15 July they sent an urgent letter to the centre announcing that thousands had died of hunger and that over 1.5 million farmers were suffering from a famine raging across half a dozen coun-ties. The chief responsible for this famine was Zhang Zhongliang, who as leader of the province had ratified inflated crop figures, increased state procurements, condoned cadre abuses on the ground and failed to act when starvation had appeared in April 1959. Before Mao's own eyes, in the middle of the Lushan meeting, one of his most zealous followers was thus being undermined by a provincial party committee.[18]

More bad news reached Mao. In April Peng Dehuai had visited Eastern Europe on a goodwill tour, briefly meeting with Khrushchev in Albania. Shortly after his return, during a debriefing session with Mao, Peng Dehuai uttered a clumsy remark which made the Chairman's face turn red: several dozen leaders close to Tito, he observed, had fled to Albania. Tito was the ruthless leader of Yugoslavia who had dared to oppose Stalin, alienating some of his close supporters. Mao must have interpreted the comment as a veiled criticism of his own rule.[19] A few weeks later, on 20 June, the Soviet leadership reneged on its agreement to help China develop nuclear weapons.

Then on 18 July Khrushchev publicly condemned the communes while visiting the Polish town of Poznań. He accused those who had pressed for communes in Russia in the 1920s of having a poor understanding of what communism was and how it should be built. The initial release of his speech on Polish radio did not mention the communes, but a few days later a full version was printed in *Pravda*, which to close observers could only look like a carefully planned attack on Mao. A translation in Chinese appeared a few days later in a newsletter reserved for the Beijing leadership,[20] but already on 19 July Mao circulated a report compiled by the embassy in Moscow showing how some Soviet cadres openly discussed the fact that people were dying of hunger in China as a result of the Great Leap Forward.[21] Could there be collusion between enemies within the party and revisionists abroad? Was it a coincidence that Khrushchev made his speech precisely when both Peng Dehuai and Zhang Wentian were attacking the Great Leap Forward?

Ke Qingshi, the party boss in Shanghai, was so incensed by Zhang Wentian's talk that he approached Mao and urged him to take on his enemies then and there. Li Jingquan also spoke with Mao. Liu Shaoqi and Zhou Enlai conferred with the Chairman on the evening of 22 July, although the details of what was said that evening are not known.[22] In a rather disingenuous but clever way that implicated Liu Shaoqi, Mao would claim a few weeks later that he had been puzzled by requests for greater freedom of speech by some comrades: Liu was the one who had pointed out to him that these were not isolated voices but a faction fighting the party line.[23]

On 23 July Mao gave a long and rambling speech lasting three hours in which obscure metaphors were mixed with blunt threats aimed at frightening his opponents. He opened his speech thus: 'You have spoken at great length, so how about you allow me to say a few words – what do you think?' He then rebutted Peng Dehuai's letter, reviewed all the attacks on the party since its foundation and cautioned leaders not to waver in a moment of crisis – some comrades were a mere thirty kilometres away from being rightists. He repeated the threat he had made at a party meeting three months earlier: 'If you don't attack me, I won't attack you, but if you attack me I for sure will attack you.' If every little problem in every brigade was to be reported in the *People's Daily* at the expense of any other news, he said, it would take at least a year to appear in print. And what would be the result? The country would collapse, the leadership would be overthrown. 'If we deserve to perish, I will go to the countryside to lead the peasants and overthrow the government. If the People's Liberation Army won't follow me, I will then go to find a Red Army. But I think that the

Liberation Army will follow me.' Mao admitted overall responsibility for
the Great Leap Forward, but he also implicated a string of colleagues, from
Ke Qingshi, the Shanghai boss who had first proposed a steel campaign,
Li Fuchun who was in charge of overall planning, Tan Zhenlin and Lu
Liaoyan who together oversaw agriculture, to the provincial leaders he
labelled leftist, whether the province be Yunnan, Henan, Sichuan or Hubei.
Mao delivered an ultimatum: leaders would have to choose between Peng
and himself, and the wrong choice would bring about enormous political
consequences for the party.[24]

His audience was shell-shocked. As Mao walked out with his doctor,
he bumped into Peng Dehuai. 'Minister Peng, let's have a talk,' Mao
suggested.

Peng Dehuai was livid. 'There's nothing to talk about. No more talk,'
he answered, cutting through the air by bringing down his right hand in a
chopping motion.[25]

––––––––––

On 2 August, Mao opened the plenum of the central committee in a short
but fierce speech which set the tone for the following two weeks. 'When we
first arrived in Lushan there was something in the air, as some people said
that there was no freedom to speak openly, there was pressure. At the time
I did not quite understand what this was all about. I could not make head
or tail of it and did not see why they said there was not enough freedom.
Indeed, the first two weeks felt like a meeting of immortals and there was
no tension. Only later did it become tense, as some people wanted freedom
of speech. Tension appeared because they wanted the freedom to criticise
the general line, freedom to destroy the general line. They criticised what
we did last year, and they criticised this year's work, saying that everything
we did last year was bad, fundamentally bad . . . What problems do we
have now? Today, the only problem is the rightist opportunists launching a
furious attack on the party, the people and the great and dynamic socialist
enterprise.' Mao warned his colleagues that there was a stark choice to be
made. 'You either want unity or you want to split the party.'[26]

The following week small working groups were charged with grilling Peng
Dehuai, Zhang Wentian, Huang Kecheng, Zhou Xiaozhou and others on

every detail of their plot against the party. In a series of tense confrontations and cross-examinations, the 'anti-party clique' had to subject themselves to ever more detailed self-criticisms in which every aspect of their pasts, their meetings and their talks was scrutinised. Allegations about famine had cast a shadow over provincial bosses such as Li Jingquan, Zeng Xisheng, Wang Renzhong and Zhang Zhongliang, and they needed no encouragement to attack the men who had undermined their credibility. Lin Biao proved just as ferocious. A gaunt, balding general who had destroyed the best Guomindang divisions in Manchuria in the civil war, Lin had been quietly promoted by Mao to one of the vice-chairmanships of the party a few months earlier. Suffering from all sorts of phobias about water, wind and cold, he often called in sick, living a mole-like existence, but at Lushan he rallied to the Chairman's defence, accusing Peng Dehuai of being overly 'ambitious, conspiratorial and hypocritical'. In his shrill voice he crowed that 'Only Mao is a great hero, a role to which no one else should dare to aspire. We all lag very far behind him, so don't even think about it!'[27]

Liu Shaoqi and Zhou Enlai also had their parts to play. Both had a lot to lose, and either one could be blamed for what had gone wrong in the country if Mao decided to retreat. Liu Shaoqi had enthusiastically backed the Great Leap Forward and been rewarded for his loyalty with a promotion to head of state in April. He also viewed himself as the potential inheritor of the party's leadership and had no desire to rock the boat. After Mao's outburst Liu became so nervous that he increased his use of sleeping tablets. At one point he overdosed and collapsed in the toilet.[28] But he pulled himself together, and on 17 August, the last day of the meeting, he gave a display of fawning flattery, extolling Mao's many qualities.[29]

Zhou Enlai, as premier, had been involved in the day-to-day running of the country and would have had to account for the disastrous turn of events if Peng Dehuai had had his way. He also had personal reasons to feel threatened by the old marshal. Huang Kecheng, during one of the grilling sessions, revealed that years earlier Peng had described Zhou as a weak politician who should step down from all important posts.[30] But most of all Zhou backed Mao because he had made a decision long ago never to cross the Chairman: loyalty to Mao, as he had discovered over decades of fierce political infighting, was the key to staying in power. His

position had already been weakened after Mao's withering attack on him
at Nanning over a year ago and he had no desire to incur the Chairman's
wrath again. Mao was thus the centre of an uneasy coalition of leaders
who felt threatened by Peng Dehuai. Without their support the Chairman
might not have prevailed.

As the meetings progressed and the criticisms escalated, the men who
had spoken out against Mao were gradually broken down until full confessions were obtained. Peng admitted that his letter and the comments he
had made in the early sessions were not isolated incidents, but 'anti-party,
anti-people, anti-socialist mistakes of a rightist opportunist nature'.[31]

Mao spoke again on 11 August, singling out Peng Dehuai: 'You said
that at the North China meeting I fucked your mother for forty days, and
here at Lushan you only fucked my mother for twenty days, so I still owe
you twenty days. Now we indulge your desire, and I even added five days
on top of the forty we have had so far so that you can insult us as much
as you want, otherwise we would owe you.' In the more standard jargon
of socialism, Mao claimed that Peng and his supporters were 'bourgeois
democrats' who had little in common with the proletarian socialist revolution, thereby stripping them of their positions and casting them into the
ranks of the bourgeoisie.[32]

At the closing meeting of the conference five days later a resolution was
adopted in which Mao's opponents were found guilty of having conspired
against party, state and people.[33] The next few months would unleash a
nationwide witch-hunt against 'rightist' elements.

13

Repression

The army was purged. Lin Biao, who could be depended on to ferret out any ideological opposition among the military, was rewarded for his performance at Lushan with Peng Dehuai's job. Lin knew that speaking the truth about conditions in the countryside was a naive approach bound to fail, and he showered the Chairman with flattery instead. But in private he was much more critical than Peng, confiding in his private diary – unearthed by Red Guards years later – that the Great Leap Forward was 'based on fantasy, and a total mess'.[1] Rarely was the distance between a leader's inner thoughts and his public statements so vast, but all over the country party officials scrambled to prove their allegiance to the Chairman and the Great Leap Forward as a new purge unfolded.

The tone was set at the top. In language auguring the Cultural Revolution, Peng Zhen beat the drum for a purge of the ranks: 'The struggle should be profound, and should be carried out according to our principles, whether it is against old comrades-in-arms, colleagues or even husbands and wives.' Tan Zhenlin, the zealous vice-premier overseeing agriculture, pointed out that enemies were entrenched at the very top: 'this struggle should separate us from some of our old comrades-in-arms!'[2] In Beijing alone thousands of top officials were targeted by the end of 1959, including almost 300 up to the level of central committee member, or 10 per cent of the top echelon. More than sixty were branded as rightists. Many were old veterans, but as the leadership explained they had to be smashed resolutely or else the 'construction of socialism' would be imperilled.[3]

Across the country anybody who had expressed reservations about the Great Leap Forward was hunted down. In Gansu this struggle started as soon as Zhang Zhongliang returned to Lanzhou. Huo Weide, Song

Liangcheng and others who had 'shot a poisoned arrow at Lushan' were denounced as members of an 'anti-party clique'. Well over 10,000 cadres were hounded throughout the province.[4] Where his rivals had revealed widespread famine in a letter of denunciation to Beijing, Zhang wrote instead to the Chairman: 'Work in every department is surging ahead in our province, the changes are momentous, including those concerning grain. We are looking at a bumper harvest across the province.'[5] Then, as his realm turned into a living hell in 1960, he wrote again to explain deaths by starvation, blaming them on Huo Weide, the leader of the anti-party clique. Zhang minimised what would later be revealed to be death on a massive scale by again calling it a problem of 'one finger out of ten'.[6]

Anybody who had stood in the path of the Great Leap Forward was removed. In Yunnan, the deputy of the Bureau for Commerce was dismissed for having made critical comments about food shortages and the people's communes – and for having snored while recordings of the Chairman's speeches were being played.[7] In Hebei, the vice-director of the Bureau for Water Conservancy was purged for having expressed doubts about the wisdom of dismantling central-heating systems during the steel campaign.[8] County leaders who had started to close some of the canteens were persecuted for abandoning socialism and 'reverting to a go-it-alone policy'.[9] In Anhui vice-governor Zhang Kaifan and some of his allies were sacked, as Mao suspected that 'such people are speculators who sneaked into the party . . . They scheme to sabotage the proletarian dictatorship, split the party and organise factions.'[10] Similar high-level dismissals also occurred in Fujian, Qinghai, Heilongjiang and Liaoning, among other provinces.

Provincial leaders who had managed to soften the impact of the Great Leap Forward were removed. Under constant fire from Mao and his acolytes for his caution, Zhou Xiaozhou, the reluctant leader of Hunan province, had relented and inflated the crop projections in 1958. But he rarely lost an opportunity to put a damper on the enthusiasm of local cadres during inspection trips. In Changde he had openly scoffed at all the bragging about grain output. He questioned the supply system. Approached by a woman who complained about the local canteen, he had suggested that she simply walk out and cook a meal back home. He had refused point-blank to have anybody in Hunan follow the example set by Macheng, seeing the sputnik fields as a dangerous diversion from pressing agricultural tasks. In Ningxiang, where he had discovered that only women were working in the fields, he had demanded that the menfolk be recalled from the backyard furnaces. His response to the work–study programme requiring all students in primary schools to participate in productive labour had been a mere expletive: 'Rubbish!'[11] Despite his best efforts, many local cadres had forged ahead, embracing the Leap Forward through a mixture of conviction and ambition, leading to the same kind of abuses on the ground as could be found elsewhere.

But, all in all, Hunan was in better shape than its neighbour Hubei, run by Mao's sycophant Wang Renzhong. When Mao's special train had stopped in Wuchang in May 1959, just before the Lushan meeting, the city was in a terrible state. Even in the guesthouse set aside for Mao, there was no meat, no cigarettes and few vegetables. Changsha, in Mao's home province of Hunan, was different, with open-air restaurants still serving customers. Zhou Xiaozhou was all too conscious of the contrast, prodding his rival Wang, who was accompanying Mao to Changsha: 'Hunan was criticised for not having worked as hard. Now look at Hubei. You don't even have stale cigarettes or tea. You used up all your reserves last year. Today, we may be poor, but at least we have supplies in storage.'[12] With hindsight, maybe Zhou had made too many enemies to survive in the fierce environment of a one-party regime. As a key member of the 'anti-party clique' he was purged immediately after the Lushan plenum, paving the way for leaders like Zhang Pinghua who were willing to follow Mao's every dictate – and starve the local population as a result.

Whatever remnants of reason had managed to survive the folly of the Great Leap Forward were swept aside in a frenzied witch-hunt which left farmers more vulnerable than ever to the naked power of the party. At every level – province, county, commune, brigade – ferocious purges were carried out, replacing lacklustre cadres with hard, unscrupulous elements who trimmed their sails to benefit from the radical winds blowing from Beijing. In 1959–60 some 3.6 million party members were labelled or purged as rightists, although total membership surged from 13,960,000 in 1959 to 17,380,000 in 1961.[13] In a moral universe in which the means justified the ends, many would be prepared to become the Chairman's willing instruments, casting aside every idea about right and wrong to achieve the ends he envisaged. Had the leadership reversed course in the summer of 1959 at Lushan, the number of victims claimed by famine would have been counted in the millions. Instead, as the country plunged into catastrophe, tens of millions of lives would be extinguished through exhaustion, illness, torture and hunger. War on the people was about to take on a wholly new dimension as the leadership looked away, finding in the growing rift with the Soviet Union a perfect pretext to turn a blind eye to what was happening on the ground.

The Sino-Soviet Rift

Mikhail Klochko received his recall telegram on 16 July 1960. Together with some 1,500 Soviet advisers and 2,500 dependants, he was ordered to pack up and leave by his embassy in Beijing. His hosts were courteous to the last, having been instructed to provide every assistance possible – as well as to obtain, by any means possible, all the technical information that the Russians had not already handed over.[1] At a banquet for the departing advisers, foreign minister Chen Yi thanked them warmly for their immense help and wished them good health. On a more sour note, a Soviet delegate complained, 'We've done so much for you, and you are not content.'[2]

After Mao had initiated an international crisis by shelling Quemoy and Matsu two years earlier, Khrushchev started to reconsider his offer to deliver a sample atom bomb to China. Nuclear disarmament talks between the Soviet Union and the United States prompted him to delay honouring his pledge, and in June 1959 he finally reneged on his promise altogether.[3] In late September 1959, at a summit between the USA and the Soviet Union, Khrushchev agreed to a reduction of 1 million in the total number of Soviet troops, seeking a further rapprochement with the United States. Relations further deteriorated when Khrushchev visited Beijing a few months later to commemorate the tenth anniversary of the People's Republic. The Soviet delegation clashed with their hosts over a series of issues, including a border dispute between China and India, as Moscow attempted to act as an intermediary between the two countries instead of backing its ally Beijing. In the spring of 1960, Beijing started openly to challenge Moscow for the right to lead the socialist camp, denouncing Khrushchev in increasingly vituperative terms for his 'revisionism' and his pursuit of 'appeasement with imperialists'.⁴ Angered, the Soviet leader retaliated by pulling all Soviet advisers out of China.⁵

The withdrawal came as a blow to Mao. It led to the collapse of economic relations between the two countries, the cancellation of scores of large-scale projects and a freeze in high-end military technology transfers. As Jung Chang and Jon Halliday point out in *Mao: The Unknown Story*, the population should have benefited from these cancellations, as less food would now have to be exported to pay for expensive projects.⁶ But where the agreements allowed for repayments to be made over sixteen years, Mao insisted on settling up ahead of schedule: 'Times were really tough in Yan'an [during the war], we ate hot peppers and nobody died, and now that things are much better than in those days, we want to fasten our belts and try to pay the money back within five years.'⁷ On 5 August 1960, even before the departure of all Soviet specialists was completed, provincial leaders were warned by phone that the country was not exporting enough, as it was heading towards a deficit in the balance of payments of 2 billion yuan. Every effort had to be made to honour the Soviet debt within two years, and this had to be done by increasing exports of grain, cotton and edible oils as much as possible.⁸

The true scale of early repayments to the Soviet Union has only just come to light with the opening of the archives in the Ministry of Foreign Affairs in Beijing, where an army of accountants kept detailed records of how shifting exchange rates, the changing gold content of the ruble, re-negotiations of trade agreements and the calculation of interest rates affected repayments to the Soviet Union. They show that Moscow lent some 968.6 million rubles to Beijing between 1950 and 1955 (not including interest). By the time of the recall of Soviet experts some 430.3 million rubles were still owed.⁹ But as a consequence of the trade deficit further loans were contracted during the following years, and by the end of 1962 the total owed by Beijing stood at 1,407 million rubles (1,275 million in loans plus interest estimated at 132 million). Some 1,269 million of this was amortised by 1962.¹⁰ In other words, while the total debt increased from 968 to 1,407 million rubles, China managed to pay off roughly half a billion between 1960 and 1962, as tens of millions of Chinese died of famine. It may be that this amount was actually smaller, as the figure provided for 1960 did not include interest, which was presumably repaid on top of capital, but even if we allow for a correction of 10 per cent the fact remains that large sums of money were paid to the Soviet Union. In 1960 some 160 million rubles were sent to clear part of the debt, while in 1962 about 172 million rubles were returned (the figure for 1961 is missing but is likely to be similar).[11] Large amounts of exports were also used to amortise the debt, meaning that by the end of 1962 China owed the Soviet Union only 138 million rubles: China insisted on paying 97 million in 1963, clearing the debt by 1965.[12]

But the Russians never asked for an accelerated repayment. On the contrary, they agreed in April 1961 that 288 million rubles in unpaid balances should be refinanced as a new credit, with the payments taking place over four years, the first in 1962 being no more than 8 million.[13] As the moratorium on the trade deficit worked like an unplanned loan, it actually meant that China was given more economic aid by the Soviet Union than any other country had received during a single year to date.[14]

The real damage done to the economy by the recall of all experts was minor, since few civilian specialists worked in agriculture. And even if some industrial projects were delayed by the withdrawal of foreign expertise, the economy, at this stage, was already in deep trouble. But Mao conveniently blamed the Soviet Union for China's economic collapse, starting one of the most enduring myths about the famine, namely that hunger was caused by Soviet pressure to pay back the debts. Already in November 1960 China invoked natural catastrophes as well as the immense damage done to the entire economy by the Soviet recall to explain delays in the delivery of foodstuffs to East Germany.[15] In 1964, Mikhail Suslov, the chief ideologue in foreign policy in Moscow, noted that China blamed the Soviet Union for the famine.[16] To this day, when ordinary people who survived the famine are asked what, in their opinion, caused mass starvation, the answer almost invariably points to the Soviet Union. This is how a farmer from Shajing, near the Hong Kong border, explained the famine in a recent interview: 'The government owed the Soviet Union a huge sum of money and needed to repay the loans. A very huge sum of loans. So all the produce in the country had to be submitted. All the livestock and the grain had to be given out to the government to repay the loans to the Soviet Union. The Soviet Union forced China to repay the loans.'[17]

Did the recall of foreign advisers hasten the adoption of policies in China designed to tackle the famine? Few observers, at the time or to this day, see it in that light. Khrushchev is roundly blamed for having shot himself in the foot: overnight the Soviet leader threw away whatever leverage he had over China. Especially scathing of their leader were Russian diplomats serving in Beijing at the time, for instance Stepan Chervonenko and Lev Deliusin, who relished their country's 'special relationship' with China – and hence their own positions as intermediaries between the countries.[18] Khrushchev himself certainly had no such goal in mind. He probably expected a humbled China to come back to the table to renegotiate in terms more amenable to the Soviet Union. But whether he intended to do so or not, Khrushchev's move did contribute to isolating Mao further, hitting him just when reports were coming in from all parts of the country about the effects of mass starvation. In fact, Mao became so depressed in the summer of 1960 that he took to his bed, seemingly incapable of confronting adverse news.[19] He was in retreat, trying to find a way out of the impasse.

Capitalist Grain

Almost immediately after the recall of Soviet experts in July 1960, a triumvirate consisting of Zhou Enlai, Li Fuchun and Li Xiannian was put in
charge of foreign trade.[1] Their answer to Khrushchev's action was to move
the trade structure away from the Soviet Union towards the West. By
the end of August, minister of foreign trade Ye Jizhuang instructed his
representatives abroad to reduce imports from the socialist bloc. All negotiations for new trade agreements were to cease, with the exception of a
few strategic projects such as steel from the Soviet Union for the Nanjing
bridge. No new import contracts were to be signed, on the pretext that the
price or specifications of the goods on offer were not satisfactory.[2] Some
foreign observers at the time talked about a ruthless blockade of China by
the socialist camp,[3] but the uncoupling of the economy from the Soviet
Union and its allies was entirely initiated by Beijing.

However, China could not fob off former trade partners with quib-
bles about inadequate specifications for ever. By December 1960, with
Mao in retreat, a more plausible explanation was finally offered. The official version was that China was suffering from unprecedented natural
catastrophes which had ravaged a great deal of the countryside, and no
more foodstuffs could be exported to the Soviet Union. All trade with the
socialist camp had to be reduced, with the exception of Albania.[4] Besides
deflecting attention away from the man-made dimensions of the famine,
invoking the force of nature had a further advantage. Trade agreements
usually carried a standard escape clause, Article 33, stipulating that in the
event of unforeseen circumstances beyond human control, part or all of
the contract could be terminated.[5] Article 33 was now to be used not only
to decrease trade but to cancel a whole series of agreements.[6]

The statistical tables presented in Chapter 10 show that exports to the Soviet Union fell from 761 million rubles in 1960 to 262 million the following year. A similar drop marked imports from Eastern Europe. Only when all arrears with trading partners had been cleared could trade agreements for 1961 be contemplated, Ye Jizhuang explained to his partners in East Berlin.[7] But not only had East Germany become used to rice, it was also dependent on China for edible oils. So large was the shortfall that Walter Ulbricht was forced to turn to Khrushchev for help in August 1961.

China moved away from the socialist bloc not as punishment for the withdrawal of Soviet experts but because it was bankrupt. The best gauge of the country's financial worthiness was the value of the yuan on the black market. It began a spectacular decline in 1960. Then, in January 1961, as news of food shortages leaked out to the rest of the world, it nosedived to an all-time low at about US$0.75 per ten yuan, or about one-sixth of the money's official value. Overall, by June 1961 it had dropped 50 per cent in value from the previous year.[8]

Part of the yuan's decline was caused by the need to raise hard currency to pay for grain on international markets. One way of coping with starvation had been to move grain from surplus areas to famished regions, but by the autumn of 1960, as another crop failure worsened the famine, this strategy had very little effect. Zhou Enlai and Chen Yun managed to convince Mao that grain had to be imported from capitalist countries. How they did this remains unclear, but they probably sold the idea by portraying imports of grain as a way to boost exports for cash. The first contracts were negotiated in Hong Kong at the end of 1960.[9] Close to 6 million tonnes of grain were purchased in 1960–1 at a cost of US$367 million (see Table 4). Terms of payment varied: the Canadians asked for 25 per cent down in convertible sterling while the Australians allowed 10 per cent upfront and granted credit on the remainder. But all in all about half had to be paid in 1961.[10]

Table 4: Imports of Grain by China in 1961

Exporting country	Million tonnes
Argentina	0.045
Australia	2.74
Burma	0.3
Canada	2.34
France	0.285
Germany	0.250
total	5.96

Source: BArch, Berlin, 1962, DL2-VAN-175, p. 15; see also Allan J. Barry, 'The Chinese Food Purchases', *China Quarterly*, no. 8 (Oct.–Dec. 1961), p. 21.

In order to meet these commitments China had to earn a surplus in transferable currency, and this could be done only by cutting imports of capital goods and increasing exports to the non-communist world. Throughout the famine thus far Zhou Enlai had made sure that deliveries of eggs and meat reached Hong Kong every single day.[11] Now, in the autumn of 1960, despite protests from a disgruntled Khrushchev who complained about lack of deliveries to the Soviet Union, he decided to redirect all available foodstuffs towards Hong Kong, greatly increasing trade with the crown colony.[12] Cotton and textile products too left for Hong Kong, jumping from HK$217.3 million in 1959 to HK$287 million the following year.[13] All in all, Hong Kong was the largest source of foreign currency earned during the famine, producing some US$320 million a year.[14] As in 1958, Asian markets were also swamped with cheap goods. Textiles, for instance, were dumped at prices competitors like India and Japan could not possibly match, even when these goods were badly needed on the mainland.

Beijing also emptied its reserves, sending silver bars to London. China became an exporter of bullion by the end of 1960, shipping some 50 to 60 million troy ounces in 1961, of which 46 million, valued at £15.5 million, were taken by Britain.[15] In total, if we are to rely on a report by Zhou Enlai, some US$150 million was raised through selling gold and silver by the end of 1961.[16] In a desperate attempt to raise more foreign currency, China also started a grim trade in sympathy by which overseas Chinese could buy special coupons in exchange for cash in Hong Kong banks: these coupons could then be sent to hungry relatives across the border, to be exchanged for grain and blankets.[17]

Why did China not import grain from its socialist allies? Pride and fear were the main obstacles. As we have seen, the leadership never hesitated to place the reputation of the country above the needs of the population, plundering the countryside to meet export agreements entered into with foreign partners. However, pride often does come before the proverbial fall, and in March 1961 Zhou Enlai had to execute a humiliating climb-down, explaining to his trading allies that China was no longer in a position to export foodstuffs, to meet its long-term trade agreements or to honour a number of contracts for large industrial plants. Over a million tonnes in grain and edible oils were still outstanding to the Soviet Union for the year 1960 alone, and China would not be able to catch up with food shipments in the near future. As Zhou put it diplomatically, how could his country possibly ask for grain when it had failed its socialist allies so badly?[18]

Beijing also feared that a request for help might be turned down by Moscow, since the entire Great Leap Forward had been designed to show up the Soviet Union. This fear was probably justified, although initially Moscow displayed goodwill. The Russians, for instance, offered to deliver a million tonnes of grain and half a million tonnes of sugar on an exchange basis, free of interest, the cost to be reimbursed over several years. Beijing turned down the grain but took the sugar.[19] Khrushchev repeated his offer of grain during a meeting with Ye Jizhuang at the Kremlin in April 1961. He had every sympathy for China's predicament, he told the minister of foreign trade, all the more so since the Ukraine had suffered a terrible famine in 1946. In a crude and rather thoughtless reminder which could only cause offence, he added that there had even been cases of cannibalism. Then he changed the topic of the conversation, casually mentioning that the Soviet Union was about to overtake the United States in steel produc-tion. Ye Jizhuang politely declined the offer.[20]

A few months later, as the famine failed to vanish with the arrival of summer, Zhou Enlai approached the Russians again. At a meeting with a delegation from Moscow in August 1961, he explained why, for the first time in the history of the People's Republic, grain was being imported from the imperialist camp. Then Zhou, in a rather roundabout manner, enquired about the Soviet Union's willingness to trade 2 million tonnes of grain against soybeans, bristles and tin, possibly even rice. Only a third would be paid upfront, the rest would follow over the next two years. Coming just after the delegation had baulked at a trade deficit of 70 million rubles, the timing of the request was poor. 'Do you have any foreign currency?' the Soviet side asked bluntly, forcing Zhou to admit that China had none, and that it was selling silver.[21] The delegation left the issue hanging in the air, and nothing further happened for several months, till finally someone dropped a hint by telling Deng Xiaoping that the Soviet Union was experiencing difficulties and was not in a position to help. The loss of face for China must have been tremendous.[22]

Delaying tactics in the midst of calamity were also adopted by Moscow when Zhou Enlai asked for an extra 20,000 tonnes of petrol in July 1961: Khrushchev waited for four months until after the Twenty-Second Soviet Party Congress before acceding to Beijing's request.[23] Political leverage was also extracted from a swap of grain agreed upon in June 1961. Out of all the wheat Beijing purchased from Canada, 280,000 tonnes were earmarked for the Soviet Union, which in turn exported a similar amount to China. After the wheat had been shipped directly to Russia from Canada, the Soviets acted as if the import came from North America, at the same time listing their export of grain to China in the published trade statistics for the year 1961. In the eyes of the world, with foreign experts raking over published statistics for signs of a rift between the two socialist giants, it looked as if the Soviet Union was feeding China.[24]

Not all of the grain purchased abroad was intended for home consumption. The rice bought from Burma, for instance, was shipped directly to Ceylon to meet outstanding commitments. Some 160,000 tonnes also found their way to East Germany to address the trade deficit with socialist allies. And China, in the midst of famine, continued to be generous to its friends. Two cargoes of wheat carrying some 60,000 tonnes were shipped directly to Tirana from Canadian ports as a gift. Since Albania had a population of about 1.4 million, this amount provided as much as one-fifth of domestic requirements.[25] Pupo Shyti, Tirana's chief negotiator in Beijing, later recalled that he could see the signs of famine in Beijing, but 'the Chinese gave us everything . . . When we needed anything we just asked the Chinese . . . I felt ashamed.'[26] Other countries, aside from Albania, also received rice for free at the height of the famine, for instance Guinea, the recipient of 10,000 tonnes in 1961.[27]

China never ceased to cultivate its international image with liberal aid and cheap loans to developing nations in Asia and Africa. One reason why Beijing increased foreign donations during the Great Leap Forward was to prove that it had discovered the bridge to a communist future. But the main consideration was rivalry with Moscow. In an age of decolonisation, Khrushchev had started competing for the allegiance of developing nations, trying to draw them away from the United States into the Soviet orbit by lavishing aid on prestige projects such as dams and stadiums. Mao wanted to challenge him for leadership in Asia and Africa. Dismissive of the Kremlin's notion of 'peaceful evolution', on which relations with the developing world were premised, he encouraged instead a militant theory of revolution, aiding communist revolutionaries in such countries as Algeria, Cameroon, Kenya and Uganda in determined competition with Moscow.

How much help was given in times of famine? Overall, China provided 4 billion yuan to foreign countries from 1950 to July 1960, of which 2.8 billion was free economic aid and 1.2 billion came as interest-free or low-interest loans.[28] Most of this was granted from 1958 onwards. In 1960, as a new body called the Foreign Economic Liaison Bureau with ministerial rank was created to cope with increased donations, aid to foreign countries was fixed at 420 million yuan.[29] The following year, as Beijing refused new loans or even deferment of payments offered by socialist allies aware of China's predicament, some 660 million yuan was slated for foreign aid.[30] The beneficiaries included Burma at US$84 million and Cambodia at US$11.2 million, while Vietnam was granted 142 million rubles and Albania 112.5 million rubles.[31] These sums were made available as the overall income of the state shrank by 45 per cent to 35 billion yuan, cuts having been made in a number of areas, including 1.4 billion in health and education.[32]

Such generosity meant that on the ground, where people were starving, grain was still being exported in 1960, some of it for free. In fact, with a policy of 'export above all else' (*chukou diyi*), just about every province had to export more than ever before. Hunan was instructed to export goods to the value of 423 million yuan, or 3.4 per cent of the total output value of the province, the produce to be exported including 300,000 tonnes of rice and 270,000 pigs.[33]

In the five months following Zhou Enlai's decision in August 1960 to curb the export of food to the socialist camp, well over 100,000 tonnes of grain were procured in Guangdong and sent to Cuba, Indonesia, Poland and Vietnam, representing about a quarter of the 470,000 tonnes requisitioned in the province during that period. As provincial boss Tao Zhu explained after formal diplomatic relations were established with Fidel Castro's regime in September 1960, delivering grain to the people of Cuba, besieged by American imperialism, was a matter of 'international reputation'.[34] Factory workers in Guangzhou were less enthusiastic about selfless assistance to the developing world: already bitter about the lack of cotton, exported and put on sale in the department stores of Hong Kong, they openly wondered: 'why export to Cuba when we don't have enough to eat?'[35] Even in places as far away as Gansu, villagers protested that they had to go hungry because Mao was shipping rice to Cuba.[36] At a party gathering in Beidaihe, the following month, the leadership decided to send Castro a further 100,000 tonnes of rice worth 26 million yuan in exchange for sugar.[37]

———

Could China have accepted aid instead of spending all its foreign currency on grain imports? President John Kennedy, apparently, noted coolly that Beijing was still exporting food to Africa and Cuba even in a time of famine, adding that 'we've had no indication from the Chinese Communists that they would welcome any offer of food'.[38] The Red Cross did try to assist, but approached Beijing in a blundering way by first enquiring about famine in Tibet – where a major rebellion had just been squashed by the People's Liberation Army. The response was swift and predictable. The country had witnessed an unprecedentedly rich harvest in 1960, there was absolutely no famine and rumours to the contrary were slanderous. Adding fuel to the fire, Henrik Beer, clumsy secretary general of the League of Red Cross Societies, then sent a second telegram from Geneva asking whether this was true as well for China. A furious reply followed from Beijing, pointing out that Tibet and China were not separate entities but constituted one country, throughout which the government relied on the many advantages of the people's communes to overcome the natural calamities of the previous two years.[39]

But even had the Red Cross broached the issue in a more tactful way, it is very likely that foreign help would have been refused. When the Japanese foreign minister had a quiet word with his counterpart, Chen Yi, about a discreet gift of 100,000 tonnes of wheat, to be shipped out of the public view, he was rebuffed.[40] Even gifts of clothes by schoolchildren in East Berlin, offered to help typhoon-ravaged Guangdong in 1959, were seen as a loss of face, and embassies were told to accept no further donations.[41] China was willing to patronise the developing world but would accept help from nobody.

Finding a Way Out

Faced with a bankrupt economy, Zhou Enlai, Li Fuchun and Li Xiannian, the triumvirate in charge of foreign trade, began in August 1960 to move the trade structure away from the Soviet Union towards the West. In the following months Zhou Enlai and Chen Yun managed to convince Mao that imports of grain were needed to get the economy back on its feet after the agricultural losses attributed to natural disasters. The party planners also started quietly masterminding a turnaround by tinkering, ever so prudently, with policy guidelines. Li Fuchun initiated work on a new motto that emphasised 'adjustment' instead of great leaps forward in August 1960. In a one-party state where government by slogan held sway, the very notion of adjustment would have been unthinkable only six months earlier. Zhou Enlai warily added the term 'consolidation' to make it more palatable to Mao.[1] Li Fuchun would have to navigate carefully to get the new mantra past a mercurial Chairman.

Then, on 21 October 1960, a report from the Ministry of Supervision landed on Li Fuchun's desk. It was about mass starvation in Xinyang, a region in Wu Zhipu's model province of Henan. Where an earlier investigation had mentioned 18,000 deaths in the county of Zhengyang alone, now the figure had quadrupled to 80,000 deaths. In Suiping, the seat of the hallowed Chayashan commune, one in ten villagers had starved to death.[2]

When Li Fuchun handed over the report to Mao Zedong three days later, the Chairman was visibly shaken: here were counter-revolutionaries who had seized control of an entire region, carrying out horrific acts of revenge against class enemies. After an urgent meeting with Liu Shaoqi and Zhou Enlai, a team was dispatched under the leadership of Li Xiannian, who was joined en route by Tao Zhu and Wang Renzhong.

In Xinyang they found a nightmare. In Guangshan county, ground zero of the famine, they were met by quiet sobs of despair from famished survivors, huddled in the bitter cold among the rubble of their destroyed homes, surrounded by barren fields marked by graves. The hearths were stone cold, as everything from doors, windows and lintels to the straw roofs had been ripped out for fuel. The food was gone. In a reign of terror after the Lushan plenum, the local militias had rampaged through the villages searching for hidden grain, confiscating everything to make up for the shortfall in output. In a hamlet once humming with activity, two children with drumstick limbs and skeletal heads, lying by their cadaverous grandmother, were the only survivors.[3] One in four people in a local population of half a million had perished in Guangshan.[4] Mass graves were dug. Ten infants, still breathing, had been thrown into the frozen ground in Chengguan.[5] In total in 1960 over a million people died in the Xinyang region. Of these victims 67,000 were clubbed to death with sticks.[6] Li Xiannian cried: 'The defeat of the Western Route Army was so cruel yet I did not shed a tear, but after seeing such horror in Guangshan even I am unable to control myself.'[7]

'Bad people have seized power, causing beatings, deaths, grain shortages and hunger. The democratic revolution has not been completed, as feudal forces, full of hatred towards socialism, are stirring up trouble, sabotaging socialist productive forces': Mao could no longer deny the extent of the disaster, but as a paranoid leader who saw the world in terms of plots and conspiracies, he blamed the trouble on class enemies.[8] Rich farmers and counter-revolutionary elements had taken advantage of the anti-rightist campaign to worm their way back into power and carry out acts of class revenge. At no point did the Chairman acknowledge that the regime of terror he modelled at the top was being mirrored at every level down the party hierarchy.

Mao ordered power to be taken back. Across the country a campaign unfolded to root out 'class enemies', often backed by powerful delegations sent by Beijing. Li Xiannian and Wang Renzhong supervised a purge in Henan in which county leaders were overthrown and thousands of cadres investigated, some arrested on the spot.[9] A general with a forty-man team was dispatched by Beijing to clean up the militia.[10] In Gansu a delegation sent by the Ministry of Inspection led by Qian Ying oversaw a major purge, which resulted in the downgrading of Zhang Zhongliang to third secretary of the provincial party committee. Other regions followed, as one urgent order after another pressed for an overthrow of 'abusive cadres' in the people's communes. On 3 November 1960 an emergency directive was finally issued allowing villagers to keep private plots, engage in side occupations, rest for eight hours a day and restore local markets, among other measures designed to weaken the power of the communes over villagers.[11]

It was the beginning of the end of mass starvation. Sensing a change in the wind, Li Fuchun pushed through his policy of economic adjustment for the year 1961.[12] He had been the first planner to back Mao in the launch of the Great Leap Forward. Now he was the first one to backtrack, prudently steering a policy of economic revival past the Chairman.

At this stage Liu Shaoqi was still looking from the sidelines. He shared the Chairman's view that the countryside had become a breeding ground for counter-revolution. Like other leaders, he had preferred to ignore what happened on the ground after the confrontation at Lushan, and instead devoted much of his energy to stridently denouncing the revisionist path taken by the Soviet Union. He was not oblivious to the famine. Malnourishment was evident even inside the vermilion walls of Zhongnanhai, the compound which served as the headquarters of the party in Beijing. Meat, eggs and cooking oil were scarce, and famine oedema and hepatitis were endemic.[13] But it was politically safer to interpret the signs of starvation as the result of environmental disasters. On 20 January 1961, Liu Shaoqi harangued an audience from Gansu about the dangers of feudalism, which had led to the calamity witnessed in Xinyang: 'This is a revolution: the key is in mobilising the masses. We should mobilise the masses and allow them to free themselves.'[14]

Only days before, Mao had voiced his surprise at the extent of the bourgeois backlash in the countryside: 'Who would have thought that the countryside harboured so many counter-revolutionaries? We did not expect that the counter-revolution would usurp power at the village level and carry out cruel acts of class revenge.'[15] Instead of relying on the reports from the grass-roots which, Mao claimed, had obviously misled the leadership, the Chairman decided to dispatch several high-powered teams to investigate the countryside. Deng Xiaoping, Zhou Enlai and Peng Zhen were all sent off to visit communes around Beijing. Mao himself spent several weeks in Hunan. In the hope that farmers would speak to him without inhibition, Liu Shaoqi headed back to his home in Huaminglou, Hunan. It would be a revelatory experience with far-reaching repercussions.

———————

Determined to avoid the large retinue of bodyguards and local officials that inevitably came with every visit from a top dignitary, Liu set off on 2 April 1961 from Changsha, travelling in two jeeps in the company of his wife and a few close assistants, bowl and chopsticks tucked away in light luggage, ready for a spartan regime in the countryside. Soon the convoy came across a sign announcing a giant pig farm. On closer inspection, it turned out that the farm consisted of no more than a dozen scrawny hogs foraging in the mud. Liu decided to spend the night in the fodder store, and his escorts combed the place in vain for some rice straw to soften the plank beds. Liu noted that even the dried human excrement piled up for fertiliser consisted of nothing but rough fibre, another telltale sign of wide-spread want. Nearby a few children in rags were digging for wild herbs.[16]

Liu Shaoqi's fears were confirmed over the following weeks, however difficult it was to get wary farmers to tell the truth. In one village where he stopped on his way home, he found that the number of deaths had been covered up by local leaders, while an official report drew a picture of everyday life which had nothing to do with the destitution Liu saw on the ground. He clashed with the local boss, who tried to steer the team away from speaking with villagers. He tracked down a cadre who had been dismissed as a rightist in 1959: Duan Shucheng spoke up, explaining how the brigade had earned a red flag during the Great Leap Forward. To protect their privileged status, Duan explained, local leaders had system-atically persecuted anybody who dared to voice a dissenting view. In 1960 a meagre crop of 360 tonnes of grain was talked up to 600 tonnes. After requisitions villagers were left with a paltry 180 kilos, out of which seed and fodder had to be taken, leaving a handful of rice a day.[17]

In his home village Tanzichong, friends and relatives were less reluctant to speak out. They denied that there had been a drought the year before, blaming cadres instead for the food shortages: 'Man-made disasters are the main reason, not natural calamities.' In the canteen cooking utensils, dirty bowls and chopsticks were tossed in a pile on the floor. A few asparagus leaves were the only vegetable available, to be prepared without cooking oil. Liu was shaken by what he saw. A few days later, he apologised to his fellow villagers in a mass meeting: 'I haven't returned home for nearly forty years. I really wanted to come home for a visit. Now I have seen how bitter your lives are. We have not done our jobs well, and we beg for your pardon.' That very evening the canteen was dissolved on Liu's orders.[18]

A committed party man, Liu Shaoqi was genuinely shocked by the disastrous state in which he found his home village. He had dedicated his every waking moment to the party, only to find that it had brought widespread abuse, destitution and starvation to the people he was meant to serve. What he also discovered was a complete lack of connection between people and party: he had been deliberately kept in the dark – or so he claimed.

While the details of his trip to the countryside are well known, his clash with the local officials is not. Liu first deflected blame on to party boss Zhang Pinghua, who had taken charge of the province after Zhou Xiaozhou's fall from power: 'My home town is in such a mess but nobody has sent me a report, not even a single letter or a complaint. In the past people used to send me letters, then it all stopped. I don't think that they didn't want to write, or refused to write, I am afraid that they simply were not allowed to write, or they did write and their letters were inspected and confiscated.' With the provincial Bureau for Public Security he was blunt, accusing the security apparatus of being 'completely rotten'. How could the local police be allowed to check and retain personal letters, and how could they get away with investigating and beating people for trying to bring local malpractices to his attention? Later Liu confronted Xie Fuzhi, the powerful minister of public security and close ally of Mao, asking him why abuse was allowed to go on unchecked in his home town. Gone was the patient party builder Liu: here was a man shaken in his faith who had promised to speak out on behalf of his fellow villagers.[19]

Back in Beijing Liu continued to speak his mind. On 31 May 1961, at a gathering of leaders, he made an emotional speech in which he bluntly placed the blame for the famine on the shoulders of the party. 'Are the problems that have appeared over the past few years actually due to natural disasters or to shortcomings and errors we have made in our work? In Hunan the peasants have a saying that "30 per cent is due to natural calamities, 70 per cent to man-made disasters."' Liu dismissed the attempt to gloss over the scale of the calamity by dogmatically insisting that the overall policy of the party was a great success, touching a raw nerve by debunking one of Mao's favourite aphorisms: 'Some comrades say that these problems are merely one finger out of ten. But right now I am afraid that this is no longer a matter of one out of ten. We always say nine fingers versus one finger: the proportion never changes, but this doesn't quite fit the actual reality. We should be realistic and talk about things as they are.' About the party line he did not mince his words. 'In carrying out the party line, in organising the people's communes, in organising work for the Great Leap Forward, there have been many weaknesses and errors, even very serious weaknesses and errors.' And he was in no doubt as to where the responsibility lay. 'The centre is the principal culprit, we leaders are all responsible, let's not blame one department or one person alone.'[20]

Liu was parting company with Mao. He got away with his blistering critique because the horror, by now, was so evident everywhere that it could no longer be brushed aside. He would pay dearly for his challenge during the Cultural Revolution, but for the time being other leaders cautiously leaned towards the head of state, ever so slightly inflecting the balance of power away from Mao. Zhou Enlai, always circumspect, acknowledged some of the errors made in the wake of the Lushan plenum, and then, to help the Chairman save face, openly accepted blame for everything that had gone wrong.[21]

Liu Shaoqi took a chance by pushing the limits for critical debate, but Li Fuchun was the one who used the shift to engineer a strategic retreat away from the Great Leap Forward. A bookish man with self-effacing airs, he had been wary of putting forward dissenting views, but he too changed his tone, delivering a trenchant assessment of the economy at a meeting of party planners in Beidaihe in July 1961. Only a few months earlier, attentive to the moods of the Chairman, he had smoothed over widespread shortages, claiming that a socialist economy never developed in a straight line, as even the Soviet Union had gone through periods of decrease in grain output.[22] But in the wake of Liu Shaoqi's attack he no longer dodged the issue. In Shandong, Henan and Gansu, he noted, tens of millions of farmers struggled to survive on a handful of grain a day, and the famine had little to do with natural calamities. People were starving because of the mistakes made by the party. He had seven adjectives to describe the Leap Forward: too high, too big, too equal (meaning that all incentives had been erased), too dispersed, too chaotic, too fast, too inclined to transfer resources. A lengthy analysis followed, as well as concrete proposals aimed at lowering all production targets and getting the economy back on track. A close follower of Mao, he had an astute way of absolving him of all blame: 'Chairman Mao's directives are entirely correct, but we, including the central organs, have made mistakes in executing them.'[23]

Li received the Chairman's endorsement. The following month he gave a similar report at a top-level party meeting in Lushan, again exempting the Chairman from any responsibility. It was the turning point in the famine. Li was a soft-spoken, unassuming man whose loyalty towards Mao could hardly be doubted and who, unlike Peng Dehuai, had found a way of presenting the facts without incurring his wrath. Mao, a paranoid leader who suspected betrayal behind the slightest disapproval, praised the report instead.

A series of biting assessments followed Li Fuchun's speech. Li Yiqing, a senior party secretary, reported that in 1958 more than 140,000 tonnes of farming tools had been thrown into the backyard furnaces in the model province of Henan. Wu Jingtian, vice-minister of railways, explained how one in five locomotives was out of circulation because of engine damage. Peng De, vice-minister of transportation, announced that fewer than two out of three vehicles under his command actually worked. Vice-minister of metallurgy Xu Chi noted that the steelworks of Angang were forced to stop for weeks on end over the summer because of coal shortages.[24]

Mao rarely attended the meetings, following them instead through written reports compiled every evening. He was in retreat, strategically withholding judgement and finding out where his colleagues stood. But the Chairman was not pleased. Letting off steam with his doctor Li Zhisui, he said: 'All the good party members are dead. The only ones left are a bunch of zombies.'[25] But he took no action. At last, party leaders started to discuss among themselves the extent of the damage done by three years of forced collectivisation. What they discovered was destruction on a scale few could have imagined.

PART THREE

DESTRUCTION

Agriculture

The term 'command economy' comes from the German *Befehlswirtschaft*. It was originally applied to the Nazi economy, but was later used to describe the Soviet Union. Instead of allowing dispersed buyers and sellers to determine their own economic activities according to the laws of supply and demand, a higher authority would issue commands determining the overall direction of the economy following a master plan. The command principle entailed that all economic decisions were centralised for the greater good, as the state determined what should be produced, how much should be produced, who produced what and where, how resources should be allocated and what prices should be charged for materials, goods and services. A central plan replaced the market.

As planners took over the economy in China, farmers lost control over the harvest. In 1953 a monopoly over grain was introduced, decreeing that farmers must sell all surplus grain to the state at prices determined by the state. The aim behind the monopoly was to stabilise the price of grain across the country, eliminate speculation and guarantee the grain needed to feed the urban population and fuel an industrial expansion. But what was 'surplus grain' in a country where many farmers barely grew enough to scrape by? It was defined as seed, fodder and a basic grain ration set at roughly 13 to 15 kilos per head each month. However, 23 to 26 kilos of unhusked grain were required to provide 1,700 to 1,900 calories per day, an amount international aid organisations consider to be the bare minimum for subsistence.[1] The notion of a surplus, in other words, was a political construct designed to give legitimacy to the extraction of grain from the countryside. By forcing villagers to sell grain before their own subsistence needs were met, the state also made them more dependent on the collective. Extra grain above the basic ration had to be bought back from the state by villagers with work points, which were distributed on the basis of their performance in collective labour. Farmers had lost control not only of their land and their harvest, but also of their own work schedules: local cadres determined who should do what and for how many work points, from collecting manure to looking after the buffaloes in the fields. As the market was eliminated and money lost its purchasing power, grain became the currency of exchange. Most of it was in the hands of the state.

But a more insidious problem lurked behind the notion of a grain surplus, namely the enormous pressure applied to local leaders to pledge ever greater grain sales. The amount sold to the state was determined in a series of meetings which started from the village up, as a team leader passed on a quota to the brigade, where the pledges were adjusted and collated into a bid passed on to the commune, which then negotiated how much it would deliver to the county. By the time a pledge reached the level of the region and the province, the amount had been revised upwards several times as a result of peer pressure. A figure very far removed from reality finally landed on the desk of Li Fuchun, the man responsible for planning the economy and setting national production targets. He, in turn, inflated the target according to the latest policy shifts agreed on by the leadership: that new figure was the party's command.

The pressure to show sensational gains in grain output reached a climax during the Great Leap Forward. In a frenzy of competitive bidding, party officials from the village all the way up to the province tried to outdo each other, as one record after the other was announced by the propaganda machine, in turn spurring even more cautious cadres to inflate the figures. Even after the party had tried to rein in some of the more extravagant claims in early 1959, failure to project a substantial leap in output was interpreted as 'rightist conservatism', in particular during the purges which followed the Lushan plenum. In a climate of fear, village leaders followed orders rather than try to haggle over quotas. More often than not, a party secretary or deputy from the commune would simply drive up to a strip of land, have a look around and casually determine the target yield. A team leader explained the process as follows: 'In 1960 we were given a quota of

260 tonnes. This was increased by 5.5 tonnes a few days later. Then the commune held a meeting and added a further 25 tonnes. After two days, the commune phoned us to say that the quota had gone up to 315 tonnes: how this all happened we have no idea.'[2]

The higher the office, the greater the power to increase the quota, which had repercussions for every subordinate unit, and each had to juggle the figures to comply. When Xie Fuzhi, the boss in Yunnan, was told by Beijing that the national target for grain output had been raised to 300 million tonnes, he immediately convened a telephone conference to explain to county leaders that this really meant 350–400 million tonnes. Yunnan, he rapidly calculated, contained about one-thirtieth of the total population, meaning a share of 10 million tonnes. Since Yunnan did not want to trail behind the rest of the country, Xie raised this to a nicely rounded total of 25,000,000,000 *jin*, equivalent to 12.5 million tonnes.[3] Everybody from the region down to the county, commune, brigade and village had to scramble and adjust the local quotas accordingly.

With inflated crops came procurement quotas which were far too high, leading to shortages and outright famine. But if the figures were made up, how do we know what the real crop was and what proportion of the harvest was procured by the state? Kenneth Walker, a specialist in agrarian economics at the University of London, spent a decade painstakingly assembling statistical data from a whole range of local newspapers, published statistics and policy guidelines. He showed that the state imposed the highest levies in 1959–62 at a time when the average output per head was actually at its lowest.[4]

Just as his study appeared in print in 1984, a statistical yearbook was published by the National Statistical Bureau in China with a set of historical data covering the famine years. Most observers have relied on these official figures. But why should we trust a set of statistics published by a party notoriously protective of its own past? Problems with the official statistics appeared when Yang Jisheng, a retired journalist from the Xinhua agency, published a book on the famine based on party archives. He relied on a set of figures compiled in 1962 by the Bureau for Grain. But this merely transferred the problem from one set of numbers to another. The fact that a document comes from an archive does not automatically make it right. Every archive has a series of competing figures, put together in different ways by different agencies at different times. As a result of political pressure the statistical work of the Bureau for Grain disintegrated from 1958 to 1962, to such an extent that the state itself could no longer calculate a realistic level of grain production. And the distortion was at its greatest at the very top, as false reporting and inflated claims accumulated on their way up the party hierarchy. If the leaders themselves were lost in a morass of statistical invention, it seems unlikely that we can magically extract the numerical truth from a single document in the party archives. Mao Zedong, Liu Shaoqi, Deng Xiaoping and other leaders knew all too well that they were looking at the world through layers of distorted filters, and their solution was to spend more time investigating what happened on the ground in field trips to the countryside.

Table 5: Different Estimates for Grain Output and Grain Procurements in Hunan (million tonnes)

| | Total estimated crop output | | Total estimated procurements | |
	Bureau for Grain	Office for Statistics	Bureau for Grain	Office for Statistics
1956	–	10.36	–	2.39 (23.1%)
1957	11.3	11.32	2.29 (20.2%)	2.74 (24.2%)
1958	12.27	12.25	2.66 (21.7%)	3.50 (28.5%)
1959	11.09	11.09	2.99 (26.9%)	3.89 (35.1%)
1960	8	8.02	1.75 (21.9%)	2.50 (31.2%)
1961	8	8	1.55 (19.4%)	2.21 (27.6%)

Source: Hunan, May 1965, 187-1-1432, pp. 3–8; the crop figures are from Hunan, 30 June 1961, 194-1-701, pp. 3–4, which has figures which are slightly different from the 1965 estimations; the figures for the Bureau for Grain are from Yang, *Mubei*, p. 540.

On the other hand, between 1962 and 1965 local statistical bureaus tried to rebuild their credibility and often went back to the years of famine to find out what had happened. The figures they produced indicate a much higher degree of procurement than those provided by the Bureau for Grain. Table 5 compares the figures compiled by the Bureau in 1962 with the local numbers calculated in 1965 by the provincial Office for Statistics in Hunan in an attempt to determine how much farmers had actually contributed to the state. The difference in estimates for the grain output is minimal, but when it comes to the size of the levies the figures provided by the province turn out to be much higher, ranging from 28 to

35 per cent of the total harvest. Why is there a discrepancy of 4 to 10 per cent? One reason can be found in the nature of the statistical evidence. Closer scrutiny indicates that the figures provided by the Bureau for Grain were not carefully reconstructed in the aftermath of the famine, but rather mechanically compiled from the plans the Bureau had handed out in the previous years. Each plan had two sets of numbers, one set indicating the procurements 'actually realised' in the current year, the other setting targets for the coming year. The procurement figures given for 1958, for instance, come from the plan for 1959, meaning that they were rough approximations.[5] To this we should add the fact that the Bureau for Grain in Beijing was under much pressure in 1962 to show that it had not allowed excessive procurements to drain the countryside of grain, and would thus have adopted a set of low figures. But there is another reason for the mismatch: at every level of society, from the village and the commune up to the province, grain was being hidden. The figures compiled in 1965 by the Office for Statistics in Hunan were based on careful research after the famine. The Office could go back to whole sets of commune and county statistics to find out how much had actually been procured, in contrast to the numbers the province officially handed over to the centre. The discrepancy, in other words, corresponds to the amount of procured grain which escaped the gaze of the state.

Other examples confirm that the rates of procurement were much higher than those suggested by the Bureau for Grain. In Zhejiang, for instance, Zeng Shaowen, a top provincial official, admitted in 1961 that some 2.9 million tonnes, or 40.9 per cent of the harvest, was procured in 1958, followed by an even larger 43.2 per cent in the following year. The Bureau for Grain gives much lower percentages, namely 30.4 per cent for 1958 followed by 34.4 per cent.[6] A similar story comes from Guizhou. In the provincial archives, which Yang Jisheng was unable to access, a document from the provincial party committee shows that an average of 1.8 million tonnes was procured each year from 1958 to 1960, meaning 44.4 per cent, with a peak of 2.34 million tonnes in 1959 – equivalent to an enormous 56.5 per cent of the crop. The figures given by the Bureau for Grain are on average 1.4 million tonnes for the same three years, or about a quarter less.[7]

Some of these calculations may seem rather abstract, but they matter a great deal. Grain is not only the currency of exchange in a command economy; it becomes the source of survival in times of famine. When either Hunan or Zhejiang increased their procurements by 8 to 10 per cent, taking an extra 750,000 tonnes of grain from the countryside in the middle of the famine, the number of people forced into starvation grew proportionally. We have seen how one kilo of grain provided a sufficient number of calories for one person each day, meaning that a family of three could live on a tonne per year. But the real point is that many farmers could have survived famine if their rations had been only marginally increased by some 400 or 500 calories a day, equivalent to a large bowl in the evening. In short, in order to understand how people perished on such a scale, it is vital to see the role played by increased procurements in times of declining harvests.

Table 6: Different Estimates of Grain Procurement (million tonnes)

	Total output	Official statistics	Total procurements Bureau for Grain	Bureau for Statistics
1958	200	51	56.27	66.32
1959	170	67.49	60.71	72.23
1960	143.50	51.09	39.04	50.35
1961	147.47	54.52	33.96	–

Source: Walker, *Food Grain Procurement*, p. 162; Yang, *Mubei*, p. 539; Yunnan, 1962, 81-7-86, p. 13; output figures are given for unhusked grain while procurement figures are for processed grain, hiding a further loss of about a fifth of the total weight.

How much grain was procured overall? Table 6 has three sets of statistics. The first two show the overall figures reached by Kenneth Walker in 1983 following his research into published statistics as well as the numbers provided by Yang Jisheng from the Bureau for Grain. But, as we have seen, the Bureau for Grain should not be taken at its word, as it had neither the expertise nor the political inclination to collect the actual figures. The third set of statistics comes from the notes taken by the Yunnan Office for Statistics in 1962 as its members attended one of the national conferences periodically convened by the Bureau for Statistics in Beijing. No one set of true numbers will ever be discovered in the archives, since every figure was a statement bound by politics and expediency rather than by expertise.

But it seems that the Bureau for Grain compiled figures which were far below both what foreign observers managed to calculate on the basis of published regional statistics and what the Bureau for Statistics compiled in 1962. In short, evidence from different sources shows that the level of procurement varied from 30 to 37 per cent nationally, far above the more usual 20 to 25 per cent extracted up to 1958. As Mao had indicated on 25 March 1959 at a secret gathering of party leaders, 'If you don't go above a third, people won't rebel.' He himself encouraged much greater procurements than usual, at a time when it was well known that the crop figures had been inflated.[8] In other words, the idea that the state mistakenly took too much grain from the countryside because it assumed that the harvest was much bigger than it was is largely a myth – at most partially true for the autumn of 1958 only.

A proportion of the procured grain was sold back to the farmers – at a premium – but they were at the end of a long waiting list. As we have seen in Chapters 10 and 15, the party had evolved a set of political priorities which ignored the needs of the countryside. The leadership decided to increase grain exports to honour its foreign contracts and maintain its international reputation, to such an extent that a policy of 'export above all else' was adopted in 1960. It chose to increase its foreign aid to its allies, shipping grain for free to countries like Albania. Priority was also given to the growing populations of Beijing, Tianjin, Shanghai and the province of Liaoning – the heartland of heavy industry – followed by the requirements of city people in general. The consequence of these political decisions was not only an increase in the proportion of procurements, but also an increase in the overall amount of grain handed over to the state out of these procurements. In the case of Zhejiang, for instance, an annual average of 1.68 million tonnes left the province from 1958 to 1961, in contrast to 1.2 million tonnes in each of the preceding three years. In 1958 alone that meant that more than half of the procured grain was handed over to Beijing even before the province started to feed its urban residents.[9] Overall, the amount of grain taken out of the procurements by the state to feed Beijing, Shanghai, Tianjin and Liaoning province and maintain its export market went up every single quarter, from 1.6 million tonnes in the third quarter of 1956 to 1.8 million tonnes in the same period in 1957, to

2.3 million tonnes in 1958, to 2.5 million tonnes a year later and to a high of 3 million tonnes in three months in 1960.[10]

The net effect of these policy priorities was that the lives of many villagers were destroyed. As Wang Renzhong put it in a meeting of the leaders of all southern provinces in August 1961, 'extraordinarily difficult conditions demand extraordinary measures', explaining that grain could be provided only to the cities, so that villages in the grip of famine would have to fend for themselves. As he saw it, some of the parts had to be sacrificed in order to keep the whole.[11]

He was not alone. Zhou Enlai, for one, was relentless in pushing for greater requisitions. He was the man in charge of making sure that enough grain was taken from the countryside to feed the cities and earn foreign currency. He badgered provincial bosses in person, over the phone, through his deputies and in a ceaseless string of telegrams marked 'urgent'. He too had a keen sense of hierarchy in which the needs of the countryside had to give way to the interests of the state – which he represented. He knew full well that the vast amounts of grain he was given by Li Jingquan, a radical follower of Mao, could lead only to a situation of mass famine in Sichuan. But others, too, clung rigidly to the view that the starvation of the people mattered less than the demands of the state. Deng Xiaoping thought that in the command economy requisitions had to be enforced ruthlessly 'as if in a war': no matter how much a provincial leader tried to defend his turf the party line had to be held, or the state would perish. Speaking at the end of 1961, when the extent of the famine was well known among the leadership, this is what Deng Xiaoping had to say about Sichuan, where huge requisitions caused the deaths of many millions of people: 'In the past, procurements have been too heavy in some regions, for instance in Sichuan, where they have been heavy for quite a few years, including this year, but there was no alternative. I approve of the Sichuan style, they never moan about hardship, we should all learn from Sichuan. And I am not saying this because I myself am from Sichuan.'[12] As we have seen, Mao phrased it differently: 'When there is not enough to eat, people starve to death. It is better to let half of the people die so that the other half can eat their fill.'[13]

The procurement prices paid by the state for grain varied from province to province. In the case of maize, for instance, it ranged from 124 yuan per tonne in Guangxi to 152 yuan just across the border in Guangdong in early 1961. The difference for rice could be up to 50 per cent, for instance 124 yuan per tonne in Guangxi versus 180 yuan for the same quantity in Shanghai.[14] The state made a substantial profit by exporting rice for 400 yuan per tonne.[15] These prices were periodically adjusted, but the procurement prices remained so low that more often than not farmers produced grain at a loss. As late as 1976 it was unprofitable simply for that reason to cultivate wheat, barley, maize and sorghum. The income on rice was marginal.[16] But in a command economy farmers no longer decided for themselves which crop they could grow, as they had to follow the orders of local cadres instead – who in turn had to apply the commands of the party. And the planners were transfixed by grain output, deciding to force an ever greater proportion of farmers to concentrate on grain – to the detriment of the overall economy. This vision was translated in 1959 into a policy of encouraging grain production above all else, leading many provinces to extend the surface cultivated with grain by some 10 per cent.[17] Farmers who were asked to abandon more remunerative crops for maize, rice or wheat lost out. For instance, after some villages in Zhejiang were told to grow grain instead of the melons, sugarcane and tobacco they had habitually cultivated, they saw their income plunge.[18]

Another problem with the command economy was that officials on the ground did not always know what they were doing, and they imposed decisions which turned out to be disastrous. We have already seen how close cropping and deep ploughing were insisted on by the regime at the height of the Great Leap Forward. This was compounded by capricious interventions by local cadres with little knowledge of agriculture. In 1959 in Luokang commune a local leader decided to replace the existing crop with sweet potatoes on half of the available acreage, only to change his mind later and substitute the potatoes with peanuts. These were then torn out to make room for rice instead. The previous year the commune had tried deep ploughing, using vast concentrations of manpower on small strips of land to dig deep furrows, much of it by hand. Huge amounts of fertiliser were applied, in some cases up to 30 tonnes a hectare. It all came to nothing.[19] In Kaiping county, Guangdong, thousands of villagers were repeatedly forced to plant a crop in the early spring of 1959 despite bitterly cold weather: the seeds froze on three occasions, and in the end fields yielded a paltry 450 kilos per hectare.[20]

But even more disastrous was the command to plant less. Mao was so convinced that the countryside was heaving under the weight of grain that he suggested that a third of the land be allowed to lie fallow. 'People in China on average cultivate three *mu*, but I think that two *mu* is enough.'[21] Combined with an exodus of farmers towards the cities, the overall acreage under cultivation plummeted. In Hunan in 1958 some 5.78 million hectares were cultivated with grain, but by 1962 this was down by 15 per cent to 4.92 million hectares.[22] In Zhejiang province some 65,000 hectares of cultivated land vanished every year, leading to a loss of about a tenth of the total acreage by 1961.[23] These provincial averages masked deep regional differences. In the Wuhan region, for instance, just over half of the available 37,000 hectares were tilled.[24] Tan Zhenlin, the man in charge of agriculture, noted in 1959 that some 7.3 million hectares were allowed to lie fallow.[25] Speaking in early 1961 Peng Zhen estimated that the total sown area stood at 107 million hectares: if true this would have meant a waste of 23 million hectares since 1958.[26]

To this loss had to be added a change in the proportion of grains grown. The urban population much preferred fine grains – rice, wheat, soybeans – although in the north considerable amounts of coarse grain – sorghum, maize and millet – were also consumed. But sweet potatoes were regarded as peasant fare and were not generally eaten in significant amounts.[27] Sweet potatoes, moreover, were a perishable commodity, meaning that the state had a limited interest in them: most of the procurements were in fine grains. But the proportion of sweet potatoes grew during the years of famine, as cadres responded to pressure to increase the yield by switching to the tuber, which was easy to cultivate. More often than not farmers were left with potatoes only.

By imposing a monopoly on the sale of grain the state undertook a task of mammoth proportions. State employees had to buy the grain, store it, transport it to different destinations across the country, store it again and distribute it against ration coupons – all according to a master plan rather than the incentives created by the market. Even a wealthy country might have baulked at the immensity of the task, but China was a poor nation, and a very large one at that. State storage – as opposed to small inventories distributed across a wide range of private and public producers, retailers and consumers – contributed in no small measure to the destruction of grain. Insects were common, rats abounded. A detailed investigation by the Guangdong Provincial People's Congress showed that in Nanxiong county an astonishing 2,533 of all 2,832 local granaries had rats. Insects infested a third of all 123 state granaries and an even larger proportion of the 728 commune granaries in Chao'an county.[28] In Yunnan in the first half of 1961 some 240,000 tonnes were contaminated by vermin.[29] In Zhucheng county, Shandong, each kilo of grain was crawling with hundreds of insects.[30]

And then there was rot. Poor storage conditions contributed to it, as well as the practice, not always successfully detected by grain inspectors, of bulking up grain with water. In Guangdong close to a third of 1.5 million tonnes of state grain contained too much water, so that one granary after another succumbed to rot.[31] In Hunan one-fifth of all grain in state granaries was either infested with insects or corrupted by a high water content. In Changsha, the provincial capital, over half of all stored grain was contaminated.[32] Temperatures in the state granaries were often too high, accelerating the blight, and in turn benefiting the insects, which took advantage of the heat and moisture. In Yunnan the temperature in some of the granaries reached 39–43 degrees Celsius.[33] Even far away from the humidity of subtropical China, in the cold winter of the northern plain, rot was common. Just outside the capital, in the middle of the worst year of famine, well over 50 tonnes of sweet potatoes decayed in a dozen villages in Yanqing county. A further 6 tonnes putrefied in storage facilities across the Haidian district in Beijing.[34]

Significant losses were also caused by fire, through arson or accident. In Yunnan alone 70 tonnes of food went up in smoke each month in 1961; more than 300 tonnes were completely written off each and every month in 1960 and in 1961 due to blight, insects and fire. The Bureau for Security calculated that the grain lost to fire in 1960 alone in that province would have been sufficient to feed 1.5 million people adequately for a whole month.[35] Yunnan was not the worst offender. In the Anshan region, Liaoning province, 400 tonnes were destroyed each month in 1960, although this figure included only losses that could be attributed to theft and corruption – a topic we will address later.[36]

The transportation system was disastrously affected by the programmes of the Great Leap Forward. The railway system was paralysed by early 1959, overwhelmed by the amount of goods the plan directed from one end of the country to the other. Lorries rapidly ran out of fuel. All over the country grain was going to waste on railway sidings. In the small provincial capital of Kunming, some 15 tonnes were lost on trains and lorries each month.[37] But this was nothing compared to what happened in the countryside after the harvest. In Hunan, the entire system seized up in the summer of 1959 because of a shortage of hundreds of freight wagons which were needed every day. Lorries were lacking too, so that only half the grain could be transported from the countryside to the main railway stations. Some 200,000 tonnes of grain accumulated by the roadside, although only 60,000 tonnes could be loaded every month.[38]

In the end farmers did not even have enough seed left to plant the crop. Travelling by train from Beijing to Shanghai in early spring 1962, foreign visitors noted that swathes of farmland along the tracks were sparsely planted at best, field after field lying fallow.[39] Across the country, once carefully manicured fields now looked desolate, with clumps of stunted wheat or rice withering for lack of fertiliser. Large plots lay abandoned because the farmers had nothing to plant. Everywhere vast amounts of seed normally put aside for sowing in the following season had been eaten by desperate farmers. Even in Zhejiang, relatively sheltered from the worst effects of the famine, one in five villages lacked the seed necessary to plant the fields.[40] In subtropical Guangdong, normally ablaze in every shade of green in spring, 10 per cent of the sprouts routinely rotted, the seed weak and impoverished, the land leached of all nutrients. In some communes in Zhongshan county half the fields wilted, as fledging plants turned yellow and then slowly decomposed into a brown mush.[41]

As the planners directed an ever larger proportion of the farmland to be cultivated with grain, the output in commercial crops and edible oils plummeted. But unlike grain, there was no notion of a subsistence threshold below which the state should not intervene, and procurements soared as a result.

Cotton is a good example. We have already noted how textile products from China flooded the international market in 1958, as the country declared a trade offensive by exporting goods at prices below economic cost. The strategy backfired, but exports of textiles nonetheless increased in order to settle the trade agreements entered into with foreign partners. China shipped 1 million metres of cotton cloth to the Soviet Union in 1957, then 2 million metres in 1959 and a huge 149 million metres in 1960.[42] The cost of importing 10,000 tonnes of raw cotton to feed the textile industries was US$8 million. The mathematics was simple. As finance minister Li Xiannian exclaimed in November 1961, calculating the equivalent import cost of an extra 50,000 tonnes of cotton that had been procured from the countryside that year, '40 million US dollars is really wonderful!'[43]

Table 7: Cotton Output and Cotton Procurements in Hunan (tonnes)

	Output	Procurement
1957	21,557	17,235 (80%)
1958	23,681	15,330 (64.7%)
1959	32,500	28,410 (87.4%)
1960	21,000	19,950 (95%)
1961	15,130	15,530 (102.6%)

Source: Hunan, 1962, 187-1-1021, p. 33; March 1964, 187-1-1154, pp. 80 and 97.

The lure of the greenback was irresistible. Procurements increased from 1.64 million tonnes in 1957 to 2.1 million tonnes the following year. Although only half of that amount was levied in 1960, as the cotton crop collapsed, it still meant that between 82 and 90 per cent of the total cotton output ended up in the hands of the state.[44] Take the example of Hunan (Table 7). As the actual output plunged after a peak in 1959, the percentage taken by the state shot up from 80 per cent to 95 per cent in 1960. In 1961, Hunan officials managed to procure more than the total cotton output by fanning out all over the province and sweeping up every bale of cotton, including reserves set aside by teams and communes from the previous crop. This strategy had been adopted by Hebei in 1959 and was highly commended by the leadership. As the State Council explained in February 1959, Hebei had managed to increase its procurements by a third by commandeering reserves found in collective storage facilities and by 'taking the cotton still in the hands of the masses'.[45]

The masses were left without much clothing. Just as grain was distributed according to political priorities which favoured the export market above domestic needs, a large proportion of the cotton was fed to the textile industries and sold on the international market. What remained was rationed and distributed in dribs and drabs following a well-established pecking order which placed party and army at the top followed by the urban population, each of these categories being further fine-tuned into an intricate hierarchy which had one thing in common: the producers of cotton, namely people in the countryside, were generally excluded. Out of the 3.5 million cotton pieces (*jian*) produced in 1961, about half were reserved for party and army uniforms and 1 million were put aside for the export market, leaving 800,000 for a population of 600 million.[46] In Guangzhou ration coupons were required for towels, socks, shirts, vests and raincoats. Cotton cloth was rationed to a metre a year, those living in the suburbs getting one-third less than city dwellers. Before the Great Leap Forward, by contrast, anyone could buy more than seven metres of cotton a year.[47]

By 1960, the situation in the countryside had become so desperate that farmers ate the cotton seeds. In Cixi county, Zhejiang, some 2,000 villagers were poisoned in a single month by eating cakes made of seeds, an indication of the extent of despair reached in one of the most sheltered provinces of China. In Henan they poisoned over 100,000 people in the region around Xinxiang alone, killing more than 150.[48] Across the land desperately hungry villagers ate anything they could get their hands on, from leather belts and straw roofs to cotton padding. Spending a month travelling through some of the most devastated regions along the Huai River in September 1961, Hu Yaobang, a party chief and associate of Deng Xiaoping who would soar to pre-eminence decades later by steering the country away from orthodox Marxism, reported seeing women and children stark naked. Many families of five or six shared one blanket. 'It is hard to imagine if you do not see it with your own eyes. There are several places where we should urgently address this issue, to avoid people freezing to death.'[49] Throughout the country those who died of starvation often did so naked, even in the middle of the winter.

———

Although slaughtered in significant quantities during the Great Leap Forward in 1958, over the years poultry, pigs and cattle mainly succumbed to neglect, hunger, cold and disease. Numbers give a sense of the extent of the devastation. Whereas some 12.7 million pigs were rooting about in 1958, a mere 3.4 million scrawny animals were alive in 1961 in Hunan province (Table 8). Hebei had 3.8 million pigs in 1961, half of what the province boasted five years earlier. A million cattle had also vanished.[50] Shandong lost 50 per cent of its cattle during the famine.[51]

Table 8: Pigs in Hunan Province (millions)

1957	1958	1959	1960	1961
10.9	12.7	7.95	4.4	3.4

Source: Hunan, 1962, 187-1-1021, p. 59.

Neglect was widespread, as incentives to look after livestock were removed once all the animals had been turned over to the people's communes. In Huaxian, just outside Guangzhou, pigs stood in a foot of excrement. In some villages the pig sheds were destroyed for fertiliser, leaving the animals exposed to the elements.[52] Routine quarantine measures broke down, as veterinary services lay in disarray. Rinderpest and swine fever spread; chicken flu was common.[53] The winter exacted the highest toll. Tens of thousands of pigs died of hunger in Cixi county, Zhejiang, in a single winter month.[54] In December 1960 alone 600,000 pigs died in Hunan province.[55]

Even more revealing are the disease rates, which rocketed sharply. In Dongguan, Guangdong, the death rate for pigs was just over 9 per cent in 1956. Three years later a quarter of all pigs died, and by 1960 well over half of all pigs perished. The county was left with a million pigs where more than 4.2 million had existed a few years earlier.[56] In Zhejiang, the death rate in some counties was 600 per cent, meaning that for every birth six pigs died; the entire herd was soon eliminated.[57] In all of Henan the situation with livestock was better in 1940, in the middle of the war against Japan, than it was in 1961 – according to Zhou Enlai himself.[58]

Before the pigs died of hunger they turned on each other. More often than not livestock was not segregated by weight, meaning that they were all locked up in a common space where the smaller ones were pushed aside, trampled on, mauled to death and devoured. In parts of Jiangyin county, for instance, many of the pigs froze to death, but quite a few were cannibalised by larger hogs.[59] When large numbers of pigs are thrown together in a harsh environment, apparently no pecking order develops, and each animal regards all others as its enemy. In Beijing's Red Star commune, where the death rate for livestock was 45 per cent, villagers noticed that hogs ate piglets, as all were confined together indiscriminately.[60]

A small proportion of the deaths were caused by innovations in animal husbandry. Like close cropping and deep ploughing, these were supposed to propel the country past its rivals. All sorts of experiments were carried out to increase the weight of pigs, some of them inspired by the fraudulent theories of Trofim Lysenko. A protégé of Stalin, Lysenko rejected genetics and believed that inheritance was shaped by the environment (Lysenko, it might be added, openly expressed his contempt for the Great Leap Forward in 1958, to the great irritation of the leadership in Beijing).[61] Just as seeds of hybrid varieties were developed for greater resistance, hybrid breeding of livestock was envisaged by senior leaders. Jiang Hua, party secretary of Zhejiang, thus asked the county leaders to take steps to 'actively shape nature': he suggested cross-breeding sows with bulls to produce heavier piglets.[62] Local cadres, eager to fulfil impossible quotas for meat delivery, also artificially inseminated animals that had not even reached maturity, including ones weighing a mere 15 kilos (a healthy adult pig should weigh between 100 and 120 kilos). Many of the animals were crippled as a result.[63]

Despite a precipitous decline in livestock, state procurements were relentless. In Hebei and Shandong a ban on the slaughter of animals was imposed in the countryside for a period of three months in early 1959.

As we have seen, Mao applauded the ban, going so far as to suggest that a resolution be passed that nobody should eat meat: all of it should be exported to honour foreign commitments.[64] Mao did not quite get his way, although the rations for the urban population were slashed several times. Even in Shanghai, a city where on average each person consumed some twenty kilos of meat annually in 1953, a mere 4.5 kilos in ration tickets were allocated by the plan in 1960, although in reality much less was available.[65] But party members continued to receive a regular supply of meat. Guangdong was thus ordered in 1961 to deliver 2,500 pigs to the capital, all earmarked for state banquets and foreign guests: this was in addition to the more regular state procurement quotas.[66]

The fishing industry was also badly damaged by collectivisation, as the equipment was either confiscated or poorly maintained. In Wuxing, a district of the prosperous silk city of Huzhou situated on the south of Lake Tai, one in five boats was no longer seaworthy because of insufficient tong oil to repair sprung seams. The number of leaks steadily increased, since the marine nails were no longer being made of forged iron.[67] The overall catch tumbled. On Chaohu Lake, Anhui, a single team of fishermen routinely caught some 215 tonnes of fish in 1958. Two years later no more than 9 tonnes were hauled aboard, as boats and nets rotted away without any care being taken. Many fishermen abandoned the trade because of a lack of incentives.[68]

———

Ploughs, rakes, sickles, hoes, shovels, buckets, baskets, mats, carts and tools of every kind were collectivised, but which collectivity actually owned them? A tug of war began between teams, brigades and communes, with mutual recriminations and random repossessions, the result of which was that in the end nobody really cared. Some villagers would simply throw their ploughs and rakes aside in the field at the end of the day. Whereas in the past a good tool could last up to ten years – some ploughs managing to survive for sixty years with careful repairs – they no longer lasted for much more than a year or two. A mat used to dry millet, when carefully maintained, might only have to be repaired after ten years, but with the advent of the people's communes most were worn out after one season.

Some rakes, it was reported by a team of investigators from Shanghai, had to be repaired after a day.[69]

And those were the tools that had not been devoured in the backyard furnaces during the frenzied iron and steel movement in 1958. At the Lushan plenum held in the summer of 1961, Li Yiqing, secretary of the south-central region, told the party leaders that 140,000 tonnes of farming tools had been thrown into the fires in the model province of Henan.[70] When these losses were tallied with what was destroyed through neglect, the total varied from about a third to half of all equipment. In Shandong a third of all tools were useless within a year of the Great Leap Forward.[71] In the Shaoguan region, Guangdong, 40 per cent of all necessary equipment was gone by 1961, meaning a loss of some 34 million tools. A third of what was left was broken.[72] The number of waterwheels in Hebei was halved, while carts were also reduced by 50 per cent.[73] In Zhejiang province half of all water pumps, over half of all planting machines and more than a third of all threshing machines were damaged beyond recovery.[74]

Besides the fact that there were few incentives to repair tools that belonged to everybody in general and nobody in particular, other reasons stood in the way of recovery. Widespread shortages of natural resources, especially timber, meant galloping inflation – despite the fixed prices of the planned economy. In Zhejiang, for instance, bamboo was 40 per cent more expensive than before the Great Leap Forward, and the iron allocated to the countryside for tool production was of inferior quality.[75] Their homes already stripped of cooking utensils and agricultural implements to feed the backyard furnaces, the villagers were then handed back useless ingots of brittle iron. Half the metal allocated to villages in Guangdong in 1961 was defective.[76] Tool production in state enterprises, as we shall see, did not fare any better.

18

Industry

Ever greater output targets were assigned to factories, foundries, work-shops, mines and power plants all over China. How a production unit was rewarded was determined by the percentage of the quota it managed to fulfil. The output total was the magic number that determined the rise and fall of any one factory. And just as cadres in the people's communes pledged ever increasing amounts of grain, all over the country factories tried to outperform each other in fulfilling the plan. Lists of output figures were broadcast on a daily basis by the propaganda machine, reproduced on chalkboard messages and wall newspapers for everybody to see. Charts and diagrams with growth projections were displayed in factory shops. Photos of model workers were enshrined under glass on a 'board of honour', while posters, stars, ribbons and slogans adorned the walls of every workshop. Underachievers were identified at factory meetings, while workers who overfulfilled the targets were commended, some of them attending mass meetings in Beijing reviewed by the Chairman himself. Above the hissing molten metal, the clang of crucibles and the whistling steam an incessant racket would come from loudspeakers, spewing out propaganda and radio programmes to encourage workers to increase production.[1]

As the supreme goal of the red factory was output, the cost of input was often neglected. In the sprawling bureaucracy in charge of industry, from the central economic ministries to the different administrative departments within the factories, nobody quite managed to keep track of the stagger-ing amount of equipment ordered from abroad. Even Zhou Enlai, who so ruthlessly pressed for the extraction of foodstuffs from the countryside to meet export targets, seemed unable to curb the import of machinery effectively. Enterprises also borrowed money to fund constant expansion, build prestige buildings and purchase more equipment. In the case of the Luoyang Mining Machinery Factory, the monthly interest owed to the bank was equal to the factory's entire wage package.[2]

But, once installed, the new equipment was subjected to poor maintenance and relentless maltreatment. On a visit to a wharf in Shanghai in 1961, the otherwise sympathetic delegation from East Germany were taken aback by the state in which they found imported machinery. New materials like sheet metal, tubes and profile iron rusted in the open.[3] The Iron and Steel Plant in Wuhan, inaugurated with much fanfare by Mao at the height of the Great Leap Forward in September 1958, gave a similar impression of extreme neglect, a mere two out of six Siemens-Martin furnaces operating at full capacity by 1962.[4] More detailed reports by investigation teams confirmed that materials, tools and machinery were neglected or even deliberately damaged. In the Shijiazhuang Iron and Steel Company, for instance, half of all engines broke down frequently.[5] A culture of waste developed. In Luoyang, three factories alone had accumulated more than 2,500 tonnes of scrap metal that went nowhere.[6] In Shenyang, sloppy streamlets of molten copper and nickel solutions ran between heaps of scrap metal.[7]

Waste developed not only because raw resources and supplies were poorly allocated, but because factory bosses deliberately bent the rules to increase output. The brand-new iron and steel plant in Jinan, according to a team of auditors, wasted a fifth of total state investment, or 12.4 million yuan, in its first two years by adding sand to hundreds of tonnes of manganese ore, resulting in a useless mixture which had to be discarded.[8]

As everyone worked feverishly towards higher production levels, mountains of substandard goods accumulated. Many a factory spewed out inferior goods as corners were cut in the relentless pursuit of higher output. The very fabric of material culture was shot through with shoddy goods, from ramshackle housing, rickety buses, wobbly furniture and faulty electric wiring to flimsy windows. The State Planning Commission found that a mere fifth of all the steel produced in Beijing was first rate. Most was second or third rate, and over 20 per cent was classified as defective. In Henan more than half of all the steel produced in factories was third rate or worse. Inferior material churned out by the steel-producing giants had a knock-on effect for a whole range of related industries. At Angang, the sprawling steel and iron complex in Anshan, the rails produced in 1957 were generally of first-rate quality, but by 1960 a mere third corresponded to the requisite standards. As the quality of the rails suffered, several sections of the railway network became too dangerous for heavy traffic and had to be closed down; a few collapsed altogether.[9]

Not only did the quantity of inferior goods increase, but larger proportions of them found their way into society. In Henan only 0.25 per cent of the cement which did not fulfil production criteria actually left the premises in 1957. This ballooned to over 5 per cent in 1960, as large quantities of substandard material were used on building sites. A survey of a whole series of industries in Kaifeng, Henan, reached an even more astounding conclusion: more than 70 per cent of all the output consisted of reject products.[10]

And just as faulty rails, warped beams and fake cement perilously weakened the material structure of everyday life, inferior consumer goods became part and parcel of socialist culture. In Shanghai clocks sounded the alarm at random, enamel basins were sold with splits and bubbles on the surface, while half of all knitwear and cotton goods were defective.[11] In Wuhan zips jammed, knives bent and blades broke off the handles of agricultural tools.[12] Sometimes factories cut costs by churning out products without any identifying label. This was the case with a fifth of the tinned meat sold in Beijing. Sometimes the labels were wrong, for instance when fruit was substituted for pork, leading to large amounts of rotten goods.[13] Even more worrying were problems caused by the addition of chemicals to processed food. In one year a Beijing dye factory sold 120 tonnes of harmful pigments specifically designed as food additives. Many of these were banned, for instance Sudan yellow, a dye used in inks. Lax procedures over quality control also meant that contaminated food and medicine were allowed to leave the factory floor, one example being a batch of 78 million bottles of penicillin gone bad. A third was sent out from a Shanghai factory before the problem was even spotted.[14] Mao scoffed at the very notion of a defective product: 'there is no such thing as a reject product, one man's reject is another man's grain'.[15]

Mao may have dismissed concerns about quality, but a reject culture damaged the country's reputation on the international market. As we have seen, the cost of making good on the leaky batteries, contaminated eggs, infected meat, fake coal and other tainted merchandise delivered in 1959 alone amounted to 200 or 300 million yuan. But reject culture also corrupted the inner workings of military industry. As a report by Marshal He Long showed, it was not only assault rifles that failed to fire, but also nineteen jet fighters produced in Shenyang that were substandard. In Factory 908 well over 100,000 gas masks were unusable. Nie Rongzhen, who ran the nuclear weapons programme, in turn complained about the poor quality of wireless devices and measuring gauges, which were often unreliable because of dust particles trapped inside. Even in top-secret factories rubbish was found everywhere, and the slightest breeze blew the dirt resting on propaganda banners hanging on the wall on to sensitive equipment: 'The Americans doubt that we can make guided missiles because the Chinese are too dirty.'[16]

Living conditions for workers were appalling. Stupendous imports of foreign machinery were meant to catapult the country forward, as gleaming new plants, from steel mills and cement kilns to oil refineries, were purchased from the Soviet Union and Eastern Europe. But very little was invested in the housing and feeding of ordinary workers and their families – despite the fact that the workforce exploded with the arrival of millions from the countryside.

Take the iron and steel plant in Jinan, the capital of Shandong. Established at the height of the Great Leap Forward in 1958 with the most technologically advanced equipment, it should have been a haven for its new recruits. But conditions deteriorated rapidly. There were inadequate toilet facilities, so workers urinated and defecated directly on the factory floor. Filth and stench permeated the premises, lice and scabies were common. Chaos reigned on the ground. Scuffles were a frequent occurrence, windows were broken and doors smashed in. A pecking order emerged in which the strongest workers grabbed the best beds in the dormitories. Fear was pervasive, in particular among women, who were commonly teased, humiliated and abused by local cadres in their offices, in their dormitories or sometimes on the factory floor in full view of other workers. None of them dared to sleep or go out on their own.[17]

A similar scene could be found in Nanjing. When the Federation of Trade Unions looked into the lives of iron, steel and coal workers in 1960, they found filthy canteens infected with insects and rodents. Queues were interminable, up to a thousand workers lining up in front of a single canteen window at the Lingshan Coal Mine. As the canteen was open for only an hour, workers would tussle and wrangle for space, sometimes coming to blows. In the Guantang Coal Mine, miners who were late were deprived of their meal, and had to go down the shafts for a ten-hour shift on an empty stomach. Dormitories were cramped. On average each worker had a space of 1 to 1.5 square metres, although some slept on boards jammed between beds or against the pillars. Many rested in shifts, having to share a bed. Straw roofs would leak, forcing some of the workers to move their bunk beds around the dripping pools. Others slept under an umbrella. Protective equipment was either lacking or wholly inadequate. Many miners had no shoes and had no alternative but to go down the shafts barefoot. Those made to hew coal in open pits were drenched when it rained, their jackets soaked with water. In the dormitories there were no blankets, and the humidity was so high that clothes would never quite dry. Some of the steel workers who had to work in front of blast furnaces burned their feet because they had no shoes.[18]

Further south, in subtropical Guangzhou, the dormitories were so crowded that a bunk bed provided no more than half a square metre per worker. Shoddy construction work meant that the premises were hot and damp during the rainy season, causing mould to spread like a rash, infecting clothes and bedding. The humidity was such that some of the facilities were described as mere 'ponds', with water dripping from the walls to form puddles on the floor.[19] In the Quren coal mine, located near Shaoguan, workers cannibalised the pit props and mine timber to build furniture or provide heating. One in seven workers suffered from silicosis, also known as potter's rot, caused by inhalation of dust particles, as no protective masks were provided.[20]

The situation was no better in the north. In the capital itself, a detailed study of four factories by the Federation of Trade Unions showed that there were four times as many workers as before the Great Leap Forward, although dormitory space had failed to keep pace with the increase. In Changxindian, in the Fengtai district, a railway factory allocated just over half a square metre to each of its workers. Throughout Beijing, workers slept in storage rooms, libraries and even in air shelters, often on bunk beds arranged in three layers. They were packed like sardines, so tightly that there was no room to turn at night. In order to get through a door, workers had to queue up. The toilets were permanently engaged and more often than not blocked. Many would wrap their faeces in a sheet of newspaper and chuck the package through a window.

Few factories provided sufficient heating: one of the four enterprises inspected had none in the bitterly cold winter of 1958–9. Workers would resort to burning coal balls in small stoves, which resulted in several deaths from coal-gas poisoning. Influenza was common. Rubbish accumulated everywhere; theft was widespread. Bullying was rife, in particular in the case of new arrivals. In the Liulihe Cement Plant, separately inspected by the Federation of Trade Unions in March 1959, three canteens designed for a total of a thousand people had to provide for over 5,700 workers. Older workers were simply pushed aside by young men eager to jump the queue, many never eating anything but cold food.[21] A year later a similar investigation noted few changes, adding that 'hooliganism' – a criminal offence taken from the Soviet penal code and covering a wide range of acts such as foul language, destruction of property and illegal sexual behaviour – was common in dormitories. Workers used power and influence to upgrade from one bed to another, finding space for friends and family despite overcrowding.[22]

By 1961 up to half of the workforce in Beijing suffered from famine oedema.[23] Industrial diseases were common, some 40,000 workers having been exposed to silicon dust. A report written by the city's People's Congress estimated that one in ten workers suffered from a chronic disease.[24] The real situation was probably much worse.

Many new factories opened during the Great Leap Forward were described as 'run by the people' rather than 'run by the state'. They fared no better. Most were jerry-built affairs, quickly set up in buildings confiscated from the public and often inadequate for industrial production. One chemical workshop in Nanjing, put together in a residential dwelling, had a bamboo roof and paint peeling from mud walls. It employed some 275 workers. Radioactive waste permeated nooks and crannies, accumulated on the floor of the common room or lay in open vats, from where it was spread by wind and rain. Workers suffered from throat and nose irritations, as the protective equipment they were meant to wear was not used properly. The masks and gloves were often turned inside out, and were carried to the dormitories without thorough cleansing. Of the seventy-seven female workers medically inspected, eight were pregnant or breast feeding, although they were in contact with radioactive material for several hours daily. No showers were taken in the winter.[25]

This was not an isolated example. In the twenty-eight factories 'run by the people' in the Gulou district, the old centre of town where drums used to mark the night watches, rubbish was found everywhere. Ventilation was non-existent in the smaller concerns. Many of the workers were women who had joined during the Great Leap Forward. Most had no work experience and were given very little protective equipment, some only donning straw hats. Exposure to chemical components and silicon dust commonly caused red eyes, headaches, itches and rashes. Some of the women had the cartilage separating their nostrils eaten away by constant inhalation of chemicals. Heatstroke, with temperatures near the furnaces ranging from 38 to 46 degrees Celsius even in the middle of the winter, was a frequent occurrence.[26] In a health check carried out on 450 women working in a factory producing electron tubes in Nanjing, more than a third suffered from lack of menstrual periods, a symptom of malnutrition. In the Nanjing Chemical Plant a quarter had tuberculosis, while one in two suffered from low blood pressure. Half had worms.[27]

However abysmal their living conditions, workers were better off than the farmers who produced the food they ate. But few could afford to support their families or remit money to the village many had left behind. Their salaries were eroded by inflation and depleted by food purchases, necessary to complement the meagre rations they were given in the canteen. In the Shijiazhuang Iron and Steel Company, workers spent three-quarters of their salaries on food.[28] In Nanjing many workers had to borrow money, incurring debts ranging from 30 to 200 yuan. Given the paltry salaries that most workers earned, these were crippling liabilities. A Grade Three worker made 43 yuan a month, although the food alone for a family of five cost 46 yuan. No savings were made in the canteen, where the fare was often poor and expensive.[29] But few people ever managed to rise to a Grade Three. The majority of salaries ranged from 12.7 to 22 yuan a month.[30] In the more deprived factories 'run by the people' over a third of the work-force were paid less than 10 yuan a month. Many had to borrow money or pawn the few personal items they had left, selling spare clothing during the summer only to shiver through the winter.[31]

And then came the medical fees, for which workers often had to pay. A close look at one chemical plant in Beijing in 1960 showed that hundreds of workers were in debt as a result of medical treatment. Chong Qingtian looked after his sick wife but owed some 1,700 yuan by the time she died. He was taken to court and was required to pay 20 yuan each month, leaving him with just over 40 yuan to live on. He was an excellent worker, but many were in a less enviable position, ending up being ruined by the medical fees incurred to treat illnesses caused by appalling working conditions.[32]

When all the problems inherent in the planned economy were taken into account – uncontrolled capital spending, enormous wastage, defective products, transportation bottlenecks, woeful labour discipline – the performance of most factories was dismal. The actual costs were difficult to calculate in the financial morass created by central planning. Not only did accountants cook the books, but sometimes they did not even know how to handle the sums. In Nanjing some forty large production units had a total of only fourteen accountants, of whom a mere six were able to keep track of the money. Many factories did not even maintain a log for outgoings and incomings, and nobody had the faintest idea of the costs incurred.[33]

But some approximations indicate the extent of the damage, as the example of steel, which is basically iron reinforced with carbon and hardening metals, shows. In Hunan 2.2 tonnes of iron were used to produce a tonne of steel, meaning enormous waste. The cost of making a tonne of steel was 1,226 yuan, which had to be sold at a state-mandated price of

250 yuan – or a loss of about 1,000 yuan per tonne. In 1959 the province lost about 4 million yuan each month on steel.[34] Better prepared to make steel in a cost-effective way were the technologically advanced mills and furnaces of Shijiazhuang. Founded in 1957, Shijiazhuang Iron and Steel made a profit before the Great Leap Forward, but soaring costs soon sent it plunging into the red. In 1958 a tonne of steel cost 112 yuan, turning a profit for the plant of some 16 million yuan. In 1959 the cost per tonne went up to 154 yuan, pushing the plant into a deficit of 23 million yuan, followed in 1960 by costs of 172 yuan per tonne and losses in excess of 40 million yuan. By that time the plant relied on a variety of poor iron ores coming from mines as far away as Hainan Island.[35]

As the losses started piling up, output collapsed. After several years of breakneck growth, the economy moved into a deep slump in 1961. The supply of coal – the fuel of modern industry – dried up. In the coal mines the equipment had been so badly treated during the Great Leap Forward that most of it was defective. New machinery often did not last longer than six months on account of the low-grade brittle steel used in its production. The miners themselves were leaving in droves, disgusted at the soaring cost of food and housing, fed up with the shortages of such basic items as soap, uniforms and rubber shoes.[36] And even if the coal was hauled out of the mines, fuel shortages consigned much of it to pile up unused. The four big coal mines in Guangdong province produced some 1.7 million tonnes of coal in 1959 but managed to transport less than a million.[37] In Gansu the radical leadership of Zhang Zhongliang made sure that coal production soared from 1.5 million tonnes in 1958 to 7.3 million tonnes in 1960, at considerable human cost, but after the petrol ran out some 2 million tonnes were abandoned in the mines.[38]

Table 9: Industrial Output for Hunan Province (million yuan)

1957	1958	1959	1960	1961	1962
1,819	2,959	4,023	4,542	2,426	2,068

Source: Hunan, 1964, 187-1-1260.

As coal production plummeted, factories around the country came to a standstill. In Shanghai in December 1960 the China Machinery Plant worked at a third of its capacity because of a lack of electricity. The Number One Cotton Mill had 2,000 workers idle all day long.[39] In the first half of 1961 the mandated amount of coal delivered to Shanghai was decreased by 15 per cent, but a third of that reduced amount was never actually delivered. Close to half of all the iron and timber needed to feed the city's heavy industry was missing as well.[40]

Because it was an industrial centre of strategic importance, Shanghai was given the highest priority by the planners. The situation was worse elsewhere, as the shortcomings of the economy spiralled out of control. In Shaoguan, the heavy-industry city of Guangdong, a survey of thirty-two state enterprises in the summer of 1961 showed that production had nosedived, with soap down by 52 per cent on the previous year, bricks by 53 per cent, pig iron by 80 per cent, matches by 36 per cent, leather shoes by 65 per cent. In the shoe factory each worker produced one pair a day where three had been made before the Great Leap Forward.[41] Table 9 shows what happened in the whole of Hunan province. These figures refer only to output, which more than doubled from 1957 to 1960, only to be halved again in the following two years. Had the cost of this obsession with quantity over quality been calculated, it would have pointed to a disaster of gargantuan proportions, inversely commensurate with the ambitions of the master plan. But no factories went bankrupt: that was a capitalist phenomenon associated with the boom-and-bust cycles that the planned economy was designed to avoid.

19

Trade

Many goods never reached the shops. The Bank of China calculated that some 300 million yuan was missing in Hunan in 1960 as a result of fake receipts, goods lost en route, sold on credit without permission or simply misappropriated. That was just in one province. At a national level the State Council estimated that some 7 billion yuan in funds was held that year by state factories instead of contributing to the circulation of goods.[1] At every level of the distribution network, corruption and mismanagement took their share, nibbling away at the supply of goods that the plan had allocated to the people.

When goods actually managed to leave the workshop floor, their first call was in a depot, where special storage companies accredited by the state sorted them according to their final destinations. In the Storage and Transportation Company in Shanghai, hundreds of objects worth well over 100,000 yuan – telephones, refrigerators, medical equipment, cranes – accumulated in boxes because of sloppy paperwork, incorrect accounts and illegible inventories. A hundred vats of shrimp paste rotted outside in the rain for a month, the documents having gone astray and the company having forgotten all about them. But, above all, goods vanished because the profit motive never quite disappeared: what was 'lost' could be traded privately on the black market.[2]

Then there was the wait for a train or a lorry. China was a poor agrarian country that never had the capacity to send goods and supplies from one end of the realm to the other, and the flow was rapidly dislocated by a crumbling transportation system. As early as the end of 1958 the economy ground to a halt, and mountains of goods were heaped everywhere about stations and ports. Each day some 38,000 freight vehicles were required by the plan, but only 28,000 were available. Having inspected only the loading areas along the coast north of Shanghai, the planners found that a million tonnes of material was waiting for transport.[3]

Lack of equipment, spare parts and fuel only made the situation worse over the next three years. By 1960 in Tianjin, Beijing, Hankou, Guangzhou and other cities, goods entering the railway stations exceeded those leaving by an amount equivalent to 10,000 tonnes each and every day. Much of this was simply piled up in makeshift storage facilities, which reached a quarter of a million tonnes by mid-October. In Dalian 70,000 tonnes of uncollected freight languished in the station, while hundreds of tonnes of expensive imported rubber had been lying around the port of Qinhuangdao for six months. In the transportation hub of Zhengzhou a ditch six metres deep was dug to dump goods, from cement bags to machinery. Much of it was damaged, a forlorn mound of bags and bundles, crates, barrels and drums.[4] In Shanghai, by the summer of 1961, goods estimated to be worth 280 million yuan had accumulated in canteens, dormitories and even on the streets, including 120 million metres of much-needed cotton. Much of the stock simply rotted or rusted away.[5]

Such was the breakdown in the transportation system that trains had to queue for their turn to enter a station. Both the tools and the manpower to move cargo were lacking. Brand-new unloading equipment turned out to be defective, a problem compounded by the fact that 100,000 porters and haulers had hastily been made redundant to save on salaries. Logistics and co-ordination were not among the strengths of the planned economy.[6] To this had to be added a lack of incentives and downright hunger. Engine drivers, normally pampered by the regime, had generally been entitled to a personal allowance of some 25 kilos of grain a month in the past, but this was lowered to 15 kilos. In Dahushan, Liaoning, the grain was substituted by sorghum or millet, while in Shijiazhuang, Hebei, half of the monthly ration was delivered in sweet potatoes. Workers did the bare minimum, besides being weakened by poor diet.[7] The mayhem also affected international shipping. Lost income as a consequence of chartered ships having to wait for days on end in the main ports of China alone amounted to £300,000.[8]

Local networks also collapsed. In Yunnan before 1958, more than 200,000 mules and donkeys carried food, clothes and supplies to the many villages tucked away in the mountains. They were replaced by horse carts, which grew from a mere 3,000 to well over 30,000. But horses cost far more in fodder, and they were badly managed by state enterprises, many dying during the famine. Carthorses, moreover, were ill suited to negotiate the steep mountain paths and rugged landscapes of the southern province, leaving many of the small villages isolated.[9]

Lorries foundered. Yunnan was given only half the petrol it needed in 1960, and by September some 1,500 were running on alternative fuels, from charcoal to lignite as well as sugarcane and ethanol.[10] In Hunan vegetable oil instead of machine oil was added to engines, causing widespread damage.[11] Even in Shanghai motorised rickshaws were taken off the streets while many of the buses changed to gas, some of it carried in enormous improvised gunny bags rather than in cylinders.[12] Neglect also undermined deliveries. The Vehicle Transport Company in Guangzhou, for instance, boasted forty cars, most of them acquired since the Great Leap Forward. Of these three had already been ruined by 1961, while an average of twenty-five were in repair around the clock, leaving about a dozen in use.[13] As the vehicles were pushed to the limit in the race to fulfil a faltering plan, the actual running costs increased. In 1957, by one estimate, a car cost just 2.2 yuan per 100 kilometres in spare parts and replacements, but 9.7 yuan by 1961. The main reason was constant use and poor maintenance.[14]

All manner of goods were delivered to the door in pre-revolutionary China, carried in baskets swung from a shoulder pole, carted on wheelbarrows or occasionally in donkey panniers. Itinerant traders reached even isolated villages in the hinterland, carrying cloth, crockery, baskets, coal, toys, candy and nuts as well as cigarettes, soap and lotions. In the cities vendors thronged the streets, offering every possible item from socks, handkerchiefs, towels and soap to women's underwear.

When hawkers and traders gathered at regular intervals at an agreed location in the countryside, a periodic market emerged: a multitude of farmers, craftsmen and traders, all with their goods on back or cart, swarmed into a silent hamlet which was transformed into a busy scene with wares sold by the wayside or displayed on temporary stalls. In the towns and cities, hundreds of boutiques, shops, bazaars and department stores competed for attention, from hatters, shoemakers and drapers to photographers, all mixing with fortune-tellers, magicians, acrobats and wrestlers to offer amusement and commerce.

While traditional shops were low and open with the living quarters above, new department stores were towers of commerce, monuments of trade standing tall above the surrounding buildings. They could be found in every large city, illuminated at night with rows of electric lights, offering local and imported goods ranging from American canned sardines to child-size motor cars. The striking contrast between the elaborate department stores and traditional single-storey shops, often only next door, was typical of the diversity that ran through the whole structure of everyday life in the republican era.[15]

Most of this busy, bustling world vanished after 1949. Free trade was replaced by a planned economy. Markets were closed down. Spontaneous gatherings were forbidden. Hawkers and pedlars were taken off the streets, often forced into collective enterprises controlled by the state. The itinerant trader and the once ubiquitous blacksmith became relics of the past. Department stores were nationalised, their steady supply of goods from all over the world drying up and being replaced by state-mandated goods produced in state-owned enterprises to be sold at state-mandated prices. The owners of small shops were forced to become government employees. Mikhail Klochko remembered going to an obscure little store with hardly any goods at all in Beijing. He bought a pencil box out of pity for the wan shopkeeper and his two sickly children.[16] The only prosperous shops were near the tourist hotels in cities like Beijing and Shanghai, offering furs, enamelware, watches, jewellery, embroidered silk pictures of landscapes and portraits of Marx, Engels, Lenin and Mao. Called Friendship Stores, they were reserved for foreign visitors and elite party members.

For ordinary people the choice was dire. Take the example of Nanjing, a once flourishing city on the south bank of the Yangzi which had served as the capital of the republic. Although the government clamped down on the free market, there were still well over 700 shops on the eve of the Great Leap Forward, selling their wares directly to the public. By 1961 a mere 130 had survived. Where a sophisticated network of manufacturers, traders and retailers had linked the city with some seventy counties and over forty cities across the country, the advent of rigid collectivisation led to a turning inward, as a mere six counties and three cities contributed to the local handicraft industry. As the plan replaced the market, the range of handicraft products halved to about 1,200. Even well-known heritage brands, from Golden Chicken hairpins to Yangzi River spring locks, buckled under the weight of the state. Variety in design suffered. Whereas some 120 different locks had been available before 1958, by 1961 only a dozen survived. Most were so similar that one key could open several padlocks. But prices for all products were higher, generally by about a third, in some cases double.[17] The same could be said of foodstuffs. Since the launch of the Great Leap Forward some 2,000 food pedlars had been forced to change jobs in Nanjing. Previously individual hawkers had an intimate knowledge of complex market conditions and efficiently transported the vegetables to key delivery points in the city, but now a clumsy and rigid command economy only compounded the problems caused by famine in the countryside.[18]

The trade in surplus goods and waste material, thriving before 1949, also disintegrated. Lauding the widespread practice of recycling every conceivable object, Dyer Ball observed before the fall of the empire that poverty encouraged care to be given to the most insignificant trifle, turning everybody into a merchant.[19] But the exact opposite happened during the famine: obsession with a master plan produced mountains of waste on the ground, since few people were given any incentives to recycle. In Guangzhou some 170 tonnes of waste material – from iron oxide to graphite powder – was heaped about the city in the summer of 1959. Before the Great Leap Forward, every scrap of metal or shred of cloth would have been recycled by a small army of independent pedlars, who made sure that rags, cans, plastic, paper and tyres reached a potential buyer. Many abandoned the trade after they had been forced to enrol in a large and unresponsive collective.[20]

While the rubbish accumulated, shortages of the most basic necessities became endemic. In Nanjing everything was scarce by the summer of 1959, even ordinary objects such as shoes and pots.[21] Queues – the hallmark of socialism – were part of everyday life. As famine set in, they grew longer. In Jinan some factory workers took two days off work to wait in line to buy grain. Li Shujun queued for three days but failed even to get a ticket, which had to be exchanged for a number, which in turn had to be exchanged for grain – all in different queues.[22] In Shanghai too working men and women had to queue for the few goods which reached the shops. The ritual started before daybreak, as everybody knew that the shops would be empty by the afternoon.[23] Patience could wear thin. Fights broke out when some people used bricks to mark their place in a queue and these were then kicked over by others.[24] In Wuhan, where up to 200 people had to wait in a single queue all night to buy rice towards the end of 1960, tempers flared and scuffles erupted.[25]

The state rather than the market determined the price of goods. This was supposed to stabilise prices and enhance the purchasing power of the people. But farmers bought manufactured goods at inflated prices, although they were forced to sell grain and other foodstuffs to the state at rock-bottom prices – often so low that they made a loss, as we have seen. A colossal transfer of wealth took place from the countryside to the cities. A sense of the scale of this was indicated by Lan Ling, an official with the inspectorate in Qingdao. By compiling and adjusting the prices paid for food and goods since 1949, he found that the price for coal had increased by 18.5 per cent, soap by 21.4 per cent, shoes by up to 53 per cent, rope by 55 per cent, household goods by up to 157 per cent and ordinary tools by up to 225 per cent. In contrast the price paid by the state for grain had actually decreased, ranging from 4.5 per cent for wheat to 10.5 per cent for maize.[26]

Prices fixed by the state were rarely respected, if only because all sorts of additional charges could be made. A detailed investigation by the People's Congress in Guangzhou found that there could be up to forty different transfer prices for the exact same type of metal bar. In the steel and iron industry many of the prices actually charged were 50 per cent higher than those mandated by the state. In some cases the price rocketed by a factor of ten, contributing to a slump in industrial production as company managers had a hard time adjusting a rigid budget to the violent fluctuations in the supply costs. The price of coal, too, was fixed, but private deals struck between different enterprises led to relentless upward pressure. The actual cost of production thus soared, forcing the state to subsidise industries even further by trying to keep the prices of finished goods down. This too failed, as just about everything became more expensive yet increasingly shoddy, from glass bottles and mothballs to hairpins and wooden clogs.[27] In Wuhan, as everywhere else, the cost of a water bucket, an iron kettle or a small fruit knife had doubled in a year or so since the launch of the Great Leap Forward. In the smelting capital of the new China, an iron pot cost twenty-two yuan when five yuan would have sufficed in 1957.[28] As Li Fuchun acknowledged in the summer of 1961, annual inflation was at least 10 per cent for everything from food and commodities to services, but it reached 40 to 50 per cent in some places. Some 12.5 billion yuan was squandered on goods worth only 7 billion.[29]

Other side effects of the planned economy appeared, because the profit motive rather than selfless dedication to the people's needs always lurked just under the surface of the paper plan. In the midst of humanity's greatest famine, a whole range of deluxe products were sold at a premium, from vegetables, cinema tickets and tea leaves to simple pails. State-owned enterprises used widespread shortages to upgrade some of their goods and boost profits.[30] When the People's Congress of Beijing decided to have a close look at the Beijing Department Store, the Stalinist flagship on Wangfujing, it found out how enterprises responded to inflationary pressure rather than to consumer demand. In 1958 around 10 per cent of all underwear in the store was in the higher price bracket. The bulk, 60 per cent, consisted of mid-range products accessible to most city dwellers. In 1961 more than half were luxury items, with a mere third carrying a mid-range price tag. This structural change came on top of inflation, which was estimated at 2.7 per cent each month.[31]

As state-owned behemoths replaced small shops, the responsibility for defective goods shifted away from the street towards remote and impenetrable bureaucracies.[32] The plan, of course, had an answer to this problem, setting up 'service stations' (*fuwuzu*) for the benefit of the great masses. But they were few and far between, unable to cope with a deluge of shoddy goods and, most of all, utterly uninterested in serving the people. So in a poor country the cost of fixing an object often exceeded the cost of replacing it. In Wuhan the expense of having shoes resoled, pots repaired or keys cut was double the state-mandated prices, as service stations effectively enjoyed a monopoly over repair work. In Xiangtan, Hunan, it cost eight yuan to repair a fire pot but only nine yuan to buy a new one, while in many regions the cost of having socks darned was about the same as buying a new pair.[33] Over the winter of 1960–1, as everybody was shivering from fuel shortages and inadequate clothing, repair centres in the capital were buried beneath heaps of defective goods. Apathetic employees merely pushed the stuff around, lacking the incentives, the tools and the supplies to tackle their jobs. Even simple nails to resole a pair of shoes were unavailable. In the Qianmen commune, in the heart of the capital, some sixty stoves lay about rotting. Broken furniture was strewn about the place, which was short of saws, planes and chisels.[34]

Even when service stations undertook to launder clothes, what should have been a relatively straightforward matter became caught in a hopeless quagmire. A cumbersome bureaucracy involved a whole series of separate steps, from registering the items and issuing a receipt to handing out the washed clothes, all these operations being performed by different people, involving a third of the workforce. Those who actually did the washing rarely managed more than ten items a day. Everything was run at a loss and charged to the state, despite the high prices. On Shantou Road, Shanghai, a small laundry paid 140 yuan in salaries each month, although it made only about 100 yuan a month in income, not counting numerous lost items of clothing that had to be compensated for.[35] Of course most ordinary people would have preferred to repair their clothes, shoes and furniture themselves, but their tools had been taken away during the iron and steel campaign. Lao Tian remembered that in Xushui – one of the country's model communes – for several years his mother had to queue up to borrow the only needle that had not been confiscated in the neighbourhood.[36]

Housing

Every dictator needs a square. Military parades are at the heart of state rituals in communist regimes: power is evinced by a show of military might, with leaders gathering on the rostrum to greet the cadenced tread of thousands of marching soldiers and model workers, while jet fighters scream and whine overhead. Stalin had the Resurrection Gate on Red Square bulldozed and Kazan Cathedral demolished in order to make room for heavy tanks to clatter past Lenin's tomb. Mao was Khrushchev's guest of honour at the fortieth anniversary of the October Revolution, celebrated in Red Square in 1957, but he had no intention of lagging behind his rival. Tiananmen Square had to be bigger, he decided: was China not the most populous nation on earth?[1] The square was expanded to hold 400,000 people in 1959, as a maze of medieval walls, gates and roads were levelled to create a vast concrete area the size of sixty football fields.[2]

The expansion of Tiananmen Square was one of ten gigantic achievements designed to overawe Khrushchev at the tenth anniversary of the Chinese Revolution, to be celebrated in October 1959 in the presence of hundreds of foreign guests – one edifice for each year of liberation. A brand-new railway station, capable of handling 200,000 passengers a day, was built in a matter of months. A Great Hall of the People appeared on the western side of Tiananmen Square, a Museum of Chinese History on the eastern side. The Zhonghua Gate was erased to make room for the Monument to the People's Heroes, a granite obelisk some thirty-seven metres high at the centre of the square.

The leadership bragged to the foreign press eagerly anticipating the anniversary that sufficient new buildings had been erected to give the capital a total of thirty-seven square kilometres of new floor space – more than fourteen times that of all the office buildings put up in Manhattan since the Second World War.[3] It was an empty boast, as Beijing was turned into a giant Potemkin village designed to fool foreign visitors. But there was no denying that the party was spellbound by a vision in which soaring skyscrapers of steepled glass and concrete would transform Beijing overnight, relegating to oblivion the shameful mud huts and grey brick houses clustered along narrow lanes. Plans were drawn up for the systematic destruction of the entire city within ten years. At one point even the Imperial Palace was threatened by the wrecking ball.[4] Tens of thousands of houses, offices and factories were pulled down, as the capital became a giant building site permanently covered in dust. Foreign embassy staff were taken aback by the rate of demolition, as some of the buildings that were pulverised had only recently been completed. 'The general picture is one of chaos,' commented an observer. All work was concentrated in Tiananmen Square, while elsewhere long-established building sites were deserted.[5] More often than not pillars and beams went up for the first and second floor, and were then abandoned because of shortages of materials, leaving skeletal frames to stand forlorn as so many monuments to delusion.[6]

While most of the prestige buildings were ready in time for the October 1959 celebrations, they came at considerable cost. The planners were effective at creating an illusion of order on paper, but chaos reigned on the ground. In a fitting tribute to the folly of the Great Leap Forward, defective steel was incorporated into the party's new nerve centre. Close to 1,700 tonnes of the steel beams used for the Great Hall of the People were either bent out of shape or insufficiently thick. Threaded steel produced in Tianjin was so weak that it had to be discarded. Across the square thousands of bags of cement were wasted, while a third of the equipment used on the building site was routinely out of order. And even at the heart of power, the party could not get more than three-quarters of the workforce to arrive on time in the morning. When they finally got to their posts, many slacked and skimped. A team of twenty carpenters called in from Wenzhou took three days to install fifteen window casements. Only one actually fitted.[7]

Across the country vast amounts of money were lavished on prestige buildings. Stadiums, museums, hotels and auditoria were built specifically to mark the tenth anniversary of liberation in 1959. In Harbin 5 million yuan was spent on a National Day Hotel, more than the total cost of the Beijing Hotel. A further 7 million was thrown at a National Day Stadium. In Tianjin, too, a National Day Stadium was planned, with seats to hold 80,000 spectators. Stadiums went up in Taiyuan and Shenyang, among other cities. Jiangsu decided to allocate 20 million yuan to National Day projects.[8]

Every local dictator, it seemed, wanted to have his ten pet projects in slavish imitation of the capital. The accoutrements of power in Beijing were widely duplicated at lower levels, as many leaders aspired to become a smaller version of Mao Zedong. Another reason was that officials were accountable to their bosses higher up in Beijing, not to the people below them. Big, tangible structures and flashy projects were a sure way to foster the illusion of effective governance. In Lanzhou, the capital of impoverished Gansu, provincial boss Zhang Zhongliang pushed for ten big edifices, although this rapidly spiralled up to sixteen schemes, including a People's Hall designed to be exactly half the size of the Great Hall of the People in Tiananmen Square, a People's Square, an East Railway Station, a Culture Palace for Workers, a Culture Palace for Minorities, a stadium, a library and a luxury hotel, as well as new buildings for the provincial committee, the provincial People's Congress, a Television Tower and a central park. The cost was set at 160 million yuan. Thousands of houses were destroyed, leaving many of the inhabitants homeless in the middle of the winter. Very little was achieved. After construction work was stopped in the wake of Zhang Zhongliang's fall from power in December 1960, nothing but rubble remained in the centre of the city.[9] Dozens of other prestige buildings were also started without any sort of approved plan. One example was a brand-new Friendship Hotel for foreign experts. The number of guests was misjudged by a factor of three, so that in the end the 170 foreigners were given an average of sixty square metres of luxurious accommodation while villagers were dying of cold and hunger just outside Lanzhou. After the recall of Soviet experts the building was eerily quiet.[10]

A step further down the ladder of power was the commune, and there was no shortage of radical leaders willing to transform them into models of communist utopia. In Huaminglou, where Liu Shaoqi was born, party secretary Hu Renqin initiated his own ten construction projects. These included a 'pig city', a giant pig shed stretching for ten kilometres along the main road. Many hundreds of houses set back from the street were destroyed to make room for the project. Stopping here on an inspection tour in April 1961, as we have seen, Liu Shaoqi found nothing but a few dozen scrawny animals. A water pavilion was built on the lake, as well as a large reception hall for visiting officials. In the meantime, half a million kilos of grain rotted in the fields. The death rate in some teams was as high as 9 per cent in 1960.[11] All over the country similar monuments to party extravagance appeared. In Diaofang commune, Guangdong, where thousands starved to death, some eighty houses were ripped up for timber and bricks, all of which were earmarked for a People's Hall spacious enough to convene a gathering of 1,500 people.[12]

In the three years up to September 1961, a total of 99.6 billion yuan was spent on capital construction, to which had to be added a further 9.2 billion in housing projects ostensibly earmarked for ordinary people. Most of the money ended up being invested in prestige buildings and offices with no tangible benefit for anyone but party members.[13] But that did not take into account all sorts of accounting tricks used to fund even more construction. In Guizhou the Zunyi region appropriated some 4 million yuan of state funds, including financial assistance for the poor, to indulge in a building spree, sprucing up leading cities with new buildings, dancing halls, photo studios, private toilets and elevators. In Tongzi county funding reserved for six middle schools was embezzled to set up a brand-new theatre.[14] Li Fuchun, on reviewing the many billions spent on prestige projects without state approval, felt sheer despair: 'People cannot eat their fill and we are still building skyscrapers – how can we communists have the heart to do that! Does it still look like communism? Is it not empty talk when we go on all day long about the interests of the masses?'[15]

As private property became a thing of the past, collective units moved into the mansions that had once been the pride and joy of the moneyed elite. As a sense of ownership evaporated, no one individual being held accountable for any one property, a form of destruction appeared that was more insidious than the muffled thud of the sledgehammer. Once one of the most magnificent estates in Shanghai, Huaihai Middle Road nos 1154–1170 were taken over by an electric machinery unit in November 1958. In less than a year the windows were broken, the marble and ceramic tiles were smashed, and the building was stripped and gutted of expensive imported kitchen equipment, its heating system, the fridge and all the toilets. Stench permeated the premises, and rubbish was strewn all over the compound. The army was just as careless. Once it had claimed control of a garden villa on Fenyang Road, the place was left to crumble. The staircase fell apart, railings were broken, the chimney collapsed, all removable property was stolen, the trees in the garden died and the lotus pond turned into a smelly swamp. After a manor on Hongqiao Road had been occupied by the air force, the floorboards were broken up, the water taps and electricity switches dismantled, while the toilet overflowed with faeces. There were many other examples, 'too many to be enumerated', according to a report by the housing authorities.[16]

Lack of maintenance spread beyond individual houses. In Wuhan termites literally ate their way through many old buildings. In Station Street, half of one thousand buildings were infested. No. 14 Renhe Street simply caved in on its inhabitants. Architectural landmarks such as the Hong Kong and Shanghai Bank in Hankou were in danger of being over-run by vermin.[17]

Places of worship were no exception. Religion had no place in the people's communes: churches, temples and mosques were turned into workshops, canteens and dormitories. In Zhengzhou, eighteen out of all twenty-seven places of worship for Catholics, Protestants, Buddhists and Muslims were taken over, and a further 680 rooms privately rented out by religious congregations were confiscated. The city was proud to announce by 1960 that the number of Christian and Muslim worshippers had shrunk from 5,500 to a mere 377. All eighteen religious leaders now participated in 'productive labour' – except for three who had died.[18]

Destruction also extended to historic monuments. In Qujiang, Guangdong, the tomb of Zhang Jiuling, the famous Tang-dynasty minister, was damaged by a people's commune digging for treasures, while a

Ming-dynasty Buddhist temple in Shaoguan was torn down for building material. Further south in Guangdong a cannon built by Lin Zexu to fight the British during the Opium War was blown up and used as scrap iron.[19] In Dujiangyan, Sichuan, the scene of an irrigation system dating back to the third century AD, a string of ancient temples were dismantled and burned for fuel.[20] The Erwang temple, abounding in cultural relics and surrounded by ancient trees, was declared an historical monument in 1957 – and partly blown up with explosives a few years later.[21] In the north the Great Wall of China was plundered for building material, while bricks from the Ming Tombs were carted away with the approval of local party secretaries. A stretch of wall measuring forty metres long and nine metres high at Dingling Tomb, where the Yongle Emperor was buried, was razed to the ground, while hundreds of cubic metres were dug from the Baocheng Tomb, also known as the Precious Hall. 'Bricks belong to the masses' was the clinching argument.[22]

City walls too were an object of official wrath. Their crenellated parapets, erstwhile symbols of imperial grandeur, overgrown with vines and shrubbery, were now seen as monuments to backwardness. Mao Zedong set the tone, pointing out at the Nanning conference in January 1958 that the walls around Beijing should be destroyed. Large sections of the vermilion gates and walls would be taken down in the following years. Other cities followed suit: parts of the wall that girdled the old city of Nanjing were dismantled by collective units in search of building material.[23]

———

But most of the devastation was in the countryside. Destruction came in waves. As we have seen, buildings were torn down to provide nutrients for the soil during the fertiliser campaign in early 1958. To allow a continuous revolution to take hold, buildings were used as a source of fuel: as farmers ploughed deep furrows throughout the night, bonfires flared and sparkled. Then, as the people's communes were established, private property was turned into offices, meeting halls, canteens, nurseries or kindergartens. Some were stripped for building material, others torn down to make way for a vision of modernity that never quite managed to migrate from paper to the village. With the drive to produce more iron and steel, metal window frames and door knobs were stripped, then the floorboards were taken for fuel. When the Great Leap Forward acquired a second life after the summer of 1959, the militia went from house to house searching for hidden grain as if it were a weapon of insurrection, breaking through walls, prodding the floor for hidden holes, digging up cellars, often taking down part or all of the building as compensation. As famine set in, the villagers themselves started cannibalising their homes, either bartering the bricks for food or burning the wood for fuel. If the thatch on the roofs had not yet been consumed by fire, it was taken down and eaten in desperation. Villagers also ate the plaster from the walls.

At best people were compelled to make a 'voluntary' contribution, as happened in a village in Xinhui, Guangdong, where each household was asked for thirty bricks towards a new school. As local cadres 'borrowed' more and more building material there was no house left in the end.[24] Sometimes villagers were compensated for their contributions. One villager in Sichuan dared to ask for both a tea cup and a towel in exchange for half a straw hut. He was given the tea cup. A neighbour received a small washbasin for four rooms.[25]

But most of the time coercion was the order of the day in the village. In Guangdong, where Zhao Ziyang pioneered an anti-hiding campaign in early 1959, the militia confiscated everything from a single peanut to entire mansions.[26] In Longgui commune, Shaoguan, party secretary Lin Jianhua abolished private property, sending the militia on a rampage through the villages. In a typical team of eighty-five households, some fifty-six rooms and outdoor toilets were sequestered. Farmers were tied up and beaten if they refused to follow orders.[27]

It is difficult to estimate how much was destroyed. The situation varied tremendously from place to place, but overall the Great Leap Forward constitutes, by far, the greatest demolition of property in human history. As a rough approximation between 30 and 40 per cent of all houses were turned into rubble. Here is what Liu Shaoqi, the head of state, wrote to Chairman Mao on 11 May 1959, after having spent a month investigating the region of his birth: 'According to comrades from the provincial party committee 40 per cent of all houses in Hunan have been destroyed. Besides this there is also a portion that has been appropriated by state organs, enterprises, communes and brigades.'[28] The number of people per room in Hunan doubled during the years of the Great Leap Forward, as entire families crowded into a single room the size of a wardrobe – despite the space created by the loss of several million people to starvation.[29] In Sichuan the situation was worse, with families living in toilets or under the eaves of somebody else's house. In Yanyuan (near Xichang), an area dominated by the Yi, a minority people who lived scattered in mountain areas, the situation was dire after thousands of houses were handed over to the state: 'According to statistics 1,147 families share one room with another family, 629 families share one room with three or four other families, 100 families share one room with five or more families.'[30] In the province as a whole, the rate of destruction varied from 45 to 70 per cent in some of the most affected counties.[31]

Many never found a new home, surviving as well as they could on the margins of society, seeking temporary accommodation in ragged shacks cobbled together from debris or living in pig sheds. In the Huanggang region of Hubei, where temperatures dropped to freezing, about 100,000 families had no home in the winter of 1960–1. Half of the population there had no firewood for heating, and people had to survive the bitter cold wearing miserable rags.[32]

––––––––

A special group of victims were displaced by the irrigation and reservoir schemes launched during the Great Leap Forward. There were several million of them. In Hunan alone well over half a million people were evacuated.[33] A third of a million, if not more, were evicted as each of the giant projects were started at the Three Gate Gorge in Henan, Xin'anjiang in Zhejiang and Danjiangkou in Hubei.[34] In the Zhanjiang region in Guangdong, some 300,000 houses were needed for evacuee families by the end of 1961.[35]

Most were moved without much planning and generally without compensation. In Yueyang county, Hunan, some 22,000 people lost their homes during the building of Tieshan Reservoir. The bricks, furniture, tools and cattle of the villages to be inundated by the reservoir were commandeered and used to set up a collective farm in the mountains, to which the displaced people were relegated by the county authorities. Marooned in the mountains, without arable land to survive on and with all ties to their home villages cut off, they found life miserable, and many started flocking back to the plain. Then the reservoir project was abandoned. Most of the evacuees decided to return home, but were left stranded in ghost towns from which every removable asset had been stripped. They sought shelter in makeshift huts, outdoor toilets, pig sheds and even caves, some of which periodically collapsed and buried their occupants. Many had to beg or steal to get by, sharing a few cooking utensils and surviving on a paltry ration of 10 kilos of grain a month. Few had any padded clothes or blankets for the winter.[36]

Many of the displaced people roamed the countryside, but some eventually returned home, pulled by ties to their native place. About a hundred kilometres north-east of Beijing, set in a picturesque valley with chestnut, pear and crab-apple orchards against the wooded mountains, the residents of some sixty-five villages were uprooted to make way for the Miyun Reservoir, built between September 1958 and June 1959. As many as 57,000 people lost their homes. As if this were not bad enough, local cadres requisitioned all the tools and stole the furniture. Farmers who resisted were locked up. Only a quarter of the villagers were relocated, but the makeshift camps were so confined that their inhabitants referred to them as 'pig sheds'.

Two years later many were still traipsing homeless and adrift in the countryside. In March 1961, a group of 1,500 families returned home, men, women and children shuffling along dirt roads, carrying in ragged bundles and shabby bags whatever clothes and belongings they had managed to salvage. A few went back to their original villages – the reservoir was still without water – and built mud huts or slept in the open.[37] Millions of such refugees lived in similar squalor all over the country.

The dead were also evicted. This flew in the face of a deep-rooted concern with the afterlife, expressed through complex mourning practices, funeral rites and ancestor rituals. Burial was the preferred means of dealing with a corpse, as the body was seen as a valued gift to be placed whole under the soil near one's ancestral village. Mutual obligations were thought to exist between ancestral souls and their descendants. The dead had specific needs that had to be respected. At funerals spirit money was burned, as well as a whole array of goods, from furniture to entire houses, all made of paper and designed to help the deceased to settle in the hereafter. The coffin had to be airtight. Graves had to be swept, and food and gifts regularly offered to ancestors.[38]

Some of these practices were observed during the Great Leap Forward. As much as the party decried popular religion as superstition, some local cadres indulged in expensive burials. For the burial of his grandmother one official in Hebei summoned a funeral band of thirty musicians. A canteen was commandeered for the occasion, 120 guests being treated to wine and cigarettes – in the midst of the famine. As if this could not quite assuage his grief, Li Jianjian had the remains of his parents, buried some five years earlier, exhumed, transferred to new coffins and reburied. Li Yongfu, the deputy party secretary of a knitting factory in Beijing, not only erected a tent with electric lighting to welcome a funeral band, but also burned a paper car, a paper cow and paper militia to assist the passage of his mother to the next world. Five monks chanted scriptures.[39]

But many of the burial places were destroyed, for stone, timber or even fertiliser. In Hunan, for instance, gravestones were taken to build a dam, and party activists set the example by destroying the resting places of their own ancestors. In Yueyang, in hundreds of desecrated graves, bones stuck out of the coffins.[40] Wei Shu remembered in an interview how he was made to erase graves in the Sichuan countryside: 'You know, graves for dead people, they usually look like little hills. We had to flatten them, that was one of the things we had to do in 1958. At night, we were ordered to go around to destroy the graveyards and turn them into farming land.'[41] In many parts of the country agricultural land occupied by ancestral graves was systematically reclaimed. In Beijing the crematoriums worked full time during the Great Leap Forward. In 1958 over 7,000 bodies were cremated, almost three times more than in 1956, and twenty times more than in 1952. A third of these corpses had been disinterred to make way for agriculture.[42]

But in the countryside the authorities did not always bother to cremate the bodies that they had unearthed in their frantic search for timber. As a restricted publication edited by the secretarial office of the State Council noted, in Mouping, Shandong, local cadres used corpses to fertilise the land: 'they have tossed a few not yet fully decomposed bodies on to the crops'. An elderly lady who had been buried only days earlier was stripped of her clothes, her naked body dumped by the roadside.[43]

This was by no means an exceptional case. In his report to the commissar of the military division in Shaanxi where he worked, party member Hou Shixiang explained that when he returned to his village in Fengxian county, Hunan, he noticed that many of the coffins had been disinterred and had been left strewn about the field in front of his house. The lids were ajar, the remains gone. A few days later, on a rainy afternoon, he noticed a plume of smoke from the chimney of the local deputy secretary. Inside the house were four large cauldrons in which corpses were being simmered into fertiliser, the extract to be evenly distributed over the fields.[44]

21

Nature

Travelling extensively through the Qing Empire in the 1870s, Baron von Richthofen reported that the entire north of the country was destitute of trees, the barren mountains and hills offering a desolate view.[1] Securing fuel for the long, cold winters was always a problem in imperial China. Farmers raised large quantities of maize and sorghum: seeds were used for food, while the stalks served as fuel to heat the *kang*, a hypocaust bed which the family slept on at night and sat on during the winter when it was heated by flues built inside.[2] In a country depleted of forests, lack of fuel was widely felt: the scarcity of wood meant that every chip, twig, root and shaving was eagerly gleaned by children or elderly women, who stripped the ground bare.

Forest destruction – for clearing, fuel and timber – was made worse after 1949 by rash interference in the natural environment. Mao viewed nature as an enemy to be overcome, an adversary to be brought to heel, an entity fundamentally separate from humans which should be reshaped and harnessed through mass mobilisation. War had to be waged against nature by people pitted against the environment in a ceaseless struggle for survival. A voluntarist philosophy held that human will and the bound-less energy of the revolutionary masses could radically transform material conditions and overcome whatever difficulties were thrown in the path to a communist future. The physical world itself could be reshaped, hills erased, mountains levelled, rivers raised – bucket by bucket if necessary.[3] Launching the Great Leap Forward, Mao declared that 'there is a new war: we should open fire on nature'.[4]

The Great Leap Forward decimated the forests. In the drive to increase steel output, the backyard furnaces that mushroomed everywhere had to be fed, farmers fanning out into the mountains to cut down trees for fuel. In Yizhang county, Hunan, the mountains were covered in lush primeval forest. A great cutting followed, some units felling two-thirds of the trees to feed the furnaces. By 1959 nothing but bare mountains remained.[5] In Anhua, to the west of Changsha, an entire forest was turned into a vast expanse of mud.[6] Being driven through thick ancestral forests along the road from Yunnan to Sichuan, Soviet specialists in forestry and soil preservation noted that trees had been randomly felled, resulting in landslides.[7] Forests were brutalised everywhere, sometimes beyond recovery.

But random logging did not stop with the end of the steel campaign. The famine was not just a matter of hunger, but rather of shortages of all essentials, fuel in particular. As farmers were desperate for firewood and timber, they reproduced habits acquired during the steel campaign, returning to the woods to cut and slash. Stealing was easier than ever before because lines of responsibility for forestry had become blurred with collectivisation: the forest belonged to the people.[8] In Wudu county, in arid Gansu, there had been some 760 people in charge of forestry before the Great Leap Forward; by 1962 about a hundred remained. The situation was the same all over China. In 1957 Jilin province was covered in dense forests and beautiful woodlands managed by 247 forestry stations. Only eight of these survived collectivisation.[9]

Not only were local brigades powerless to stop depredations of natural resources, but they were often complicit in them. When walking through the gates of Sihai commune in Yanqing county, up in the mountains just outside Beijing, a visitor in March 1961 was met with the sight of some 180,000 stumps of trees – linden and mulberry – cut an inch or two above the ground. This was the work of a mere two units.[10] Farmers were so desperate for warmth that they even cut down fruit trees in the middle of the winter. As the Forestry Bureau from Beijing reported, 50,000 apple, apricot and walnut trees were hacked down by one village in Changping, while a brigade used a tractor to uproot 890,000 plants and seedlings for fuel.[11] More often than not, communes would send teams to poach from neighbours: from Huairou a hundred farmers were dispatched across the county border to Yanqing, where they cut down 180,000 trees in less than three weeks.[12] Closer to the capital, trees along the railway were felled,

10,000 vanishing along the line in Daxing county.[13] Further south even telephone poles were taken down for fuel.[14] Far inland, in Gansu, a single brigade destroyed two-thirds of all 120,000 varnish trees, crippling the local economy, while another team managed to fell 40 per cent of the tea-oil trees on which local villages had depended for their livelihoods.[15]

People were desperate for kindling. Some villages burned not only their furniture but even some of their houses after cutting down the trees: 'What is under the pot is more scarce even than what is in the pot,' farmers lamented.[16] Even in Panyu, Guangdong, surrounded by subtropical vegetation, two-thirds of all households had no fuel to start a fire, some even lacking a match. Fire had to be borrowed from neighbours. Once started, it was guarded like a precious commodity, as entire villages sank back into a primitive barter economy.[17]

In cities too trees were felled, but for different reasons. As we have seen, many companies used the Great Leap Forward to expand their facilities, often out of all proportion to their actual needs. One arm of the Commercial Bureau of Nanjing destroyed a fruit yard with 6,000 cherry, peach, pomegranate and pear trees. The cleared field remained empty. Such destruction was common in Nanjing. As an investigation at the end of 1958 showed, a few dozen units were responsible for illegally hacking down 75,000 trees. Most were factories in need of timber, but some sold the wood on the black market to raise much-needed income.[18]

Although there were periodic campaigns to turn the denuded countryside green – barren deserts would be transformed into lush forests – widespread famine, poor planning and a more general collapse of authority combined to defeat efforts at afforestation. Trees that had just been planted instantly disappeared. In 1959, for example, Beijing sent thousands of people to plant 2,600 hectares of protective greenery at the Ming Tombs Reservoir. The local commune destroyed more than half within a year. Outside Beijing between a third and four-fifths of all reforestation and seedling projects were lost. The damage in regions further removed from the seat of power must have been even greater.[19] In Heilongjiang, with its mountains clad in dense forest harbouring virgin larch, purple linden and Manchurian ash, one-third of all seedlings in new shelter forests died because they were poorly managed.[20] In Hubei, some 15,000 trees planted to stabilise the banks of a dam in E'cheng were illegally felled as soon as they were put in the ground. They were replanted, but the job was carried out so badly that most simply tilted over and dried out.[21]

To the many causes of denudation must be added fire, cases of which soared as a result of greater human activity in forests and a collapse in effective forestry management. Some 56,000 hectares were destroyed in thousands of fires in Hunan during the first two years of the Great Leap Forward.[22] In the arid northern plains of Shaanxi and Gansu, where forest was already rare, 2,400 fires claimed more than 15,000 hectares in the spring of 1962.[23] Fires could be accidental, but often the forest was burned on purpose to produce fertiliser or hunt down wildlife. As fire advanced and the forest receded, so the animals were slaughtered. Even rare species were fair game for hunters, and some of them – golden monkey, wild elephant and sable – were driven to the edge of extinction.[24]

Fire was also used to clear the land for cereal grain, although most of the reclamation took place in pastoral areas. Elsewhere the cultivated surface actually shrank since collectivisation was supposed to bring about such astonishing jumps in productivity that a third of all fields could be abandoned. In the Gansu corridor and the Ningxia plain, for instance, winter wheat intruded on the steppes, hastening desertification. The county of Yanchi – to take but one example from Ningxia – doubled its farmland to 50,000 hectares during the Great Leap Forward, cutting away the highland grasses and driving the sheep up the hills to graze: the county now faced the sand. Further to the west, in the arid Qaidam basin, a bleak expanse pockmarked by salt marshes and surrounded by mountains so cold that little could grow, communes destroyed 100,000 hectares of shrubbery and desert vegetation to make way for grain cultivation. The risk of being buried by drift sand then forced several collective farms to move.[25]

The extent of forest coverage lost during the famine is difficult to estimate.[26] Up to 70 per cent of the shelter forest was destroyed in some counties in Liaoning province. In east Henan, 80 per cent of all shelter forests vanished; in Kaifeng it had gone altogether, and some 27,000 hectares were given up to the desert.[27] Throughout the immense expanse of the north-west – from Xinjiang to Shanxi – a fifth of all trees were cut down.[28] In Hunan half of the forest was felled.[29] In Guangdong just under a third had disappeared.[30] Yu Xiguang, an expert on the famine, claims that 80 per cent of the forest coverage went up in smoke, although that may be an overestimate.[31] The damage varied from place to place, and even in the archives statistics are political artefacts rather than objective reflections of reality. What is certain is that never before had such a large diversity of forests, from the bamboo groves in the south to the alpine meadows and boreal stands of fir and pine in the north, suffered such a prolonged and intense attack.

After dark clouds filled the skies, thunder and rain exploded over Hebei in the early summer of 1959. As the torrential downpour continued unabated, the drainage system choked with mud, excrement and foliage, irrigation canals caved in, streets turned into rivers and the region north of the capital flooded. The monsoon dissolved the houses made of mud and destroyed the fields, either waterlogging them or washing away the topsoil. Streets were coated with silt and heaped with wreckage. A third of all farmers in Tongzhou were affected, as homes collapsed, crops were lost and animals drowned.[32] Other catastrophes besieged China during the summer. Heavy rain lashed Guangdong. Typhoons pummelled the coast further north. Extreme variations in the weather had unforeseen consequences, causing the worst drought in Hubei in several decades.[33] Much was made of the impact of nature on the economy, as the leadership deflected attention away from politics by attributing economic setbacks to these calamities. The exact proportion of blame to be assigned to nature became a point of contention, and Liu Shaoqi would later get into trouble by openly claiming that only 30 per cent of 'difficulties in production' were caused by natural disasters, the remaining 70 per cent being due to man-made factors.

But Liu's explanation, while quite common, reproduced rather than challenged the notion which lay at the root of environmental degradation in China at the time, namely that humans were an entity separate from nature altogether.[34] Both were intertwined, as detailed studies carried out on 'natural calamities' at the time show. When an investigation team revisited Tongzhou the following summer, they found extreme destitution, as the state had all but abandoned the villagers, who barely survived without adequate food, clothing or shelter.[35] Traditional coping mechanisms in times of disaster – private charity, state assistance, mutual help, family savings and migration – had failed to take effect, and the flooding had a far more profound and prolonged effect as a result of collectivisation. But none of this explained why Tongzhou had been hit so badly. Did it rain more over that part of the region? The answer came a year later, after Liu Shaoqi pointed out the marginal role played by catastrophes in a speech attended by thousands of top cadres. In the more open political climate of 1962, the Water Conservancy Bureau started taking stock of how the Great Leap Forward had affected the irrigation system. It singled out Tongzhou for special attention. The conclusion was unambiguous: poorly conceived irrigation projects, hastily implemented during the water-conservancy movement of 1957–8, had disturbed a carefully balanced natural water system. Combined with a huge extension of agriculture, more water than ever before was forced to go underground. When the clouds burst over Tongzhou in 1959 the water had nowhere to go, inundating fields and villages.[36]

The same happened all over the country. In Hebei, the Cangzhou region was so devastated by a typhoon in July 1961 that a team of twenty-four men was immediately sent from the provincial party committee. They spent ten days in the region, where close to half of all the fields stood under water. The team quickly realised that the natural drainage system had been destroyed by irrigation work undertaken since the Great Leap Forward. Poorly designed reservoirs, canals and ditches contributed to the disaster, but increased cultivation made it worse, as big, square fields had replaced the small and uneven plots that traditionally followed the topography of the terrain. Even villages which had never suffered from inundation now stood waterlogged. Mud houses topped by heavy stone roofs caved in on their inhabitants. As the team noted, nature and people paid the price of past policies: everything was 'emaciated' (*shou*): 'people are emaciated, the earth is barren, animals are skinny and houses are thin'.[37]

Tongzhou and Cangzhou are two well-documented examples, but even greater belts of starvation ran along the Huai River and Yellow River plains: from Shangqiu in Henan to Jining in Shandong, from Fuyang in Anhui to Xuzhou in Jiangsu, Hu Yaobang spent a month travelling some 1,800 kilometres inspecting the devastation caused by heavy rain in September 1961. As we shall see, many of the sites of horror where the death rate was at least 10 per cent were located in those two areas. Some of these names – Fengyang, Fuyang, Jining – have since become symbols for mass starvation. The first thing Hu Yaobang observed was that the rainfall that autumn had hardly been exceptional. In some of the most devastated counties such as Fengyang 'the rainfall was basically normal'. Further enquiries revealed that the main reason these regions were devastated by inundations of no more than 700 millimetres was the extraordinary extent of water-conservancy projects carried out since the autumn of 1957. These vast irrigation networks trapped the water, then silted up and became 'an evil dragon turning the land into a sea'. So bad was the situation that any rainfall exceeding 300 millimetres could cause devastation. The local villagers deeply resented the canals and channels built over the past few years, seeing them as the main reason for the inundations. Hu noted that 'some of the cadres are honest and are learning the lesson, but others are confused, some even insisting that it is a natural catastrophe'.[38]

Throughout the country the irrigation projects, built by hundreds of millions of farmers at great human and economic cost, were for the main part useless or downright dangerous. Many violated the laws of nature, resulting in soil erosion, landslides and river siltation. We saw how in Hunan, a province blessed with fertile soil, river valleys and terraced fields, lush mountains covered with primeval forest were defaced by local communes during the steel drive. The denuded mountains were washed bare by torrents, since there was no longer a canopy to intercept rainwater. As the capacity of forests to retain water was degraded, natural hazards were amplified into disasters. Large irrigation projects that had disrupted the natural flow of water with stopbanks, culverts, reservoirs and irrigation channels only aggravated matters. Accumulated deposits heightened the bed of local rivers in Hunan by up to 80 centimetres, so that water threatened to spill over and flood the neighbouring villages.[39]

Local reclamation projects made things worse. Launched by the state and local communes in response to food shortages, they showed little sense of stewardship of nature. In Hunan over 100,000 hectares were opened up, much of it on steep mountain slopes. The rain then flushed the soil and took it to the newly built reservoirs, choking them with sediment. One team in Longhui reclaimed ten hectares on a gradient against the mountain: the runoff from torrential rain in May 1962 took enough soil to silt up thirty dams and five roads.[40]

Shortages of different goods also tended to reinforce each other in a vicious circle of want. Once all the fertiliser had been squandered in the Great Leap Forward of 1958, the fields turned barren. Paths between the rice paddies were poorly maintained, as farmers lost control over the land and crops were randomly planted and frequently changed. Close cropping and deep ploughing further stripped the farmland, as the soil was played out. In the past a field could retain carefully irrigated water for four to five days, but by 1962 the water seeped through the earth in less than seventy-two hours. This meant that twice as much water was needed, precisely as the system was silting up.[41] The Bureau for Water Conservancy and Hydroelectricity in Hunan concluded that some 57,000 square kilometres suffered from soil erosion, including most of the river basin of the Yangzi and between a quarter and a third of the Xiang, the Zijiang and the Yuanjiang – three of the four largest rivers in the province. Up to half of all devices for water and soil conservation had silted up and been washed away. In the wake of the irrigation campaign the amount of soil erosion had increased by 50 per cent.[42]

Shabby workmanship, carried out by starved farmers without much planning and often in disregard of expert opinion, also marred new irrigation projects. In Hunan, by the end of the famine, less than half of all pumps actually worked. Many were broken, others simply stopped working in the absence of any supervision.[43] In the Hengyang region, two-thirds of all medium-sized reservoirs and a third of all small dykes were dysfunctional, as water was lost through leaks and seepages.[44] In the province as a whole, a tenth of all medium reservoirs were described as completely wasted projects, and they were abandoned halfway through. None of the ten large ones had much of an impact, as they submerged large cultivated surfaces but actually irrigated very little, causing great anger among local people who had been forced to resettle.[45] In many cases the building material was so brittle that the movement of the waves inside the reservoirs created grooves of a depth of fifty to seventy centimetres inside the dam.[46] The use of dynamite by hungry farmers to fish near dams and sluices did not improve the situation.[47]

Hunan was no exception. In neighbouring Hubei, during the drought of 1959 which the party leadership identified as one of the catastrophes to have ravaged the country, water from the mighty Yangzi could not be diverted into the fields because more than three-quarters of all new sluices were too high. The river passed along arid fields, as people and cattle went thirsty.[48] Along the 100-kilometre stretch between Jianli and Jingzhou, in the midst of the drought, farmers dug holes into local dykes to irrigate the fields, but later these were flooded during heavy rains.[49] By 1961 an estimated 400,000 small reservoirs were in a state of disrepair; roughly one in three either collapsed, silted up or leaked dry.[50]

But as in other parts of a country in the grip of gigantism, large projects also mushroomed. In Hubei they swelled from a few dozen before 1957 to well over 500. Once these were completed they were often simply abandoned to local communes, many of which failed to provide any supervision whatsoever. Stones were carted away from embankments, aqueducts were left to silt up, holes were dug in retaining walls, and cowsheds, pigsties and even entire houses were built on top of dams. The rubber used to seal sluices hermetically was cut away, while the telecommunication equipment from unmanned sentry posts was stolen.[51] The conclusion was inescapable: despite the huge efforts devoted to irrigation schemes with the forced enlistment of millions of farmers throughout the province, by 1961 less than a million hectares were irrigated, in contrast to the 2 million in 1957.[52] The position in Hunan was only marginally better: after massive investment in water conservancy the overall irrigated surface in the province increased from 2.66 million hectares in 1957 to about 2.68 million in 1962, or less than 1 per cent.[53]

Dams throughout the country lacked spillways, used shoddy material and were built without regard for the local geology. Many collapsed. In Guangdong, the dam at Fenghuang, Chao'an county, burst in 1960, followed by another at Huangdan, Dongxing county. These were large reservoirs, but medium-sized and small ones also caved in, for instance in Lingshan, Huiyang and Raoping.[54] Nationwide, 115 large reservoirs, or

38 per cent of the total, were unable to hold back the floodwaters during the rainy season.[55] According to a report from the central leadership, three large, nine medium and 223 small dams or reservoirs collapsed in 1960 because they were badly built.[56]

While many of those erected with earth collapsed almost immediately, some were dangerous time bombs ticking away for decades. This happened with the Banqiao and Shimantan dams in Zhumadian, Henan, built as part of the 'Harness the Huai River' campaign in 1957–9, as we have seen in an earlier chapter. When a typhoon hit the region in August 1975, these dams broke, unleashing a tidal wave which drowned an estimated 230,000 people.[57] By 1980 some 2,976 dams had collapsed in Henan. As the chief of the provincial Bureau for Water Resources later put it, referring to the Great Leap Forward, 'the crap from that era has not yet been cleared up'.[58]

———————

Interference with nature increased the alkalisation – also known as salinisation or sodification – of farmlands, although this was a phenomenon more commonly associated with the semi-arid plains of the north. Alkalisation is often seen as a drawback of irrigation in dry regions where a lack of rainfall allows the soluble salts contained in water to accumulate in the soil, severely reducing its fertility. New irrigation schemes had a disastrous effect on the alkalisation of the North China Plain. In Henan, some two-thirds of a million hectares of soil turned into alkaline land.[59] In Beijing and the surrounding suburbs, as the Water Conservancy Bureau found out, the amount of soil lost to alkalisation had doubled to 10 per cent during the Great Leap Forward.[60] But along the coast, too, salinisation increased through the intrusion of marine water, a consequence of the half-baked schemes of local cadres courting the attention of their superiors. In a Hebei commune located twenty kilometres from the sea, tradition was brushed aside in the pursuit of a vision of symmetry, as grand canals were dug to criss-cross square paddy fields rebuilt from uneven plots that customarily hugged the contours of the land. The crop plummeted as the proportion of alkaline land doubled.[61] Throughout the province the amount of alkaline land jumped by 1.5 million hectares.[62]

Hebei was hardly exceptional: in his report on salinisation, Liu Jianxun noted that in many counties in northern Henan the extent of salinisation had doubled, reaching as high as 28 per cent.[63] Hu Yaobang, inspecting counties along the Yellow River, found that huge irrigation schemes in some counties in Shandong had increased the overall proportion of alkaline soil from 8 per cent to as much as 24 per cent.[64] This was confirmed in a more detailed report on the northern and western parts of the province, where on average salinisation was above 20 per cent by 1962, having doubled since the Great Leap Forward. In Huimin county it was close to half of all cultivated land. There was little doubt about the reasons for this: 'Over the last couple of years the development of irrigation schemes has disturbed the natural drainage system.'[65] How many millions of hectares were lost to salt during the great famine is not clear, but it is likely to have reached 10 to 15 per cent of all irrigated cropland.

———

No nationwide or even provincial figures exist, but qualitative evidence suggests that air and water pollution also contributed to an environmental crisis of considerable proportions. China had no treatment plants, and both urban sewage and industrial waste were discharged directly into local rivers. In the drive to transform a predominantly agricultural society into an industrial powerhouse capable of leading the socialist camp in its conquest of the world, the amount of pollutants such as phenol, cyanide, arsenic, fluorides, nitrates and sulphates released into water streams surged. Phenol is one of the most common contaminants: 0.001 milligrams per litre is advisable for drinking water and 0.01 for farming fish. In spillages in the Songhua and Mudan rivers, which flow through the bleak industrial heartland of the north, the amount of phenol ranged from two to twenty-four milligrams per litre. Where carp, catfish and sturgeon once teemed, nothing but a noisome flow of toxic materials remained. In a 150-kilometre stretch of the Nen River, a major tributary of the Songhua, some 600 tonnes of dead fish were removed by fishermen in less than a day in the spring of 1959. In Liaoning fish disappeared completely from the rivers near the industrial cities of Fushun and Shenyang. Along the coast near Dalian, it was not unusual to harvest some 20 tonnes of sea cucumber each year, but the delicacy vanished during the Great Leap Forward.[66] Further south, in Beijing, the State Council complained about pollution: the powerful Anshan iron and steel complex discharged such large amounts of waste that the rivers reeked of petrol, with dead fish floating belly up on the slimy surface.[67]

So great was the amount of alkaline waste released by paper mills in Jiamusi that even the bottoms of boats corroded. The mills themselves were no longer able to produce high-quality paper because they relied on the river water they so heavily polluted. This was the case for all factories in the belt stretching from Shanghai down to Hangzhou. Oil companies were also culprits, a single plant in Maoming releasing 24,000 tonnes of kerosene into rivers each year. Other scarce resources in the midst of famine were emptied into the water: smelting plants in dirty, dusty Shenyang, the State Council calculated, could have saved 240 tonnes of copper and 590 tonnes of sulphuric acid a year – simply by recycling the water they used.[68]

Few comparative studies were made at the time to measure the increase of pollution after 1957, but one case study illustrates the impact of the Great Leap Forward. The leather, knitting, paper and chemical factories in Lanzhou, the industrial centre of the north-west, generated some 1,680 tonnes of waste water a day in 1957. This had rocketed up to 12,750 tonnes a day by 1959. Lanzhou is the first large city along the Yellow River, which contained eight times more pollutants than was allowed by the Ministry of Hygiene. The river slowly wound its way through the deserts and grasslands of Inner Mongolia before entering the North China Plain, where the water was diverted for irrigation through endless conduits and culverts, the pollutants becoming embedded deep in the cultivated soil.[69]

People too were poisoned, as rivers were often the only source of drinking water. Workers living near steel plants in the north suffered from chronic poisoning. In Zibo, Shandong, a hundred farmers became ill after drinking water polluted with contaminants from a pharmaceutical factory upstream.[70] In Nanjing, a single factory employing a mere 275 workers produced 80 to 90 tonnes of sewage containing radioactive material each day. No measures for waste disposal existed, and all of it was dumped straight down the drain, ending up in the Qinhuai River, which turned into a cesspool. Even groundwater was poisoned: used by local people to wash their rice, the water in the wells near the factory turned red or green.[71] In Baoshan, Shanghai, the waste water produced by steel plants leached into workers' dormitories. Outside, heaps of corrugated iron waste accumulated, so that workers had to climb over the rubbish to gain access to their sleeping quarters.[72] While slag was of less concern compared to pollution caused by waste discharges, a quarter of a million tonnes accumulated every day in busy Shanghai.[73]

The air too was polluted, although we have fewer specific examples since water was a far more precious resource than air and thus was monitored in greater detail. But one study shows that in Shanghai the equivalent of 20 tonnes of sulphuric acid mist, created in the production of phosphate fertilisers, was spewed into the air each day by a number of factories.[74]

Some of these factories also produced pesticides, which contaminated animals, people, soil and air. In Shanghai, for instance, thousands of tonnes of Dipterex and DDT were produced, as well as benzene hexachloride (BHC), a highly toxic farm chemical labelled 666 which degraded only slowly in the soil.[75] The effects of pesticides on livestock, agricultural land and aquatic products are well known, but in times of famine chemical poison found new applications, spreading far beyond the farm. Desperate for food, some communes used pesticides to catch fish, birds and animals. In Hubei, insecticides such as Systox and Demeton, commonly called 1605 and 1059 powders, as well as a hypertoxic pesticide known as 3911, were deliberately spread to capture ducks, which were then sold to the cities. In Shakou alone dozens of customers were poisoned and several died after eating the contaminated fowl. Famished farmers also foraged independently for food, releasing chemicals in ponds and lakes to kill the wildlife. In some places the water turned green, killing all.[76]

But the most popular form of pest control was mass mobilisation. Enthralled by the power of the masses to conquer nature, Mao had raised the call to eliminate rats, flies, mosquitoes and sparrows in 1958. Sparrows were targeted because they ate grain seeds, depriving the people of the fruits of their labour. In what is one of the most bizarre and ecologically damaging episodes of the Great Leap Forward, the country was mobilised in an all-out war against the birds. Banging on drums, clashing pots or beating gongs, a giant din was raised to keep the sparrows flying till they were so exhausted that they simply dropped from the sky. Eggs were broken and nestlings destroyed; the birds were also shot out of the air. Timing was of the essence, as the entire country was made to march in lockstep in the battle against the enemy, making sure that the sparrows had nowhere to escape. In cities people took to the roofs, while in the countryside farmers dispersed to the hillsides and climbed trees in the forests, all at the same hour to ensure complete victory.

Soviet expert Mikhail Klochko witnessed the beginning of the campaign in Beijing. He was awakened in the early morning by the bloodcurdling screams of a woman running to and fro on the roof of a building next to his hotel. A drum started beating, as the woman frantically waved a large sheet tied to a bamboo pole. For three days the entire hotel was mobilised in the campaign to do away with sparrows, from bellboys and maids to the official interpreters. Children came out with slings, shooting at any kind of winged creature.[77]

Accidents happened as people fell from roofs, poles and ladders. In Nanjing, Li Haodong climbed on the roof of a school building to get at a sparrow's nest, only to lose his footing and tumble down three floors. Local cadre He Delin, furiously waving a sheet to scare the birds, tripped and fell from a rooftop, breaking his back. Guns were deployed to shoot at birds, also resulting in accidents. In Nanjing some 330 kilos of gunpowder were used in a mere two days, indicating the extent of the campaign. But the real victim was the environment, as guns were taken to any kind of feathered creature. The extent of damage was exacerbated by the indiscriminate use of farm poison: in Nanjing, bait killed wolves, rabbits, snakes, lambs, chicken, ducks, dogs and pigeons, some in large quantities.[78]

The main casualty was the humble sparrow. We do not have any reliable figures, as numbers were part of a campaign in which rhetorical inflation combined with specious precision to produce digits as surreal as the campaign itself. Shanghai thus triumphantly reported that it had eliminated 48,695.49 kilos of flies, 930,486 rats, 1213.05 kilos of cockroaches and 1,367,440 sparrows in one of their periodic wars against all pests (one wonders how many people secretly bred flies or cockroaches to obtain a medal of honour).[79] Sparrows were probably driven to near extinction, and few were seen for years afterwards. By April 1960, as the leaders realised that the birds also ate insects, they were removed from the list of harmful pests and bedbugs substituted instead.[80]

But the reversal came too late: insect infestations spread after 1958, ruining a significant proportion of the crop. The biggest damage was done before the harvest, as swarms of locusts would obscure the sky and cover the country-side under a bristling blanket, devouring the crop. Taking advantage of the drought in Hubei in the summer of 1961, they infested some 13,000 hectares in the Xiaogan region alone. In the Jingzhou region more than 50,000 hectares were devastated. Overall, in the province, some 15 per cent of the rice crop was lost to the voracious grasshopper. Everything was stripped bare, over half of all cotton being lost in the Yichang region.[81] Around Nanjing, where a ferocious campaign had been fought against sparrows, some 60 per cent of all fields suffered from insect damage in the autumn of 1960, which led to severe shortages of vegetables.[82] All sorts of harmful species thrived: in Zhejiang province 500,000 to 750,000 tonnes of grain, or roughly 10 per cent of the harvest, were lost in 1960 to snout moth, leafhopper, pink boll-worm and red spider, among other pests. Preventive measures were hampered by lack of insecticide: farm chemicals had first been squandered in the assault on nature in 1958–9, and then shortages of all commodities extended by 1960 to pesticides, just as they were needed more than ever.[83]

In the war on nature, different factors thus combined to amplify dramatically what the leadership described as 'natural catastrophes'. The steel campaign caused deforestation, leading in turn to soil erosion and water loss. Grandiose irrigation schemes further disturbed the ecologi-cal balance, worsening the impact of inundations and droughts, both of which were drivers of locusts: drought eliminated all competition, while the heavy rains that followed allowed locusts to hatch more quickly than other insects and take over a mauled landscape. Because sparrows had vanished and pesticides had been misused, the insects descended unop-posed on whatever meagre crop the farmers had managed to grow.

Mao lost his war against nature. The campaign backfired by breaking the delicate balance between humans and the environment, decimating human life as a result.

PART FOUR

SURVIVAL

Feasting through Famine

Equality may have been a pillar of communist ideology, but all communist states built elaborate hierarchical orders on the ground. One reason for this was that most of these regimes lived in constant fear of real or imagined enemies, justifying the regimentation of society along military lines in which each subordinate unit was expected to carry out orders without questioning: 'each official is the anvil of his superiors and the hammer of his subordinates'.[1] Another reason was that the command economy distributed goods and services according to need rather than demand. And the needs of different groups were assigned different priorities by the party, whether the country was defending the realm against imperialist powers or busy building a communist future. In the People's Republic access to food, goods and services was largely determined by a household registration system – the rough equivalent of the internal passport instituted in December 1932 in the Soviet Union. Introduced to the cities in 1951, it was extended to the countryside in 1955 and became law in 1958, just when farmers were being pitchforked into communes. It divided people into two separate worlds by classing them either as 'city dwellers' (*jumin*) or as 'peasants' (*nongmin*).[2] The status conferred by the registration system was inherited through the mother, meaning that even if a village girl married a city dweller she and her children remained farmers.

The household registration system was a linchpin of the planned economy. As the state was in charge of the distribution of goods, it had to have a rough idea of the needs of different sectors of the economy. If large flows of people moved about the country in complete freedom it would upset the production quotas and distribution charts so meticulously mapped by central planners. But another function of the system was to tie the cultivators to the land, making sure that cheap labour was available in the collective farms from which a surplus was taken to pay for industrialisation. Farmers were treated as an hereditary caste deprived of the privileges given to city dwellers, which included subsidised housing, food rations and access to health, education and disability benefits. In the midst of famine the state left farmers to fend for themselves.

A wall was created between cities and the countryside, but an equally important fault line ran between ordinary people and party members. And within the party – as in the army – an elaborate internal hierarchy further determined the privileges to which one was entitled, from the amount of grain, sugar, cooking oil, meat, fowl, fish and fruit to the quality of durable goods, housing, health care and access to information. Even the quality of cigarettes varied according to rank. In Guangzhou in 1962 cadres of ranks 8 and 9 received two cartons of ordinary cigarettes a month, cadres of ranks 4 to 7 two better-quality cartons, while the highest three ranks, reserved for top intellectuals, artists, scientists and party leaders, received three cartons of the finest quality.[3]

At the apex of the party stood the leadership, who had special residences ensconced behind high walls, security guards round the clock and chauffeured cars. Special shops with scarce goods at discounted prices were reserved for them and their families. Dedicated farms produced high-quality vegetables, meat, chicken and eggs, which were analysed for freshness and tested for poison before being sampled by tasters. Only then was the food served to leaders in the capital and the provinces.[4] Above them was Mao, living in opulence near the Forbidden City where emperors had once dwelled, his bedroom the size of a ballroom. Sumptuous villas, staffed with chefs and attendants all year round, were at his beck and call in every province or major city.[5] At the bottom of the scale were the millions locked away in labour camps located in the harshest parts of the countryside, from the bitterly cold plains of Manchuria to the arid deserts of Gansu. They were made to break stones, dig for coal, carry bricks or plough the desert for years on end without any recourse to the law.

As the famine developed, the ranks of the privileged swelled. Despite continuous purges, the party membership increased by almost half, from

12.45 million in 1958 to 17.38 million in 1961.[6] Party members knew how to take good care of themselves. One way to feast through famine was to attend frequent meetings, where everything was provided for by the state. Some 50,000 officials came to Shanghai in 1958, a number which had doubled to 100,000 by 1960. They stayed in state-run hotels and dined at state-sponsored banquets. A favourite haunt was the Donghu Hotel, former residence of the famous gangster Du Yuesheng: it was one of the few venues not to charge for anything at all, whether elaborate menus or a range of perfumes on offer in the toilets. Some of these conferences lasted for over a month. In 1960 roughly one high-level conference was held every day of the year, at great cost to the city.[7]

Lower-ranking cadres feasted at local meetings. In Nayong county, in famine-ravaged Guizhou province, 260 cadres spent four days working through 210 kilos of beef, 500 kilos of pork, 680 chickens, 40 kilos of ham, 130 litres of wine and 79 cartons of cigarettes as well as mountains of sugar and pastries. To that had to be added fine blankets, luxury pillows, perfumed soap and other goods specifically purchased for the conference. In Beijing an automobile factory spent more than 6,000 yuan on eight visits to top-class hotels to entertain visitors towards the end of 1960.[8] Another ploy was to organise 'product testing' sessions. In Yingkou, Liaoning, over twenty cadres convened one morning in March 1960, systematically working their way through a range of local produce, starting with cigarettes and moving on to tinned meat, fruit and biscuits, all the while helping themselves to copious portions of rice wine. By the end of the day, satiated and drunk, three of the testers had vomited.[9]

Pleasure trips were organised. In February 1960, some 250 cadres boarded a luxury ship to cruise the Yangzi, sampling culinary delights on board while admiring limestone cliffs, karst landscapes and small gorges, occasionally leaving the comfort of their cabins to visit cultural highlights along the way. A hundred rolls of film were shot. The scent of perfumed oils and incense sticks, thoughtfully positioned throughout the vessel, wafted through the air. A steady stream of high-heeled waitresses in new uniforms served dish after dish of delicacies. A band played in the background. No expense was spared. For fuel and staff alone the twenty-five-day cruise cost some 36,000 yuan, to which had to be added 5 tonnes of meat and fish, not counting endless supplies of cigarettes and alcohol. It must have been a mesmerising sight, as the cruiser was illuminated like a rainbow with lights of every colour, dazzling in the darkness of a moonlit night. The sound of laughter, chatter and clinking of glasses travelled over the waters of the Yangzi, surrounded by a stunningly beautiful landscape blighted by mass starvation.[10]

During the famine the feasting and drinking (*dachi dahe*) that took place in party meetings in the cities and the countryside was a common source of complaint. Rapacious officials were often known as 'Pigsy Cadres', after the character in the famous Ming-dynasty novel *Journey to the West* who was part human, part pig, and legendary for his laziness, gluttony and lust.[11] But outside the party some ordinary people too had opportunities to feast. In the collective canteens staff frequently abused their positions to pilfer the provisions. In one cotton factory in Zhengzhou, capital of famished Henan, those in charge regularly raided the storage room, using it as their personal larder. On one occasion a cook gobbled down twenty salt eggs in a single day, and others ate their way through kilos of tinned meat. Noodles and fried dough cakes were eaten at night, while meat, fish and vegetables earmarked for the canteen were divided up among the team in daytime. Ordinary workers had to survive on three bowls of rice gruel a day, occasionally supplemented by some dry rice or a steamed bun. Many were too weak to work.[12]

In the countryside villagers did not always stand idly by watching the pillaging. In one commune in Guangdong, where two-thirds of all pigs had been eaten by local cadres in banquets and feasts held to celebrate the advent of plenty, farmers warned: 'You cadres openly steal, we commune members secretly rob.'[13] An orgy of slaughter marked the countryside in 1958, when farmers killed off their poultry and livestock as a form of resistance against the people's communes. Spurred on by fear, rumour and example, they opted to eat the fruits of their labour, or store up a supply of meat, or sell their assets on the black market and save some cash, rather than hand over their belongings. Hu Yongming, as we have seen, systematically ate his way through his livestock in a village up in the hilly north-east of Guangdong province, slaughtering in close succession four chickens, three ducks, dogs and puppies as well as a cat. His family gorged themselves on the meat.[14]

But even after the heady days of 1958, villagers continued to find ways to have a treat occasionally – sometimes with the connivance of their local leaders. In Luoding, a county bloodied by a thuggish leadership, one brigade still managed to 'celebrate the birthday of the Communist Party', an excuse for each family to gulp down four ducks on 1 July 1959.[15] At Chinese New Year in 1961 thousands of farm cattle were slaughtered by disgruntled farmers in the Zhanjiang region, a form of protest also observed in other parts of Guangdong province, as no pork was available for the all-important dumplings traditionally used to celebrate the new lunar year.[16]

Another reason for the occasional feast was that few people saw any reason to save, as expropriation and inflation rapidly eroded any personal reserves. Chen Liugu, a thrifty old lady living in Panyu, had managed to save 300 yuan but now splurged in the early summer of 1959, treating ten people at a restaurant where bowls of fish soup were avidly consumed. 'There is no use in saving money right now and I only have a hundred yuan left to buy a coffin.'[17] In Beijing, foreign residents noticed that some of the usually quiet restaurants did a roaring trade in 1959, as rumours about the advent of urban communes sent residents scrambling to sell their furniture in state-owned shops. The proceeds were spent on a rare meal in the restaurants.[18]

Sometimes ordinary people could eat copiously because they were lucky enough to be looked after by their cadres, who used every political skill to turn their unit into a bastion of abundance in the midst of starvation. In Xuhui, Shanghai, some canteens had the comparative luxuries of glass doors and fluorescent lamps fitted throughout. Others installed radios, while one canteen in Putuo built a basin with goldfish.[19] On the other hand poor supervision of the food-supply chain in some urban units occasionally meant that workers had plenty to eat. In Hebei an investigation showed that workers sometimes moved from one canteen to the next, eating their way through a series of meals. In one dining hall the tables were routinely laden with produce, which spilled over on to the floor. When the leftovers were swept up at the end of each session three to four washbasins, weighing five kilos each, were filled. In a further case of an embarrassment of riches, some workers took food back to their dormitories, although much of this was never eaten. The floor was covered in a layer of yellow mush, as people trod on the discarded buns.[20] In Shijingshan, just outside Beijing, the offerings were rich enough for workers to pick out the filling in jujube buns, discarding the dough.[21] In the canteens of the mighty Shanghai Machine Tool Factory, rice was given such a cursory wash that several kilos were dug out of the sewers on any one day of the week. This was used to feed the pigs. Slack supervision during the night shift allowed workers to eat their fill, and some even engaged in eating contests: a true champion could manage about two kilos of rice in one sitting.[22]

23

Wheeling and Dealing

Whatever their position in the social hierarchy, virtually everybody, from top to bottom, subverted the system of distribution, covertly giving full scope to the very profit motive that the party tried to eliminate. As famine developed, the survival of an ordinary person came increasingly to depend on the ability to lie, charm, hide, steal, cheat, pilfer, forage, smuggle, slack, trick, manipulate or otherwise outwit the state.

But no one could navigate the economy on his own. In a nation of gate-keepers, obstacles were everywhere, as anybody could obstruct anybody else, from the cantankerous caretaker in an apartment block to the dour ticket seller behind the window in a railway station. So prolific and complex were the rules and regulations that ran through the system that discretionary and potentially tyrannical power was vested even in the lowliest of bureau functionaries. The simplest of transactions – buying a ticket, exchanging a coupon, entering a building – could become a nightmare when faced with a stickler for rules. Petty power corrupted petty people, who proliferated at the lower levels of the planned economy, making arbitrary and capricious decisions over goods and services in short supply which they happened to control. And higher up the chain of command, the greater the power the more dangerous the abuse.

A network of personal contacts and social connections was required to get even the simplest things done. Asking a prominent friend to help was always easier than approaching an unknown official who might be devoted to the details of administrative procedure and see no reason to bestow a benefit on a stranger. Any connection was preferable to none, as a former neighbour, an erstwhile colleague, a school friend or even a friend of a friend was more likely to accommodate a request, turn a blind eye, skirt the law or bend a rule. In the higher reaches of power, influential colleagues could help one to secure state funds, avoid paying taxes or gain access to scarce resources. At every level people expanded their social network by trading favours, exchanging gifts and paying bribes. They looked after their own. Mu Xingwu, head of a storage unit in Shanghai, recruited nineteen relatives to work under him. Half the workforce were related: here was a solid basis for wheeling and dealing in the goods he was supposed to safeguard.[1] Everywhere people were pressurising those below them to protect and further their own interests. The planned economy, with its dedication to the greater good, spawned a system in which the individual and his personal network prevailed.

But people in the party were in a better position to use the system for their own personal benefit than those outside it. And they showed endless entrepreneurial guile in devising ways to defraud the state. A common practice for enterprises was to bypass the plan and trade directly between themselves. In Wuhan the Provincial Highway Transportation Bureau agreed to move goods for the Jianghan District Number Two Commercial Office in exchange for food. The operation was worth well over a tonne of sugar, a tonne of alcohol and a thousand cartons of cigarettes as well as 350 kilos of canned meat in the first months of 1960. The Wuhan Oil Purchasing Station, on the other hand, traded hundreds of tonnes of oil, gas and coal to provision lavish banquets for its cadres.[2] In the north the Qinghe Forestry Bureau bartered hundreds of cubic metres of timber for biscuits and lemonade from a factory in Jiamusi. Others exchanged pigs for cement, or steel for timber.[3]

These practices permeated the entire country, as a parallel economy was created by travelling representatives sent to circumnavigate the rigid supply system. Purchasing agents built up social contacts, wining and dining local officials, and traded their way through a shopping list provided by the enterprise for which they were working. Bribes were common. The director of the Bureau for Goods and Materials in Shanghai regularly received presents, from deer antlers rich in velvet to white sugar, biscuits and lamb. More than 6 million yuan in goods were 'damaged' or 'lost' under his auspices in less than a year.[4] In Guangzhou, the Bureau for Transportation was accused of 'wasting' over 5 million yuan in the three years following

the Great Leap Forward.[5] In Heilongjiang province alone one investigation estimated that some 2,000 cadres were shopping for timber on behalf
of their units in late 1960, offering watches, cigarettes, soap or tinned food
in return.[6] Dozens of factories in Guangdong sent agents on acquisition
tours to Shanghai, cutting out the state from their business deals.[7] People's
communes were no exception: the Seagull Farm in Guangdong sold some
27 tonnes of citronella oil to a Shanghai perfume factory rather than deliver
it to the state.[8] Nobody knew how much trade took place in this shadow
economy, but one investigation team put the quantity of goods shipped
out of Nanjing to other units without any official approval at 850 tonnes
for the month of April 1959 alone. Hundreds of units were involved, some
actually counterfeiting shipping permits, using false names, printing fake
certificates and even shipping in the name of the army in order to make a
profit.[9]

Barter exchange, sometimes considered a very primitive form of trade,
became one of the most efficient ways of distributing goods where they
were needed. And it could be a very sophisticated operation, moving along
a nationwide network, cannibalising state structures, shadowing the planned
economy and yet managing to remain invisible thanks to creative accounting. Goods became currency. In a detailed study of a famed dumpling shop
in Shenyang, investigators showed that food was routinely exchanged for
goods from more than thirty construction units in the city, ranging from
iron pipes to cement and bricks. A steady and cheap supply of ingredients
was also secured by exchanging the dumplings directly with state providers.
The Municipal Aquatic Products Company, suffering as much as any other
distributor from severe shortages in the midst of famine, handed over its
entire supply of shrimps, normally earmarked for consumers in the suburbs,
to the shop for the promise of dumplings. The cadres went on shopping
sprees in the best department stores in Shenyang, paying with dumpling
coupons. They took care of their employees, who feasted on the produce.
The traffic police and the fire brigade were bought off, while even services
such as delivery of coal, water supply, toilet cleaning and hygiene inspections
were all carried out against an agreed amount of the shop's speciality.[10]

Creative accounting could hide misappropriation of funds. Accountants
would invent expenditures which were never incurred, in some cases

claiming funds of up to a million yuan. Another trick consisted of moving state investments away from industry towards fixed capital, as state units treated themselves to new buildings, dance halls, private toilets and elevators. This happened in the Zunyi region, where a raid revealed that 5 million yuan had been embezzled since the Great Leap Forward.[11] In Heilongjiang, one quarry entered all the capital expenditure on offices, canteens and even kindergartens into the production costs, thus passing on the bill to the state. In many other enterprises administrative and operating expenses were added on to the production costs. In Beijing alone some 700 administrative units, complete with salaries and expenses, thus vanished into a black hole called 'production'.[12] Other costs could be disguised and passed on to the state. In Luoyang, Henan province, a ball-bearing factory built a 1,250-cubic-metre swimming pool, sending the bill up as a 'heat lowering device'.[13]

Endless borrowing from state banks was also a common ploy. As Li Fuchun pointed out when he noted a deficit of 3 billion yuan in the summer of 1961, many units borrowed from the bank to feast.[14] And when a city or a county was in the red, it simply stopped paying taxes. This started in 1960, as a number of provinces passed regulations stipulating that all profits be kept. The Finance Department and the Trade Department of Liaoning province thus dictated that profits from enterprises under their control should be removed from the budget and distributed locally instead. In Shandong, Gaoyang county unilaterally determined that profits should fall outside the budget and be retained locally. Losses, on the other hand, were entered into the budget and billed to the state. Not only did collective enterprises and urban communes routinely fail to raise taxes, but entire cities decided to forgo tax collection.[15]

And then there were those who simply stole from the state, dispensing with clever accounting tricks altogether. Local factories along the Shanghai–Nanjing railway line pilfered, embezzled or smuggled well over 300 tonnes of steel, 600 tonnes of cement and 200 square metres of timber in less than a year. The New China Lock Factory from Xuzhou, for instance, hired a lorry systematically to steal all the material it needed from railway depots. Most of these activities were directed by top cadres. A large assembly hall in Nanjing East Station, entirely built from stolen material

No photographs other than those taken for propaganda purposes are known to exist from the years of the famine.

Chairman Mao pensively overlooks the Yellow River in 1952. A large dam was built in 1958–60 to attempt to tame the river known as 'China's Sorrow', but, as with many dams and dykes all over the country built during the Great Leap Forward, it was so poorly designed that it had to be rebuilt at huge expense.

Mao and Khrushchev at the Kremlin in November 1957. Mao saw himself as the leader of the socialist camp and believed that the Great Leap Forward would allow China to forge ahead and make the transition from socialism to communism, leaving the Soviet Union far behind.

On 25 May 1958 Chairman Mao galvanises the nation by appearing at the Ming Tomb Reservoir to help move earth (the original photo also shows Peng Zhen, the mayor of Beijing, but he was later airbrushed out of the picture).

Building a cofferdam of straw and mud to divert the Yellow River at the Qingtong Gorge in Gansu, December 1958. Forced labour on water conservancy schemes all over the country claimed the lives of hundreds of thousands of exhausted villagers already weakened by hunger.

The people of Beijing collect scrap iron in July 1958. In a frenzy to produce more steel, everybody was required to offer pots, pans, tools, even door knobs and window frames to feed the backyard furnaces, which more often than not produced useless lumps of pig iron.

Breaking stones for the backyard furnaces in Baofeng county, Henan, October 1958. To fuel the furnaces, the forests were denuded of trees while many houses in the countryside were stripped of wood.

Carrying fertiliser to the fields in a spirit of competitive emulation, Huaxian county, Henan, April 1959. Attempts to set new agricultural records encouraged a scramble for fertiliser, as every conceivable kind of nutrient was thrown onto the fields, from animal manure to human hair. Everywhere buildings made of mud and straw were torn down to provide fertiliser for the soil, leaving many villagers homeless.

Chairman Mao inspecting an experimental plot with close cropping in the suburbs of Tianjin in August 1958. Close cropping, whereby seeds were sown far more densely than was usual, was seen as a cornerstone of innovative tilling, but the experiment only contributed to a famine of unprecedented proportions.

On the right, Li Jingquan, leader of Sichuan province where more than 10 million people died prematurely during the famine, shows off a model farm in Pixian county, March 1958.

A bumper harvest of sugar cane in Guangxi province, November 1959. During the Great Leap Forward reports came in from all over the country of new records in cotton, rice, wheat or peanut production, although most of the crops existed on paper only.

Chairman Mao on a visit to Wuhan in April 1958, with Hubei provincial leader Wang Renzhong on the right of the photo; Shanghai mayor Ke Qingshi, also a staunch supporter of the Great Leap Forward, appears on the left behind Marxist philosopher Li Da, standing in the middle.

Peng Dehuai, who would speak out against the Great Leap Forward at the Lushan plenum in the summer of 1959, meets with party activists in December 1958.

Tan Zhenlin, a close follower of Mao and in charge of agriculture, addresses a party conference in October 1958.

Li Fuchun, the top official in charge of economic planning, meets several cadres in the suburbs of Tianjin, autumn of 1958.

Liu Shaoqi tours the countryside in his home province of Hunan and discovers the extent of the famine in April 1961.

From left to right, Zhou Enlai, Chen Yun, Liu Shaoqi, Mao Zedong and Deng Xiaoping at the party conference in January 1962, dubbed the Seven Thousand Cadres Assembly, at which Liu openly blames 'human errors' rather than nature for the catastrophe.

under the direction of station manager Du Chengliang, was a monument
to organised theft.[16]

Another way to defraud the state was to inflate the ration roster. A macabre
trade in dead souls flourished in the countryside. Just as families tried to
hide a death in order to get an extra ration of food, cadres routinely inflated
the number of farmers and appropriated the surplus. This was common
too in cities, where the state was committed to feeding urban residents.
When a team of investigators pored over the accounts of one county in
Hebei, they discovered that the state handed out an average of nine kilos
of grain a month in excess of the prescribed rations for each of the 26,000
workers. Everybody massaged the figures, one small brickyard being bold
enough to declare more than 600 workers where only 306 could be found
on the ground. Some factories classified all their workers as involved in
heavy duties because that entitled them to a larger ration, even if most of
the employees were engaged in light work.[17] In the construction industry
in Beijing, up to 5,000 workers who had died or had returned to the countryside were kept on the books. Even in the more rarefied atmosphere of
the Chinese Academy of Social Sciences, well over a third of the 459 workers who claimed their daily allowance in the Institute of Geophysics were
not regular members entitled to food rations.[18]

The obverse of this practice was to hire people outside the approved
plan. A black market in labour appeared in which supply and demand
determined the salary. Top workers and promising apprentices were lured
away with fringe benefits or monetary incentives. Thousands, according
to a report in the summer of 1960, had been hired away in Nanjing in
the first half of the year.[19] Such was the competition that, when factory
bosses refused to let good workers pursue better opportunities elsewhere,
they would complain about lack of 'employment freedom' and try to
get dismissed. A few exploded in a violent rage, directing their ire at the
cadres who stood in their way. Of the 500 apprentices in the commercial sector of Baixia District, 180 had absconded. Part and parcel of the
black market in labour were 'underground factories', which popped up in
every city, including Nanjing. Some people took on night shifts on top of

their regular jobs, others worked two shifts to make ends meet. This was the case for two-thirds of all workers in one construction unit near the centre. Students, doctors and even cadres abandoned their posts to make money on the black market, working on docks or moving goods on flatbed tricycles.[20]

One of the many paradoxes of the planned economy, therefore, was that everybody traded. People speculated by buying in bulk, betting on the fact that shortages and inflation would push the price up. An entire operation was run by Hubei University, with telegrams instructing agents to buy or sell specific commodities according to the fluctuating demands of the black market. A research centre at the Chinese Academy of Social Science in Shanghai employed twenty students from East China Normal University to buy goods which were traded for scarce commodities with other units.[21]

Party members were well placed to undertake speculative operations, some of them on a full-time basis. Li Ke, a cadre from the Jianguomen commune to the east of Beijing, wrote himself a certificate for sick leave for nine months and started trading in sewing machines, bicycles and radios, investing the profit in a bulk acquisition of electric bulbs and cables. These he sold in Tianjin, purchasing in turn furniture which he unloaded in the suburbs precisely when the market contracted: he thus acted in a commercially astute way, all the while being in the pay of the state. Many others did the same.[22]

But most cadres had bigger fish to fry, and petty trade was left to ordinary people. In Shanghai, a once freewheeling treaty port, trading habits died hard. Zhao Jianguo, a woman entrepreneur with little money, dealt mainly in small commodities such as light bulbs, but she also made a good profit on a prestigious Phoenix bicycle. Li Chuanying, also a petty trader, bought goods in Shanghai and sold them in Anhui province. Hu Yumei travelled to Huangyan, Zhejiang, to deal in straw hats, mats, dried fish and shrimps, often doubling her money. Ma Guiyou made about 100 yuan a month buying up jewellery and watches from wealthy families downtown and dealing in ration tickets in the countryside: 'I am not a counter-revolutionary! I don't steal and I don't rob, and I don't have a job, so who cares if I do a bit of business?' The officials who compiled the report with the help of neighbourhood committees in August 1961 were taken aback not only by the range of goods on offer, but also by the quality of information about market conditions. Despite all the economic information gathered by the machinery of the central planners, petty traders were more in touch with popular demand than the party. The phenomenon was widespread, drawing participants from all social backgrounds, ranging from old rickshaw puller Chen Zhangwu, who sold fruit from the countryside to make ends meet, to influential managers who used official trips to distant places such as Inner Mongolia and Manchuria as a cover for private deals.[23]

Factory workers also traded goods. The Federation of Trade Unions was alarmed by workers keen to pursue a 'capitalist lifestyle' by spurning the principles of the planned economy and speculating on scarce commodities, carefully comparing prices in different shops and buying for profit. Some would join a queue wherever they spotted one, regardless of what was being sold. A few brought family members along to take turns. Li Lanying, a female factory worker, spent five yuan on carrot jam, hoping to resell it at a later date. A colleague acquired persimmons by the sackload. These were not exceptions but rather 'a way of life', as the report put it, because workers widely believed that 'saving money is not as effective as saving goods'. Savings were eroded by several percentage points a month.[24] In Shanghai fear of want prompted people to queue up and hoard any and all goods still available from the shops.[25]

When workers lacked the capital for speculation they resurrected a practice common before 1949, called *dahui*. Poor people would mutually borrow from a circle of trusted friends, each lending five to ten yuan a month to a different member every month, and each acting in turn as a banker about once a year. In the Dongcheng district in Beijing, some seventy such deals were struck every month among factory workers. Some splurged on luxury goods. Zhao Wenhua, a postal worker, treated herself to a watch, a bicycle, a fur coat and wedding gifts, all seen as durable objects that would keep their value. The practice spread on the understanding that, in times of dearth, goods were a safer bet than money.[26]

Even children traded. Roughly one out of ten primary school children in Jilin speculated in cakes, meat, eggs, vegetables or soap.[27]

A few rolled the dice. In Lantang commune, Guangdong, two cadres gambled away a thousand kilos of grain belonging to the village, as well as several hundred kilos of vegetables. A few kilometres away a woman who lost fifty yuan gambling sold sex to meet her debts.[28] Gambling was an ingrained habit the authorities were unable to stamp out in Guangzhou, where factory workers played poker for food rather than for money. Some risked astronomical sums, up to 3,500 yuan.[29] In Liuhe, just outside Nanjing, gambling occurred almost everywhere, involving groups of up to twenty people.[30] Gambling was endemic during the famine, as people staked everything they had in sheer desperation. In the midst of the catastrophic winter of 1960–1, gambling was rife in Hunan too, with some players literally losing their trousers.[31]

As cash lost its purchasing power, ration coupons became a form of surrogate money. They were required for most essential goods, ranging from oil, grain, pork and cloth to thermos flasks, furniture and even building materials. Designed to ensure equitable distribution of basic commodities, they also tied the population into the household system, through which they were distributed. Each household was issued with a certificate or ration book on which all the family members were recorded, and this document in turn entitled the household to a monthly supply of ration coupons. Coupons were often valid for only one month. Their use was sometimes restricted to their place of issue, which could be a local canteen, a commune, a county, a city or occasionally an entire province. A rice coupon from one county had no validity in the next, forcing people to stay in their place of residence.[32]

Coupons were traded, just as goods were bartered. In some communes, for instance in Jinghai county, Hebei, coupons became a substitute for salaries, as money was all but phased out. A huge variety of coupons for goods and services from pumpkin seeds to haircuts was issued in lieu of payment, ranging in value from one fen to five yuan.[33]

One of the purposes of coupons was to preclude hoarding. But as the Guangdong Provincial People's Congress discovered in February 1961, over a third of all coupons, distributed since September 1959, had not been exchanged, meaning that paper worth some 20,000 tonnes of grain was circulating as surrogate money.[34]

Forging coupons, which were often hastily printed on poor-quality paper, was much easier than counterfeiting money. In the East China Hydraulic Institute a dozen forgeries circulated in the canteens.[35] The phenomenon must have been common. A police raid in Shantou brought to light some 200 separate cases involving pirated coupons. As a report to the provincial People's Congress indicated, more than a third of social infractions were related to ration coupons; the security forces even blamed 'enemy speculators' for releasing a flood of fakes in Qingyuan in the autumn of 1960.[36]

Where buyers and sellers met, a black market emerged. As trade moved from the shop on to the street, markets appeared on street corners, outside department stores, by railway stations, near the factory gates. The black market ebbed and flowed in a legal twilight zone, receding with each crackdown only to reappear as soon as the pressure abated. Sellers would furtively accost buyers and pull goods from paper bags or coat pockets, while others sat on kerbs, spreading out their wares on the ground, from foodstuffs and second-hand bric-a-brac to stolen goods. The public security services would conduct regular sweeps, chasing away the black-marketeers. But they kept returning. And when the local authorities turned a blind eye, makeshift bazaars emerged, with people gathering at an agreed time to barter goods, until the whole affair grew into a more permanent market with buyers and sellers flocking in from the neighbouring villages.

In Beijing black markets appeared in Tianqiao, Xizhimenwai and Dongzhimenwai, where hundreds of traders offered goods that could fetch up to fifteen times the price fixed by the state. This did not deter an enthusiastic throng of housewives, workers and even cadres from shopping around. As bemused agents from the Public Security Bureau noted, people actually liked black markets.[37] They were tolerated but not allowed to flourish in the capital, unlike in Guangzhou, where buyers came from all over the region. In the southern city hundreds of buyers from Hunan province alone could be found specifically buying sweet potatoes in the summer of 1961, many of them having been sent directly by their home units.[38] Trade was openly conducted, and many of the sellers were children, including some who were only six or seven years old, and older ones who smoked and haggled with prospective buyers.[39]

In Tianjin local officials uncovered around 8,000 cases of black-market activity in the first weeks of January 1961. On some occasions more than 800 people were selling goods in one market alone, surrounded by thousands of customers examining the goods and generally blocking the traffic. 'There is nothing that the black market does not have,' according to one investigator.[40] The police who patrolled the streets were fighting a losing battle, and in July 1962 the authorities finally decided to legalise dozens of markets they had never quite managed to eradicate. By the end of the year half of the fruit and a quarter of all the pork sold in Tianjin came from more than 7,000 pedlars. They made almost double the money a state worker earned.[41] Thousands of people travelled to Tianjin from Beijing each day, such was the reputation of its market.[42]

———

As the famine gained ground and hunger gradually eroded the social fabric of everyday life, people turned inward. Everything was on sale. Nothing escaped the realm of trade, as bricks, clothes and fuel were bartered for food. In Hubei a third of the workers in big factories survived on loans. Some were so deeply in debt that they sold their blood to survive.[43] In a unit in Chongqing, Sichuan, one in twenty workers sold their blood. The percentage was even higher in Chengdu, as working men and women exchanged their blood for a morsel to feed their families. Construction worker Wang Yuting was known in all the hospitals, having sold several litres over a period of seven months.[44]

But the situation was infinitely worse in the countryside. From a single district in Huangpi, Hubei, 3,000 families took their spare clothes to sell in Wuchang, where they also begged for food.[45] In Cangxian county, Hebei, a third of villagers sold all their furniture, some even the roofs over their heads.[46] People bartered all they had in Changshou county, Sichuan, including the clothes from their backs.[47]

Before they died they sold their offspring, more often than not to couples who could not have children of their own. In Shandong, Yan Xizhi gave away his three daughters, and sold his five-year-old son for fifteen yuan to a man in a neighbouring village. His youngest son, a ten-month-old toddler, was sold to a cadre for a pittance. Wu Jingxi got five yuan for his nine-year-old son from a stranger, a sum which covered the cost of a bowl of rice and two kilos of peanuts. His heartbroken wife, an inquiry discovered, cried so much that her swollen eyes were losing their vision. Wang Weitong, mother of two, sold one of her sons for 1.5 yuan and four steamed dough buns. But many, of course, never found a buyer for their children.[48]

24

On the Sly

Under the cloak of collectivisation, backed up by the naked power of the militia, party officials proceeded to strip people of every conceivable possession – in particular in the countryside, where farmers were more often than not defenceless in the face of rapacious cadres. It was a war of attrition waged against the people, as every new wave of plunder nipped in the bud even a faint hope of actually owning something private. In Xiangtan, Hunan, local people remembered six 'winds of communism' blowing over the villages. The first came in the winter of 1957–8, as money, china, silver and other valuable objects had to be handed over for 'capital accumulation'. The second took place in the summer of 1958 with the advent of the communes. A third 'wind' blew away pots, pans and iron utensils as the steel campaign gripped the county. Then, in March 1959, all savings in state banks were frozen. By the autumn of that year large irrigation projects were launched again, and tools and timber were commandeered. Finally, in the spring of 1960, a project for a giant pigsty was hatched by a local leader, who seized pigs and building materials.[1]

Most people had little recourse against open pillage. But they were not passive victims, and many devised a whole range of strategies of survival. The most common one was to slack at work, allowing natural inertia to take over. Loudspeakers might be blaring exhortations to work, propaganda posters might extol the model worker who overfulfilled the plan, but apathy more often than not governed the factory floor. In a typical workshop of forty workers in Beijing, half a dozen would habitually crouch around the stove to warm up in winter, while others would leave the factory in daytime to queue for goods or watch a movie. Cadres simply did not have the means to control every worker and punish every disciplinary breach.[2] A more comprehensive study by the Propaganda Department showed that in Shanghai up to half of all workers failed to pay much heed to work discipline. Some would arrive several hours late, others spent time chatting with each other. A few loafers failed to do any work at all, simply waiting for the next meal. Many disappeared well before the end of the day.[3]

The deeper the country sank into famine, the greater the shirking became. By 1961 each worker in Shanghai was contributing 40 per cent less value than in 1959, as more workers managed to produce fewer goods. Slacking, of course, was only one of several reasons why productivity plummeted, as we have seen in Chapter 18, but by 1961 factory workers had become masters of time theft.[4]

In the countryside, by 1959, many villagers had to work all day without eating. Apathy at work, besides being a result of malnutrition, was essential for survival, as every bit of energy had to be saved to get through the day. Farmers would till the fields under the watchful eye of a passing cadre, but as soon as he was out of sight they would drop their tools and sit by the road, waiting for the end of their shift. In parts of the countryside people slept all afternoon, placing their own sentries at key intersections along the fields.[5] Where cadres were lenient, up to half the local population managed to avoid work.[6] In some villages under a tolerant leadership, entire families would huddle together and sleep for days on end, literally hibernating through the winter months.[7]

Some historians have interpreted black-marketeering, obstruction, slacking and theft as acts of 'resistance', or 'weapons of the weak' pitting 'peasants' against 'the state'. But these survival techniques pervaded the social spectrum, so much so that if these were acts of 'resistance' the party would already have collapsed. In the conditions of starvation created by the regime, many people had little choice but to ignore customary moral standards and steal as much as they could.

Theft was endemic, its frequency determined by need and opportunity. Transportation workers were in the best position to pilfer state property, as millions of tons of goods passed through their hands. In the Wuhan

Harbour Number Six Dock over 280 of the 1,200 employees systemati-cally stripped freight trains while pretending to carry out maintenance and repair work.[8] In Hohhot, Inner Mongolia, half of the 864 porters at the railway station stole goods.[9] Mail theft was common, and was often organised by party members. In the Guangzhou Post Office a team of four was responsible for opening more than 10,000 overseas parcels, taking watches, pens, ginseng, milk powder, dried abalone and other gifts. Many of the stolen wares were then sold at auction to postal workers. The entire leadership at the post office, or more than a hundred cadres, had a hand in the operation.[10]

Students stole from the canteen, fifty cases a month being brought to light in Nanjing University in 1960.[11] In Hushu Middle School in Jiangning county, just outside Nanjing, petty theft was the norm among students, a way of life that started with a simple carrot pilfered from the kitchen.[12] In state shops and department stores clerks at the counter subtly doctored receipts or even produced counterfeits, while in the back assist-ants rummaged through the storage rooms. Xu Jishu, a sales assistant at the Friendship Store in Shanghai, tampered with receipts, adding small sums of money that amounted, over time, to around 300 yuan. Li Shandi, employed in a pharmacy, confessed to putting away one yuan each day over several years, almost doubling her salary.[13]

Opportunity was greatest in the city, but need ruled the countryside, where many farmers had to survive famine by living on their wits. At every stage of the production cycle, villagers tried to keep back some of the grain from the demands of the state. This started in the field, even before the wheat or maize was fully ripened. Harking back to a traditional practice called *chiqing*, or 'eating green', villagers quietly clipped off spikes of grain straight from the field, husked and ground it in their hands and ate the raw, green kernels when out of sight of the militia. Eating the crop before it reached maturity was more common in the north, as it was easier to hide among dense rows of maize or in a field thick with wheat than in a rice paddy. Maize was also a more durable crop, standing in the fields for a longer period of time, and thus allowing for a greater number of thefts to take place.[14]

The autumn harvest in 1960 almost vanished in some communes as a result of crop eating. In Guangrao, Shandong province, several brigades took up to 80 per cent of the maize before it ripened, while crops of millet and green beans vanished altogether. In Jiaoxian county, also in Shandong, up to 90 per cent of all grains disappeared. Thousands of similar incidents rocked the province, as many of those discovered eating from the fields were beaten to death by the local militia.[15] In Xuancheng, Anhui, entire fields were eaten clean, as if a swarm of locusts had passed over them.[16] Recollecting the years of hunger, farmer Zeng Mu captured the importance of theft: 'Those who could not steal died. Those who managed to steal some food did not die.'[17]

Once the grain had been threshed and bagged, it was bulked up with water and sold to the state – with or without the complicity of local inspectors. As we have already seen, in Guangdong alone almost a third of 1.5 million tonnes of state grain suffered from a high water content, although poor storage conditions no doubt contributed to the rot in the subtropical south.[18] Once sold to the state, grain on the move was exposed to a plethora of thieving hands. In Xinxing county, Guangdong, close to 900 incidents of theft were reported in 1960. Lin Si, a boatman from Xinhe, took about half a tonne of grain on dozens of occasions. Others were more prudent, replacing stolen foodstuffs with sand and stones. In Guangzhou shippers would extract the grain with a bamboo tube and pour sand back into the bags.[19] In Gaoyao, Jiangsu, just about every boatman helped himself to the grain, each taking an average of 300 kilos a year.[20]

Guards in charge of state granaries stole. In Zhangjiakou, bordering Hebei and Inner Mongolia, a fifth of all watchmen were dishonest, sometimes stealing with the complicity of party members. Half of all cadres in charge of collection points in Qiuxian county were corrupt.[21] In the end, with the grain passing through so many grasping hands, one wonders how much actually reached the canteen table. In Suzhou local investigators estimated that out of a kilo of rice only about half made it to its final destination. It was pilfered from the granaries, taken during transportation, pocketed by accountants, confiscated by cadres and finally filched by cooks before a bowl of rice was ever served in a canteen.[22]

When local cadres colluded with the farmers, powerful forms of collective theft, subterfuge and deception could emerge, shielding the village from the worst effects of the famine. Some cadres kept two sets of books, one with the real figures in the village and another with fake numbers for the eyes of grain inspectors. This was widespread in several counties in Guangdong province.[23] In Xuan'en county, Hubei, one in three book-keepers falsified the accounts. In Chongyang county, one party secretary took the initiative by declaring some 250 tonnes to the commune higher up but pencilling 315 tonnes into the local account book.[24] In June 1959 the office of the Hebei provincial committee concluded from a discrepancy between the amount of grain actually stored and the official inventory that 160,000 tonnes were missing, much of it as a consequence of false report-ing and creative accounting.[25]

Then the grain had to be hidden, which was no easy task in the midst of ferocious and often bloody campaigns to take it from the farmers. In Xiaogan, Hubei, one of the largest stashes discovered by inspection teams contained some 60 tonnes of grain. In Yitang commune, 110 tonnes were hidden behind false walls, inside coffins or in wardrobes. A search in Wuluo among fifteen households yielded 26 tonnes. In some cases local leaders distributed the grain immediately after the harvest and urged farm-ers to eat as much as they could before the militia could strike.[26]

Throughout the country there were cases of local leaders quietly distrib-uting grain to the farmers, helping many to survive the famine. In Yixian county, Hebei, 150 to 200 kilos of harvested grain per hectare were handed out in one commune. Elsewhere inspection teams commonly found 'black granaries'. In Jiaohe county, virtually every team had 'underground grain' of around 750 kilos.[27] Near Tianjin, the leader of Sunshi commune put it in simple terms when he withheld 200 tonnes of seed: 'the state's grain is also the people's grain, and what belongs to the people also belongs to the state'.[28] In Hunan some twenty-three counties were discovered to have 5 to 10 per cent of grain above what had been declared, totalling 36,000 tonnes. One of the most extreme cases was Liuyang, where 7,500 tonnes turned up after a painstaking check of 30,000 granaries.[29] But all too often the reverse was true. In many villages local leaders preferred to lower the grain consumption rather than ask for help higher up the chain of command, as they feared being seen as slackers who would beg rather than work towards a higher crop.[30]

Another stratagem used by local cadres was to 'borrow' grain from state granaries. In Hebei some 357,000 tonnes were thus 'borrowed' up to April 1959, often under pressure from highly placed party members. Party secretary Li Jianzhong from Sungu commune, near Tianjin, thus phoned the granary for a 'loan', which the employees flatly refused, only to be visited by the local boss who exerted the power of his position: 'When you are asked for a loan you should lend; even when you are not asked for a loan you should lend. From now on if there is a problem I will come and sort it out.' A loan of 35 tonnes was agreed on the spot. Units and institutions in cities too were keen to borrow without ever paying back. One middle school borrowed grain to feed its students, incurring a debt of 35,000 yuan.[31]

But in the end, when the food ran out, people turned on each other, stealing from other villagers, neighbours or even relatives. In Nanjing half of all conflicts between neighbours involved food, as people stole from each other, some of the incidents leading to fist fights.[32] Children and the elderly suffered most, for instance when a blind grandmother was robbed of the little rice she had been able to buy with relief coupons in Danyang city.[33] In the countryside, fierce competition for survival gradually eroded any sense of social cohesion. In Liaojia village, just outside Changsha, larceny was so bad that desperate cadres could do nothing but tell the farmers to steal from other villages instead, for which they would not be punished.[34] And once community bonds in the countryside unravelled, the family became an arena for strife, jealousy and conflict. One woman remembered how her mother-in-law slept with food coupons in a pouch tied around her neck. A nephew cut the string and stole the coupons one cold winter night, exchanging the lot for sweets. The woman died several days later.[35]

Communes, villages, families: all were seething with tension and resentment, as famine increasingly pitted erstwhile neighbours, friends and relatives against each other. As one party official noted in Hubei during the distribution of the summer crop, 'between the state and collectives, between brigades, between individuals, up, down, left, right and centre: at all levels there are disputes'.[36] Violence flared, fights over the crop tearing apart units or teams. Sticks and knives were produced as villagers confronted each other in fights over food.[37] In Yingshan county, Hubei, two poor men were hung from a tree after they were found stealing millet.[38]

In times of famine one person's gain was another's loss. Even when it seemed that petty theft took place against a faceless state, somebody down the chain of distribution paid the price. In Xuanwei county, Yunnan, a number of village leaders pumped up the figures when making grain deliveries in December 1958. The grain was earmarked to feed 80,000 railway workers. The plan on paper had pencilled in enough calories for each worker, but it failed to predict that the amounts delivered by the neighbouring villages were below the planned requirements. The railway workers – ordinary farmers conscripted from the countryside – went hungry for several days, and some seventy died of hunger before the end of the month.[39] Throughout the countryside, radical collectivisation created conditions of extreme shortage in which one person's survival depended on another person's starvation. In the end, through a combination of destructive policies initiated from above and covert forms of self-help pursued from below, the country imploded. But while self-defence and self-destruction in the famished countryside were often hard to disentangle, it was the weak, vulnerable and poor who suffered the most.

'Dear Chairman Mao'

Truth had met its end in Lushan. Although speaking out is never advisable in a one-party state, the clash among leaders in the summer of 1959 left nobody in any doubt about the danger of offering an opinion that diverged from the party line. And as Mao was often cryptic in his pronouncements, it was prudent to veer to the left rather than stray to the right. In the midst of mass starvation nobody actually mentioned famine, as leaders used euphemisms such as 'natural disasters' or 'temporary difficulties'. Lower down the ladder famine was such a taboo that local cadres went to great lengths to hide the starving and the sick from the prying eyes of inspection teams. When the party committee of Longhua county, Hebei, sent a group of officials to investigate the countryside, some villages herded the sick together and hid them in the mountains.[1]

A string of foreign visitors – carefully screened by the party and given a lavish tour of model communes – were all too willing to jump to the defence of Maoism.[2] François Mitterrand, a left-wing politician who later became president of France, felt privileged to report the Chairman's words of wisdom to the West. In his opulent villa in Hangzhou, Mao, 'a great scholar known in the entire world for the diversity of his genius', told him in 1961 that there was no famine, but only 'a period of scarcity'.[3] At the other end of the political spectrum, the Englishman John Temple, Conservative MP for Chester, toured the country in late 1960 and declared that communism worked and the country was making 'great progress'.[4]

But not everybody was so willing to be duped. Foreign students with a Chinese background were far less gullible. The majority of the 1,500 foreign students in Nanjing – most from Indonesia, others from Thailand, Malaysia and Vietnam – expressed doubts about the Great Leap Forward, openly wondering about the viability of the communes and questioning the whole idea of collectivisation. As early as March 1959 quite a few were acutely aware of the effects of hunger on the countryside.[5]

Some foreign students were less inhibited than their local counterparts, but critical views were widespread in schools around the country – despite repeated campaigns against 'rightist conservatism'. As an investigation team dispatched by the Communist Youth League found, misgivings about the Great Leap Forward, the communist party and socialism in general were common. University students openly asked why, if the people's communes were such a superior form of organisation, food was short and peasants were abandoning their villages. Why was the supply of goods so poor in a socialist system? Why was the standard of living so low if the rate of development was higher than in capitalist countries? 'Indonesia may be a colony but people there live a good life,' one student opined.[6]

In the cities talk about the famine was muffled by the roar of propaganda, but was clearly audible to the many agents of the party. As informers working for a street committee noted in the Putuo district of Shanghai, ordinary factory workers like Chen Ruhang speculated openly about the number of deaths caused by the famine. Mass starvation was the main topic of conversation in his household, with visitors coming from the famished countryside in 1961.[7] In Hubei – as the Federation of Trade Unions discovered – half of all workers were talking critically about the famine by the end of 1961. Some openly defied their leaders. In one case, a man who was reprimanded for shirking work patted his stomach, then looked the cadre right in the eye and said 'It's empty!'[8]

In the south, closer to Hong Kong and Macau, talk about the free world beckoning just across the border was common by 1962. In Zhongshan county young people tilling the fields swapped stories about the crown colony, and hundreds actually attempted to make the passage each year. Many were arrested and sent back to their villages, where they regaled their friends with tales from their odyssey.[9] In Guangzhou young workers openly admired Hong Kong, allowing flights of fancy to take them to a mythical place where the food was bountiful and the work was easy.[10] 'Hong Kong is a good world!' somebody scribbled on the wall of a primary school.[11]

Other scribblers appeared determined to leave behind more permanent traces of their discontent. Messages of opposition were scrawled on toilet walls. In Xingning city one angry hand etched a slogan in a public toilet insulting Mao.[12] A lengthy diatribe against the export of food was found on the wall of a toilet in the Nanjing Automobile Factory.[13]

More daring were those who came out at night to post flyers and posters critical of the party. In Shanghai somebody left a two-metre poster inciting rebellion.[14] Sometimes hundreds of leaflets were involved. In Gaoyang a hundred flyers with handwritten slogans on pink or red paper appeared overnight, prominently posted on walls or pinned on trees around the city: 'Why are the people of our country starving? Because all the grain is being shipped to the Soviet Union!' Another sounded a warning: 'The harvest is coming up soon and we must organise a movement to steal the wheat: he who wishes to join in, please be prepared!'[15] In Lanzhou over 2,700 flyers advocated a general strike in May 1962.[16] In Hainan, the large island off the coast of Guangdong, some 40,000 anti-party leaflets were reportedly distributed, some apparently dropped from planes sent by Chiang Kai-shek.[17] The extent of these subversive activities is difficult to gauge, as traces of opposition must have been erased as soon as they were spotted. But in Nanjing, in a mere three months, some forty separate slogans and flyers about the famine were reported by the police.[18]

Farmers too used posters to seek redress, vent their anger or denounce a cadre. In Ningjin county, Hebei, Zhang Xirong was brave enough to post a long wall-essay, called a *dazibao*, in protest over the conditions of his local canteen. He immediately attracted the attention of the local Public Security Bureau and was dragged away. His plea, in any event, was a lonely one, lost in a sea of 1.7 million flyers, posters and slogans the county deployed in its campaign to heighten public security.[19] Just as stubborn was farmer Wang Yutang. His response to an anti-rightist campaign, with its millions of official propaganda posters and ceaseless radio broadcasts, was to post his own *dazibao* in Shishou county. 'The Great Leap Forward in 1958 was all bragging, workers suffer greatly and our stomachs go hungry,' it boldly proclaimed.[20] But even if the balance of power was heavily tilted towards the party, which used a sea of propaganda to drown out the slightest grumbling of discontent, posters could sometimes achieve their goal.

In Dazhu county, Sichuan, villagers effectively turned some of the propaganda weapons of the party against a local leader, denouncing him in more than twenty posters for embezzling six yuan. The public humiliation was such that the man refused to oversee the harvest and went fishing instead. Farmers immediately took possession of the crop.[21]

But more popular were verses. Just as Mao had demanded that everyone be a soldier, he proclaimed every man and woman a poet. The population was forced to produce millions of verses in the autumn of 1958, as festivals were organised and prizes handed out for the best folksongs that rhapsodised bumper harvests, steel plants or water-conservancy measures. A frenzied vision of a socialist future was conjured up in rhymed quatrains churned out by the million. In Shanghai alone it was claimed that a mere 200,000 workers had composed some 5 million poems.[22] While much of the officially sponsored poetry was rather trite, a truly creative spirit did appear in some of the ditties spontaneously created by villagers in response to collectivisation. Here, in the midst of famine, was a playful sense of humour that helped people get through times of misery. In Shanghai a popular saying was 'All is well under Chairman Mao, a shame no one can eat his fill.'[23] In Jiangmen county, Guangdong, farmers sang the following song:

> Collectivisation, collectivisation,
> Nobody earns, somebody spends,
> Members earn but teams spend,
> Teams earn but brigades spend,
> Brigades earn but communes spend,
> Only fools become party activists![24]

An illiterate villager came up with a poem to describe the thin gruel served in the canteen:

> We enter the canteen,
> We see a big pot of gruel,
> Waves swell on each side of the pot,
> In the middle people drown.[25]

Local cadres were given satirical nicknames that mocked their greed, bad temper or gluttony. In Kaiping county, Guangdong, farmers referred to one particularly rotund cadre as 'Cooked Food Dog' (*yanhuogou*). 'Golden Fly' and 'Chopping Block Aunt' were also used. Elsewhere, 'Big Belly' was common, while every commune seemed to have a demon from the ghostly underworld. Many a cadre was called 'King Yan', the King of Hell.[26] Irony was not uncommon. In Sichuan – where, as we have seen, provincial leader Li Jingquan noted how people became even more corpulent than Mao Zedong thanks to the bounty brought about by collectivisation – some of the villagers mocked the canteens, saying that 'the advantage of the mess hall is that we are all much fatter', referring to the swelling of bodies in famine oedema.[27]

––––––––––

Just beneath the surface of official propaganda lay a shadow world of rumours. They turned the world upside down, offering an alternative, dissident form of truth which subverted the censored information emanating from the state.[28] Everybody listened to rumours, trying to make sense of the wider world and waiting for an end to the folly of collectivisation. Rumours questioned the legitimacy of the party and discredited the people's communes. In Wuhan it was feared that even wives might be shared.[29]

Rumours encouraged acts of opposition to the state. Informal news about farmers who took possession of their land or grabbed grain from state granaries were common. In Chaoyang, Guangdong, one prophetic woman proclaimed that taking food in times of hunger would be condoned by the party.[30] In Songzi, Hubei, some seven brigades decided in the winter of 1959–60 to dissolve the collectives and divide up the land.[31] Rumours about land distribution also ran rampant in Anlu, Chongyang and Tongshan.[32] 'Mao has died, the land will be returned to the people!' was the message relayed by villagers in the midst of famine in Jiang'an, Sichuan.[33]

Deafening noise about shortages also contributed to a state of permanent chaos on the ground which, in turn, prompted the propaganda machine to churn out even louder slogans. People and party were locked in a war of words, as every dogma found its obverse in rumour. Panics, for instance, were triggered when ration coupons for certain goods were said to be phased out. Some workers in the Angang Steel Works bought up to thirty-five pairs of socks in June 1960 as long queues spontaneously appeared out of nowhere to stockpile all cotton goods.[34] Similarly, in a commune in Changle, Guangdong, a rumour that salt might be withdrawn led to local panic in January 1961, with people struggling to hoard some 35 tonnes of salt in five days, forty times more than usual.[35]

Rumours of war and impending invasion engulfed entire communities, spreading fear by turning the party propaganda upside down. And fear, in turn, promoted a sense of cohesion, as apocalyptic imagery united a disgruntled countryside. In Guangdong farmers heard that Guangzhou was up in arms and Shantou had been taken, as Chiang Kai-shek had invaded the country. Banners wishing the Guomindang a long life appeared by the roadside. The information was precise: 'The Guomindang has reached Dongxi Village on the 14th!' or 'Chiang Kai-shek will come back in August!'[36] Defying common assumptions about the parochial lives that peasants allegedly lived in isolated villages, these rumours spread like wildfire, leaping from county to county and across provinces, reaching Hunan in a matter of days.[37] In Putian, Fujian, the province opposite Taiwan, a secret society distributed yellow banners to be prominently displayed after the fall of the communist party. Apparently the banners also protected against the effects of nuclear radiation.[38]

Some wronged villagers were confident enough to appeal to the law. In Liuhe, near Nanjing, a cadre snatched and later ate the chicken an old woman was trying to sell. Incensed, she went straight to court and lodged a complaint.[39] But more often than not litigation was meaningless, all the more so since the judicial system had crumbled under political pressure – even leading to the abolition of the Ministry of Justice in 1959. Politics was in command, curtailing formal justice – as well as formal recourse. In Ningjin county, for instance, the number of cadres in charge of the police, the inspectorate and the courts was halved in 1958. The local courts were overwhelmed with civil cases brought by ordinary people.[40]

In response, many turned instead to a tradition of complaint in the form of letters and petitions. As misinformation proliferated within the party bureaucracy, every level feeding false reports and inflated statistics to the next one up, the state security tried to bypass official organs and reach straight down to street level. It paid close attention to popular opinion and encouraged anonymous letters of denunciation.[41] Class enemies, after all, could worm their way into the ranks of the party, while spies and saboteurs were lurking among the masses. Popular vigilance was necessary to ferret them out: the people monitored the party. Even the most insignificant nobody had the power to put pen to paper and bring down a mighty cadre, a negligent local official or an abusive bureaucrat. Arbitrary denunciation could strike at any time up the ladder of power. And people wrote furiously, sending bags of letters each month to beg, protest, denounce or complain, sometimes coyly and humbly, occasionally vociferously. Some denounced their neighbours over a trifle, others merely sought help in changing jobs or moving house, and a few went into a long tirade against the entire system, peppering their letters with anti-communist slogans. They wrote to newspapers, the police, the courts and the party. Some wrote to the State Council, and not a few addressed their letters to Mao Zedong personally.

In Changsha the provincial authorities received some 1,500 letters or visitors a month. Many wrote to seek redress from a perceived injustice, and a few even ventured to write letters critical enough to be deemed 'reactionary'. Those who presented a specific case with a concrete request had a chance of receiving an answer. After all, within the huge monitoring system of the party bureaucracy, local authorities had to show that they acted on 'requests from the masses'.[42] By March 1961 in Nanjing, around 130,000 letters had been received since the start of the Great Leap Forward. The majority of complaints concerned work, food, goods and services, but a more detailed analysis of 400 letters 'by the masses' showed that one in ten made a direct accusation or threatened to sue.[43] In Shanghai the bureau for handling letters from the public received well over 40,000 items in 1959. People complained about lack of food, poor housing and work conditions, with a few attacking the party and its representatives.[44] The point of a denunciation was to prompt an investigation, and some letters carried enough conviction to spur the authorities into action. After a complaint was sent to the provincial governor of Guangdong alleging that the Institute for Nationalities included dozens of fictitious students on its roster to increase its grain allocation, a local security team was dispatched, and managed to extract several confessions and an apology from the Institute's leaders.[45]

Some readers sent letters to the *People's Daily*. Few of these were published, but their contents were summarised and circulated among the leadership. Coal miners from Guangxi province, for instance, wrote to complain that some of them fainted on the job because the food rations had been slashed even though their working hours had increased.[46] The State Council received hundreds of letters each month. Some writers were bold enough to attack the policies of the Great Leap Forward and lament the export of grain in the midst of hunger.[47] Some wrote directly to the top leaders. In doing so they reproduced a long-standing imperial tradition of petitioning the emperor, but they also demonstrated their belief that abuses of power were local, not the result of a campaign of collectivisation initiated by Mao himself: 'if only Mao knew'. Justice, surely, had survived in the capital. Letters offered hope. Xiang Xianzhi, a poor girl from Hunan, had a letter addressed to the Chairman stitched inside her coat for a full year before handing it over to an investigation team sent by the provincial party committee.[48] 'Dear Chairman Mao' was a standard opening greeting, for instance in the case of Ye Lizhuang's letter about the starvation and corruption in Hainan. His appeal worked. It led to a lengthy investigation by a high-powered team, which brought to light 'oppression of the people' by local party members.[49]

But many letters never reached their destination. After Liu Shaoqi personally complained to the minister of public security, Xie Fuzhi, that letters sent to him by fellow villagers had been opened by the local police (see Chapter 16), the full extent of the abuse came to light. In Guizhou the post office and the Public Security Bureau routinely opened the mail, which led to the arrest of the authors of denunciations for 'anti-party' or 'counter-revolutionary' activities. When a cadre wrote about mass starvation in Zunyi, he was interrogated for several months and sent to work in a kiln factory.[50] More than 2,000 letters were opened by the police every month in Gaotai county, Gansu. Anonymity, apparently, offered little protection. In one case, He Jingfang mailed eight unsigned letters, but the local police still managed to track him down, extract a confession and send him off to a labour camp.[51] In Sichuan, Du Xingmin's letter denouncing party secretary Song Youyu led to a frantic search throughout the brigade in which writing samples were compared. Du was unmasked and accused of being a saboteur. But before being handed over to the Public Security Bureau, Du had both his eyes gouged out by an enraged Song. He died a few days later in prison.[52] No wonder some people turned to violence instead.

Robbers and Rebels

Violence was an act of last resort, as desperate farmers assaulted granaries, raided trains or plundered communes. After Cangzhou, Hebei, had been hit by a typhoon in 1961, some villagers armed themselves with sickles to steal the corn from the fields. One party secretary took charge of a brigade and organised raids against neighbouring villages, plundering dozens of sheep and several tonnes of vegetables.[1] Some of these incursions were armed: in one incident a leader in Shaanxi provided the rifles with which a hundred villagers ransacked an adjacent commune and hauled away 5 tonnes of grain. Another local leader headed an armed gang of 260 men who slept rough in the daytime and pillaged at night.[2] In parts of the countryside, large groups would assemble along county and provincial boundaries and make forays across the border, leaving behind a trail of destruction.[3]

But more often than not the target of peasant violence was the state granary. The scale of the attacks was staggering. In one Hunanese county alone thirty out of 500 state granaries were assailed in two months.[4] In the same province the Xiangtan region witnessed over 800 cases of grain theft in the winter of 1960–1. In Huaihua farmers forced open a whole series of barns, taking several tonnes of millet.[5]

Raids on trains were also common. Farmers would gather along a railway and rob freight trains, using the sheer weight of their numbers to overwhelm the guards. This became increasingly common from the end of 1960 onwards, as the regime started to realise the extent of mass starvation and launched a purge of some of the most abusive party members. After provincial boss Zhang Zhongliang had been demoted in Gansu province, some 500 cases of train robbery were reported by the local police in January 1961 alone. The total losses were estimated at roughly 500 tonnes of grain and 2,300 tonnes of coal. And with each assault the crowds grew bolder. At the Wuwei railway station, only a few dozen people caused trouble in early January, but as others joined the fray the crowds swelled into the hundreds. Then, by the end of the month, 4,000 villagers ran amok, bringing to a halt a train from which every detachable portion of property was removed. Elsewhere, near Zhangye, a granary was pillaged from dusk to dawn by 2,000 irate farmers, who killed one of the guards in the process. In another case military uniforms were stolen from a wagon. On the prowl days later, the villagers were mistaken for special forces by the guards in charge of a warehouse and given access to the grain unopposed.[6]

All along the railway line, granaries were attacked, livestock stolen, weapons seized and account books burned. Armed forces and special militia had to be sent in to establish order.[7] Some of the train robberies had diplomatic repercussions, for instance when the assailants of a freight train burned the exhibition goods that were in transit from the Democratic People's Republic of Korea to the People's Republic of Mongolia.[8] To the credit of the Ministry of Public Security, nobody was ordered to shoot into the crowds, and the police were instructed instead to focus on the 'ringleaders'.[9]

Violence begets violence: sometimes the protective shield outsiders mistook for passivity and submissiveness broke down, and villagers erupted in a blind fury. In heated meetings at which higher quotas were introduced, farmers accused their leaders of starving them to death, some of the more disgruntled ones going so far as to assault and kill local cadres with cleavers.[10] Others armed themselves with sticks and chased cadres suspected of skimming public funds. In Yunyang county, Sichuan, local people unleashed a collective anger upon their leader, who jumped into a pond to his death together with his wife.[11] In the mountainous county of Tongjiang, local team leader Liu Funian was made to kneel on stones and was beaten with a flagpole.[12] But such examples were unusual. Ordinary people may have pilfered, stolen, lied and on occasion torched and pillaged, but they were rarely the perpetrators of violence. They were the ones who had to find ways of 'eating bitterness' – the Chinese saying for enduring hardship – by absorbing grief, accepting pain and living with loss on a devastating scale.

Less overt but equally destructive was arson, although it was not always possible to distinguish between fires started accidentally, for instance by poor villagers trying to stay warm during the winter, and those ignited deliberately as a form of protest. The Ministry of Public Security estimated that at least 7,000 fires caused 100 million yuan worth of losses in 1958 – although it was unable to tell what proportion should be attributed to intentional burning.[13] Dozens of cases of arson were reported every year by the public security organs in Hebei.[14] Towards the end of 1959 there were three times more fires in Nanjing than there had been the previous year. Many were caused by neglect, but not a few were attributed to arsonists. Zhao Zhihai, for instance, started a fire in the dormitory of his factory as a form of protest.[15] Xu Minghong burned four haystacks and was shot dead by the local militia.[16] In Songzi, Hubei, the house of a party secretary was torched.[17] Elsewhere in the province angry farmers doused a statue of Mao with petrol and set it ablaze.[18] In Sichuan, Li Huaiwen set fire to the local canteen, which had once been his home, shouting: 'Get the hell out of here, this canteen belongs to me!'[19]

By 1961 pyromania possessed the countryside. Around Guangzhou, hundreds of fires flickered at night in the weeks following the Chinese New Year, many started by farmers demanding their own private plot.[20] In Wengyuan county the villagers scribbled a message on a wall near the granary they had just torched, proclaiming that the grain that was no longer theirs might as well be burned.[21]

As starvation sets in, famished people are often too weak and too focused on their own survival to contemplate rebellion. But inside the vaults of the party archives is plenty of evidence of underground organisations springing up in the last two years of the famine. They never posed a genuine threat to the party and were easily crushed, but they did act as a barometer for popular discontent. Many of these organisations never even got off the ground. In Hunan, for instance, 150 people along a county border armed themselves for rebellion in the winter of 1960–1, but were immediately swept up by local security forces. Near the provincial capital a Love the People Party was set up by a few disgruntled farmers in favour of the freedom to cultivate and trade in agricultural products. They too never stood a chance.[22]

But more credible challenges came from the provinces near Tibet, where an armed uprising in March 1959 was quelled with heavy artillery, resulting in the Dalai Lama's flight to exile. In Qinghai in 1958 open rebellion continued for months on end, at places ranging from Yegainnyin (Henan), close to the Gansu border in the east, to Gyêgu (Yushu) and Nangqen (Nangqian) up in the Tibetan plateau. Some of the rebels were inspired by Lhasa, others were fuelled by Islam. The armed forces in the province were insufficient to deal with the uprisings, and the army initially focused on regaining control of all vital highways.[23]

The region continued to be rocked periodically by local uprisings. In the autumn of 1960, villagers in Xuanwei county, Yunnan, rebelled, an act of subversion that rapidly spread to several communes. The movement was backed by local cadres, including party secretaries in the higher echelons of power. Weapons were seized, and hundreds of discontented villagers rallied around slogans promising the abolition of the people's communes, a free market and a return of the land to the farmers. The army swiftly intervened, capturing and eliminating all but one of the leaders. In his report to Zhou Enlai, top security boss Xie Fuzhi mentioned a dozen similar incidents in the south-western provinces that year.[24] To this had to be added over 3,000 'counter-revolutionary groups' detected by the public security forces: Yunnan alone harboured a hundred groups that referred to themselves as a 'party' (dang).[25]

Secret societies were ruthlessly crushed after 1949, but a long history of state suppression had prepared them for survival against all odds. A survey of one northern province gives an indication of the extent of their continued influence – although the numbers may have been inflated by overzealous cadres keen on more resources to fight the counter-revolution. In Hebei province about forty groups dubbed 'counter-revolutionary' were unmasked within the first few months of 1959. Half of these belonged to secret societies the party had tried to extirpate. Huanxingdao,

Shengxiandao, Baguadao, Xiantiandao, Jiugongdao – there were about a dozen popular religious sects and secret societies active in the province. In Ningjin county alone, close to 4 per cent of the local population was thought to belong to one sect or another, many of them swearing allegiance to the Yiguandao.[26] Some of these societies extended their influence across provincial boundaries. Despite restrictions on the movement of people from the countryside, followers would travel from Hebei to Shandong to pray at the grave of a leader of a village sect called the Heaven and Earth Teaching Society.[27] Everywhere people turned to popular religion, despite party strictures against 'superstition'. In Guangdong, where a ceremony to mark the birthday of the Mother Dragon remained popular, some 3,000 worshippers gathered for the occasion in Deqing in 1960. Even students and cadres joined in.[28]

But nothing could destabilise the regime even in its darkest hour. As in other famines, from Bengal and Ireland to the Ukraine, most villagers, by the time it became clear that starvation was there to stay, were already too weak even to walk down the road to the next village, let alone find weapons and organise an uprising. In any event, even a mild form of opposition was brutally repressed and severely dealt with: leaders of riots or uprisings faced execution, while others were given an indefinite sentence in a labour camp. What also prevented the country from imploding, even as tens of millions perished, was the absence of any viable alternative to the communist party. Whether they were dispersed secret religions or poorly organised underground parties, none except the regime could control this huge expanse of land. And the potential for a coup from within the army had been averted by extensive purges carried out by Lin Biao after the Lushan plenum in 1959.

Yet something more tenacious than mere geopolitics prevented the appearance of a credible threat to the rule of the party. The most common technique of self-help in times of mass starvation was a simple device called hope. And hope dictated that, however bad the situation was in the village, Mao had the best interests of his people at heart. A common conviction in imperial times was that the emperor was benevolent, but his servants could be corrupt. Even more so in the People's Republic, the population had to reconcile a vision of utopia trumpeted by the media with the everyday reality of catastrophe on the ground. The belief that cadres who were abusive failed to carry out the orders of a beneficent Chairman was widespread. A distant entity called 'the government' and a semi-god called 'Mao' were on the side of good. If only he knew, everything would be different.

Exodus

The most effective strategy of survival in times of famine was to leave the village. Ironically, for millions of farmers the Great Leap Forward meant departure to the city rather than entry into a commune. As targets for industrial output were ceaselessly revised upwards, urban enterprises started recruiting cheap labour from the countryside, creating a migration of tidal dimensions. More than 15 million farmers moved to the city in 1958 alone, lured by the prospect of a better life.[1] From Changchun, Beijing, Tianjin and Shanghai to Guangzhou, cities exploded as, according to the official census, the total urban population ballooned from 99 million in 1957 to 130 million in 1960.[2]

The great outflow from the countryside happened despite formal restrictions on the movement of people. The household registration rules described in Chapter 22 were brushed aside in the rush to industrialisation. But few migrants managed officially to change their place of residence from the village to the city. A great underclass was created, relegated to dirty, arduous and sometimes dangerous jobs on the margins of the urban landscape, and facing discriminatory barriers against assimilation in their place of work. Migrant workers were deprived of the same entitlements accorded city dwellers, for instance subsidised housing, food rations and access to health, education and disability benefits. Most of all they had no secure status, dwelling in a twilight zone of legality and risking expulsion back to the countryside at any time.

This happened in early 1959, as food reserves ran out and the country faced its first winter of hunger. In all major cities, as we have seen, grain reserves fell to historic lows, shortages in industrial centres such as Wuhan being so severe that they risked running out of food within a matter of weeks.³ The mounting crisis prompted the leadership to ramp up the household registration system, erecting a great wall between city and countryside. As it could provide food, housing and employment only to urban residents, it left farmers to fend for themselves. In order to ease the burden further, the state capped the growth of the urban population. Tough restrictions on the movement of people were imposed by the State Council on 4 February 1959 and again on 11 March 1959, stipulating that the free market in labour could no longer be tolerated and villagers had to be sent back to the countryside.⁴ As the police started enforcing the household registration system in Shanghai, it was revealed that in some districts up to a fifth of all families had only temporary residence permits, the majority being farmers from Jiangsu province.⁵ An estimated 60,000 villagers resided in the city illegally, most working in the freight and construction industries. In the wake of the State Council's repeated directives, a quarter of a million farmers were rounded up and sent back to the countryside.⁶ Adrift between two worlds in the midst of starvation, migrants throughout the country were being forcibly returned to their villages. In the countryside, in turn, local authorities did their best to prevent anybody from leaving for the city, locking people into the famine.

The attempt to impose a cordon sanitaire around cities was defeated by a myriad of factors. The great outflow in 1958 had created patterns of migration and networks of contacts which were used by villagers to return to the city. In Hebei in early 1959 one in every twenty-five agricultural workers was roaming the countryside in search of employment. Those who returned to the village over the Chinese New Year encouraged others to follow, heading back as a group to enterprises where good connections had been established and few questions were asked. Letters were sent from the city, including money and detailed instructions on how to join the exodus. In Xinyang, one of the most devastated regions in Henan, letters came 'incessantly' from Qinghai, Gansu and Beijing, according to local officials – who opened the mail. Li Mingyi sent three letters, including 130 yuan, to his brother, urging him and four other relatives to join him in working for the railway bureau in Xining.⁷

In the village tales were told about life in the city, seen as a haven where rice was plentiful and jobs abounded. Some communes actually supported a form of chain migration by agreeing to take care of children and the elderly, as remittances from workers in the city contributed to the survival of the entire village. From Zhangjiakou, a major hub along the railway to the west of Beijing, a third of a million people vanished during the 1958–9 winter, representing some 7 per cent of the entire workforce.[8]

Even in relatively sheltered provinces such as Zhejiang villagers took to the road in the winter of 1958–9. Some 145,000 people were known to be on the move, although many more must have escaped the attention of the local authorities tasked with arresting them. As elsewhere, most were headed for a city in search of employment. They were ambitious, the majority intending to travel as far as Qinghai, Xinjiang and Ningxia, where the famine was less intense. But proximity to a city remained a key factor in prompting villagers to flee. In Longquan, for instance, one in ten of all able-bodied villagers crossed into Fujian province, a mere forty kilometres away, while others trekked to the cities of Xiaoshan, Fenghua and Jinhua. Most were young, male workers; the women were left behind to look after the family and the village. In Buxia Village, forty kilometres south of Xiaoshan, 230 workers left in several large groups, including local cadres and members of the Youth League. A significant proportion of these had already experienced the city as factories eagerly recruited from the surrounding villages during the Great Leap Forward. Many absconded in the middle of the night, while others walked away in broad daylight, claiming to visit a sick relative in town. In a few cases cadres themselves wrote letters of reference and provided travel permits, encouraging villagers to pull up stakes and take their chances in the city. Some made a profit by selling blank permits bearing an official stamp.[9] Elsewhere, for instance further south in Guangdong, local cadres adopted a lenient attitude, sensing that more movement of people could alleviate the famine. In Lantang commune a mere one in seven of all workers in a brigade participated in collective labour. The others performed private work or traded with neighbouring counties, some going as far as Haifeng, over 100 kilometres down the coastline.[10]

Many left in groups, boarding freight trains headed for the city. On one day in March 1959, a group of about a hundred farmers managed to board a train at Kongjiazhuang, Hebei, without buying a single ticket. A few days later, a similar number boarded from Zhoujiahe station, a tiny village in Huai'an.[11] In Hubei, on the stretch from Xiaogan to Shekou, hundreds of farmers would congregate at the station each day and board en masse. Some intended to flee the village, but many simply went to the city to sell wood or visit friends. When asking for a ticket, collectors faced verbal abuse and physical assault. In the chaos of boarding, accidents happened, as weaker fare dodgers fell off the train, including a five-year-old child who had a leg severed in the process.[12]

All these groups amounted to a large number of people on the move. In the first four months of 1960, for instance, over 170,000 farmers escaping from the countryside were found ticketless on trains in Beijing alone, most of them hailing from Shandong, Hebei and Henan. Once on board, every available bit of property was used in the struggle for survival. As one official noted in disgust, they 'wantonly spoil and damage goods, some urinating and defecating on them, a few using high-quality stockings as toilet paper'.[13]

After they had arrived at their destination, many migrants would be met at the station by a friend or by a tout recruiting labour.[14] Others found a job on the black market. Called 'human markets' (renshi) in Beijing, they opened early in the morning as a mob of unemployed men pushed, shoved and jostled for attention as soon as a prospective employer turned up. Most lived in temporary shelters, a few stayed with friends and family. They would work for as little as 1.3 yuan a day, although carpenters could fetch up to 2.5 yuan, the highest salary for skilled labour being 4 yuan. Some were recruited underground by state companies, others were hired by private individuals for menial jobs or domestic service.[15]

The cumulative effect of this outflow could overwhelm the city, despite the cordon sanitaire designed to keep the urban population insulated from the rural famine. Thousands found their way into Nanjing every month, and by the spring of 1959 some 60,000–70,000 refugees had either arrived or transited through the city, overrunning the temporary shelters hastily erected by the municipality. On a single day in February 1959 around 1,500 refugees disembarked. Two-thirds were young men, and most came from the surrounding counties, although a number also hailed from Anhui, Henan and Shandong, the three provinces most affected by famine. A few wanted to visit friends and family, most had no money, and all were in search of a job. Factories and mines secretly recruited them, paying them by piece rate, less than workers with residence permits. Some enterprises actually faked the necessary papers to register them locally, but the vast majority – some 90 per cent of all factories – simply inflated the official number of workers in order to secure sufficient food to feed illegal workers.[16]

Not every migrant found a job on the black market, and some were forced to live a marginal existence in the shadows of the city, stealing, begging, scavenging or selling themselves in order to survive. Kong Fanshun, a twenty-eight-year-old male, was described as a vagrant who would climb walls at night to steal clothes and money. Su Yuyou was caught after he entered a shop, grabbed a large flatbread and stuffed the whole thing into his mouth while making a run for it. Young women could be found soliciting customers in the centre of the city. For a ration coupon worth ten or twenty cents or for a pound of rice they would perform a sexual favour in a quiet corner of a public park. Those who failed faced starvation: some twenty bodies were collected each month during the harsh winter.[17] All were described as a threat to social order by the local authorities, reinforcing the negative imagery associated with country folk. When they were caught they were sent back to their villages, only to return to the city again after a few weeks.[18]

Some of the refugees, when questioned by officials, told their stories. Yu Yiming, interviewed in May 1959, had been surviving on two bowls of gruel a day in her village in Anxian county. After the cadres turned over all the grain to the state, nothing but cabbage remained. Then all the bark on elm trees and the chestnut tubers vanished, leaving the village depleted. Wang Xiulan, a fellow villager, broke down in tears, crying that 'we are not lying, we have not had any food for several months, everything has been eaten – what can we do?' Other escapees explained how they had managed to abscond under the cover of night. Tao Mintang, from Lishui county, recounted how eleven of them fled as a group one evening, lured by rumours that in Heilongjiang young workers could make up to seventy yuan a month.[19]

Not all migrants lived in the city's dark underbelly, eking out a miserable existence at the mercy of rapacious factory bosses. In the rush towards industrialisation during the Great Leap Forward, some of the most able men recruited from the countryside were given good salaries as incentives to stay.[20] In Pukou, Nanjing's busy port, a team of loaders working on the docks had no right to food rations, reserved for city residents, but they earned about 100 yuan a month, enough to eat in some of the top restaurants. Some made two salaries, making a better living for themselves than most of the registered workers in local factories.[21] A few even specialised in trading ration coupons on the black market. One woman was caught with coupons worth 180 kilos of rice, which she bought in Shanghai to double her money in Nanjing, exploiting one of the countless loopholes in the planned economy by which the same basic commodity was sold at vastly different prices across the country. Most migrants in factories and construction sites were men, but the majority of villagers who left the rural areas to trade were women.[22]

On the other hand, as the famine went on, whatever leverage some young migrants might have had on a black market desperately short of labour simply vanished, replaced by desperation for a scrap of food. By 1960 in Lanzhou some 210,000 migrants worked in factories without any pay, being given no more than board and lodging. Zhang Zhongliang, the gung-ho boss of Gansu, personally endorsed the arrangement. But outside the provincial capital complicity from the leaders led to conditions of slave labour. In Tongwei, a steel factory locked up migrants and forced them to work themselves to death, refusing to feed them: a thousand died that year, as factory bosses were assured of a steady supply of vagrants and drifters looking for work.[23] Who knows how many factories operated in similar conditions?

As the years of famine went by, the motivations behind migration changed. In a nutshell, the lure of employment was replaced by the compulsion of famine. As a sense of despair grew, some would steal off into the mountains, hoping to survive on berries, insects and possibly small animals. But few actually made it, some being forced to return to the village, emerging from the forest with dishevelled hair and torn clothes, sometimes entirely naked, a wild look in the eyes, so changed that they were no longer recognised.[24] On the other hand, when disaster struck, people left en masse, children in tow, their meagre possessions strapped on their backs; local authorities could only stand by and watch the exodus. After the Cangzhou region in Hebei was hit by a typhoon in 1961, listless masses of humanity took to the roads, trailing along in total silence, the only sound being the shuffle of their feet. Entire brigades left collectively – cadres, men, women and children, trading their clothes for taro along the way, with many of the adults and most of the children ending up stark naked.[25] All over the country people died by the roadside.

What was the effect of the exodus on the village? In many cases, villagers and even local cadres supported mass emigration, as they hoped that remittances would allow them to survive. But the countless tales of life in the city, where jobs were easy, the pay was generous and food limitless, must have contributed to a general sense of demoralisation. The revolution, after all, had been fought for the farmers, but all too obviously life in the countryside was inferior to that in the city. The imposition of a cordon, shielding towns from villages, can only have worsened a pervasive feeling of worthlessness; in effect, the countryside was quarantined, as if peopled by lepers. As the best workers were poached by recruiters from the city, villages were sometimes split, as jealous farmers turned against families with migrants in the city, beating them or depriving them of food.[26] And even if some communities may have welcomed migration, they soon found themselves crippled by labour shortages: those who left were overwhelmingly healthy, enterprising young men. Organised flight, on the other hand, had a domino effect which could deplete some villages of all working adults. In Huai'an county, strategically located by the Beijing–Baotou railway, one village had some fifty working men but a mere seven remained by the spring of 1959; even the head of the village and the party secretary had become drifters looking for work in the city.[27] Where people left because of famine, nothing but ghost villages survived; only those who were too weak to walk stayed behind.

With jobs crying out to be filled during the initial rush of the Great Leap Forward, some of the village officials went after the migrants, trying to persuade them to return home during the busy season. A great many people crossed the border from Hunan into Hubei, following an earlier pattern of migration established during severe shortages in 1957.[28] A team of cadres was dispatched to find the villagers, but they were met with a volley of abuse: the migrants refused to go back to the village where food was rationed. The cadres then turned against the local authorities, accusing them of poaching their people to help build a reservoir. They, instead of the migrants, were thrown behind bars; once released they were forced to make a humiliating retreat back to Hunan.[29] A more subtle approach was tried elsewhere, for instance in Hengshui, Hebei, where half of all the 50,000 migrants from Qingliangdian commune were wheedled into returning home in 1960. Relatives were made to write letters imploring them to come back to the village. Sometimes these letters were hand-delivered by local cadres anxious to ensure that they reached their destination.[30]

But most of the time brute force was used to prevent villagers from leaving. As we shall see in greater detail in a subsequent chapter, local cadres beat, starved and tortured those who tried to flee, or exacted punishment from family members. Throughout the countryside, located at strategic junctions, 'dissuasion stations' (*quanzuzhan*) or 'custody and deportation stations' (*shourong qiansong zhan*) were set up by the militia, responsible for arresting people on the run and escorting them back to the village. These centres could arbitrarily detain people without judicial supervision or legal charge, even if they held a temporary residence permit: they survive to this day, specifically targeting beggars and migrant workers. Over 600 were in operation throughout the country at the height of the famine. Eight cities alone – from Guangzhou to Harbin – held more than 50,000 people in such stations by the spring of 1961.[31] In Sichuan in 1960 some 380,000 people were detained and sent back.[32]

Cut off from a social network which could provide a measure of protection, adrift on the road with only the bare essentials, escapees were ideal prey. As the Ministry of the Interior reported in May 1960, in Shandong these stations not only confiscated food coupons, rations and train tickets, but also strung drifters and migrants up and beat them black and blue. Women were molested.[33] In Tianshui, Gansu, one in every eight guards said they had raped a woman, while all of them routinely beat villagers in their custody. A special 'school' was even set up to reform the escapees:

they were insulted, spat upon, tied up and forced to kneel or stand for hours on end. Their few possessions were stolen, from small knives, eggs, noodles, wine and rope to socks and trousers. Women were threatened, beaten or starved in order to obtain sexual favours. Many were put to work to cook meals, launder clothes, clean the toilets and wash the feet of the guards. Failure to prepare the noodles of guard Li Guocang properly led three of the inmates to be sent to a 'school' where they were beaten for a whole day.[34]

But however harsh the treatment meted out to refugees, they rarely gave up, and often managed to burst through the fetters of the system. When a group of seventy-five villagers were sent back to Wuhu from Shanghai, sixty managed to escape.[35] A month later 150 out of 250 refugees escorted back north to Shenyang from Tianjin succeeded in absconding. Many were what party officials referred to as 'habitual' refugees (*guanliu*), escaping from the village again and again.[36] Life on the road might have been bitter, but it was better than waiting for death in the village.

———

The tide turned in 1961: surrounded by famine, beleaguered by migrants and facing a growing population that could no longer be fed, the leadership in Beijing decided to send back 20 million people from the cities to the countryside. The order came on 18 June 1961, the target being a reduction of 10 million people before the end of the year, leading to savings of 2 million tonnes of grain. The rest would follow in 1962, and stragglers would be swept up by 1963.[37]

The authorities moved fast. In Yunnan, where cities had ballooned from 1.8 million inhabitants in 1957 to 2.5 million by 1961, around 300,000 people, many of them unemployed, were selected in order to fill the quota.[38] Those sent back included 30,000 prisoners from Kunming, relocated to labour camps in the countryside.[39] In the cities of Guangdong close to 3 million people were unemployed: some 600,000 were moved to the countryside by the end of 1961.[40] In Anhui, where 1.6 million had been added to an urban population of 3.1 million after 1957, some 600,000 people were removed.[41] By the end of the year, state planner Li

Fuchun announced that 12.3 million people had been moved, another 7.8 million being targeted for 1962.[42] In the end, the state proved more resilient than the villagers, mercilessly employing new methods of coercion to keep the urban population at an historic low for years to come.

———

The lucky ones managed to cross the border, but this came at a cost. In Yunnan, where minorities living near Vietnam, Laos and Burma voted with their feet as soon as the Great Leap Forward started, punishment was brutal. Some 115,000 people left the country in 1958 from villages adjacent to the border, protesting against the lack of free trade, restrictions on the freedom of movement, forced collectivisation and hard labour on irrigation schemes. Those caught fleeing were routinely beaten. A young woman with a baby daughter was bayoneted to death in Jinghong, while others were locked up in a house which was then blown up with dynamite. Even those who voluntarily returned to their villages were tortured and executed, their bodies left by the side of the road. The stench of rotting corpses was pervasive.[43] Numbers are hard to obtain, but according to the British Foreign Office some 20,000 refugees arrived in Burma in 1958, most of whom were sent back across the border into China.[44] Given that many of the ethnic minority peoples had relatives on both sides of the border, the total is likely to have been much higher. In the southern provinces frontier people fled to Vietnam. Many were smugglers, but when hunger became too intense they used their knowledge of the terrain to cross the border, never to return.[45]

The exodus took place all along China's extended borders, in particular during a lull in policy enforcement in 1962. What began as a trickle of refugees from Xinjiang became a flood, and by May some 64,000 people had made the crossing, often in large groups, as families with children and their meagre possessions stumbled into the Soviet Union.[46] Half the population of Chuguchak (Tacheng), from cadres to toddlers, marched along the ancient silk road to the border, leaving behind a wasteland.[47] Thousands crossed the border every day at the Bakhta and Khorgos checkpoints on the Kazakhstani–Chinese border, overwhelming the border patrols. Many were weak and ill, turning to the Soviet authorities for help.[48] Millions of

rubles were made available to provide the refugees with jobs and temporary housing.[49] In Kulja (Yining) chaos ensued after the Soviet consulate
was invaded by an armed mob, eager to take away all archives relating
to the nationality of minority people, as only those registered as Soviets
could cross the border. Granaries were robbed and shots were fired at the
militia.[50] According to Soviet sources, rumours that the local authorities
actually sold bus tickets to the border caused mayhem. As crowds gathered
around the party offices to demand transportation, they were fired upon,
and some of them were killed.[51]

A similar scramble to escape took place at the border in Hong Kong
in May 1962. Throughout the famine people managed to make their
way to the British colony: in 1959 illegal immigration was estimated at
some 30,000.[52] This was on top of legal immigration, with the mainland
handing out around 1,500 visas a month to those it no longer needed at
home.[53] But in May 1962, as the mainland temporarily relaxed its border
controls, a steady flow became a flood, reaching a peak of over 5,000 a day.
Overnight, Hong Kong became the free Berlin of the East. The great exodus
was well planned, and those who undertook it tended to be young urban
residents recently sent to the countryside following factory closures: faced
with severe food shortages and abandoned by the system, some decided
to flee. Many had money, biscuits, tinned food and a map. Speculators
in Guangzhou even sold improvised compasses called Paradise Pointers.[54]
Tickets for the border area were on sale at the railway station, although
clashes occurred between mobs and police in early June during a riot put
down by troops.[55] Those lucky enough to have a ticket boarded a train, but
others trekked along the coast or hiked through the hills for several days.
When a crowd large enough to overpower the guards had gathered by the
border, the refugees made a run for it, swimming across the river that separated the mainland from Hong Kong, scrambling through the barbed-wire
entanglements and working their way under the steel mesh of the border
fence. Accidents happened. Some refugees mistook a reservoir near the
border for the river, and tried to swim across it at night: some 200 bodies
were later found floating or washed up against the abutment.[56] Others
were smuggled on sampans for a fee, some landing on offshore islands, the
unlucky ones capsizing in rough seas and drowning.[57]

Once they had reached Hong Kong, the refugees had to evade British border patrols. Most were arrested on the spot, but a few slipped into the hills, poor, in rags, mostly barefoot, and some with broken ankles. Unlike in Berlin, they were not welcome, as the crown colony feared being swamped by mainlanders. Nobody else offered to take them, with the United States and Canada rigidly sticking to their quotas, and even Taiwan accepting very few for resettlement.[58] The United Nations refugee agency, on the other hand, did not recognise the People's Republic: 'refugees from China' could not exist in political terms and therefore could not be aided under the UNHCR's system.[59] As Hong Kong's colonial secretary Claude Burgess put it, the refugee problem was one that 'no country in the world is in practice willing to share with us'.[60] Only those who could be vouched for by relatives in Hong Kong were allowed to stay, and the vast majority were eventually returned to the mainland. Crowds sympathised with the plight of the refugees, providing food and shelter or obstructing vehicles returning them to the border point at Lo Wu. By June China had closed its border again and the influx ceased as suddenly as it had started.

PART FIVE

THE VULNERABLE

28

Children

Communal nurseries and kindergartens were set up everywhere in the summer of 1958, allowing women to step out of their homes and join the Great Leap Forward. Problems appeared right away, as children were separated from their parents all day long, in some cases for weeks on end. In the countryside retired women and unmarried girls were given crash courses in childcare, but they were quickly overwhelmed by the number of toddlers that parents were required to hand over to the state. And as labour shortages became acute in the rush towards industrialisation, even they were forced to work in the fields and factories, leaving children in minimal care. The buildings of childcare centres were often ramshackle, in some cases not having any fixed premises at all, but making do with a mud hut or an abandoned shed, and allowing the children to run wild.[1] Outside the capital, in Daxing county, a mere dozen out of 475 boarding kindergartens had rudimentary equipment, and more often than not children simply ate and slept on the floor. Many of the buildings had leaking roofs, and some lacked doors and windowpanes altogether. As carers had only a rudimentary training, accidents were frequent, with children bumping into boiling kettles and suffering burns. Neglect was such that in one facility several children aged three to four were unable to walk. In the suburbs clustered around Beijing, a third of all kindergartens were described by the Women's Federation as 'backward'.[2] Even in the capital childcare was basic in the extreme. In the nurseries everybody cried, one report noted: the children forced away from their families would burst into tears first, quickly followed by inexperienced young carers who felt utterly overwhelmed by the pressure, and finally mothers reluctant to entrust their offspring to the state would also start crying.[3]

Lack of qualified staff also led to the use of corporal punishment to maintain a semblance of order in overcrowded kindergartens. This was common even in the cities, one of the worst cases being a female supervisor who used a hot iron to discipline recalcitrant children, and burned a three-year-old on the arm.[4] Poor standards of care and shabby facilities also combined to produce disease. Eating utensils were shared while infected children were not segregated, allowing germs to colonise the kindergarten. Even in the relative oasis of Shanghai, toddlers risked going about all day with faeces in their pants.[5] In Beijing infection rates were high. In the Number Two Cotton Factory, 90 per cent of the children were sick, commonly with measles and chickenpox. Scabies and worms were also widespread. Death rates were high.[6] In the suburbs flies abounded and the kindergartens reeked of urine. Food poisoning was a common occurrence, killing many children. Diarrhoea infected four in five children; some of them also suffered from rickets.[7] With the advance of the famine, oedema became widespread, as bodies started swelling up with water. In Nanjing, two out of three children inspected in a kindergarten suffered from water retention; many also had trachoma (an infectious eye disease) and hepatitis.[8]

Abuse was rife. Food was commonly stolen from kindergartens, as hardened adults pilfered the rations designated for helpless children. This happened in three-quarters of all kindergartens in Guangzhou, either through blatant theft or more subtly via accounting irregularities.[9] In one case in Nanjing, all the meat rationed for the children was taken home by director Li Darao, who also appropriated the entire soap ration. Elsewhere in the city all the meat and sugar was evenly divided up between members of staff.[10] In the countryside abuse was more frequent but less well documented. In November 1960 one or two infants died every day in Qichun county, Hubei: the workers in charge of the premises ate most of the food.[11] In the end, as the state receded in the midst of chaos, the kindergartens simply folded, leaving villagers to fend for their children. To take but one example, the number of childcare institutions in Guangdong declined from 35,000 to 5,400 in 1961 alone.[12]

Children old enough to be sent to school were made to work. A work–study programme, launched by the central government in the autumn of 1957, required all students to participate in productive labour, which in practice could amount to half of all time spent in school. This was before the Great Leap Forward had even started.[13] As the country was mobilised in the steel campaign in the autumn of 1958, children not only collected scrap iron and old bricks, but actually operated the furnaces, a task so gruelling that some fainted after long shifts in the heat. Hundreds of primary schools in Wuhan opened several factories each in a burst of industrialisation. In the schools children were kept on the premises all day long, sleeping in primitive conditions, sometimes three to a bed in leaking buildings. Teaching was suspended for weeks on end, as the world of collective labour was deemed to be the centre of individual development. Anxious parents had no alternative but to sneak into the school buildings at night to check on the well-being of their children.[14] Then passive resistance took effect, and by early 1959 some students attended formal classes only, opting to skip work experience; a few left school altogether.[15] In Nanjing, many of the truants simply stayed at home, but a quarter found work in factories. Several students worked for the police.[16]

Schoolchildren had to participate in productive labour, but were often put to work without adequate safety measures. Accidents were common and hundreds died throughout the Great Leap Forward. While digging a canal in Gansu, seven students perished as a bank collapsed. In Shandong eight met their ends working in an abandoned kiln when a wall caved in.[17]

In the countryside most children did not have the luxury of school at all. They were expected to work in the fields, carry manure, look after cattle or collect firewood for the canteen. Much of this followed traditional practice, as children in poor families had always been expected to help out. But collectivisation brought in its wake a much harsher regime, one in which labour was the property of the collective rather than the individual or the family. Children were no longer asked to work by parents but bossed around by local cadres instead. Many treated children as if they were adults. Tang Suoqun, a thirteen-year-old girl, was made to carry a forty-one-kilo load of cut grass. Not far away a boy aged fourteen had to haul manure weighing fifty kilos.[18]

Throughout the country a stark logic governed relationships between the rulers and ruled. As there was not enough food to go around, the most able workers were given preferential treatment while those considered to be idlers – children, the sick and the elderly – were abused. The party archives provide long and painful lists of examples. Ailong, a thirteen-year-old boy who looked after the ducks in Guangdong, was caught digging up roots for food. He was forced to assume the aeroplane position, was covered in excrement and had bamboo inserted under his nails. The beatings he received were so ferocious that he was crippled for life.[19] In Luoding county, Guangdong, local cadre Qu Bendi beat to death an eight-year-old who had stolen a handful of rice.[20] In Hunan, Tan Yunqing, aged twelve, was drowned in a pond like a puppy for having pilfered food from the canteen.[21] Sometimes parents were forced to inflict the punishment. When a boy stole a handful of grain in the same village in Hunan where Tan Yunqing was drowned, local boss Xiong Changming forced his father to bury him alive. The father died of grief a few days later.[22]

Reprisals were also taken against children as a form of collective punishment. Guo Huansheng, on her own with three children, was refused leave of absence to take her five-year-old son to the hospital. She was a stubborn woman and made her way all alone to Guangzhou without permission, but nonetheless lost her child to disease in the hospital. When she returned home after an absence of ten days she discovered that her two other children had been ignored by the entire village. Covered in excrement, they had worms crawling on their anuses and armpits. Both soon died. Local cadre He Liming then started appearing at her house to bang on the door and denounce her as a shirker. The woman lost her mind.[23] In Liaojia village, near Changsha, one parent escaped to the city, leaving behind two children. The local cadres locked them inside the house, and they starved to death a few days later.[24]

Recalcitrant children were also locked up. In subtropical Guangdong children could be placed inside a hog's cage simply for talking during a meeting.[25] The police helped, putting children aged seven to ten behind bars for stealing small amounts of food in Shuicheng county, Guizhou. One eleven-year-old was locked up for eight months for the theft of a kilo of corn.[26] Larger correctional facilities were established at the county level, designed specifically for children deemed to be incorrigible. In Fengxian county, under the jurisdiction of Shanghai, some 200 children aged six to ten ended up in a re-education camp under the control of the Public Security Bureau: physical punishment included being kicked, standing, kneeling and the insertion of needles into palms; some were handcuffed.[27]

Pressure also came from inside the family. When the parents were too busy working in the fields or taken ill and confined to their beds, the children were in charge of fetching the allocated ration from the canteen, which could be many kilometres away. The children – sometimes as young as four – had to jostle with adults in the canteen, and then carry the food back to the family. The strain was immense, and many of those interviewed today remember vividly how they let their families down on one or another occasion. Ding Qiao'er was a small girl of eight when she had to look after her entire family, as her father was taken ill and her mother had kidney stones and bound feet, which meant that she could not work for the commune and earn a living. Every day the girl had to queue in the canteen for up to an hour, all the while being pushed aside and bullied by hungry adults. The entire family of six depended on the one bowl of watery porridge she was handed, but one day, after a heavy downpour, the scrawny girl slipped on her way back home and spilt the entire contents. 'I cried, but then I remembered that my parents and the whole family were still waiting for me to bring the food back for them to eat. So I picked myself up and scraped the food up from the ground. It was full of sand.' Her family got angry, blaming her for having wasted the ration on which all depended. 'But in the end they ate the food, slowly, because it was full of sand. If they did not eat it, they would be so hungry that they might go crazy.'[28]

Children fought with each other for food. Although Ding Qiao'er was the child who brought home the family ration, sometimes her parents would give more food to her brothers, depriving her and her younger sister. They argued, they cried and sometimes they even fought with each other over the rations. Liu Shu, who grew up in Renshou county, Sichuan, also remembers how his younger brother filled up his bowl first, leaving next to nothing for the others. 'At each meal, he screamed loudly. Every meal was like that. Because he screamed, he was often beaten.'[29] Li

Erjie, a mother of three, recalled that her two sons fought over food every day. 'They fought fiercely. My youngest daughter received the smallest ration, although she always cried for the biggest amount. She cried very loudly to get her way. My other children cursed her for that and still remember it to this day.'[30]

Violence against children inside the family could go much further, as family members became competitors in the presence of insufficient food.[31] Information is difficult to come by, but police reports sometimes get close to the complex family dynamics that developed in times of hunger. In Nanjing about two cases of murder inside the family were reported every month in the middle of the famine. Most of the violence was committed by men and directed against women and children, although one in five victims was an elderly person. In the majority of cases the reason behind murder was that the victims had become a burden. In Liuhe a paralysed girl was thrown into a pond by her parents. In Jiangpu, a dumb and probably retarded child aged eight stole repeatedly from both parents and neighbours, putting the family at risk: he was strangled in the night. A few cases show deliberate starving of a weaker family member. Wang Jiuchang, for instance, regularly ate the ration allocated to his eight-year-old daughter. He also took her cotton jacket and trousers in the middle of the winter. In the end she succumbed to hunger and cold.[32]

In the countryside, following an established tradition the communist party could do little about, children were sold or given away when they could no longer be supported by their own families. In Neiqiu county, Hebei, Chen Zhenyuan was strained to the limit by his family of six, and he gave his four-year-old son to a fellow villager. His seven-year-old was handed over to an uncle in a neighbouring county.[33] In Chengdu, Li Erjie gave one of her three daughters to her sister. But other family members did not like the child, and the mother-in-law was a fierce woman who openly favoured her own grandson: 'We have no food for ourselves, why should we keep another little bitch?' she complained. She took away all of the food earmarked for the adopted child. The girl, who was only four years old, was also sent to fetch vegetables from the canteen every day, having to deal with adults pushing and shoving in the queue. She often fainted from hunger. She was neglected by her adoptive family and was found covered in lice a few months later, when she was taken back by her mother.[34]

Few families were willing to take on an extra burden in the famished countryside, prompting some people to abandon their children. The lucky ones were left behind in a city, some families making a great effort to break through the cordon fencing off the countryside. In Nanjing over 2,000 children were found abandoned in 1959, four times more than in the entire decade of communist rule up to the Great Leap Forward. Six out of ten were girls, and about a third were aged three or older; most were sick, a few blind or handicapped. Judging by the accents of those able to speak, many came from Anhui province, others from villages neighbouring Nanjing. Some of the families were interviewed by community workers. The most common rationale was the very logic of collectivisation, as some villagers gave official propaganda a twist by arguing that 'children belong to the state'. Utopian images of abundance beyond the village, of wealth and happiness ensconced behind city walls, were also important. A common folk notion in the countryside was that a child could 'enter town and enjoy a happy life', as it would be brought up in prosperity.

But more tragic stories lurked behind such rationalisations, for instance in the case of a thirteen-year-old boy called Shi Liuhong. He was taken on a trek across the mountains from his home village in Hujiang. Tired and hungry, he fell asleep by the side of the road, only to find that his mother had gone when he woke up. This was one of the most common ways of 'losing' a child. The verb 'lose' (*diu*) was often used as a euphemism for abandonment. As a thirteen-year-old girl recounted, her father had died three years earlier and there was no food in the village. Her mother had first 'lost' her blind brother, aged fourteen; then her younger brother and sister were 'lost' in the mountains, before she too was left behind.[35]

As the last example shows, some children were abandoned in pairs, perhaps because the parents hoped that they might stay together. On the streets of Nanjing a six-year-old was thus found crying for his mother and holding on to two younger toddlers. But other reasons also accounted for the abandonment of siblings. Some were left on the streets because women from the countryside – desperate for food and shelter – 'remarried' men in the city who did not welcome children.[36] Some had their date of birth scribbled on a piece of paper pinned to their clothes, others carried a written note in a pocket. In a few rare cases, desperate mothers took their children straight to the police station.[37]

There are no reliable statistics on the number of abandoned children, but in a city like Nanjing several thousand were found in a single year. In Wuhan, the capital of Hunan, four or five were picked up by the authorities each day by the summer of 1959.[38] In the province as a whole some 21,000 children were placed in state orphanages by the summer of 1961, although many more were never recorded by the authorities.[39]

But in most cases children stayed with their parents to the very end. Across the countryside, in countless villages, starving children with swollen bellies and pipe-stem limbs, their heavy heads wobbling on thin little necks, were left to die in peasant huts, by empty fields or along dusty roadsides. In some villages in Jinghai county, Hebei, children aged four to five were unable to walk. Those who could wore nothing but an unlined garment, shuffling barefoot through the snow in the winter.[40] Even in cities such as Shijiazhuang half of the babies died because their mothers had no milk.[41] In some cases, children were almost the only ones to die. In a small village in Qionghai county, Guangdong, forty-seven people, or one in ten, died in the winter of 1958–9: of these, forty-one were infants and children, six were elderly.[42]

Yet, against all odds, sometimes the children were the ones who survived. In Sichuan it was estimated that 0.3 to 0.5 per cent of the rural population were orphans – meaning roughly 180,000 to 200,000 children without parents. Many roamed the villages in ragged groups, unwashed and unkempt, surviving on their wits – which, most of the time, meant theft. Children on their own were easy prey, stripped of their meagre belongings – cups, shoes, blankets, clothes – by their guardians or neighbours. Discarded by acquaintances once they had robbed her of her every possession, Gao Yuhua, a girl aged eleven, slept on a hay bed and had a mere loincloth to cover herself. She stayed alive by crushing grains of millet which she ate raw, and was described by an investigation team as resembling a 'primitive child' from the Stone Age.[43] Xiang Qingping was adopted by a poor farmer in Fuling, but after the twelve-year-old had complained to neighbours that the man abused him and gave him mud to eat, his head was bashed in. Elsewhere in the county an orphan had his spine broken by angry villagers who caught him stealing from the fields.[44] When siblings survived it was not uncommon for them to turn on each other. Among many reported cases, Jiang Laosan, aged seven, was beaten and robbed by his brother aged sixteen, dying a few months after becoming an orphan.[45]

Some of the orphans showed extraordinary resilience, as the story of Zhao Xiaobai, a soft-spoken woman with sad eyes, shows. A few years before the Great Leap Forward her family left their native village in Henan to join a migration programme encouraging farmers to settle in Gansu province. Her father was made to break ice in the mountains but died of hunger in 1959. Her mother was too ill to work. One of the local cadres came to the house, banging on the door to announce that slackers would not be fed. Another local bully came at night, pestering her mother for sexual favours. In the end, exhausted, she seems to have given up. In the middle of a freezing night in January 1960, she got up and went to the toilet. Her daughter Zhao Xiaobai, aged eleven, woke up and asked her mother where she was going. Then she fell asleep again, but two hours later her mother was still in the toilet. 'I called out to her, but she did not answer. She just sat there, with her head towards one side, but she said nothing.'

Surrounded by strangers speaking an alien dialect, Zhao and her sister aged six ended up living with an uncle, who had also migrated to Gansu. 'He was reasonable towards me, because I was old enough to go out and work. But he was not nice to my sister. You know in Gansu, it was very cold, minus 20 Celsius. He asked my sister to go out looking for kindling in such freezing weather. How could she find any wood? One day, as it was freezing, she came home empty-handed. So he beat her on the head, and she bled pretty badly.' To protect her sister from her uncle's abuse, Zhao took the six-year-old with her as she went to work like an adult, digging canals and ploughing fields. Here too she was unsafe. 'Once, as I was working, I heard my little sister crying, and I saw somebody hurting her. Somebody was using sand balls to hit my sister, and she was surrounded by clumps of sand. Her eyes were covered in grit, and she just cried and cried.' Zhao found a couple who were planning to return to Henan. She sold everything they had and bought two tickets at ten yuan. Back in Henan, at last, they found her grandmother who took the two girls under her wing.

When asked how she had become the woman she is now, Zhao Xiaobai answered without hesitation: 'Through suffering.'[46]

Some children never found anybody willing to look after them and were placed in orphanages, where conditions – rather predictably – were appalling. Physical punishment was common, for instance causing a dozen to die at the hands of their guardians in one commune in Dianjiang county, Sichuan.[47] In Hubei orphans were sheltered in ramshackle buildings with leaking roofs and left to survive the winter without padded cotton clothes or blankets. Medical care was non-existent. Many thousands died of disease.[48]

Although infants died in disproportionate numbers, fewer of them were actually born during the famine. Demographic experts have relied on the published census figures of 1953, 1964 and 1982 to try to piece together the decline in births during the famine, but much more reliable figures are available from the archives, as in a command economy local authorities had to keep track of the population. In the Qujing region, Yunnan, where the famine appeared in 1958, births dropped from 106,000 in 1957 to 59,000 the following year. In Yunnan as a whole the number of births plummeted from 678,000 in 1957 to 450,000 in 1958.[49]

Another way to look at it is to find age-related statistics compiled after the famine. In Hunan, a province which was not among the worst-hit regions, a very clear gap appears among children aged three in 1964, that is born in 1961: there were some 600,000 fewer of them than six-year-olds, although they too must have suffered. On the other hand there were four times more children aged one, and four times more children under the age of one.[50] But none of these statistics recorded what must have been countless unreported cases of infants dying within weeks of being born: who had any incentive to count the deaths of newborns whose births had not even been recorded in the middle of starvation?

Women

Collectivisation, designed in part to liberate women from the shackles of patriarchy, made matters worse. Although work patterns varied hugely from one end of the country to the other, in most of the north women rarely worked in the fields before the Great Leap Forward. Even in the southern regions, it was often only the poor who joined the menfolk outdoors. Besides taking care of domestic work, women and even children usually engaged in other occupations, making handicrafts in their spare time to supplement the family's income. Entire villages sometimes specialised in producing a defined range of commodities for local markets, from paper umbrellas, cloth shoes and silk hats to rattan chairs, wicker creels and twig baskets, all from the safety of the household.[1] Even in more isolated villages, women by custom worked from home, weaving, spinning and embroidering for family and for cash.

As women who had never worked in the fields were mobilised in the rush to modernise, they were required to turn up every day at the sound of the bugle, and march off in teams to plough, sow, rake, weed and winnow. But despite full employment in communes, women were paid less than men, no matter how hard they toiled. The work-point system devised by the communes systematically devalued their contribution, since only strong men were able to reach the top of the scale. And as women joined the collective workforce, the state did very little to lighten the load at home, as there was no shortage of domestic tasks which still needed to be carried out, from mending clothes to raising children. Kindergartens, for instance, were supposed to help with babysitting, but, as we have seen, many were far from adequate, which meant that women often had to juggle childcare with full employment.[2] As family life was buffeted by constant campaigns, the exigencies of mobilisation took a heavy toll on women, exhausting many even before famine began to bite. In those villages drained of able-bodied men who joined the exodus to the city, women were left to look after relatives and dependants.

Most of all, women were vulnerable because in a regime which mercilessly traded food for work every weakness led to hunger. In the relentless drive to achieve ever higher targets, at the furnace, in the field or on the factory floor, menstruation was widely seen as a flaw. Menstrual taboos of popular religion, which feared the polluting potential of women during their periods, were swept aside seemingly overnight. Failure to come out to the field was punished, the most common form of retribution being a reduction of work points for each day of absence. Some male cadres abused their positions of power, humiliating those women who asked for sick leave. Xu Yingjie, party secretary of the Chengdong People's Commune in Hunan, forced those who requested a rest on the grounds of menstruation to drop their trousers and undergo a cursory inspection. Few were willing to undergo the humiliation, and many became ill as a result, several dying under the strain of labouring while suffering severe menstrual pain or gynaecological problems.[3] Expectant mothers were also compelled to work, often until the last stage of pregnancy, although they too were commonly penalised. In one district in Sichuan alone twenty-four women miscarried after being compelled to work in the fields. Chen Yuanming, who objected, was kicked between her legs by the cadre in charge and crippled for life.[4]

Where abusive cadres assumed power unopposed, punishment could go much further. In the same Hunan commune just mentioned, pregnant women who did not appear at work were made to undress in the middle of the winter and then forced to break ice.[5] In Qingyuan, Guangdong, hundreds of villagers at a time were made to work in the middle of the winter without cotton-padded clothing; no exceptions were made for pregnant women or those with small children, and people who protested were deprived of food.[6] In Panyu county, just outside Guangzhou, a cadre grabbed seven-months-pregnant Du Jinhao by her hair and forced her to the ground for not working sufficiently hard. He kept her pinned down and shouted abuse at her until she passed out; her husband cried with fear but was powerless to intervene. After she regained consciousness she staggered back home looking dazed, then sank to her knees, collapsed and died.[7] Some women were so desperate that they preferred to die: Liang Xianü, pregnant yet obliged to work in the winter, jumped to her death in a cold river.[8]

Exhausted and hungry, women became so weak that they stopped menstruating altogether. This was common everywhere, even in the cities, where women were given some medical care. In the Tianqiao district, to the south of Beijing, half of all female workers in a metallurgy factory suffered from lack of menstrual periods, vaginal infections or a prolapsed uterus. As the only available washroom was always occupied, some of the women went for months without ever washing. When combined with endless hours in a poorly ventilated environment, even political activists like Yuan Bianhua would spit blood and sometimes even lacked the strength to stand up on their own.[9] Other studies, conducted by the Women's Federation, made similar observations. In the Beijing Electron Tubes Plant, for instance, half of all 6,600 women had some form of gynaecological disorder. Wu Yufang, aged twenty-five, had arrived at the factory as a sturdy young girl in 1956 but in 1961 suffered from headaches, irregular menses, sleeplessness, irritability and lack of strength. Married for five years, she was still without children – a medical examination showed that she, like many of the other workers, had mercury poisoning.[10]

The physical decline among rural women was so extreme that many suffered from a prolapsed uterus, meaning that the womb, held in place inside the pelvis by muscles and ligaments, collapsed inside the vaginal canal. Even without overwork and lack of food, weakness can cause the uterus to sag or slip out of its normal position. This happens when women experience a difficult childbirth or suffer from a loss of oestrogen. But the term refers to a variety of different stages, from a drooping cervix to the uterus coming completely outside the vagina: the latter was the syndrome observed again and again by medical authorities. The statistics they provided – even if classified – could not possibly reflect the reality, and varied from 3 to 4 per cent of women in the countryside just outside Shanghai to one in every five working women in Hunan.[11] The real incidence must have been much higher, given that many women would have felt too ashamed to report the condition, many cadres would have been reluctant to report medical disorders associated with starvation, and too few trained doctors actually existed in the countryside to have even a rough idea of what was happening.

A prolapsed uterus was difficult to cure because the underlying causes – lack of food and lack of rest – were hard to remedy in times of famine. Even if they had money to pay the fees, many women simply did not have the time to leave their children and their work to visit a hospital, which were few and far between in the countryside. Many villagers also feared hospitals, and they resorted instead to local treatments. In Hubei, female healers used a variety of recipes, some handed down from generation to generation, to assist women suffering from gynaecological problems, heating and grinding ingredients into a powder that was smeared on to the vaginal walls and mixing medicinal herbs to cure menstrual disorders. Aunt Wang, as she was known in a village in Zhongxiang county, helped hundreds of women, her house often harbouring four or five patients being nursed back to health as her husband went foraging for leaves and roots in the forest.[12] But such traditional remedies were rarely tolerated under forced collectivisation, and in the absence of effective medical care most women simply had to bear their condition and labour on.

———

Women were vulnerable in other ways. Socially marginalised in what remained, after all, a tough, male-oriented world, they were prone to sexual abuse. Huge power was given to local cadres, while famine gradually eroded the moral fabric of society. As if this combination were not bad enough, many families were separated or broken up as menfolk joined the exodus, enrolled in the army or laboured on distant irrigation projects. As the layers of social protection surrounding women gradually crumbled, they were left almost entirely defenceless to confront the naked power of the local bully.

Rape spread like a contagion through a distressed moral landscape. A few examples will suffice. Two party secretaries of a commune in Wengcheng, north of Guangzhou, raped or coerced into sex thirty-four women in 1960.[13] In Hengshui county, Hebei, three party secretaries and a deputy county head were known to have sexually abused women routinely, one of them having had sex with several dozen.[14] Further north, a secretary of Gujiaying village raped twenty-seven women, and an investigation showed that he had 'taken liberties' with almost every unmarried woman in the village.[15] Li Dengmin, party secretary of Qumo, raped some twenty women, two being under age.[16] In Leiyang, Hunan, girls as young as eleven or twelve were sexually abused.[17] In Xiangtan, a cadre set up a 'special team' (*zhuanyedui*) of ten girls whom he sexually abused at whim.[18]

And even if women were not raped, they were subjected to sex-specific humiliations, as collectivisation swept aside the customary moral values of sexual restraint and bodily propriety. China was undergoing a revolution, turning upside down moral codes of behaviour passed down from generation to generation, which led to perversions that would have been unthinkable before 1949. In a factory in Wugang county, Hunan, local bosses forced women to work naked. On a single day in November 1958 more than 300 went about their jobs in the nude. Those who refused were tied up. A competitive system was even devised by which the women most eager to strip were granted a reward, the top gift consisting of cash to the value of fifty yuan, more or less equivalent to a month's salary. While some women may have embraced the opportunity to advance their careers, many were no doubt repelled, although nobody dared to speak their mind. But a few did write. After some of the women fell ill – Hunan can be bitterly cold during the winter – a series of anonymous letters were sent to Mao Zedong. Whether he actually read these letters we do not know, but someone highly placed in Beijing phoned the provincial committee in Changsha and demanded an inquiry. The factory leaders, it came to light in the course of an investigation, had apparently 'encouraged' the women to take off their clothes in a 'spirit of emulation' which aimed to 'break feudal taboos'.[19] Seemingly anything could be justified in the name of emancipation.

Equally crude and humiliating were the nude parades, which happened across the country: women, occasionally men, were made to march through the village entirely naked. In Suichang county, Zhejiang, men and women accused of larceny were stripped naked and paraded. Zhou Moying, a grandmother aged sixty, was forced to undress and then lead the procession by beating a gong – despite the pleas for pardon from fellow villagers.[20] Some of the abused women felt too ashamed to return to their homes. Twenty-four-year-old Zhu Renjiao, stripped and paraded for petty theft, 'felt too ashamed to face people' and asked to be moved to another village. She killed herself when her request was turned down.[21] In another small village in Guangdong, the militia stripped two young women and tied them to a tree, using a flashlight to explore one of the girl's private parts, and drawing a large turtle – symbol of the male organ – on the other woman's body. Both committed suicide.[22]

Less often mentioned in the archives or in interviews, but part of a distinct social trend in any famine, was the trade in sex. Women provided favours for almost anything, from a morsel of food and a better job to a regular but illicit relationship with a man who could offer some sense of security. Most of these transactions went on undetected, but there was also a whole underworld of prostitution which the authorities tried to monitor. One correctional facility in Chengdu kept well over a hundred prostitutes and delinquent female children. More than a dozen were sex workers who had been 're-educated' after the communist victory in 1949, but refused to reform themselves. Wang Qingzhi, who went by the nickname of 'Old Mother', in turn introduced other women to the trade. Some of the new sex workers formed bands with male thieves and roamed the country, travelling to Xi'an, Beijing and Tianjin to make a living. A few worked independently, one or two even regularly handing over money to their parents – who turned a blind eye to the source of the income.[23]

Village women also offered their bodies for food after escaping to the city, as we have already seen. The logical extension of this trade in sex was bigamy, as country girls lied about their age or their marital status in order to secure a husband in town. Some were only fifteen or sixteen, well below the legal age of marriage. Others were already married but committed bigamy to survive. A few were prepared to abandon their children from a previous marriage, but not all of them deserted their families: some returned home only a few days after the wedding had taken place.[24]

Trade in sex flimsily disguised by the pretence of marriage was even more common in the countryside. In one closely studied Hebei village the number of weddings increased seven-fold in 1960, the worst year of the famine. Women poured into the village from distressed areas, marrying for goods, clothes or food for relatives. Some were as young as sixteen, others left soon after the wedding. A few of the women introduced other family members to the groom, resulting in half a dozen cases of bigamy.[25]

And then there was trafficking in women. From Inner Mongolia, for instance, teams spread out over the country, hauling back hundreds of women every month. Most came from famished Gansu, a few from Shandong. Some were mere children, others were widows, although married women were also trafficked. The victims ranged across all social categories, including students, teachers and even cadres. Few came voluntarily, and some were traded several times. Forty-five women were sold to a mere six villages in less than half a year.[26]

───────────

Always marginalised, sometimes humiliated, invariably exhausted and often abandoned by the men, women, in the end, were the ones who had to make the most heart-rending decision, namely how the meagre food ration should be divided. This was not so at the onset of famine, as men were normally in charge and demanded to be fed first. In the same way that women were systematically given fewer work points than men under collectivisation, a patriarchal society expected that priority be given to the feeding of all male members of the household. As men provided, women abided, a cultural imperative that dictated that even in normal times women were given a smaller share of the food. And as famine took over, women were deliberately neglected in the interests of male survival, a choice that was justified on the grounds that the entire family ultimately depended on the ability of men to go out and find food. But once the men were gone, women had to endure the agony of their starving children without being able to help. Not all could live with the constant crying and pleading for food by their children, made so much more unbearable by the stark choices they had to make about the distribution of scarce resources. Liu Xiliu, deprived of food for six days as punishment for being too sick to work, finally succumbed to the pangs of hunger and devoured the ration allocated to her child, who

soon started crying of misery. Unable to suffer the torment she swal-
lowed caustic soda to put an end to her life.[27]

There is no doubt that the emotional distress and physical pain – to say
nothing of the self-abasement and humiliation many had to endure – were
enormous, and much of this was a direct consequence of sex discrimi-
nation. But historians have shown that in many other poor, patriarchal
societies women did not die in much greater numbers than men, however
problematic recorded rates of mortality may be. In the Bengal famine, male
mortality even exceeded that of females, leading the historian Michelle
McAlpin to write that 'females may be better able than males to withstand
the trials of a period of famine'.[28] As we have seen in previous chapters,
women excelled at devising everyday strategies of survival, from foraging
in the forest and preparing substitute foodstuffs to trading on the black
market. In the end, the greatest victims of the famine were the young and
the elderly.

The Elderly

Life in the countryside has always been tough in China, and strict observance of traditional notions of filial piety would simply have been beyond the reach of all but the wealthiest households before the communist takeover. Proverbs suggested the limits of respect for the elderly in traditional society: 'With nine sons and twenty-three grandchildren, a man may still have to dig a grave for himself.'[1] Even if children were the family pension, the elderly continued to rely for the most part on their own work to eke out a frugal life. And while some prestige may have been associated with old age, in a society that heavily emphasised earning power many people must have felt a decline in respect when moving into old age. As elsewhere, the elderly feared loneliness, impoverishment and abandonment, in particular those who were more vulnerable than others – the ones without family. But in most cases, before 1949, they could count on a measure of care and dignity: their mere survival commanded respect.

Yet by the time of the Cultural Revolution a completely different set of values seemed to dominate, as young students tortured their teachers and Red Guards attacked elderly people. When did the moral universe turn upside down? While the party was steeped in a culture of violence, fostered by decades of ruthless warfare and ceaseless purges, the real watershed was the Great Leap Forward. As villagers in Macheng complained, the people's communes left children without their mothers, women without their husbands, and the elderly without relatives:[2] these three family bonds were destroyed as the state was substituted for the family. As if this were not bad enough, collectivisation was followed by the agony of famine. As hunger stalked an already distressed social landscape, family cohesion unravelled further; starvation tested every tie to the limit.

The prospects for the elderly without children were particularly grim, so much so that many traditionally tried to join monasteries or nunneries, while others established fictitious ties of kinship with adopted children. These age-old customs were swept away with collectivisation. In the summer of 1958 retirement homes for the childless elderly appeared throughout the villages of rural China; at the peak of the Great Leap Forward over 100,000 of them were reportedly established.[3]

Abuse was rife. Some of the elderly were beaten, even those with only a few meagre possessions were robbed, and others were put on a slow starvation diet. In Tongzhou, just outside Beijing, the head of the retirement home systematically stole food and clothes earmarked for the elderly, condemning the inmates to a winter without heating or cotton-padded jackets. Most passed away as soon as frost appeared, although their bodies were not buried for a week.[4] Further south, in Qionghai county, Guangdong, the entire village was put to work in the absence of able-bodied men, who were all conscripted on a distant irrigation project. The elderly slaved day and night, a seventy-year-old going for ten days without any sleep at all. A tenth of the village died in the winter of 1958–9, the majority of them children and those elderly people kept in retirement homes.[5] In Chongqing county, Sichuan, the director of one home made the residents work nine hours a day followed by two hours of study in the evening. In another case the elderly were forced to work throughout the night, according to the demands of 'militarisation'. Slackers were tied up and beaten or deprived of food. In Hunan too they were routinely tied up and beaten.[6] In Chengdu, in the winter, the inmates of one retirement home slept on a muddy floor: they had no blankets, no cotton-padded clothes, no cotton hats and no shoes.[7] In Hengyang, Hunan, the medicine, eggs and meat reserved for the elderly went to the cadres in charge of the home. As the cook succinctly put it, 'What point is there in feeding you? If we feed the pigs at least we will get some meat!' In the province as a whole, by the end of the famine a mere 1,058 had managed to survive in the remaining seven homes.[8]

Many of the homes collapsed almost as soon as they had appeared, besieged by the same systemic problems of funding and corruption which undermined kindergartens. The childless elderly who were abandoned to the care of collective entities had to scramble for survival by the winter of 1958–9. But life outside the retirement home was no better. Just as children were treated like adults, the elderly too had to prove their worth to the collective, as rations in the canteen were dished out against work points. Hunger was never simply a matter of lack of resources, but rather of their distribution: confronted with shortages in both labour and food, local cadres all too often decided to exchange the one for the other, in effect creating a regime in which those unable to perform at full capacity were being slowly starved to death. The elderly, in short, were dispensable. And just as children were harshly chastised even for small misdemeanours, so the elderly were subjected to an exacting regime of discipline and punishment, in which the family often shared. In Liuyang county, Hunan, a seventy-eight-year-old who complained about working in the mountains was detained and his daughter-in-law ordered to hit him. After she had refused she was beaten bloody. Then she was ordered to spit on the old man, who had also been beaten to a pulp: he died shortly afterwards.[9]

Inside the family the fortunes of the elderly depended on the goodwill of their children. All sorts of quarrels developed in times of famine, but new bonds also developed. Jiang Guihua remembered that her mother did not get on well with her blind grandmother. The grandfather was a cripple. Both were dependent on others for food but also for help in getting dressed and using the toilet. Jiang Guihua was the one to provide help, as her mother often lost her temper and tried to cut their food rations. But there was little she could do, and after a while her grandparents died of eating soil. They were buried without a coffin, wrapped in some straw and lowered into a shallow pit.[10]

In the end, when everybody left the village in a desperate search for food, only the elderly and the handicapped stayed behind, often unable to walk. In Dangyang, Hubei, seven people were all that remained of a once lively and noisy village, four being elderly, two blind and one handicapped. They ate leaves from the trees.[11]

PART SIX

WAYS OF DYING

31

Accidents

Poor safety was endemic to the command economy, despite detailed labour legislation and meticulous rules on every aspect of industrial work, from the provision of protective clothing to the standards of lighting. An extensive network of labour inspectors – from the Federation of Trade Unions, the Women's Federation and the Communist Youth League, as well as from the Ministry of Health and the Ministry of Labour – periodically toured workshops, monitored health hazards and looked into the living standards of workers. They operated under huge political pressure and often preferred to turn a blind eye to widespread abuse, but they could file hard-hitting reports. Despite this vast apparatus, factory managers and team leaders, regardless of their personal sympathies for their workers, remained obsessed with increased output.

On the ground both zealots and dawdlers set the tone. Party activists cut corners, reduced standards, ignored safety and abused the workforce as well as every piece of equipment in their relentless quest to meet higher production targets. On the factory floor and in the fields, ordinary people tried to counter the blow of each new production drive with the force of collective inertia. But widespread apathy and negligence, while easing the pressure from above, also had a corrosive effect on safety in the workplace, as people abdicated responsibility for anything that did not concern them directly. And as collectivisation produced growing shortages of food, clothes and fuel, much riskier techniques of self-help appeared, from lighting a stove in a thatched hut to stealing safety equipment, leading in turn to more accidents. Worker fatigue only made matters worse, as people fell asleep by the furnace or at the wheel.

To this should be added a simple if grisly calculation: failure to fulfil a target could cost a manager his career, while violation of labour safety attracted a mere slap on the wrist. Life was cheap, costing a lot less than installing safety equipment or enforcing labour legislation. After all, what were a few deaths in the battle for a better future? As we have seen, foreign minister Chen Yi, comparing the Great Leap Forward to a battlefield, was adamant that a few industrial accidents were not going to hold back the revolution: 'it's nothing!' he said with a shrug.[1]

Take the case of fire. We have noted how the Ministry of Public Security estimated that some 7,000 fires destroyed 100 million yuan in property in 1958, the year of the Great Leap Forward. One reason for the extent of the damage was a lack of firefighting equipment. Most of the fire hoses, pumps, extinguishers, sprinklers and other tools had been imported, but foreign purchases were suspended in a drive towards local self-sufficiency. By the end of 1958, however, all but seven out of the eighty national factories making the equipment had closed down. In some cases firefighters had to stand by empty-handed and watch the flames spread, powerless to intervene.[2]

The situation did not improve over the following years. Workers in overcrowded shacks cobbled together from mud, bamboo and straw huddled around improvised fires, which sometimes got out of control. Hundreds of fires raged through Nanjing in a single month in 1959.[3] Accidents also happened when people sneaked away from the canteen to cook their own meals on the sly. When a young girl lit a fire in dry weather, the wind carried a spark and set fire to her hut, which erupted into a blaze destroying lives and property.[4] When a kerosene lamp was kicked over during engineering work at Jingmen, Hubei, an inferno claimed sixty lives.[5] Villagers recruited to work on large irrigation sites lived in hastily erected straw huts, which regularly went up in flames as exhausted workers bumped into lamps or furtively lit a cigarette.[6] Few reliable statistics exist about actual death rates, but in Jiangxi a mere twenty-four incidents burned or asphyxiated 139 people in a single month.[7] In Hunan about fifty people died each month; the Public Security Bureau listed some ten fires a day in the first half of 1959.[8]

Industrial accidents soared, as safety was considered a 'rightist conservative' concern. In Guizhou the provincial party committee estimated that the number of accidental deaths had multiplied by a factor of seventeen in early 1959 compared to a year earlier.[9] The exact number of casualties was unknown, as few inspectors wanted to pour cold water on the Great Leap Forward with talk of death, while enterprises routinely concealed accidents. Li Rui, one of Mao's secretaries purged in the wake of the Lushan plenum, later estimated the total of fatal industrial mishaps in 1958 at 50,000.[10] According to the Ministry of Labour, some 13,000 workers died in the first eight months of 1960, equivalent to over fifty deaths each day. Although this was probably only a fraction of the actual accidents, the report highlighted some of the problems which beset the mining and steel industries. In the Tangshan Iron Plant more than forty powerful blast furnaces were jammed together in a square kilometre, but no protective fences were erected around the cooling basins. Workers slipped and fell into the boiling sludge. In coal mines across the country, inadequate ventilation allowed asphyxiant and highly inflammable gases to accumulate. Coal-gas explosions ripped through the mines, sometimes ignited by the sparks coming from faulty electrical equipment. Flooding was another mining hazard which claimed numerous lives, while badly maintained mine stopes collapsed and buried the miners alive.[11] In March 1962, a blast tore through the Badaojiang mine, Tonghua county, Jilin, claiming seventy-seven lives, although the worst case was probably in the Laobaitong mine in Datong, where 677 miners died on 9 May 1960.[12]

But explosions also happened routinely in smaller concerns, although such cases were no doubt excluded from the statistics gathered by the Ministry of Labour. In Hunan a critical report noted how mining accidents had increased every quarter since the launch of the Great Leap Forward. By early 1959 an average of two miners every day were killed in an accident somewhere in the province.[13] In the Guantang mine in Nanjing – opened during the Great Leap Forward – three heavy detonations occurred in a fortnight, among other accidents described as 'avoidable'. Lamps fell down shafts, safety belts were discarded and inexperienced workers were sent down into the mines without proper training, sometimes barefoot. Shafts and tunnels were dug in a manner described a few years later as 'chaotic', in utter disregard of local geology.[14]

The coal mines claimed more lives than any other industry, but everywhere death was on the increase. Dirt and clutter encumbered the workshops, uncollected litter and abandoned parts were strewn about passageways, while a chronic lack of lighting, heating and ventilation turned the factory floor into an intrinsically hazardous environment. Most workers did not even have a uniform, let alone protective clothing. In Nanjing lethal blasts occurred every month from 1958 onwards, as concerns over the safety of workers were discarded in the pursuit of higher targets.[15] Many of the factories were hastily set up and badly conceived during the Great Leap Forward: in several cases entire roofs caved in on the workers.[16]

The situation was not much better when it came to public transportation. Inexperienced drivers joined an expanding fleet; weight and speed limits were flouted if not denounced as rightist; while trucks, trains and boats were poorly maintained and driven beyond endurance, often breaking down only to be patched back together with substandard equipment and scavenged pieces. Figures, again, are missing, but the extent of the problem is indicated by a summary report from Hunan. On the roads and rivers criss-crossing the province, more than 4,000 accidents were reported in 1958, claiming 572 lives. In one case a blind man and his handicapped colleague operated a ferry.[17] In the neighbouring province of Hubei, boats often navigated in the dark, as lamps and lighting were missing. On Macang Lake, Wuhan, an overloaded passenger ship without any safety equipment caught fire, and twenty passengers drowned in August 1960. Similar accidents happened throughout Hubei.[18] In Tianshui, Gansu, more than a hundred people, most of them students, died in two separate incidents in less than a month in the winter of 1961–2. The ferries across the Wei River were three times over the passenger limit.[19] Buses were just as congested. On those in Guangzhou, people were crammed 'like pigs', and breakdowns were so common that crowds of waiting passengers slept for days on end outside the station. Fatal accidents were common.[20]

Train disasters were less frequent, but as famine worsened railway wagons too became conveyors of death. In January 1961 passengers were marooned in the middle of the frozen countryside of Gansu, suffering delays of up to thirty hours as engines broke down or ran out of fuel. No food or water was provided on board, urine and excrement spread through the carriages, and the corpses of starved travellers rapidly accumulated. As the railway system clogged up, unruly crowds were also left stranded at railway stations. In Lanzhou, up to 10,000 people were put up in temporary accommodation because of the huge delays. The station itself was packed with thousands of waiting travellers without adequate provisions. Several died each day.[21]

For each accidental death several people barely escaped with their lives. But in the midst of the famine, even a minor injury could spell doom. Workers rarely received compensation for an industrial accident, and were often ruined by medical expenses or sacked from their jobs. In the countryside food could be used as a weapon by rapacious cadres. Absence from work, even for a medical reason, was met with a reduced food ration. Infections, malnutrition or partial invalidity reinforced each other, putting sick people at a disadvantage in the struggle for survival and all too often dragging them down in a vicious circle of want.

32

Disease

Not all people who die in times of famine die of hunger. Common illnesses such as diarrhoea, dysentery, fever and typhus claim many lives first. The precise impact of each disease in China at this time is extremely difficult to ascertain, not only because of the size of the country and the diversity of conditions on the ground, but also because some of the most problematic archives happen to belong to the health services. In a climate of fear in which millions of party members were purged or labelled as rightists, few subjects could be more sensitive than that of disease and death. When malnourishment reached the inner recesses of power in Zhongnanhai and Li Zhisui told the Chairman that hepatitis and oedema were everywhere, Mao quipped: 'You doctors are just upsetting people by talking about disease. You're making it difficult for everybody. I just don't believe you.'[1]

Of course party officials continued to produce damning reports on all sorts of topics throughout the Great Leap Forward, often at great personal risk, but reliable surveys of medical conditions are hard to find. First the health services were battered by collectivisation, then they were overwhelmed by famine victims, and finally they simply collapsed. Hospitals, even in major cities, were stripped of resources, and by 1960 doctors and nurses were fighting for their own survival. In Nanjing, for instance, up to two-thirds of all nurses and doctors were sick. They were ill because the hospitals had become catalysts in the spread of disease and death. As one report indicated, flies and other vermin could 'frequently' be found in the food, causing diarrhoea among staff and patients. Even in top hospitals reserved for party members the heating had broken down, while staff wore dirty patches and rags stitched together. Few uniforms were ever laundered.[2] In Wuhan severe shortages were compounded by criminal neglect, as most doctors and nurses in the People's Hospitals seemed to lack what a report called a 'sense of responsibility'. They turned a profit by diluting medicine with water. They stole from patients. They beat the sick. Male doctors abused female patients. Hospital finances were a shambles.[3]

In these conditions, it does not come as a surprise that few if any medical experts were inclined to spend time in famished villages armed with scalpels and test tubes, trying to establish the determinants of mortality. The countryside, where most of the people died, was cut adrift. When the extent of the famine was finally recognised in the winter of 1960–1, emergency centres were set up in abandoned cow sheds or disused farms to help the starving. In Rongxian county, Sichuan, those brought in were dumped on a thin layer of straw directly on the floor. There were no blankets despite the bitter cold. The stench was overwhelming. Pitiful moans of anguish echoed through the air. Some were left without water for days on end – not to mention food or medicine. In Tongliang the living shared beds with the dead; nobody seemed to care.[4] In Guanxian things sometimes worked out the other way around: the living were locked up with the dead, as those in charge could not wait for some people to die. Yan Xishan, a mechanical worker suffering from epilepsy, was tied up and left to die in the morgue. Rats had already eaten the eyes and the noses of six cadavers in the room.[5]

———

One of the most striking features of the famine is the low incidence of epidemics. Typhus, also called gaol fever, hospital fever or famine fever, was mentioned, but did not seem to kill in large quantities. Transmitted in the faeces of lice or fleas, it appeared in crowded, unsanitary conditions, and was associated with famine, war and cold weather. It was common in detention centres for migrants fleeing the countryside, even in cities such as Beijing and Shanghai.[6] Some 10–15 per cent of victims could succumb to typhus, typhoid and relapsing fever in times of famine, but this may not have been the case in China. Could the widespread use of DDT, efficient in pest control, have helped? This is not likely, given that other insects survived the onslaught of the country's war against nature. As we have seen, locusts actually thrived in a distressed landscape, as did other pests. The rat population, which carried the flea, was culled by the campaigns of eradication launched at the beginning of the Great Leap Forward. But rats breed ferociously fast and are not fussy feeders.

A more convincing reason why typhus, with its rash and high fever ending in delirium, may not have been widespread is that epidemics were rapidly isolated. Here was a military regime which openly denied the existence of famine yet pounced on suspected outbreaks of infectious diseases. This happened, for instance, in the case of cholera, which appeared in Guangdong in the summer of 1961. The epidemic started in early June when several fishermen fell ill after eating contaminated seafood. Within a matter of weeks thousands more were infected, and soon well over a hundred people were dying of the disease. The local authorities used the army to impose a cordon sanitaire around the affected region. While the quarantine could not prevent cholera from spreading as far as Jiangmen and Zhongshan – panic even broke out in Yangjiang – the overall number of casualties remained low.[7] Plague, too, spread to an area the size of a province in March 1960 but seems to have been contained.[8]

But other major epidemics that historians have come to associate with famine are also noticeable for their absence from the archives. There were higher incidences of smallpox, dysentery and cholera, but there is little archival evidence, so far, of millions being swept away by major epidemics. And the official gazetteers published decades after the famine by local party committees do not mention them frequently either. On the contrary, where disease is mentioned the set sentence is invariably that 'deaths by oedema caused by inadequate nutrition were high'.[9]

The picture which emerges from the record is that of a country in the grip of a whole variety of diseases, rather than suffering from the impact of two or three epidemics historically associated with famine alone. And this wide-ranging increase was as much due to the destructive effects of collectivisation on virtually every aspect of daily life, from crowded kindergartens, filthy canteens and hazardous workshops to under-equipped, overcrowded and understaffed hospitals, as it was a consequence of widespread starvation per se. In Hunan some 7,500 children died of measles in 1958, twice as many as in the previous year, as families were forced to leave their offspring in congested kindergartens. Cases of polio were fifteen times higher in 1959 than in 1958. The incidence of meningitis doubled, attributable, again, to disastrous conditions in boarding kinder-gartens.[10] Snippets of information from other regions confirm this trend. Thousands of cases of meningitis, for instance, also appeared in Nanjing in the winter of 1958–9, claiming 140 lives.[11] The rate of diphtheria also increased hugely, causing seven times more deaths in Nanjing in 1959 than in the previous year.[12]

Hepatitis soared, but tended to affect privileged city residents rather than the impoverished masses in the countryside. In the cities of Hubei one in five suffered from the disease in 1961. In Wuhan alone some 270,000 out of 900,000 people tested positive.[13] In Shanghai too the number of infections was high enough to prompt some state enterprises to request special medical facilities to treat the illness.[14]

Malaria was endemic. In the summer of 1960 up to a quarter of all villagers in parts of Wuxi suffered from the disease.[15] Snail fever, or schis-tosomiasis, caused by a parasitic worm that attacks the blood and liver, was prevalent. There were thousands of cases in many a county in Hubei, where people came into contact with freshwater snails when wading bare-foot through irrigated rice fields or when they went fishing. In Hanyang, hungry factory workers descended upon the many lakes surrounding the city to cut barley in the summer of 1961. Three thousand people were infected, a dozen died.[16] Hookworm, which sucks blood so voraciously that it leads to anaemia in the host, was common, even though reliable statistics remain elusive. But the problem was serious enough for the health authorities in Hunan to set a target of curing 3 million infected people in 1960 – in a mere eight counties.[17]

Everywhere the effects of collectivisation led to higher rates of illness. We have seen how people died from the heat of the backyard furnaces during the iron and steel campaign in 1958, but in the following years heatstroke continued to claim lives. Malnourished and exhausted workers were exposed to high temperatures all day long, and in Nanjing dozens of cases of heatstroke, several fatal, occurred in just two days in the summer of 1959.[18] In Hubei even simple straw hats were lacking, but cultivators were compelled to work at noon in the blazing sun. Thousands suffered from the heat, some thirty cases being fatal.[19]

Even leprosy was on the increase. Caused by a bacterium that leaves permanent damage to the skin, nerves, limbs and eyes, it spread because of inadequate care, contaminated water and insufficient diet. Hospitals were creaking under the workload, turning away leprosy patients. In Nanjing some 250 cases were hospitalised, but lack of resources meant that they could not be segregated from other patients.[20] Well over 2,000 lepers were known to exist in Wuhan, but a severe shortage of hospital beds condemned them to roam the city, scavenging for food.[21] Lepers in the countryside could be less fortunate. In Qigong commune, Guangdong, a sixteen-year-old boy and an adult, both suffering from leprosy, were escorted up into the mountains and shot in the back of the head.[22]

Mental illness, however difficult to define, was widespread, no doubt because the incessant depredations of the state combined with widespread loss, pain and grief to drive famished people to insanity. Few meaningful studies were produced, but one Huazhou commune in Guangdong claimed that more than 500 villagers suffered from mental illness in 1959.[23] In one curious case of mass hysteria, a third of some 600 students in a middle school in Rui'an county, Zhejiang, started crying and laughing without apparent reason in May 1960.[24] Similar reports came from Sichuan, where hundreds of villagers in several counties went berserk, talking gibberish and bursting out in convulsive laughter.[25] One estimate placed the national rate of mental illness at one per thousand, but as the case of Huazhou shows many more people must have been unable to cope with the sheer violence of collectivisation and the horror of famine (that much is clear from very high rates of suicide, as we shall see in the next chapter). In any event, few were ever cared for, as the medical authorities had other priorities. In Wuhan, for instance, some 2,000 known cases had no access to specialist care, as a mere thirty beds were available for psychotic cases in the entire city.[26]

Even when they were badly treated, the mad had one advantage: like the court jester, they got away with telling the truth. As one survivor from the Xinyang region remembers, only one man dared to mention the famine in his village, walking around all day in a craze, repeating to all and sundry a popular jingle: 'man eats man, dog eat dog, even rats are so hungry that they nibble away at stones'. Nobody ever bothered him.[27]

———

Major epidemics usually associated with famine did not afflict the countryside in China. Instead the destructive effects of collectivisation increased
a whole range of illnesses, including poisoning, as people took to famine
foods. Some could be quite nutritious – edible kelp eaten in Ireland during
the potato famine of 1846–8, or tulip bulbs in the Netherlands during the
hunger winter of 1944–5 – but many led to digestive diseases.

Even before people started scrounging for edible roots and wild herbs,
digestive problems could appear, caused by severe imbalances in diet.
Urban residents were sometimes given a much higher proportion of pick-
les, salted vegetables and fermented bean curd as substitutes for fresh
greens. In Nanjing, for instance, many factory workers had a salt intake
of thirty to fifty grams a day, almost ten times the amount that would
be recommended today. They added soy sauce to hot water to break a
monotonous diet. In one case a man was found to have ingested some
five litres of soy sauce in less than a month.[28] But large amounts of leafy
vegetables without sufficient carbohydrates also caused ill-health. When
grain rations ran out by the end of the month and hungry people resorted
to fresh produce instead, their skin would sometimes turn purple and they
died, victims of phosphite poisoning. Dozens of fatal cases were reported
in the countryside around Shanghai in 1961.[29]

Poor hygiene in the food industry caused diarrhoea outbreaks that
claimed the weak and vulnerable. The chaos sown by collectivisation was
felt at every level of the food-supply chain, as the state took command of
production, storage, processing, distribution and catering. Food became
just another output figure to be massaged, twisted and faked by factory
bosses, while apathy, neglect and sabotage were common among workers. In Wuhan food poisoning was frequent in the summer of 1959,
with hundreds of incidents being recorded every couple of days. Heat in
the sweltering summer played a part, but a detailed investigation of six
food producers identified widespread neglect as the main culprit. Flies
were everywhere: one zealous inspector counted about twenty insects per
square metre. Jugs and vats destined for the market had broken seals, their
contents wriggling with worms. In one factory maggots were found in 40
tonnes of jam and maltose. Rotten eggs made their way into cakes and
candies. There was no water on many of the premises, so workers did not

wash their hands; some urinated on the floor. Once the foodstuffs reached the market, they rotted away in humid weather.[30]

A further problem was that many of the ingredients no longer came from the suburbs but were shipped over long distances instead. A batch of carrots from Zhejiang province, for instance, had rotted during transportation to Wuhan. And then the human and material tools for handling food were grossly inadequate. The pedlars who previously reached every corner of the market with fresh produce had been absorbed into a lumbering collective, while a sixth of all vegetables rotted in the streets simply because there were not enough bamboo baskets to distribute them.[31]

In the canteens the situation was no better. Flies were found in the food, while even basic utensils were missing. In one case 300 workers had to share thirty pairs of chopsticks during breakfast, which were rapidly rinsed in a washbasin filled with dirty water. Restaurants offered no escape from the cycle of neglect. The kitchens were described as chaotic, governed by flies rather than by people. When the flies were swatted they dropped into the food. In one eating place the vegetables were served covered in dirt. Insects were found in the vinegar and soy sauce containers.[32]

These examples are all from the cities – where people were relatively privileged in comparison to the abysmal conditions in the countryside. Since all the food was concentrated in large canteens, entire villages were affected by outbreaks of diarrhoea or food poisoning. In Jintang county, Sichuan, the thin gruel served to the 200 farmers in one canteen contained dozens of maggots. The reason was that the well used by the canteen was adjacent to a toilet, and drainage was poorly divided, in particular after heavy rain. Those who refused to eat the gruel went without any food for three days. The few who managed to down the concoction suffered from severe stomach pain. Dozens were taken ill. Ten died.[33] Four vats with human excrement and urine, their contents spilling on to the floor, were found in a kitchen in Pengxian county. The water used to wash the food and dishes came from a stagnant pond by the doorstep. A quarter of the villagers were sick. Flies lorded it over people.[34] In Jinyang, also in Sichuan, 'chicken excrement is everywhere, human faeces have piled up, ditches are blocked and the stench is overwhelming': local people referred to the canteen as 'shit alley'.[35] Even when there was food, canteens could run out of fuel or water. In Chengdu, where several branches of the Yangzi merged, some of the cooks had to travel half a mile to find water, and the grain was sometimes served raw.[36] But in many cases, of course, the canteens did not operate at all. After they had run out of food and fuel, the doors were closed and villagers had to fend for themselves.

Collectivisation was chequered with accidents, as we have seen in the last chapter. People were not only given contaminated products or tainted food, they also fell victim to poisoning accidents. In less than a month in 1960 some 134 fatal cases were reported to the Ministry of Hygiene, although this was a pale reflection of the reality on the ground. Pesticides were sometimes stored in canteens and granaries, while the tools used to prepare food or handle chemicals were not always kept apart. In Baodi county, Hebei, a roller contaminated with pesticides was used to mill the grain, and over a hundred villagers were poisoned. Nothing was done, the flour was sold a few days later, and another 150 people fell ill. In Wenshui, Shanxi, a pot used for poison found its way into the kitchen of a kindergarten, where more than thirty children ended up with severe intestinal pains. In Hubei fertiliser balls were mistaken for bean cakes. A thousand people fell ill, and thirty-eight died.[37]

As food ran out, the government started promoting new food technologies and substitute foods. Most of these were quite harmless. The 'double-steam method', heralded as a 'great revolution in cooking technology', enjoined cooks to steam the rice twice, adding water each time to bulk up the food.[38] Some of the substitute foods consisted merely of ground corncobs, corn stalks or the chaff from soybeans and other grains. But the government also introduced new ersatz foods. Chlorella was heralded in the early 1950s by food experts around the world as a miracle form of algae that could convert twenty times more solar energy into protein than other plants. But the plankton soup that promised to pull millions out of hunger turned out to be impossible to produce and so vile to the palate that the craze eventually subsided. In China the watery slime was elevated to the status of miracle food during the famine. It could be cultivated and skimmed from swampy ponds, but more often than not it was grown in vats of human urine, the green stuff being scooped out, washed and cooked with rice.[39] It probably contributed very little in terms of nutrition. Scientists discovered in the 1960s that the nutrients were encased in tough cell walls that were impossible for human digestion to break down.[40]

Prisoners were used as guinea pigs. Besides the green plankton, which sickened the inmates, they were also fed sawdust and wood pulp. Bao Ruowang – also known as Jean Pasqualini, the author of a memoir about life in a Chinese labour camp – remembered how brown sheets of the stuff were ground into paper pulp and mixed with flour. Mass constipation followed, killing the weaker prisoners.[41] But even in the cities the spread of substitute foods caused obstruction of the bowels or rupture of the sphincter. Workers at the Liangma factory in Beijing had to prise out their faeces by hand.[42]

Villagers scoured the forest for plants, berries and nuts. They combed the hills for edible roots and wild grasses. In desperation, they scavenged for carrion, rummaged through rubbish, scraped the bark off trees and in the end turned to mud to fill their stomachs. Even in Beijing foreigners witnessed people knocking off the leaves of acacia trees with sticks, which were then collected in bags and turned into soup.[43] Yan Shifu, a wiry man with a broad grin, was a young boy aged ten when the Great Leap Forward unfolded in Sichuan. He now works as a chef, and has a good memory for food. He recalls how ramie leaves were finely chopped and turned into pancakes, rape stalks were cooked into a thick stew, while mustard leaves were boiled. Pea stalks were milled, sieved and turned into small pancakes. Banana stalks were peeled and eaten raw, as if they were sugarcane. Radish was pickled and rare enough to be seen as a treat. Insects were popped live into the mouth, but worms and toads were grilled. Despite his family's ingenuity, his father and his younger sister died of starvation.[44]

Some of the grasses, mushrooms and roots foraged by villagers were toxic. Few people actually knew what they were eating, as children were often the ones in charge of slipping out at night and foraging for wild herbs. 'In those days,' one survivor reminisced, 'it was not possible to go out to look for known herbal remedies. We ate everything. We ate any plant that was green. We did not care, as long as we knew that the plant was not poisonous. We ate almost anything.'[45] But accidents were common. In Hebei about a hundred deaths caused by contaminated food, diseased animals and toxic roots and herbs were reported each month.[46] Cassava, a starchy tuber that could be milled into tapioca, is an excellent source of carbohydrates, but the leaves are highly toxic and cannot be eaten raw. In Guangxi province some 174 people died in a single month after eating it without proper soaking and cooking. A similar number in Fujian province succumbed to a paralytic neurological disease caused by cassava – among thousands of cases of food poisoning.[47] Cocklebur, a weedy plant, was another hazard. The seeds were highly toxic, killing unsupervised pigs rooting for food. In humans it led to nausea and vomiting as well as twisting of the neck muscles, followed by a rapid pulse, breathing difficulties and eventually death. In ten days the toxic weed claimed 160 victims in Beijing.[48]

In a strange reversal of fortune, sometimes the most politically marginalised people were in a better position to survive, as they had developed coping mechanisms against starvation for many years before the Great Leap Forward. As the offspring of an 'evil landlord', Meng Xiaoli and his brother were chased from their ancestral house in Qianjiang, Hubei, immediately after the communist takeover in 1949. He was not given the time to gather any belongings. Though he was only a young boy, his jumper was torn from his back. They wandered about the village with their mother, ostracised by all, and ended up by the lakeside digging for wild vegetables. They slept on dried straw with the village dogs on their first night, and were later allocated a shabby mud hut. At first they tried to beg but nobody dared to give them any food. 'So we tried to catch fish from the lake but couldn't catch enough to eat because we didn't have the right tools. But we still managed to survive because we could dig up lotus roots and pick up seeds. After a few months, my brother and I learned how to catch fish from the lake. Although we didn't have any rice, in fact we could eat quite well.' When the famine engulfed the village years later, the family was the only one to be prepared for survival.[49]

Straw and stalks were eaten from roofs. Zhao Xiaobai, the orphan girl aged eleven who had to work like an adult to look after her little sister, remembered how one day, tortured by hunger, she climbed up a ladder on to the roof. 'I was still quite young then. I was very hungry, so I broke a piece of maize stalk [used to cover the roof] and began to chew it. It tasted delicious! I chewed one piece after another. I was so hungry that even maize stalks tasted good.'⁵⁰ Leather was softened and eaten. Explained Zhu Erge, who witnessed half his village die of hunger in Sichuan but managed to survive because his mother was a cook in the canteen: 'We soaked the leather chairs people used to sit on. After they were soaked, we cooked the leather and cut it into small pieces to eat.'⁵¹

Infected animals were eaten by the famished, even in the outskirts of the capital. In Huairou county, lambs contaminated with anthrax were regularly devoured by starved villagers.⁵² Hundreds were poisoned after eating bits of smelly fat mixed with clumps of hair, scraped off animal hides by a Chengdu leather factory, which were bartered for vegetables with a people's canteen. Even the contaminated carcasses of diseased live-stock, culled by a slaughterhouse in Guanxian county, were quietly sold to a local commune.⁵³ When people were not eaten by rats, rats were eaten by people, dead ones sometimes being fished out of cesspits.⁵⁴

When nothing else was left, people turned to a soft mud called Guanyin soil – named after the Goddess of Mercy. A work team sent by Li Jingquan was taken aback by what they saw in Liangxian county, Sichuan. It was a vision of hell, as serried ranks of ghostly villagers queued up in front of deep pits, their shrivelled bodies pouring with sweat under the glare of the sun, waiting for their turn to scramble down the hole and carve out a few handfuls of the porcelain-white mud. Children, their ribs starting through the skin, fainted from exhaustion, their grimy bodies looking like mud sculptures shadowing the earth. Old women in ragged clothes burned paper charms and bowed, hands folded, mumbling strange incantations. A quarter of a million tonnes were dug out by more than 10,000 people. In one village alone 214 families out of a total of 262 had eaten mud, several kilos per person. Some of the villagers filled their mouths with mud as they were digging in the pit. But most of them added water and kneaded the soil after mixing it with chaff, flowers and weeds, baking mud cakes that were filling, even if they provided little sustenance. Once eaten the soil acted like cement, drying out the stomach and absorbing all the moisture inside the intestinal tract. Defecation became impossible. In every village several people died a painful death, their colons blocked up with soil.⁵⁵ In

Henan, as He Guanghua recollected, so many people took to eating a local stone called *yanglishi*, which was ground and turned into cakes, that adults would help each other prise out their faeces with twigs.[56] All over China, from Sichuan, Gansu and Anhui to Henan, people tormented by ravening hunger turned to mud.

People really did die of starvation – in contrast to many other famines where disease loomed large on the horizon of death. Starvation, in a strict clinical sense, means that the attrition of protein and fatty deposits in the body causes the muscles to waste away and eventually stop functioning, including the heart. Adults can survive for weeks without food, as long as they can drink water. The fat stored in the body provides the main source of energy and is broken down first. A small amount of calories are also stashed away in the liver as glycogen, which is generally converted within a day. But as soon as the fatty deposits have been exhausted, proteins are stripped from muscles and other tissues and used by the liver to produce sugars needed by the brain – the body's first priority. The brain quite literally starts cannibalising the body, taking bits of this or that tissue to come up with the glucose it needs to survive. Blood pressure lowers, which means that the heart has to work harder. The body weakens and progressively becomes emaciated. As proteins are depleted, fluids start leaking out of the blood vessels and from disintegrating tissues, accumulating beneath the skin and in cavities around the body, producing oedema. The swelling first appears in the face, the feet and the legs, but fluids can also gravitate around the stomach and chest. Swollen knees make walking painful. Taking extra salt or watering down a meal to make it last longer only worsens the condition. But some of the starving do not suffer from oedema and dehydrate instead, their skin turning to parchment, shrivelled and scaly, sometimes covered with brown spots. As the throat muscles weaken and the larynx dries up, the voice grows hoarse before falling silent. People tend to curl up to save energy. The lungs weaken. The face caves in, cheekbones stand out and bulging eyeballs are a gruesome white, staring vacantly and seemingly without emotion. The ribs poke through the skin, which hangs in folds. Arms and legs look like twigs. Black hair loses its colour and falls out. The heart has to work harder still, as the volume of blood actually increases relative to a declining body weight. In the end the organs are so damaged that they fail.[57]

Starvation may have been a taboo topic, but the archives are replete with reports about oedema (*shuizhongbing*) and death by starvation (*esi*). Wu Ningkun, a professor of English literature, described what happened as he went through hunger: 'I was the first to come down with a serious case of oedema. I became emaciated, my ankles swelled, and my legs got so weak that I often fell while walking to the fields for forced labor. I did not know what I looked like, as there were no mirrors around, but I could tell from the ghastly looks of the other inmates that I must have been quite a sight.'[58] Few victims were as eloquent, but the symptoms were observed everywhere. In a commune in Qingyuan – once considered Guangdong's granary – 40 per cent of the villagers suffered from oedema in 1960.[59] Even in cities it was common. We have already seen how half the workforce suffered from oedema in Beijing. Among high school students in Shanghai oedema spread in 1960–1.[60] In Nankai University, Tianjin's top institution of higher learning, one in five suffered from oedema.[61] So common was the disease that when the famished did not develop it, an explanation was warranted. Hu Kaiming, an outspoken official appointed as the first secretary of Zhangjiakou in 1959, observed how in the winter of 1960–1 starving villagers would suddenly drop dead as a consequence of low blood sugar, without the usual signs of oedema.[62]

Why did villagers not succumb to epidemics in much greater numbers before terminal starvation set in? One reason, suggested above, is that the party closely monitored infectious diseases. But collectivisation also brought about organisational chaos and the collapse of rural health care, which was rudimentary in the best of cases. A more plausible explanation is that people in the countryside starved to death much more quickly than elsewhere, reducing the window of opportunity during which germs could prey on a lowered immunity. The only available food was in the collective canteens, and access to these was controlled by local cadres. Under immense pressure to come up with tangible results, many local officials used food as a weapon. As we shall see in the chapter on violence, villagers who did not work were not given any food. And those who could no longer work were often exhausted. Death followed promptly.

The Gulag

Shen Shanqing, a fifty-four-year-old man working on a collective farm in Shanghai, made a fatal mistake on a summer's day in 1958. Rather than adding water to manure to reduce the solids, he poured the undiluted fertiliser directly over a row of carrots. The leaves wilted. Shen was obviously more interested in collecting work points than in selfless devotion to the Great Leap Forward in agriculture. And he was brazen as well. Rather than show contrition after his arrest, he defiantly claimed that food was scarce and prison would at least provide him with bed and board. Closer scrutiny revealed that he had also slandered the party two years earlier. He was promptly packed off to a labour camp for ten years in the windswept plains of Qinghai, 2,000 kilometres to the north-east of Shanghai. His file shows that he was released in September 1968, a sick and broken man willing to write the most demeaning confessions, from his 'deliberate act of sabotage' ten years earlier to what appeared to be his biggest infraction during a decade of forced labour, namely the accidental breaking of 'government property' in the form of a pane of glass.[1]

His sentence was severe, but many ordinary people faced a spell of one to five years in a camp for the slightest misdemeanour. Most of the evidence is securely locked away in the closed archives belonging to the public security bureaus, but reports on crime and punishment were occasionally copied to other party organs, for instance a document detailing that even petty thieves in Nanjing were sentenced to terms ranging from five to ten years in the summer of 1959.[2] In Beijing an internal prison registry with details of 400 male prisoners shows that a sentence of five to ten years for a minor offence was nothing out of the ordinary. Ding Baozhen, a farmer who had joined the People's Liberation Army in 1945 and was demobilised a decade later, pilfered two pairs of trousers worth a grand total of seventeen yuan. He was jailed for twelve years on 11 February 1958. Chen Zhiwen, an illiterate villager who stole from travellers at the Qianmen bus station in the capital, was given fifteen years. Another pauper who eked out a living as a cowherd before making his way to the capital in 1957 was found thieving in front of the Beijing Department Store: he too was locked away for fifteen years.[3]

But fewer people were shot than in the previous years – at least after 1958. The policy was to 'arrest fewer, kill fewer, and supervise fewer', Xie Fuzhi, minister of public security, explained to his staff in April 1960. Death by execution, like everything else in the planned economy, was a figure, a target to be fulfilled, a table of statistics in which the numbers had to add up: 4,000 should be killed in 1960, he announced. This was lower than the previous year. In 1959 some 4,500 people were killed (the term was always kill, *sha*, for communist regimes rarely felt the need to disguise judicial killing with euphemisms such as 'death penalty' or 'capital punishment'), while 213,000 people were arrested and a further 677,000 were humiliated in public.[4]

None of these sensitive data are easy to come by, but a public security document from Hebei shows how this worked out at the provincial level. In the province surrounding the capital some 16,000 'counter-revolutionaries' were arrested in 1958, three times more than in the preceding two years, as well as 20,000 common criminals, the highest figure since 1949 with the exception of 1955. These numbers dropped drastically in 1959, which saw the authorities apprehend 1,900 'counter-revolutionaries' and 5,000 common criminals. Little changed in 1960 and 1961, except that the number of common criminals went down to just over 1,000.[5] About 800 were shot in 1959.[6]

Few may have been killed, but even a short stint in a labour camp could spell disease and death. A constellation of labour camps stretched across the country's most inhospitable regions, from the 'great northern wilderness', as the vast swampy expanses of Heilongjiang were called, to the arid mountains and deserts of Qinghai and Gansu in the north-west. Life was miserable if not tenuous outside the gulag system, but inside the salt and uranium mines, the brick factories, the state farms and labour camps a brutal regime combined with widespread starvation to bury one out of every four or five inmates. In Huangshui, Sichuan, more than a third of all inmates starved to death.[7] In Jiabiangou, a sand dune area near the Gobi Desert in Gansu, the first batch of 2,300 prisoners arrived in December 1957. By the time the inmates were moved to another farm in September 1960, a thousand had died in abject conditions. This was followed by a further 640 deaths in November and December, when the camp was finally closed down in the wake of Zhang Zhongliang's fall from power.[8] Overall, in the entire province, some 82,000 prisoners worked in a hundred reform-through-labour camps in June 1960.[9] By December 1960 only 72,000 prisoners remained, close to 4,000 having died that month alone.[10] The lowest annual death rates in labour camps recorded in the archives consulted for this book were 4 to 8 per cent a year from 1959 to 1961 in Hebei, which held only a few thousand prisoners.[11]

How large was the population in the *laogai*, or reform-through-labour camps? Xie Fuzhi put the total – excluding Tibet – at 1.8 million in 1960. Prisoners worked in 1,077 factories, mines and quarries, as well as on 440 farms.[12] A rough death rate of 5 per cent in 1958 and 1962 and 10 per cent a year from 1959 to 1961 would amount to 700,000 deaths from disease and starvation. No wonder some wished to escape. But overall surveillance was tight, if only because the labour camps made a crucial contribution to the national economy – estimated by Xie Fuzhi in 1960 at 3 billion yuan per annum, not counting the 750,000 tonnes of produce from farms.[13]

Reform-through-labour camps were only one part of a much larger gulag system. People who were subjected to struggle sessions or put under formal surveillance – just under a million in 1959 – were all too often dispatched to a local prison.[14] And, more importantly, from 1957 to 1962 formal justice was curtailed. This started, as always, at the top, in the person of Mao Zedong. In August 1958 he pronounced that 'Every one of our party resolutions is a law. When we have a conference it becomes the law . . . The great majority of rules and regulations (90 per cent) are drafted by the judicial administration. We should not rely on these, we should rely mainly on resolutions and conferences, four [conferences] a year instead of common law and criminal law to keep order.'[15]

The Chairman's word was law indeed, as party committees – 'with the help of the masses' – took charge of judicial matters. It was this political pressure that brought about the abolition of the Ministry of Justice in 1959. In the countryside this meant that power shifted from the judicial authorities towards the local militias. In the entire county of Ningjin, Hebei, with a population of 830,000 people, a mere eighty cadres were in charge of the police, the inspectorate and the courts. This was half as many as in the days prior to the advent of the people's communes.[16]

The local militia relied on a whole new dimension added to the world of incarceration from August 1957, namely re-education-through-labour camps, called *laojiao*. Common criminals like Shen Shanqing were handed a sentence by a people's tribunal, but prisoners in re-education camps were not subject to any judicial procedures and could be kept indefinitely – until fully 're-educated'. In contrast to the reform-through-labour camps, they were organised not by the Ministry of Public Security, but by provinces, cities, counties, people's communes and even villages. Anybody suspected of pilfering, vagrancy, slandering the party, daubing reactionary slogans on walls, obstructing labour or committing an act regarded as against the spirit of the Great Leap Forward could be locked away in a re-education camp. These were just as harsh as the more formal labour camps, and they sprouted up everywhere after 1957. Xie Fuzhi mentioned 440,000 prisoners in re-education camps in 1960, but what he saw from the distance of his office in Beijing was no more than the tip of an iceberg.[17]

It was not until work teams were sent into the countryside from late 1960 onwards to supervise a purge of local cadres that the dimensions of local incarceration finally come to light. There was hardly a collective that did not run its own private gulag, backed up by the powerful militia created in the summer of 1958. Report after report mentioned how this or that unit – local police offices, village teams, people's communes – had established a 'private punishment camp' (*sili xingchang*). For every criminal like Shen Shanqing formally handed over to the courts, several bypassed the judicial system and ended up in a local prison. The size of this shadow world will never be known. In the model commune of Xushui, as we have seen, Zhang Guozhong built an elaborate gulag system, extending from the county down to every brigade. It held 1.5 per cent of the local population.[18] In Fengxian, near Shanghai, villagers were routinely carried off to special labour camps, one of them set up specifically to lock up recalcitrant children.[19] In Kaiping county, one brigade alone boasted no fewer than four camps, as hundreds of people were sent away for a couple of days or longer stretches of up to 150 days. Once inside the camps many were beaten and tortured; some were crippled for life.[20] Sometimes people were not even locked up in a formal prison. To set an example, a cadre in Kaiping chained up a grandmother accused of theft for ten days in the canteen using 4.5-kilo fetters. A young militiaman struck matches to burn her feet.[21]

Special camps and special sanctions were devised throughout the country, as local justice was allowed to run rampant. In Yinjiang county, Guizhou, the inmates of one camp had the character for 'thief' imprinted on their forehead in red ink. Throughout the province, people's communes set up 'training centres' (*jixundui*) where those who expressed critical views or refused to attend meetings were sent for 're-education' and compelled to undertake hard labour.[22] Several 'training camps' were also established by the Public Security Bureau in Liuzhou in 1959, to take care of subversive elements who objected to collectivisation.[23] In Yanqing county, north of Beijing, the merest suspicion of slacking resulted in detention: a sixty-two-year-old man spent a month in confinement for not having caught enough sparrows.[24]

If for every criminal handed over to the formal justice system some three or four people were locked away in a local re-education camp, the total prisoner population would have reached 8 to 9 million in any one year during the Great Leap Forward (1.8 to 2 million in labour camps, 6 to 8 million in re-education camps). The total number of deaths due to disease and starvation, conservatively estimated earlier at about a million in formal labour camps, would have to be multiplied by three or four, meaning that at least 3 million died in the gulag during the famine.[25] The death rate was high, but compared to the Soviet Union in the 1930s the incarceration rate was relatively low. This is because comparatively few people actually did time for crime. They were beaten and starved instead.

34

Violence

Terror and violence were the foundations of the regime. Terror, to be effective, had to be arbitrary and ruthless. It had to be widespread enough to reach everyone but did not have to claim many lives. This principle was well understood. 'Kill a chicken to scare the monkey' was a traditional saying. Cadres who forced villagers in Tongzhou – just outside the capital – to kneel before beating them called it 'punish one to deter a hundred'.[1]

However, during the Great Leap Forward something of an altogether different nature happened in the countryside. Violence became a routine tool of control. It was not used occasionally on a few to instil fear in the many, rather it was directed systematically and habitually against anybody seen to dawdle, obstruct or protest, let alone pilfer or steal – a majority of villagers. Every meaningful incentive to work was destroyed for the cultivator – the land belonged to the state, the grain he produced was procured at a price that was often below cost of production, his livestock, tools and utensils were no longer his, often even his home was confiscated. The local cadre, on the other hand, faced ever greater pressure to fulfil and overfulfil the plan, having to whip up the workforce in one relentless drive after another.

The constant hammering of propaganda may have helped in the early days of the Great Leap Forward, but the daily meetings villagers were required to attend contributed to widespread sleep deprivation. 'Meetings every day, loudspeakers everywhere,' remembered Li Popo when interviewed about the famine in Sichuan.[2] Meetings, some of them lasting several days, were indeed at the heart of collectivisation, but they were not so much a forum of socialist democracy, where the peasant masses openly voiced their views, as a site of intimidation where cadres could lecture, bully, threaten and shout themselves hoarse for hours on end. All too often farmers were woken in the middle of the night to work in the fields after an evening at a village meeting, so that they slept for less than three or four hours a day in the ploughing season.[3]

In any event, as the promise of utopia was followed by yet another spell of back-breaking labour, the willingness to trade hard work for empty promises gradually eroded. Soon, the only way to extract compliance from an exhausted workforce was the threat of violence. Nothing short of fear of hunger, pain or death seemed to be able to galvanise them. In some places both villagers and cadres became so brutalised that the scope and degree of coercion had to be constantly expanded, creating a mounting spiral of violence. With far fewer carrots to offer, the party relied more heavily on the stick.

The stick was the weapon of choice in the countryside. It was cheap and versatile. A swing of the baton would punish a straggler, while a series of blows could lacerate the back of more stubborn elements. In serious cases victims could be strung up and beaten black and blue. People were forced to kneel on broken shells and beaten. This happened, for instance, to Chen Wuxiong, who refused to work on an irrigation project far away from home. He was forced to kneel and hold a heavy log above his head, all the while being beaten with a stick by local cadre Chen Longxiang.[4] As famished villagers often suffered from oedema, liquid seeped through their pores with every stroke of the stick. It was a common expression that someone 'was beaten until all the water came out', for instance in the case of Lu Jingfu, a farmer chased by a team of thugs. So enraged was their leader Ren Zhongguang, first party secretary of Napeng commune, Qin county, that he beat the man for twenty minutes.[5]

Party officials often took a lead. The report compiled by the local party committee which investigated abuses in a commune in Qingyuan explained that the first party secretary Deng Zhongxing personally beat more than 200 farmers, killing fourteen in an attempt to fulfil the quotas.[6] The brains of Liu Shengmao, too sick to work at the reservoir in Huaminglou, Hunan, were widely spattered by the beating he received from the brigade secretary, who continued to pummel his lifeless body in a blind fury.[7] Ou Desheng, party secretary of a commune in Hunan, single-handedly punched 150 people, of whom four died. 'If you want to be a party member you must know how to beat people' was his advice to new recruits.[8] In Daoxian county – 'everywhere is a torture field', an investigation team wrote – farmers were clubbed on a regular basis. One team leader personally beat thirteen people to death (a further nine subsequently died of their injuries).[9] Some of these cadres were veritable gangsters, their mere appearance instilling fear. In Nanhai county, brigade leader Liang Yanlong toted three guns and stalked the village in a big leather coat.[10] Li Xianchun, team leader in Hebei, injected himself with morphine daily and would swagger about the village in bright red trousers, swearing loudly and randomly beating anybody who had the misfortune to catch his attention.[11]

Overall, across the country, maybe as many as half of all cadres regularly pummelled or caned the people they were meant to serve – as endless reports demonstrate. Four thousand out of 16,000 villagers working on the Huangcai reservoir in Hunan in the winter of 1959–60 were kicked and beaten, and 400 died as a result.[12] In a Luoding commune in Guangdong, more than half of all cadres beat the villagers, close to a hundred being clubbed to death.[13] A more comprehensive investigation of Xinyang, Henan, showed that over a million people died in 1960. Most died of starvation, but some 67,000 were beaten to death by the militias.[14]

The stick was common, but it was only one tool in the arsenal of horror devised by local cadres to demean and torture those who failed to keep up. As the countryside slid into starvation, ever greater violence had to be inflicted on the famished to get them into the fields. The ingenuity deployed by the few to inflict pain and suffering on the many seemed boundless. People were thrown into ponds, sometimes bound, sometimes stripped of their clothes. In Luoding a ten-year-old boy was tied up and thrown into a bog for having stolen a few stalks of wheat. He died after a few days.[15]

People were stripped naked and left in the cold. For stealing a kilo of beans, farmer Zhu Yufa was fined 120 yuan. His clothes, his blanket and his floor mat were confiscated, then he was stripped naked and subjected to a struggle session.[16] In one commune in Guangdong, where thousands of farmers were sent to do forced labour, stragglers were stripped of their clothes in the middle of the winter.[17] Elsewhere, in the rush to complete a reservoir, up to 400 villagers at a time were made to work in sub-zero temperatures without cotton-padded clothing. No exceptions were made for pregnant women. The cold, it was thought, would force the villagers to work more vigorously.[18] In Liuyang, Hunan, a team of 300 men and women were made to work bare-chested in the snow. One in seven died.[19]

And then, in the summer, people were forced to stand in the glaring sun with arms spread out (others had to kneel on stones or on broken glass). This happened from Sichuan in the south to Liaoning in the north.[20] People were also burned with incandescent tools. Hot needles were used to singe navels.[21] When farmers recruited to work on a reservoir in Lingbei commune complained about pain, the militia seared their bodies.[22] In Hebei people were branded with a hot iron.[23] In Sichuan a few were doused in petrol and set alight, some burning to death.[24]

Boiling water was poured over people. As fuel was scarce, it was more common to cover people in urine and excrement.[25] One eighty-year-old woman, who had the temerity to report her team leader for stealing rice, paid the price when she was drenched in urine.[26] In Longgui commune, near Shantou, those who failed to keep up with work were pushed into a heap of excrement, forced to drink urine or had their hands burned.[27] Elsewhere, a runny concoction of excrement diluted with water was poured down a victim's throat. Huang Bingyin, a villager weakened by starvation, stole a chicken but was caught and forced by the village leader to swallow cow dung.[28] Liu Desheng, guilty of poaching a sweet potato, was covered in urine. He, his wife and his son were also forced into a heap of excrement. Then tongs were used to prise his mouth open after he refused to swallow excrement. He died three weeks later.[29]

Mutilation was carried out everywhere. Hair was ripped out.[30] Ears and noses were lopped off. After Chen Di, a farmer in Guangdong, stole some food, he was tied up by militiaman Chen Qiu, who cut off one of his ears.[31] The case of Wang Ziyou was reported to the central leadership: one of his ears was chopped off, his legs were tied up with wire, a ten-kilo stone was dropped on his back and then he was branded with a hot iron – as punishment for digging up a potato.[32] In Yuanling county, Hunan, testicles were beaten, soles of feet were branded and noses were stuffed with hot peppers. Ears were nailed against the wall.[33] In the Liuyang region,

Hunan, iron wires were used to chain farmers.[34] In Jianyang, Sichuan, an iron wire was run through the ears of thieves, pulled down by the weight of a piece of cardboard which read 'habitual thief'.[35] Others had needles inserted under their nails.[36] In several parts of Guangdong, cadres injected salt water into people with needles normally used on cattle.[37]

Sometimes husbands and wives were forced to beat each other, a few to death.[38] One elderly man, when interviewed for this book in 2006, quietly sobbed when he recounted how as a young boy he and the other villagers had been forced to beat a grandmother, tied up in the local temple for having taken wood from the forest.[39]

People were intimidated by mock executions and mock burials.[40] They were also buried alive. This was often mentioned in reports about Hunan. People were locked up in a cellar and left to die in eerie silence after a period of frantic screaming and scratching against the hatch.[41] The practice was widespread enough to prompt a query by provincial boss Zhou Xiaozhou during a visit to Fengling county in November 1958.[42]

Humiliation was the trusted companion of pain. Everywhere people were paraded – sometimes with a dunce cap, sometimes with a placard on their chests, sometimes entirely naked.[43] Faces were smeared with black ink.[44] People were given *yin* and *yang* haircuts, as one half of the head was shaved, the other not.[45] Verbal abuse was rife. The Red Guards, ten years later during the Cultural Revolution, invented very little.

Punishment also extended to the hereafter. Sometimes the corpses of those who had been beaten to death were simply left to rot by the roadside, destined to become pariahs of the afterlife, their wandering ghosts – according to popular belief – never able to rest without proper burial rites. Signs were put up by some graves. In Longgui commune, Guangdong, where one in five died in 1959, some people were hastily buried by the roadside, the site marked by a signboard with the word 'sluggard'.[46] In Shimen, Hunan, the entire family of Mao Bingxiang starved to death, but the brigade leader refused to give them a burial. After a week rats had gnawed through their eyes. Local people later told an investigation team that 'we people are not even like dogs, nobody buries us when we die'.[47]

Family members could be punished for trying to bury a relative who had fallen foul of local justice. When a seventy-year-old mother hanged herself to escape from hunger, her child hurried back home from the fields in a panic. But the local cadre was infuriated by the breach of discipline. He chased the daughter down the road, punched her head and then, when she was down, kicked her upper body. She was crippled for life. 'You can keep her and eat her,' he said of her mother, whose body was left for days to decompose.[48] The worst form of desecration was to chop up the body and use it as fertiliser. This happened with Deng Daming, beaten to death because his child had stolen a few broad beans. Party secretary Dan Niming ordered his body to be simmered down into fertiliser for a field of pumpkins.[49]

The extent of the violence is difficult to underestimate: in a province such as Hunan, which did not rank as one of the worst in terms of overall casualties, a report by a central inspection committee addressed to Zhou Enlai at the time noted that people were beaten to death in eighty-two out of eighty-six counties and cities.[50] But it is harder to come up with reliable figures, and none are likely ever to be produced for the whole country. It was difficult enough for investigators at the time to determine how many people had died during the famine, let alone ascertain the cause of death. But some of the teams sent to the countryside probed further and came up with a rough idea of what had happened on the ground. In Daoxian county, Hunan, many thousands perished in 1960, but only 90 per cent of the deaths could be attributed to disease and starvation. Having reviewed all the evidence, the team concluded that 10 per cent had been buried alive, clubbed to death or otherwise killed by party members and the militia.[51] In Shimen county, Hunan, some 13,500 died in 1960, of whom 12 per cent were 'beaten or driven to their deaths'.[52] In Xinyang, a region subject to an inquiry headed by senior leaders such as Li Xiannian, a million people died in 1960. A formal investigation committee estimated that 6–7 per cent were beaten to death.[53] In Sichuan the rates were much higher. In Kaixian county, a close examination by a team sent by the provincial party committee at the time concluded that in Fengle commune, where 17 per cent of the population had perished in less than a year, up to 65 per cent of the victims had died because they were beaten, punished with food deprivation or forced into committing suicide.[54]

Report after report detailed the ways in which people were tortured, and the image that emerges from this mass of evidence is that at least 6 to 8 per cent of all the famine victims were directly killed or died as a result of injuries inflicted by cadres and the militia. As we shall see in Chapter 35, at least 45 million people perished above a normal death rate during the famine from 1958 to 1962. Given the extent and scope of violence so abundantly documented in the party archives, it is likely that at least 2.5 million of these victims were beaten or tortured to death.

There is no simple explanation for the violence that underpinned crash collectivisation. One might very well point to a tradition of violence stretching back many centuries in China, but how would that have been any different from the rest of the world? Europe was steeped in blood, and mass murder took an unprecedented number of lives in the first half of the twentieth century. Modern dictatorships can be particularly murderous in their combination of new technologies of power, exercised through the one-party state, with new technologies of death, from the machine gun to the gas chamber. When powerful states decide to pool these resources to exterminate entire groups of people the overall consequences can be devastating. Genocide, after all, is made possible only with the advent of the modern state.

The one-party state under Mao did not concentrate all its resources on the extermination of specific groups of people – with the exception, of course, of counter-revolutionaries, saboteurs, spies and other 'enemies of the people', political categories vague enough potentially to include anybody and everybody. But Mao did throw the country into the Great Leap Forward, extending the military structure of the party to all of society. 'Everyone a soldier,' Mao had proclaimed at the height of the campaign, brushing aside such bourgeois niceties as a salary, a day off each week or a prescribed limit on the amount of labour a worker should carry out.[55] A giant people's army in the command economy would respond to every beck and call of its generals. Every aspect of society was organised along military lines – with canteens, boarding kindergartens, collective dormitories, shock troops and villagers construed as the footsoldiers – in a continuous revolution. These were not merely martial terms rhetorically deployed to heighten group cohesion. All the leaders were military men attuned to the rigours of warfare. They had spent twenty years fighting a guerrilla war in extreme conditions of deprivation. They had coped with one extermination campaign after another unleashed by the nationalist regime of Chiang Kai-shek, and then managed to survive the onslaught of the Japanese army in the Second World War. They had come through the vicious purges and bouts of torture which periodically convulsed the party itself. They glorified violence and were inured to massive loss of life. And all of them shared an ideology in which the end justified the means. In 1962, having lost millions of people in his province, Li Jingquan compared the Great Leap Forward to the Long March, in which only one in ten had made it to the end: 'We are not weak, we are stronger, we have kept the backbone.'[56]

On the ground party officials showed the same callous disregard for human life as they had to the millions mobilised into the bloody offensives against Chiang Kai-shek. The brute force with which the country had been conquered was now to be unleashed on the economy – regardless of the casualty figures. And as sheer human willpower was deemed capable of just about any feat – mountains could be moved – any failure looked suspiciously like sabotage. A slacker in the 'war on sparrows' was a 'bad element' who could derail the entire military strategy of the Great Leap Forward. A farmer who pilfered from the canteen was a soldier gone astray, to be eliminated before the platoon was threatened with mutiny. Anybody was potentially a deserter, or a spy, or a traitor, so that the slightest infraction was met with the full rigour of martial justice. The country became a giant boot camp in which ordinary people no longer had a say in the tasks they were commanded to carry out, despite the pretence of socialist democracy. They had to follow orders, failing which they risked punishment. Whatever checks existed on violence – religion, law, community, family – were simply swept away.

As the party purged itself several times during the Great Leap Forward, it also recruited new members, many of them unsavoury characters who felt little compunction in using violence to get the job done. The village, commune or county with the most red flags was generally also the one with the most victims. But red flags could be taken away and given to a rival at any moment, forcing local cadres to keep up the pressure, although the workforce was increasingly exhausted. A vicious circle of repression was created, as ever more relentless beatings were required to get the starving to perform whatever tasks were assigned to them. In the escalation of violence, the limit was reached when the threat of punishment and the threat of starvation cancelled each other out. One villager forced to work long shifts up in the mountains in the cold of winter put it succinctly: 'We are exhausted; even if you beat me I won't work.'[57]

The way in which violence escalated at the time was analysed in an extremely interesting manuscript entitled 'How and Why Cadres Beat People', written by one of the investigation teams dispatched to the countryside in Hunan. The authors of the report not only spent time collecting incriminating evidence against cadres guilty of abuse of power, but they also interviewed them in a rare attempt to find out what had gone wrong. They discovered the reward principle: cadres beat villagers to earn praise from their superiors. However chaotic the situation was on the ground, violence always followed a line, namely from the top towards the bottom. Zhao Zhangsheng was an example. A low-ranking party member, at first he refused to hit people suspected of being 'rightists' in the purges following the 1959 Lushan plenum. He was taken to task by his superiors, and even risked being denounced as a 'conservative rightist' himself, but he continued to express reluctance at using violence against party enemies. So he was fined five yuan as a warning. Then, at long last, he succumbed to the pressure, coming back with a vengeance, bashing a small child till it was covered in blood.[58]

Peer pressure all too often dragged local cadres down to the same level, binding all in a shared camaraderie of violence. In Leiyang, county leader Zhang Donghai and his acolytes considered violence to be a 'duty' intrinsic to the 'continuous revolution': 'having a campaign is not the same as doing embroidery, it is impossible not to beat people to death'. Local cadres who refused to beat slackers were themselves subjected to struggle sessions, tied up and beaten. Some 260 were dismissed from their jobs. Thirty were beaten to death.[59] In Hechuan county, Sichuan, cadres were told that 'There are so many people working, it doesn't matter if you beat a few people to death.'[60]

Some of the interviews collected by party inspectors in 1961 confronted the perpetrators of violence with their victims. Shao Ke'nan was a young Hunanese who was beaten for the first time in the summer of 1958, at the height of the collectivisation frenzy. Dispatched to work for twelve hours a day in the middle of the winter on an irrigation project in the Huaguo mountains, he was covered in blows again. One of his tormentors was a cadre called Yi Shaohua. Shen knew Yi from his childhood, and recalled that the man had never resorted to violence before the Great Leap Forward. With the unfolding of new political campaigns he changed, beating and cursing on a mere whim. He punched hard, leaving his victims bruised, battered and bleeding.[61] When Yi Shaohua, in turn, was asked why he was so violent, he explained that the pressure had come from his superior. Yi was afraid of being labelled a rightist. His boss told him that 'if you don't beat them the work won't get done'. The pressure had to be passed along a chain of command: 'the people above us squeeze us so we squeeze the people below us'.[62] In other words, as party members were terrorised themselves, they in turn terrorised the population under their control.

Cadres had a choice. They could improve the living conditions of the villagers – against all odds – or instead try to meet the party's targets. The one came at the expense of the other. Most took the path of least resistance. Once that choice had been made, violence assumed its own logic. In conditions of widespread penury it was impossible to keep everybody alive. There simply was not enough food left in the village to provide even reliable farmers with an adequate diet, and in the climate of mass repression following the 1959 Lushan plenum it did not look as if the problem of shortages was about to be solved very quickly. An expedient way to increase the available food was to eliminate the weak and sick. The planned economy already reduced people to mere digits on a balance sheet, a resource to be exploited for the greater good, like coal or grain. The state was everything, the individual nothing, his worth being constantly assessed through work points and determined by the ability to move earth or plant rice. In the countryside farmers were treated like livestock: they had to be fed, clothed and housed, all of which came at a cost to the collective. The logical extension of these bleak calculations was to cull those judged unworthy of life. The discriminate killing of slackers, weaklings or otherwise unproductive elements increased the overall food supply for those who contributed to the regime through their labour. Violence was one way of dealing with food shortages.

Food was commonly used as a weapon. Hunger was the punishment of first resort, even more so than a beating. Li Wenming, deputy party secretary of a commune in Chuxiong county, clubbed six farmers to death, but his main tool for discipline was hunger. Two recalcitrant brothers were deprived of food for a full week, and they ended up desperately foraging for roots in the forest, where they soon died of hunger. One of their wives was sick at home. She too was banned from the canteen. An entire brigade of seventy-six people was punished with hunger for twelve days. Many died of starvation.[63] In Longgui commune, Guangdong, the party secretary of the commune ordered that those who did not work should not eat.[64] Describing what happened in several counties in Sichuan, one inspector noted that 'commune members too sick to work are deprived of food – it hastens their deaths'. In the first month the ration was reduced to 150 grams of grain a day, then in the following month to 100 grams. In the end those about to die were denied any food at all. In Jiangbei and Yongchuan, 'virtually every people's commune withholds food'. In one canteen catering for sixty-seven people, eighteen died within three months after they were barred from the premises on grounds of sickness.[65] Few reliable figures exist, but a team of inspectors who looked closely at a number of brigades in Ruijiang county, Sichuan, believed that 80 per cent of those who had died of hunger had been denied food as a form of punishment.[66] And even those who were given food in the canteen often received less than they were formally entitled to. As one farmer explained, the ladle that was dipped into the pot could 'read people's faces'. By this he meant a phenomenon that many interviewees recalled, namely that the man in charge of the canteen deliberately discriminated against those he considered to be 'bad elements'. Whereas the spoon reached deep to the bottom of the pot for good workers, it merely skimmed the surface for 'bad elements', who were given a watery concoction: 'The water looked greenish and was undrinkable.'[67]

Report after report alleges that the sick were also forced to come out and work in the fields. Of the twenty-four villagers suffering from oedema who were compelled by cadre Zhao Xuedong to take part in labour all but four died. In Jinchang commune those who were lucky enough to be given medical treatment were driven to perform heavy labour by the local party secretary as soon as they were released from medical care.[68] Throughout the country those who were too ill to work were routinely cut off from the food supply – a decision easily reached by those cadres who interpreted illness as opposition to the regime. In the worst places even those who managed to accomplish their daily task were given only a bowl of watery rice.

───────────

'To each according to his needs' was the slogan heralded by model counties such as Xushui, but all too often the reality was much closer to Lenin's dictum that 'he who does not work shall not eat'. Some collectives even divided the local population into different groups according to their work performance, each being given a different ration. Calories were distributed according to muscle. The idea was to cut the ration from those who underperformed and use it as a bonus to encourage the better workers. It was a simple and effective system to manage scarcity, rewarding the strong at the expense of the weak. A similar system had been devised in similar circumstances when the Nazis were confronted with such food shortages that they could no longer feed their slave labourers. Günther Falkenhahn, director of a mine that supplied IG Farben's chemicals complex, divided his *Ostarbeiter* into three classes, concentrating the available food on those workers who provided the best return per unit of calories. Those at the bottom fell into a fatal spiral of malnutrition and underperformance. By 1943 he had received national recognition, and the idea of *Leistungsernährung*, or 'performance feeding', was promulgated as standard practice in the employment of *Ostarbeiter*.[69]

No order ever came from above, instructing party members to restrict adequate feeding to above-average workers, but it seemed an effective enough strategy to some cadres keen to obtain maximum output for minimal expense. In Peach Village, Guangdong, the cadres divided the farmers into twelve different grades, calibrated according to performance. Workers in the top grade were given just under 500 grams of grain a day. Those lingering at the bottom received a mere 150 grams a day, a starvation diet that weeded out the most vulnerable elements. They were replaced by others who inexorably slipped down the ranks, edging closer to the end. One in ten were starved to death in 1960.[70] In fact, throughout the country, as we have seen, units were divided into different ranks, red, grey and white flags being handed out to advanced, mediocre and backward units. It was a small step to elaborate the system further and make calorie income dependent on rank. In Jintang county, for instance, one village divided its members into 'superior', 'middle' and 'inferior' groups, their names respectively listed on red, green or white paper. Members of different ranks were not allowed to mix. Red names were praised, but white names were relentlessly persecuted, many ending up in makeshift labour camps for 're-education'.[71]

Suicide reached epidemic proportions. For every murder, an untold number suffered in one way or another, and some of these opted to end their lives. Often it was not so much the pain that pushed a person to end it all as the shame and humiliation endured in front of other villagers. A set phrase was that such and such, having strayed from the path, 'was afraid of punishment and committed suicide'. 'Driven to their deaths' or 'driven against the wall' were also common expressions used to describe self-murder. In Fengxian, Shanghai, of the 960 people who were killed in the space of a few months in the summer of 1958, ninety-five 'were forced into an impasse and committed suicide', while the others died of untreated illnesses, torture or exhaustion.[72] As a very rough rule of thumb (figures, again, are woefully unreliable), about 3 to 6 per cent of avoidable deaths were caused by suicide, meaning that between 1 and 3 million people took their lives during the Great Leap Forward.

In Puning, Guangdong, suicides were described as 'ceaseless'; some people ended their lives out of shame for having stolen from fellow villagers.[73] When collective punishment was meted out, those who felt guilty for having endangered others committed suicide. In Kaiping county, a fifty-six-year-old lady pilfered two handfuls of grain. Her entire household was banned from the canteen for five days and sent to a labour camp. She committed suicide.[74] Sometimes women took their children with them, knowing that they would not survive on their own. In Shantou a woman accused of theft tied her two children to her body before jumping into the river.[75]

In cities, too, suicide rates rocketed, although there are few reliable figures. The Bureau of Public Security in Nanjing, for instance, was alarmed when it reported that in the first half of 1959 some 200 people had jumped into the river to commit suicide. The majority were women.[76] Many killed themselves because their families had been torn apart by collectivisation. Tang Guiying, for instance, lost her son to illness. Then her house was destroyed to make way for an irrigation project. She joined her husband who worked in a Nanjing factory. When the authorities launched a campaign to send villagers back to the countryside, he did nothing to protect her. She hanged herself.[77]

Sites of Horror

The horror of mass destruction was first encountered by the party leadership in Xinyang: it reduced Li Xiannian, a tough veteran of the Red Army, to tears. The immediate reaction was to blame counter-revolutionaries. Soon a campaign unfolded across the country to take power back from the forces of reaction, often with military backing from the centre. But in a clever move designed to portray Xinyang as an exception, reports were released within the party relating to the 'Xinyang incident'. To this was added the 'Fengyang incident', named after a dusty county in a plain by the Huai River in Anhui province. Here too a reign of terror had claimed a quarter of the 335,000 villagers. A compilation of party reports on both cases started circulating in the 1980s, including a 600-page document that was smuggled out of China in the wake of the Tiananmen Square massacre in 1989. These subsequently became the basis for most studies of the period. Xinyang became a byword for the famine.

However, local cadres who convened across the country to discuss the Xinyang report in 1961 were unimpressed. In Xiangtan, Hunan, a county where tens of thousands had died, some cadres thought that the Xinyang incident paled in comparison to what had happened in their own backyard. Why should it be called an 'incident', some wondered?[1]

There are, indeed, vast numbers of villages where death claimed more than 30 per cent of the population in a single year – in some cases entire hamlets were wiped out. But counties are much larger political entities, their populations typically ranging from 120,000 to 350,000. A death rate of 10 per cent in one year across an entire county, composed of many hundreds of villages, some tightly clustered together, others divided by hills, rivers or forests, could have occurred only under immense political pressure. These sites of horror, where deceit and terror combined to produce mass killings, existed across the country. Every province under the leadership of a political zealot had several, some even boasted a dozen. There is unlikely to be a complete list of such cases any time soon, given that so much of the party archives remains locked away, but below is a provisional list of fifty-six counties, which will no doubt grow as better sources become available. It is based on a compilation of forty counties by Wang Weizhi, a demographer who worked for the Public Security Bureau in Beijing.[2] But his information is incomplete, as it is derived from official figures sent to the capital rather than on local findings. A number of counties have been added to the list on the basis of the archival material consulted for this book (they are marked with an asterisk). Several of these cases will be examined in this chapter.

Sichuan: Shizhu, Yingjing, Fuling*, Rongxian, Dazu*, Ziyang, Xiushan, Youyang, Nanxi, Dianjiang, Leshan, Jianwei, Muchuan, Pingshan*, Bixian*, Ya'an*, Lushan*, Seda*

Anhui: Chaoxian, Taihe, Dingyuan, Wuwei, Xuancheng, Haoxian, Suxian, Fengyang, Fuyang, Feidong, Wuhe

Henan: Guangshan, Shangcheng, Xincai, Runan, Tanghe, Xixian, Gushi, Zhengyang, Shangcai, Suiping

Gansu: Tongwei*, Longxi*, Wuwei*

Guizhou: Meitan, Chishui, Jinsha, Tongzi

Qinghai: Huangzhong, Zaduo, Zhenghe

Shandong: Juye*, Jining*, Qihe*, Pingyuan*

Hunan: Guzhang*

Guangxi: Huanjiang

———

Tongwei, in the north-west of Gansu, was one of the poorest areas in the country. Set among undulating hills and divided by ravines on an arid loess plateau, it was once an important stop on the ancient silk road. Before the centre of gravity moved away towards the lush south, the region had heaved with human activity, as good use was made of the rich loess. Signs of the past are everywhere, as the soil is easy to dig. Walls, houses and mounds for tombs were made of loess and seemed to be carved straight out of the landscape. Caves were sculpted out of brittle hills, some with arched openings and dusty courtyards. Over time wind and rain eroded the mountain, and the dwellings ended up standing on their own. Terraces on top of hills and roads through deep valleys blended into a landscape of dirt that was moulded over the ages by busy hands. The Red Army occupied Tongwei in September 1935, where Mao composed an ode to the Long March.

Xi Daolong, head of the county, was a model party member, selected in May 1958 by the province to attend one of the communist party's most prestigious meetings in Beijing. When the Chairman's call for radical collectivisation came a few months later, Xi responded with zeal, amalgamating all the co-operatives into fourteen giant communes. Under the watchful eyes of the militia, everything was collectivised, land, livestock, homes, tools and even pots, tins and jars were confiscated. Farmers had to follow every dictate from party leaders. As Tongwei was a key link in the province's plan to divert a tributary of the Yellow River up the mountains to create a water highway which would turn the arid plateau into a green garden, one in five farmers was dispatched to work on a reservoir. In order to please an inspection team, sent to spur on work on the irrigation scheme, half of all villagers were dragged out to distant construction sites in the midst of the harvest. The crop was allowed to rot in the fields. In a poverty-stricken county where farmers only just managed to eke out a living, more than 13,000 hectares were abandoned in the first year of the Great Leap Forward alone. Over the years the harvest shrank, from 82,000 tonnes in 1957 to 58,000 tonnes in 1958, to 42,000 in 1959 and finally to a miserable 18,000 tonnes in 1960. But the procurements increased. Xi Daolong reported a bumper harvest of 130,000 tonnes in 1958. The state took a third. In 1959 Xi again reported twice as much. As the state now took almost half, there was hardly any grain left.[3]

Villagers who complained were branded rightists, saboteurs or anti-party agitators. The head of the county, a man called Tian Buxiao, was deeply shaken by what he saw in the countryside. He was denounced as an anti-party element and repeatedly subjected to struggle sessions as a 'small Peng Dehuai'. He committed suicide in October 1959. Over a thousand cadres who objected in one way or another were taken to task. Some were dismissed, others locked up, but torture was also widespread, in particular against villagers. People were buried alive in the caves carved from the loess hills. In the winter they were buried under the snow. Other forms of torture were used, including bamboo needles. In the unedited report appended to the file containing the final version sent up to the provincial committee, a sentence mentions that 'people were beaten to death and made into compost'.[4] More than 1,300 were beaten or tortured to death. By the winter of 1959–60 people were eating bark, roots and chaff.[5]

According to a report compiled by the county committee in Tongwei a few years after the famine, some 60,000 people died in 1959 and 1960 (the county had 210,000 villagers in 1957). Few households escaped starvation. Almost everyone had several relatives who died of hunger, and more than 2,000 families were entirely wiped out.[6]

Xi Daolong was eventually arrested, but he could hardly have presided over a reign of terror lasting several years without the support of his superiors. One rung above him stood Dou Minghai, party secretary of the Dingxi region to which Tongwei belonged. Dou himself was under constant scrutiny from Zhang Zhongliang, the boss in Gansu. So intense was the pressure that he considered villagers who tried to escape from the region to be 'all bad', every one of them guilty of 'opposing the party'. He kept on pressing for higher procurement rates, declaring that 'I would rather that people die of hunger than ask the state for grain.'[7] But in the end even his superiors could no longer ignore the extent of the starvation, and a hundred-strong team was sent from the provincial capital Lanzhou in February 1960. Xi Daolong and his aides were arrested.[8] A month later a report was sent to Beijing. The central leadership declared Tongwei to be 'completely rotten'.[9]

Sichuan, unlike Gansu, is a rich and fertile province traditionally known as the 'land of abundance', with subtropical forests and hundreds of rivers that have been diverted since ancient times for irrigation purposes. But in this huge province the size of France, there are vast variations, with deep valleys and rugged mountains on the Western Sichuan Plateau, sparsely

populated with ethnic minority people, in contrast to the basin around
Chengdu, where low hills and alluvial plains support tens of millions of
farmers. More counties in Sichuan than anywhere else had a death rate of
over 10 per cent a year. Most were impoverished areas in the mountains
around the basin area, but quite a few were scattered around Chongqing, a
city clinging higgledy-piggledy to steep cliffs by the Yangzi.

This was the case, for instance, with Fuling, a relatively prosperous
county with terraced fields along the Yangzi River in the hinterland outside
Chongqing. Baozi, a commune of 15,000 people known as 'Fuling's grain
storage', produced such abundant harvests that it usually sent half of its
produce as tribute to the state. Along the main road up to 400 people
could be found on any one day, busy bringing grain, vegetables and pigs
to market. But by 1961 grain output had plummeted by some 87 per
cent. The fields were overgrown with weeds, and half of the population
had vanished. A 'wind of communism' had blown over the commune, as
bricks, wood, pots, tools and even needles and nappies for babies had been
confiscated in a mad scramble for collectivisation in which the very notion
of individual property was seen as 'rightist conservatism'. 'We can eat our
fill even without agriculture for three years', was the slogan of the day, as
70 per cent of the workforce was diverted away from agriculture towards
the building of large canteens, piggeries and markets. People still working
in the fields had to follow commands from the commune, for instance
tearing out acres of maize because a deputy party secretary thought that
the leaves were turned in the wrong direction. Close planting, on the other
hand, killed the rice crop on some of the most fertile plots. In parts of
the commune 80 per cent of the rice terraces were converted to dry land
for vegetables, with disastrous results. Then, as an order came from Li
Jingquan that advanced units should help turn the mountains into a rich
green, with slopes covered with wheat, farmers were made to abandon the
fertile terraces to scrape the rocky earth up in the highlands many miles
away.

To conceal the precipitous decline in agricultural output, in 1959 the
commune leaders declared a crop of 11,000 tonnes instead of the 3,500
tonnes in storage. The state took 3,000 tonnes. The militia went around
checking for hidden stashes of grain, taking whatever they could get their

hands on. Struggle sessions punctuated the daily schedule. Body weight was the class line demarcating the poor from the rich: to be fat was to be a rightist, and rightists were ceaselessly pursued – often to the death. In the end people had nothing to eat but bark and mud. Up to a third of the population died in some of the villages in Baozi.[10]

Baozi was by no means exceptional. Throughout Fuling county, death rates were high, with some villages losing 9 per cent of their people in a single month in 1960.[11] An average death rate of 40 to 50 per cent was not uncommon in brigades across the region.[12]

Other counties in the Chongqing area also had death rates of over 10 per cent in 1960, for instance Shizhu, Xiushan and Youyang. In Shizhu the militia forbade villagers from foraging for roots and wild herbs, searching every home for pots and pans to prevent cooking outside the canteens. Violence was common, as 'beating squads' (*darendui*) in parts of the county took charge of discipline; some carried pincers and bamboo needles. Chen Zhilin, a deputy secretary of one of the communes, beat several hundred people, killing eight. Some were buried alive. In the county as a whole – according to the Public Security Bureau – some 64,000 people died in 1959–60 alone, or 20 per cent of the population. So overwhelmed by waves of death were the authorities that in the end the dead were cast into mass graves. Forty bodies were tossed into a pit in Shuitian commune. Near the road to the county capital, another sixty corpses were buried in a shallow trench, but the job was carried out so badly that twenty of the bodies had parts sticking out of the ground, which were soon attacked by ravenous dogs. As coffin wood was scarce, several dead toddlers at a time were carried out in rattan containers to be buried.[13]

Far away from the lush valleys along the Yangzi, pitched battles bloodied the grasslands up in the Tibetan plateau to the west. In 1959 in Serthar (Seda), a county in the Ganzi autonomous region, Tibetans were rounded up and forced into collectives, after Lhasa had been rocked by rebellion and the Dalai Lama forced to flee on foot over the Himalayan mountains into India. Dozens of uprisings took place in Ganzi by the end of 1958, leading to thousands of arrests and many executions.[14] In Serthar widespread slaughter preceded collectivisation, since herdsmen preferred to kill their sheep rather than hand them over to the state. Tens of thousands of animals were butchered and eaten. The cadres, in control of the grain, refused to feed the nomads, using the militia to extract every possible hint of wealth from those they considered to be their enemies. Corralled into makeshift communes, many people died of disease. Whereas the nomads had had access to clean water all year round, they were now packed into shoddy encampments without adequate facilities, and quickly overrun with excrement and detritus. Out of a population of some 16,000, about 15 per cent died in 1960 alone. About 40 per cent of those who died were beaten or tortured to death.[15]

Guizhou, unlike its northern neighbour Sichuan, is an impoverished province, historically rocked by rebellions from the minority people who compose at least a third of the population – many of them living in poverty in the hills and highlands that dominate what is known as the 'kingdom of mountains'. Chishui, once prosperous as a strategically located pass for the transportation of salt, is a forlorn outpost on the border with Sichuan. The river that flows through a red sandstone valley picks up the sediment and gives the place its name, which means 'Red Water'. In March 1935 the Red Army crossed the river several times, turning the county into a holy ground keenly promoted by local leaders after the revolution. Up in the scarlet mountains, small villages were hidden among giant tree ferns and bright-green bamboo, but most of the people grew paddy and sugarcane along the river and its tributaries. Between October 1959 and April 1960, around 24,000 people died – more than 10 per cent of the population.[16]

Wang Linchi, a relatively young man at thirty-five, was in charge of the county. He was given a coveted red flag in 1958 and was commended by the central leadership for having transformed a backwater into a 'Five-Thousand-Kilo County' thanks to the many innovations heralded by the Great Leap Forward. In Chishui, under Wang Linchi, deep ploughing meant digging to a depth of 1 to 1.5 metres: the deeper the better. Large quantities of seed were used, often 200 to 450 kilos per hectare, but at times as much as a tonne or two, sometimes even three tonnes. Among other great schemes devised by the county leadership was an irrigation project in which water would be conveyed through a network of bamboo pipes to every plot in the county. 'Water pipes in the skies of Chishui' was the slogan, but the scheme failed miserably after acres of bamboo forest were chopped down, depriving the villagers of a much-needed resource.

The result of the Great Leap Forward in Chishui was a plummeting grain output and the virtual extermination of the livestock. But Wang was determined to maintain his reputation. As early as September 1958, many months before Zhao Ziyang's report on the hiding of grain in Guangdong, he decreed that a part of the crop was being withheld by 'rich peasants' and 'bad elements' in a sustained attack on the socialist system. A merciless counter-attack with armed cadres was required to save the communes and prevent a counter-revolution. People on the ground were terrorised. A year later, in the wake of the Lushan plenum, villagers were divided into 'poor peasants' and 'rich peasants'. Behind the backs of rich peasants stood the landlords, saboteurs, counter-revolutionaries and other elements who were bent on wrecking the revolution: 'Poor and Rich Peasants, This Struggle is to the Death!' Several thousand cadres were expelled from the party for having the wrong class background, while mass demonstrations, struggle meetings and anti-hiding campaigns were organised to root out every class enemy. Like Mao, Wang Linchi was a poet, composing verses to celebrate the working class and organising a traditional opera in which he starred as the main actor – before hundreds of invited guests tucking into a lavish banquet. In the meantime, agriculture was neglected: although in January 1960 Wang announced to his superiors in Guiyang a bumper crop of 33,500 tonnes, 80 per cent of this amount existed on paper only.[17]

Wang Linchi was hardly a unique case in Guizhou, a radical province led by Zhou Lin, a close follower of Mao. Everywhere Zhou Lin tacitly encouraged a radical approach to the Great Leap Forward, resulting in one of the highest death rates in the country. In Meitan, famous for its tea, 45,000 people died in six months. Wang Qingchen, the first party secretary, deployed a labour force of 50,000 at will, building giant tea gardens, orchards, irrigation systems and communal buildings that would turn Meitan into a national model. Forty thousand pigs were requisitioned for a 'Ten-Thousand-Hog City'. Anybody critical of these schemes was accused of 'stirring an evil revisionist trend' and given the label of 'rightist opportunist'. In 1960 an 'Arrest Many and Detain Many' campaign was organised by the police and the militia, sweeping across the region and locking up close to 3,000 people in a month. A simple slogan seemed to capture the Meitan spirit: 'Those Who are Unable to Produce Grain will Not be Given Any Grain'.[18]

The figure of 45,000 deaths is very high, but even so it may be an under-estimate. According to an investigation by the provincial party committee, in one commune alone 12,000 people 'died of starvation', representing 22 per cent of the population.[19] Focusing on one village, a more detailed inquest showed how over a third of the farmers died. Nongcha was once a relatively prosperous village, in which each family owned a few ducks and chickens, but by 1961 the crop had decreased to a third of what had been produced in 1957. Vegetables were hard to come by. Sugarcane produc-tion, indispensable for local farmers to trade against food and goods, was virtually wiped out. Many of the fields lay destroyed after experiments in deep ploughing and land reclamation. Some were called 'moon plots' because the pockmarked terrain would no longer retain any water. No work points were ever kept, and villages were fed according to the whims of local cadres in chaotic canteens. Personal property was seized, private plots were abolished. State procurements were sky high despite falling grain production: in 1959 three-quarters of the crop was dragged away by state agents, leaving the villagers to starve. By 1961 one pig was left in the entire village.[20]

When an inspection team was scheduled to visit Meitan in April 1960, the local leaders scurried about day and night to bury corpses in mass graves by the side of the road. Sick villagers and neglected children were locked up and guarded by the militia, while telltale trees without bark were torn out, roots and all.[21] Travelling through the region in March 1960, Nie Rongzhen was ecstatic about Guizhou in a letter to Mao: 'In fact Guizhou is not poor at all, it is very rich – in future it should be our industrial base in the south-west!'[22]

As the Yellow River nears the end of its long journey across the loess plateau, it intersects with the Grand Canal, an ancient man-made river completed in the seventh century to haul the grain tribute from the south to the imperial capital in the north. It is said that more than 47,000 labourers were needed to maintain the canal system, which was used, at its height in the mid-fifteenth century, by some 11,000 grain barges. Qihe is the main river port in Shandong, lying just north-west of Jinan, and it should have fared well thanks to its strategic location on the Yellow River. Before the Great Leap Forward it was known as a 'grain store' with an abundant crop that managed to reach 200,000 tonnes in a good year for a population of roughly half a million. Cotton, tobacco and fruit were also widely cultivated. By 1961 Qihe county had lost well over 100,000 people, or a fifth of its population compared to 1957. Half of the workers who had survived or stayed behind were sick. The economy lay in tatters. The 200,000 tonnes of grain harvested in 1956 had dwindled to a mere 16,000 a few years later. The collapse in peanut production was even more dramatic: whereas 7,780 tonnes had been taken from the fields in 1956, a pitiful 10 tonnes was all that could be gathered by 1961. Everything, it seemed, was reduced to about one-tenth of what could have been expected before 1958. Even the land under cultivation had shrunk, as a fifth was taken away for waterworks and roads, most of which were never finished. As everywhere in the north, the amount of alkaline soil doubled, reaching almost a third of the surface under cultivation. Despite – or rather as a consequence of – massive investment in water-conservancy projects, the overall irrigated surface shrank by 70 per cent. Off the fields the devastation was just as visible. Livestock was more than halved, the number of carts dwindled, while tens of thousands of simple tools such as rakes and hoes had vanished. Over half of all trees had been felled. Of all the housing in the county 38 per cent had been destroyed. Of what was left standing, a quarter was heavily damaged and needed urgent attention. Some 13,000 families did not even have a single room left to themselves.[23]

Hanzhuang was one of the many hamlets in Qihe county. It had 240 villagers in 1957, but by 1961 only 141 remained. A quarter of the village had died of hunger, one in six families having been entirely extinguished – a fact which always carried a great deal of weight in a culture which continued to emphasise descent, despite all the official rhetoric of class war. Between 1958 and 1961 only four children had been born in the

village, one of whom had died in infancy. Many villagers were single, most
were weak or sick, and few women from other villages were willing to
marry local men. The village had lost some 40 per cent of its land, and well
over half of what remained was almost barren through heavy salinisation.
According to a local saying, 'on leaving the house one beholds a white
expanse', as the salt whitened the earth for as far as the eye could see. In the
midst of this thin, exhausted land stood derelict mud huts.

The village had boasted a total of 240 rooms, but a mere eighty
remained standing, most of them with leaky roofs or walls that had caved
in. There was nothing inside these miserable dwellings, as an inspection
team revealed: 'All the families have gone bankrupt through the famine.
Those least affected have sold all their clothes and furniture, while the most
damaged ones have had to sell their pots, bowls and basins, as well as the
wood stripped from their houses. In the village twenty-seven families have
sold everything they had.' Yang Jimao, for instance, left the village in 1960.
His wife and child could survive only by selling every possession. They had
no bed, no pots and no tools to cultivate the land. They shared a ragged
blanket and a threadbare coat. Others were worse off. Among the few
people who had stayed in Hanzhuang was Liu Zailin, aged thirty-three,
who soon died of hunger. His wife hanged herself from a rafter, leaving
behind two children who were adopted by local villagers.

In Shandong the teams sent to investigate what had happened during the
famine were coy about pointing the finger at abusive cadres, unlike their
peers in Gansu or Guangdong. But the political dimensions of the famine
were clear. The head of the village had changed fifteen times since the Great
Leap Forward. Few could do anything to resist punitive procurements
imposed from above, and in 1959 the villagers were left with an average
of twenty-five kilos of grain per person – for the entire year. Widespread
conscription of labour on irrigation projects did not help. In the winter of
1959–60 forty-six of the best labourers were recruited from Hanzhuang.
They worked for forty days and nights on end, in the snow, but were not
given any grain, which had to be supplied by the village, already depleted
by state requisitions. Some died while digging earth outside in the cold,
others dropped dead by the roadside on the way home.[24]

Across the Shandong countryside there were countless villages in a similar predicament, broken by four years of mass abuse. Early warning signs had appeared in April 1959. Tan Qilong, a senior leader in Shandong, personally witnessed how in several counties in the Jining region the trees had been stripped bare, children were abandoned and farmers died along the roadside, their faces sallow from hunger. In Juye people ate the straw from their pillows; thousands died of hunger. Tan Qilong reported this situation to provincial boss Shu Tong, but also took the exceptional step of sending a copy to Mao Zedong.[25] A few weeks later, a contrite Shu Tong had to explain the 'Jining incident' to the Chairman, who was passing through the region in his special train.[26]

But Shu Tong did nothing to alleviate the famine. By his own admission, he detested bad news and refused even to talk about 'one finger' of shortcomings in Shandong, threatening those who were critical of the Great Leap Forward with the label of 'rightist conservatism'.[27] According to others who had to work alongside Shu Tong, the regional tsar exploded in a violent rage when anybody prevented him from enforcing a utopian vision that had cost the lives of countless people. 'He who strikes first prevails, he who strikes last fails': Shu Tong religiously followed Mao's advice about seizing the grain before the farmers could eat it, enforcing vast procurements to satisfy the demands from Beijing.[28]

Gansu, Sichuan, Guizhou, Shandong – all these provinces contained counties where the death rate was above 10 per cent in 1960. But nothing was as bad as Anhui, run by Zeng Xisheng, one of Mao's most devoted followers. Like other provinces, Anhui was divided into regions, having over a dozen. One of these regions was Fuyang. Fuyang had a population of 8 million in 1958. Three years later more than 2.4 million people had died.[29]

One of the reasons for the high death rate was the landscape itself. Flat and generally barren, it offered few places to hide. Many of those who wanted to flee the area followed the river into Xinyang, in neighbouring Henan, where the famine was even worse. The Huai River itself was a web of death. In 1957 it became the focus of a huge irrigation project which commanded up to 80 per cent of the labour force. Every hectare would have a duct, every ten hectares a canal and every hundred hectares a large waterway. Fields would be as smooth as a mirror, deep ploughing making the soil as pliable as dough. Fuyang would catch up with the future in a mere year or two.[30] Slogans such as 'On a Rainy Day We See a Bright Day, the Night Becomes the Day' and 'In Daytime We Fight the Sun, At Night We Battle the Stars' were behind the ceaseless exploitation of the best workers along the river. Many succumbed to disease, exhaustion and death.[31]

To prevent workers from returning home over the Chinese New Year, the militia sealed their homes. With the inexorable advance of dams, dykes and channels, everything in the way was flattened. Trees, graves, even large bridges were torn down, forcing farmers to walk for several kilometres each day to attend to the fields.[32] Entire villages were compelled to relocate overnight at the whim of a cadre: hundreds simply vanished from the map.[33]

Other giant schemes took away the best workers from the fields before the sowing or reaping was even completed. So abundant was the crop – the party line went – that grain should be turned into alcohol. Hao county, striving to become a 'Five-Thousand-Tonne County', built more than 3,200 alcohol factories in January 1959. Less than half ever worked, and many tonnes of grain went to waste.[34]

Just as ruinous were efforts to mechanise agriculture. Clunky iron wheels were added to some 10,000 carts, which were so heavy that bulls could no longer pull them.[35] To compound the problem, the old carts were banned from the roads, and farmers seen to use them were denounced as rightists.[36]

The grain output plunged, but zealous cadres doubled it on paper. Punitive requisitions followed; carried out with routine violence, they sometimes extracted close to 90 per cent of the actual crop.[37] To compensate for the shortage in grain, cadres burst into local households and carried away tables, chairs and beds. Farmers were even forced to turn in a set amount of cotton clothes, up to several kilos per family. Failure to fulfil the quota led to a ban from the canteen. Zhao Huairen had to hand over the cotton jackets of his seventy-year-old mother and his child. In the freezing cold they had to bury themselves underneath some straw to keep warm. By 1960 there was so little left to collect that in one commune the biggest haul consisted of a hundred coffins.[38]

Torture was rampant. Iron wire was used to pierce the ears of 'bad elements', while women were stripped and suspended by their hair. In the words of a leader in Jieshou county, 'their breasts were twisted until liquid oozed out'.[39] In Linquan, the use of violence was summarised as follows by the local party boss: 'People died in tragic circumstances, being beaten and hanged to death, deprived of food or buried alive. Some were severely tortured and beaten, having their ears chopped off, their noses dug out, their mouths torn off, and so on, which often caused death. We discovered how extremely serious all of this was once we started investigating.'[40] Murder was common. In Dahuangzhuang, a small village in Linquan, nine out of nineteen cadres had killed at least one villager during the famine. Li Fengying, a team leader, killed five people.[41]

In some cases villagers were deliberately entrapped. In late 1959, at the height of the famine, one of the food-processing factories belonging to the local grain bureau in Funan county left bean cakes in a courtyard with the gates wide open. As starving farmers tried to pilfer the food, the gates were suddenly locked behind them. 'Some of those who were caught were forced into a grain sack that was tied at the end. Then they were beaten with iron bars. The sacks were covered in blood. Others had their faces carved by knives and then oil rubbed into the wounds.'[42]

Help for the famished was withheld. Fifteen tonnes of grain sent to support those in need in one county alone were confiscated, hastening the deaths of thousands.[43] People also died when the local authorities tried to hide the famine from inspection teams. The militia, for instance, were instructed to seal off the villages and not to allow anyone with signs of starvation on to the streets.[44] In one commune targeted for a visit by the Ministry of Interior in 1960, the county head scrambled to round up and hide more than 3,000 villagers with oedema. Locked up without any medical support, several hundred died in a matter of days.[45] A local cadre had a quick look at Qin Zonghuai, who was one of those suffering from oedema. 'He won't live, bury him quickly,' he ordered, as an inspection team was on its way. 'He was still breathing while being buried,' concluded the local party secretary.[46]

36

Cannibalism

The countryside was a world of noise before the famine. Hawkers filled the air with their chants, some using rattles to advertise their wares. The din of gongs, cymbals and firecrackers traditionally accompanied popular events, whether a burial or a wedding. Loudspeakers nailed to trees by street corners and village squares blasted out propaganda and revolutionary music. Passing trucks and buses, clouds of yellow dust billowing behind them, would have worked their horns incessantly. Boisterous conversations were yelled across fields, so loud that outsiders might mistake them for a bitter argument.

But after years of famine an eerie, unnatural silence descended upon the countryside. The few pigs that had not been confiscated had died of hunger and disease. Chickens and ducks had long since been slaughtered. There were no birds left in the trees, which had been stripped of their leaves and bark, their bare and bony spines standing stark against an empty sky. People were often famished beyond speech.

In this world plundered of every layer that might offer sustenance, down to bark and mud, corpses often ended up in shallow graves or simply by the roadside. A few people ate human flesh. This began in Yunnan, where the famine started in the summer of 1958. At first the carcasses of diseased livestock were unearthed, but as famine tightened its grip some people eventually dug up, boiled and ate human bodies.[1] Soon the practice appeared in every region decimated by starvation, even in a relatively prosperous province such as Guangdong. For example in Tanbin, Luoding, a commune where one in twenty villagers died in 1960, several children were eaten.[2]

Few archives offer more than an oblique reference to cannibalism, but some police reports are quite detailed. In a small village in Xili county,

Gansu, villagers caught the whiff of boiling meat from the hut of a neighbour. They reported the man to the village secretary, who suspected that a
sheep might have been stolen and proceeded to inspect the premises. He
discovered flesh stored in vats, as well as a hair clip, ornaments and a scarf
buried at the bottom of a pit. The artefacts were immediately identified
as the belongings of a young girl who had vanished from the village days
earlier. The man not only confessed to the murder, but also owned up to
having unearthed and eaten the corpses of young children on two previous
occasions. After the village had taken measures to protect the graves from
desecration, he had turned to murder.[3]

Human flesh, like everything else, was traded on the black market. A
farmer who bartered a pair of shoes for a kilo of meat at the Zhangye railway station found that the package contained a human nose and several
ears. He decided to report the finding to the local Public Security Bureau.[4]
To escape detection, human flesh was sometimes mixed with dog meat
when sold on the black market.[5]

But few reports were ever systematically compiled. Under a regime in
which the mere mention of famine could land a cadre in trouble, cases of
cannibalism were covered up wherever they appeared. In Gansu province
the provincial leader Zhang Zhongliang was personally told of a string of
cases in Tongwei, Yumen, Wushan, Jingning and Wudu, but he dismissed
the evidence out of hand, blaming 'bad elements'.[6] Shu Tong, leader of
Shandong, also suppressed evidence about cannibalism, fearing that
adverse news would harm his reputation.[7] Wang Linchi, the county leader
of Chishui, one of the sites of horror covered in the previous chapter, took
the local security forces to task for arresting villagers guilty of cannibalism.[8]
So unmentionable was the topic that in a report distributed to the party
leadership the blame for the practice was placed on saboteurs who had
tried to tarnish the reputation of the party by exhuming human bodies,
pretending to eat them in order to publicise the extent of the famine.[9]

A few fairly comprehensive documents have survived. One of these
was compiled in March 1961 by a municipal unit in Linxia, a city south
of Lanzhou. Linxia was heavily influenced by Islam, populated predominantly by Hui people and the capital of a region with a dozen other ethnic
minorities, including Tibetans, Salar, Bao'an and Dongxiang. The region

suffered from mass collectivisation during the Great Leap Forward, which ran roughshod over the habits and customs of minorities. An investigation of the region in the immediate aftermath of the famine showed that 54,000 people had died in a mere two years.[10] The report listed some fifty cases – discovered in the city, not in the entire region – all comprehensively arranged in the kind of list that was so much in favour with the planners, reducing horror to a mere set of facts and figures. Here are the details of four such cases:

Date: 25 February 1960. Location: Hongtai Commune, Yaohejia Village. Name of Culprit: Yang Zhongsheng. Status: Poor Farmer. Number of People Involved: 1. Name of Victim: Yang Ershun. Relationship with Culprit: Younger Brother. Number of People Involved: 1. Manner of Crime: Killed and Eaten. Reason: Livelihood Issues.

Date: [void]. Location: [void]. Name of Culprit: Ma Manai. Status: Poor Farmer. Number of People Involved: Entire Family of 4. Name of Victim: [void]. Relationship with Culprit: [void]. Number of People Involved: 13. Manner of Crime: Corpses Exhumed and Eaten. Reason: Livelihood Issues.

Date: 9 Jan. 1960. Location: Maiji Commune, Zhangsama Village. Name of Culprit: Kang Gamai. Status: Poor Farmer. Number of People Involved: 1. Name of Victim: Maha Maiji. Relationship with Culprit: Fellow Villager. Number of People Involved: 1. Manner of Crime: Hacked to Death, Cooked and Eaten. Reason: Livelihood Issues.

Date: March 1960. Location: Hongtai Commune, Xiaogou Gate. Name of Culprit: Zhu Shuangxi. Status: Poor Farmer. Number of People Involved: 2. Name of Victim: [void]. Relationship with Culprit: Husband and Elder Son. Number of People Involved: 2. Manner of Crime: Corpses Exhumed and Eaten. Reason: Livelihood Issues.

Most of the culprits on the list practised necrophagy, either eating those who had passed away or exhuming and eating cadavers after burial. The seventy-six victims fell into three categories: killed and eaten (twelve), eaten after death (sixteen) and exhumed and eaten (forty-eight). Among those who were murdered roughly half were fellow villagers and half were strangers passing through. Only one murder took place inside the family.[11]

Linxia was no exception. When a team of inspectors was sent to review the Qiaotou commune in Shizhu county, Sichuan, in early 1961, they were startled by the extent of cannibalism. Rather than take note of a few cases to signal the practice, as was usual, they made the effort to investigate one brigade in depth with the help of the local Public Security Bureau. The list they compiled provided the details of sixteen victims and eighteen perpetrators. Necrophagy had apparently started after Luo Wenxiu, a seventy-year-old woman, unearthed the bodies of two small children and cooked them for herself. In some cases only parts of a body were eaten. Ma Zemin's heart, for instance, was scooped out. Much of this may have been related to the fact that most of these corpses were already in an advanced stage of putrefaction. Some people covered the meat in hot peppers.[12]

In Russian there is a distinction between *liudoedstvo*, literally 'people eating', and *trupoedstvo*, or 'corpse eating'. It is a very useful distinction, one which introduces much-needed nuance into a topic stigmatised not only by the party, but also by its enemies, keen to portray cannibalism as a metaphor for the very system itself. And as the villagers themselves told and retold stories about body snatchers, cannibals with red eyes or families swapping their children between them before eating them, the whole business was sensationalised to the point where it was placed under a cloud of scepticism.[13]

But as the cases of Linxia and Qiaotou show, very few people were actually cannibals who killed to eat. Most were scavengers, extending their survival techniques to the eating of cadavers. How they reached their decision to eat human flesh must surely have varied from one person to the next. But as desperate survivors all of them would have witnessed many of the horrors being inflicted on living human beings, from body parts being chopped off to people being buried alive. Surely, in the midst of state-sponsored violence, necrophagy was neither the most common nor the most widespread way of degrading a human being.

The Final Tally

How many died? There will never be a satisfactory answer to that question, if only because in the midst of the great famine so few reliable statistics were kept.

So far, every noteworthy estimate has been based on the official figures on population size and on birth and death rates for 1950–82, published for the first time in the 1984 *Statistical Yearbook* by the National Statistical Bureau, or on the official figures of the 1953, 1964 and 1982 censuses. Immediately following the publication of the *Statistical Yearbook*, Basil Ashton used the official evidence to propose a figure of 30 million premature deaths during the 1958–62 period, when the overall population stood at roughly 650 million.[1] Judith Banister, a professional demographer, also looked at the population statistics and concluded that an estimated 30 million excess deaths appeared during 1958–61.[2] Since the data present a whole range of problems, from lack of internal consistency to the under-registration of births and deaths and the exclusion of the armed forces, different authors have tinkered with this or that variable either to lower or to heighten the number. Peng Xizhi, an expert in population studies, proposed an estimate of 23 million in 1987, while Jung Chang, in her book on Mao, reached a figure of 38 million.[3] More recently, retired journalist Yang Jisheng suggested a figure of about 36 million – also based on published statistics.[4]

New evidence was produced in 2005 when Cao Shuji, an historical demographer from Shanghai, systematically worked his way through more than a thousand gazetteers – official local histories published after 1979 by county or city party committees. While acknowledging that this widely diverse set of data, too, ultimately rests on figures made public by the party, it introduced a much more fine-tuned analysis of regional differences. Cao's estimate was 32.5 million premature deaths.[5]

How reliable are official numbers? In the Soviet Union the Central Office of Statistics produced two sets of demographic statistics, one for internal use and one for publication. But as we have already seen in the case of grain procurements, the party archives in China have widely different sets of statistics at every level, from the commune, the county and the province up to the centre. Some were compiled at the height of the collectivisation craze and were intended to convey political zeal. Others were assembled by investigation teams sent to the countryside to oversee the removal of abusive party officials. In other words, debates about whether the released figures are doctored or not miss a very basic point. There is no need for anybody to falsify figures, it is merely a matter of compiling a set of statistics which appears to be the least politically damaging. Or, to put it slightly differently, the fact that public data in a one-party state are not falsified does not necessarily make them reliable.

At least three different sets of unpublished data exist in the archives, namely those compiled by the provincial Public Security Bureau, those from the local party committee and those from the local Statistical Bureau. Nobody has ever gained access to all three sets. But after 1979, as the new leadership wanted to find out more about the Maoist era, a team of 200 was instructed by Zhao Ziyang to go around every province to examine internal party documents. The erstwhile secretary of Guangdong who had pioneered an anti-hiding campaign in 1959 was now premier, and he asked the team to draw a picture of rural China. The team's report was never published, but one of its members, a senior party official called Chen Yizi, fled to America in the wake of the Tiananmen massacre in 1989. In exile, he claimed that the team had arrived at a death toll of 43 to 46 million people for the famine.[6] Only one person who has investigated the famine has taken Chen Yizi's claim seriously – namely Jasper Becker, who interviewed him for his book *Hungry Ghosts* published in 1996. The archival evidence presented for the first time below vindicates Chen Yizi's findings and conservatively puts the number of premature deaths at a minimum of 45 million for the great famine of 1958–62.

Even Chen Yizi and his team would have encountered difficulties in carrying out their research. Archives, in a one-party state, are not public. They
belong to the party and are controlled by the party. Except for those under
the remit of the Public Security Bureaus, most of them are located in a
building inside the party headquarters. Even a high-powered delegation
from Beijing could have been fobbed off or deliberately misled by experienced archivists, all the more so since a catalogue would not have existed
for every collection. But, most of all, some sets were simply missing. In
Hubei, for instance, the file from the party committee which should have
contained the figures for all excess deaths during the famine is incomplete.
Inside the brown folder is a handwritten note appended by an archivist,
dated June 1979, which regrets that the item is 'missing'.[7] As to the Public
Security Bureau, in Hubei it offered no more than a vague estimate, speculating that the death rate in 1961 was two to three times lower than the
preceding year. The report wonders about the total death toll but provides
no answers.[8]

In any event, all three organisations – the provincial public security, the
provincial party committee and the provincial Statistical Bureau – would
have had to rely on units lower down the party hierarchy to compile their
reports. And obstruction from below was rife. In Gansu province, the
provincial party committee sent out a request for estimates in 1962 for
excess deaths during the famine. The project foundered, as only a handful
of counties ever replied.[9]

But even when numbers were sent in by county authorities there
were problems. First among these was the distinction between 'normal'
and 'abnormal' deaths. Demographers distinguish between 'natural' and
'unnatural' deaths to tease out a rough estimate of how many people
died prematurely as a consequence of famine. But in China the distinction was political. Industrial accidents, suicides, fatal epidemics or deaths
from starvation were all a matter of great concern to the authorities. They
stood as indices of social and political health, and they were diligently
monitored by the party's regulators. Even a single case of suicide could
signal that something was amiss, warranting a political investigation from
above. In the middle of mass death in Fuyang, one of the sites of horror in
Anhui where up to 70 per cent of some villages were wiped out, the region

reported 10,890 deaths for the first quarter of 1961 – of which a mere 524 were described as 'abnormal', including 103 deaths due to 'emaciation' and 'oedema'.[10] In Rongxian, Sichuan, the county head Xu Wenzheng simply dictated that in the official statistics two rules had to be followed: birth rates had to exceed death rates, and the death rate could not be higher than 2 per cent. In Fuling, also in Sichuan, two sets of statistics were kept. For 1960 local cadres managed to count a total population of 594,324 people but reported 697,590, a difference of more than 100,000.[11]

Even when cadres were willing to confront the harsh reality of famine, who could have kept track of an avalanche of death? In Jiangjin and Jiangbei counties in Sichuan, up to 250 people died each day in December 1960: the last thing on the minds of local officials would have been to do the rounds each day to produce a neat list of mortality figures, even if they were specifically asked by their superiors to do so.[12] When local cadres or police officers did try to report the full extent of death they were generally labelled rightists. Zhao Jian, head of the Public Security Bureau in Wenjiang county, Sichuan, systematically compiled statistics for 1959 and discovered that 27,000 people, or 16 per cent, were missing compared to the previous year. He was taken to task by his superior at the provincial level but refused to modify his findings, which led directly to his political demise.[13]

To make matters even more complicated, obfuscation went all the way to the top. Provincial boss Liu Zihou – like so many others – dutifully reported 4,700 'abnormal deaths' to Chairman Mao for all of Hebei in 1960, even though his own team of inspectors had discovered that in one county alone some 18,000 had died of hunger since 1958.[14] The irony is that he chastised county leaders for covering up the extent of the famine, all the while keeping the incriminating figures from his own superiors in Beijing.[15] At every level party officials badgered their subordinates for the truth but were deceitful with their own superiors, contributing to a maze of self-deception. To say that knowledge is power is a truism, and one that does not go very far in explaining why the more absolute power was, the less truth it managed to produce.

But death on such a scale could hardly be hidden all the time. Sometimes local leaders took a chance, sending in hard-hitting reports further up the hierarchy, occasionally directly to Zhou Enlai or Mao Zedong himself. Extraordinarily detailed reports compiled by the investigation teams that fanned out over the countryside after October 1960 led to the removal of a whole series of leaders who had presided over mass death. And sometimes retrospective investigations were carried out in the years following the famine, as the party tried to make sense of what had happened. The result is not so much a neatly arranged set of statistics revealing some absolute truth in a few telling numbers, but rather a mass of uneven and at times messy documentation compiled in different ways, at different times, for different reasons, by different entities, with different degrees of reliability. So assigning a team of 200 people to sift through the evidence would have been a good idea.

The very best of these documents were compiled by a powerful Security Bureau and covered an entire province. As we have seen, this did not happen in Hubei, but it did in Sichuan – by far the most devastated province in all of China. The head of the provincial Security Bureau authorised an investigation into the statistics from 1954 to 1961. The results undermined many of the reported totals, which underestimated the death toll by several per cent in 1960 alone. The corrected death rate for 1954 to 1957 was an average of 1 per cent. This increased to 2.5 per cent in 1958, to 4.7 per cent in 1959, to 5.4 per cent in 1960 and to 2.9 per cent in 1961. It added up to 10.6 million deaths from 1958 to 1961, of which 7.9 million were above 1 per cent and can thus be considered 'excess deaths'.[16] But in Sichuan, unlike the rest of the country, famine did not vanish in 1962. There are countless reports about continuing starvation from a range of counties until the end of 1962. The Public Security Bureau compiled figures which determined that 1.5 per cent died that year, meaning that another 300,000 perished prematurely, bringing the total to 8.2 million.[17] Yet even this figure is no doubt too low by at least 10 or 20 per cent, if only because in Sichuan – unlike in other provinces such as Gansu – the party boss Li Jingquan remained firmly in power despite his responsibility for the deaths of many millions of people. Even in 1962 few county leaders in Sichuan would have been prepared to report the full extent of the disaster.

No other similar documents are available – so far. But we do have data collected by regional statistical bureaus. In the case of Yunnan, where the famine started in 1958, the death rate recorded for the year was 2.2 per cent, double the national average for 1957: this alone would have amounted to 430,000 excess deaths, when most historians using official statistics mention only about 800,000 deaths for the entire 1958 to 1961 period.[18]

The best available evidence comes from carefully compiled reports at the village, commune and county level. Since the work of the historical demographer Cao Shuji, who used published party gazetteers to estimate death rates on a county basis, is in agreement with other population specialists who propose a death toll of roughly 32 million, it provides a very helpful baseline. Common sense indicates that local party committees had every incentive to underestimate published death rates, and in that sense Cao Shuji's estimate should be considered conservative. The purpose of what follows is to test his figures and provide a rough idea of how they should be adjusted. Not only is a focus on smaller entities such as counties much more accurate than larger aggregations at the national level, but it also allows us to eliminate so many of the variables that have confused demographers working with censuses, from internal migration to the size of the army between 1958 and 1962.

However, an average death rate is required in order to calculate 'extra' death figures. What would be reasonable? Here is what Liu Shaoqi, the head of state, thought in 1961 when discussing the famine in his home town of Huaminglou, where hundreds died every month: 'What are normal deaths? What are abnormal deaths? If you hit a man once and he dies of his injuries, or if somebody jumps into a river, it qualifies as an abnormal death. You can take the figures of the last two years to calculate a normal death rate . . . A normal death rate is below 1 per cent, in general 0.8 per cent, a normal birth rate is 2 per cent, any deaths above 0.8 per cent are abnormal.'[19] To err on the safe side, given the wide variations across the country, 1 per cent should be taken as a normal death rate.

In the case of Hebei, we have some very detailed reports for 1960, compiled after provincial boss Liu Zihou gave the green light by asking for investigations into abnormal deaths 'down to the level of the household'. Hu Kaiming, an outspoken party official in charge of Zhangjiakou who later incurred the wrath of Mao Zedong for proposing greater freedom for farmers to determine their own prices, reported that 1.9 per cent of the population had died in 1960, amounting to 59,000 people. In Weixian county, adjacent to Zhangjiakou, the death rate was 3.4 per cent in 1960, as 18,000 people died.[20] That amounted to some 40,000 excessive deaths in one year. Using official documentation, Cao Shuji's figure for excessive deaths in Zhangjiakou and Weixian is 15,000 for the entire three years of famine.[21] In Tianjin and the surrounding countryside – hardly the most deprived part of the country – 30,000 people died within three months at the end of 1960. A normal rate of attrition would have claimed less than half of these lives. The figure provided by Cao Shuji, again based on official rather than archival sources, is 30,000 excess deaths for three years.[22] Another example comes from Shijiazhuang, the seat of a region covering some fifteen counties. By reading the official data critically, Cao arrives at 15,000 deaths for the entire region over three years. But in the city of Shijiazhuang alone, close to 4,000 people died in a mere ten days in January 1961, when counting the victims of starvation was no longer politically taboo.[23]

Tianjin, Zhangjiakou and Shijiazhuang were cities nominally isolated from starvation in the countryside. A very different example comes from Gansu, where the demotion of Zhang Zhongliang in November 1960 was followed by several months of local investigations, bringing to light the extent of the famine. In Longxi county, 16,000 people died in 1959, or 7.5 per cent, followed by 23,000 in 1960, or 11 per cent of the population. So in those two years alone the excess deaths stood at 35,000. But for three years of famine Cao Shuji reaches 24,000 deaths.[24] Party archives give 32,000 deaths for Jingning county, about 7 per cent each year in 1959 and 1960. This contrasts with a figure of 19,000 excess deaths for a period of three years arrived at by Cao Shuji.[25] In Zhangye, out of a population of roughly 280,000, some 5,000 people died in November, followed by 6,000 in December 1960. Even if we double the normal rate of attrition to 2 per cent, that would still represent over 10,000 excess deaths in less than a quarter of a year. Cao Shuji arrives at 17,000 excess deaths – not for one county in two months, but for four counties over a period of three years.[26] In the spring of 1960 some 20,000 people died in Wuwei county alone.

Cao Shuji suggests 50,000 premature deaths for a region comprising four counties, over a period of three years.[27]

In Guizhou the provincial party committee reckoned by 1961 that some 10 per cent of the workforce was missing when compared with 1957 – meaning half a million workers, not counting children and the elderly.[28] Not all of these had died, of course, as many had migrated out of the province, but the death rates were high throughout Guizhou, in particular in regions such as Chishui and Meitan. In Chishui some 22,000 people died in half a year – or 10 per cent of the population.[29] Cao Shuji, using the official record of the county, proposes 46,000 over a period of three years, which seems reasonable enough. But in the case of Meitan, 45,000 people died in half a year. Cao Shuji suggests 105,000 for four counties over a period of three years, which must be too low.[30] Even more interesting is that in his extremely conscientious compilation of the official data for all counties, some places are missing: Yanhe, part of the Tongren region, is not mentioned, although some 40,000–50,000 people died of hunger in that county alone.[31]

In Shandong the discrepancies are of a similar magnitude – even if few of the relevant archives can be accessed by historians. In Pingyuan county, to take an example from the north-western part of the province, a high-ranking investigation noted that out of a population of 452,000 in 1957, over 46,000 people had died by 1961. Despite 24,000 births, the total population dropped to 371,000, as tens of thousands took to the roads to escape from famine – many to die elsewhere, their deaths being excluded from these figures. Cao Shuji's examination of the official annals proposes 19,000 premature deaths for Pingyuan county. Even if we take into account a normal death rate of 1 per cent per year over a period of four years, the total of excess deaths reported at the time would be equivalent to 28,000, or 50 per cent higher.[32] A similar observation can be made about Qihe, which lost a fifth of its population, or 100,000, between 1957 and 1961. If we deduct a normal death rate of 1 per cent for four years and accept that roughly half of the vanished probably migrated to other areas (the document is not clear on this issue), we are still left with a figure comparable to Pingyuan, or roughly 30,000, although Cao Shuji ventures no more than 19,000, or a third less.[33] For the entire Laizhou region, consisting of

Qingdao and thirteen counties, Cao Shuji's estimate is 164,000 premature deaths over four years. But the archives show that in Jimo county alone, according to incomplete statistics, some 47,000 people died (excluding 51,000 farmers who took to the roads) over a period of two years. Even if we deduct 15,000 normal deaths for a population of approximately 750,000 people, it still leaves the county with 32,000 premature deaths – far above Cao Shuji's estimate.[34]

In some cases the archival data and the published material are in line. In Xinxing county, Guangdong, 1.5 per cent of the population died in 1959, followed by 2.88 per cent in 1960. This would have amounted to roughly 5,000 deaths, while Cao Shuji arrives at a total of 8,000 deaths for three years.[35] For the much larger region of Jiangmen, also in Guangdong, encompassing several counties, the death rate given to the provincial party committee was 2 per cent in 1960 (or 120,000 deaths, half of which would count as 'premature'). This is difficult to compare with Cao's reconstruction of the official data, as the administrative borders of the region were extensively redrawn after 1961, but they do seem roughly to fit his estimate of 112,000 excess deaths for three years.[36] In the case of Sichuan, as noted above, political pressure under Li Jingquan meant that few if any counties reported high death rates, and none match those found in the official documentation published decades later and consulted by Cao Shuji.

None of this is intended as a criticism of Cao Shuji's work: on the contrary, his painstaking reconstruction of what happened at the county level, on the basis of well over a thousand local gazetteers, has established a baseline which is very much in accord with figures derived by demographers from more abstract sets of population statistics. A systematic comparison of these figures with archival data compiled at the time or in the immediate aftermath of the famine would not be possible without his work. And when we confront the official data with archival evidence we find a pattern of underestimation, sometimes by 30 to 50 per cent, sometimes by as much as a factor of three or four.

Perhaps some of the reports exaggerated the death rates, but it is very difficult to see why. There was no political advantage to be gained from declaring extra deaths. The death toll was not a major consideration in the purge of party members after October 1960. The manner of death mattered, as local cadres were classified according to different levels of abuse. In fact there was every advantage in inflating the overall population. When a team went to investigate the statistics in Hunan in 1964 it found that the overall population was systematically inflated by more than 1 per cent, in some counties by up to 2 or 3 per cent. The difference for 1963 was half a million people in Hunan who existed on paper alone: 'through thorough testing we found that in the past the population figures were routinely and severely inflated'.[37] When the Ministry of Public Security undertook a more widespread check on population statistics in 1963, it discovered a similar pattern of inflation across the country, sometimes as high as 2.2 per cent in the case of Gansu, for instance. 'Of a population of 681 million today, we estimate that about 1 to 1.5 per cent of those counted are fake. Many local cadres, in order to obtain greater cloth rations and other goods, intentionally increase the population figures.'[38] A year later, during the official 1964 census, the Central Census Office confirmed that 'the problem of population inflation is far worse than we thought', as at least a million was added for Hebei and Henan each, and no fewer than 700,000 for Shandong, three of the provinces that had been closely investigated: there was very little that could be done about the issue.[39]

Even if we ignore some of the most glaring disparities between archival data and official figures, the gap is in the order of 50 to 100 per cent. It is very difficult to venture an alternative death toll, all the more since so many of the key sets of archival statistics remain prudently under lock and key, far removed from the eyes of prying historians. But there is enough archival evidence, from a sufficiently large diversity of party units, to confirm that the figure of 43 to 46 million premature deaths proposed by Chen Yizi, who was a senior member of a large working group that sifted through internal party documents around 1980, is in all likelihood a reliable estimate. The death toll thus stands at a minimum of 45 million excess deaths.

It could be even worse than that. Some historians speculate that the true figure stands as high as 50 to 60 million people. It is unlikely that we will know the full extent of the disaster until the archives are completely opened. But these are the figures informally discussed by a number of party historians. And these are also, according to Chen Yizi, the figures cited at internal meetings of senior party members under Zhao Ziyang.[40] Yu Xiguang, an independent researcher with a great deal of experience, puts the figure at 55 million excess deaths.[41]

Epilogue

The turning point came in January 1962, as 7,000 cadres arrived from all parts of the country to attend the largest work conference ever held in the vast, modernistic Great Hall of the People in Beijing. Liu Shaoqi, the head of state, issued the official report to a packed audience, speaking for three hours without a break – but not without interruption. He did not confront Mao directly, which would have been unthinkable, but he openly repeated everything he had said behind closed doors to a small gathering of senior leaders half a year earlier. In Hunan, he explained, the farmers believed that the 'difficulties' were due 30 per cent to natural calamities and 70 per cent to a man-made disaster. The very use of the term 'man-made disaster' (*renhuo*) was a bombshell, drawing gasps from the audience. As Liu proceeded to dismiss the expression 'nine fingers to one', Mao's favourite phrase to emphasise achievements over setbacks, the tension became palpable. 'In general our successes have been primary, shortcomings and errors are secondary, they occupy a second position. I wonder if we can say that, generally speaking, the ratio of achievements to setbacks is seven to three, although each region is different. One finger versus nine fingers does not apply to every place. There are only a small number of regions where mistakes are equal to one finger and successes equal to nine fingers.' Mao interrupted Liu, visibly annoyed: 'It's not a small number of regions at all, for instance in Hebei only 20 per cent of regions decreased production and in Jiangsu 30 per cent of all regions increased production year after year!' But Liu refused to be intimidated, and carried on: 'In general, we cannot say it is merely one finger, but rather three, and in some places it is even more, for instance in the Xinyang region [in Henan] or in the Tianshui region [in Gansu].'

And who was responsible for this disaster? Liu squarely placed the blame on the central leadership.[1]

Liu did try to appease the Chairman by defending the general party line, postponing the verdict over the communes to five or maybe even ten years later. But Mao was furious nonetheless. 'He talks about natural disasters versus man-made disasters. This kind of talk is a disaster in itself,' he confided to his doctor.[2]

Lin Biao, the general who had rallied to the defence of the Chairman at the Lushan plenum in 1959, again lauded the Great Leap Forward, hailed as an unprecedented accomplishment when compared to any other period of the country's history. He rhapsodised: 'The thoughts of Chairman Mao are always correct ... Chairman Mao's superiority has many aspects, not just one, and I know from experience that Chairman Mao's most outstanding quality is realism. What he says is much more realistic than what others say. He is always pretty close to the mark. He is never out of touch with reality ... I feel very deeply that when in the past our work was done well, it was precisely when we thoroughly implemented and did not interfere with Chairman Mao's thought. Every time Chairman Mao's ideas were not sufficiently respected or suffered interference, there have been problems. That is essentially what the history of our party over the last few decades shows.'[3]

Zhou Enlai did what he always managed best. He tried to absolve Mao by assuming much of the blame for what had gone wrong, taking personal responsibility for excessive grain procurements, inflated production figures, the draining of grain away from the provinces and growing exports of food. 'This is my mistake,' he declared, going on to claim that the 'shortcomings and errors of the last few years have occurred precisely when we contravened the general line and Chairman Mao's precious instructions'.[4] He was trying to build a bridge across the gap that had opened between Mao and Liu, but it was to no avail.

We will never know when Mao decided to get rid of Liu, setting in motion a Cultural Revolution that would destroy the lives of all those who had opposed him during the Great Leap Forward. But a good guess is that he started plotting the elimination of his ever more threatening nemesis as soon as he realised that his entire legacy as well as his standing in history was at stake.

The defining moment may have been a summer afternoon in July 1962, when Mao was floating in his swimming pool. He had been urgently called back to Beijing by Liu, and the Chairman was in a foul mood. Liu's son recalls that his father hurriedly approached the Chairman, having been summoned to explain what the rush was all about. Liu started by reporting that Chen Yun and Tian Jiaying, two of the most outspoken critics of the Great Leap Forward, wanted formally to present their views about land distribution. Mao soon exploded into a torrent of invective. But Liu would not desist. He spoke in haste: 'So many people have died of hunger!' Then he blurted out, 'History will judge you and me, even cannibalism will go into the books!'

Mao went into a towering rage. 'The Three Red Banners have been shot down, now land is being divided up again,' he shouted. 'What have you done to resist this? What's going to happen after I'm dead?'

The two men soon calmed down, and Mao agreed that an economic policy of adjustment should continue.[5] But the Chairman was now convinced that he had found his Khrushchev, the servant who had denounced his master Stalin. Liu, he concluded, was obviously the man who would issue a secret speech denouncing all his crimes. Mao was biding his time, but the patient groundwork for launching a Cultural Revolution that would tear the party and the country apart had already begun.

Acknowledgements

I acknowledge with gratitude a Hsu Long Sing Research Grant from the Faculty of Arts, University of Hong Kong, research grant HKU743308H from the Research Grants Council, Hong Kong, and research grant RG016-P-07 from the Chiang Ching-kuo Foundation, Taiwan, which allowed me to carry out the research for this book. A number of people have read and commented on draft versions, in particular Børge Bakken, Jasper Becker, John Burns, Gail Burrowes, Chen Jian, Thomas DuBois, Louise Edwards, May Holdsworth, Christopher Hutton, Françoise Koolen, Kam Louie, Roderick MacFarquhar, Veronica Pearson, Robert Peckham, Arthur Waldron, Felix Wemheuer and Zhou Xun. Jean Hung, at the Universities Service Centre for China Studies at the Chinese University of Hong Kong, was very helpful. Michael Share, Jean-François Fayet and Elena Osokina helped me in gaining access to the archives in Moscow. Tammy Ho and Chan Yeeshan collected interviews from famine survivors in 2006. I owe a very special debt of gratitude to Zhou Xun, who not only enormously broadened the scope of the interviews on many a trip to the mainland, but also conducted additional research for me on several chapters. The Faculty of Arts at the University of Hong Kong, in particular the Department of History, has been a wonderful environment for the research, and I am grateful to all my colleagues who supported the project, in particular Daniel Chua, Peter Cunich, Maureen Sabine and Kam Louie.

There are many people in mainland China who helped my research in one way or another, but I prefer not to name them for reasons that seem obvious enough. I very much hope that the situation will be different one day. I am indebted to my publishers, namely Michael Fishwick in London and George Gibson in New York, and my copy-editor Peter James, as well as Anna Simpson, Alexa von Hirschberg and all the team at Bloomsbury. I would like to convey my deep gratitude to my literary agent Gillon Aitken, who had faith in me and the project from the very beginning. Last but not least, I wish lovingly to thank my wife Gail Burrowes.

Hong Kong, February 2010

An Essay on the Sources

The bulk of the sources come from party archives in China, and a few words about these may help the reader better to understand the foundation on which the book rests. In a one-party state, archives do not belong to the public, they belong to the party. They are often housed in a special building on the local party committee premises, which are generally set among lush and lovingly manicured grounds closely guarded by military personnel. Access to the archives is strictly regulated and would have been unthinkable until a decade or so ago, but over the past few years increasing quantities of documents older than thirty years have become available for consultation to readers with a letter of recommendation. The extent and quality of the material vary from place to place, but in general most collections distinguish between 'open', or declassified, and 'closed', or controlled files, as truly sensitive material remains out of bounds except to the eyes of the most senior party members. The very fact that this distinction removes from the scrutiny of most historians a large proportion of vital information indicates that this book has been written with relatively 'soft' material: future historians, hopefully, will be able to reveal the true scale of what happened on the basis of fully open archives.

Another complication presents itself in the fact that, with the exception of the Ministry of Foreign Affairs, most central archives are extremely difficult to access. Most historians tend to rely on provincial and county collections instead. Although a good dozen city and county archives have been used in this work, the majority of the material comes from ten provincial archives (listed in the Select Bibliography), which were chosen largely on the basis of openness. Until now no historian, to my knowledge, has been able to work on the Maoist era in the Anhui provincial archives, while the collection in Henan also remains highly restricted, to the point where even if access were granted it would remain rather meaningless, as only the most banal documents would be handed over to the researcher, often in painfully small quantities. Other collections, by contrast, have been gradually opening up, and my selection represents a good spread of provinces in terms of population density (Shandong versus Gansu), severity of the famine (Sichuan on one extreme, Zhejiang on the other) and geography (from Hebei in the north to Guangdong in the south).

The archives inside each provincial collection reflect the structure of the party machinery and are often divided into smaller groups according to the institution they belonged to – for instance the Bureau for Hygiene or the Bureau for Forestry. What the historian finds, then, is often extremely diverse material, far more so than the stark term 'archives' actually suggests. There are letters written by ordinary people, surveys of working conditions in factories by the All-China Federation of Trade Unions, investigations into cases of corruption, Bureau of Public Security reports of theft, murder, arson and assault on granaries, detailed evidence of local cadre abuses compiled by special teams sent in during rectification campaigns, general reports on peasant resistance during the collectivisation campaign, secret opinion surveys and much more.

The huge variety of material is nonetheless of official provenance. Even the letters written by ordinary farmers and workers would have been selected for some official purpose, and we have little alternative but to view everyday life through the prism of the state. This observation, of course, is true for all state archives, including those of Hitler's Germany and Stalin's Russia. It does not mean that we cannot read them against the grain. Finally, any historian worth his salt will know how to assess the authorship of official reports, their intended audience, the institutional context which engendered them and the conditions of their production. Historians are attuned to the complications which result from the distortion of social reality by official rhetoric, as terms such as 'sabotage', 'slacking', 'treason', 'enemy of the people' and 'leftist excesses' obscure what happened. Yet the sheer variety and abundance of reports about resistance demonstrate the persistence of rural strategies of survival, while the state itself was a complex, sprawling organisation which hardly ever spoke – or reported

– with one voice. Just as senior leaders such as Peng Dehuai and Mao Zedong clashed in their findings about the Great Leap Forward, different individuals, units and organisations varied enormously in how they reported what they found on the ground.

Provincial archives are not only much richer than the smaller collections which can be found in counties, cities or even villages, but they also tend to keep copies of important files that were sent to them from above, namely Beijing, or from below, for instance when counties reported on important matters such as grain shortages or the collapse of a dam. In the bureaucratic maze of communist China, a document was hardly ever 'unique', in the sense that copies were made and circulated to many institutions who might have claimed a stake in the case at hand. Many of the reports compiled by work teams, for instance, would have been sent to several dozen party members. An important central document was distributed to every province and county, while more sensitive material might have been copied only to the first secretaries of each province. In other words, a wealth of material which does not necessarily pertain to the region in question can be found in provincial collections, including minutes of speeches and gatherings at the highest level. These minutes can vary considerably, as they were taken by different people, sometimes from tape recordings. Some are more detailed than others. I have tried to make it as easy as possible for the interested reader to find out the provenance of each document. In the Notes the first number in the archival location data refers to the general collection, the name of which is provided in the list of archives at the end of this book. As an example, 'Hunan, 6 Oct. 1962, 207-1-750, pp. 44–9' indicates that the document is contained in a file from the Hunan provincial archives in collection 207, which stands for the Bureau for Water Conservancy and Hydroelectricity.

What happened at the highest level, inside the corridors of power in Beijing? So far, to understand court politics under Mao most historians have relied on official publications, internal documents (*neibu*) or Red Guard material released during the Cultural Revolution. In contrast I prefer to use archival material as far as possible, and I do so for three reasons. First, entire sentences or sections have been omitted from the published speeches of senior leaders, in particular, but not only, in Red

Guard material. There are countless examples of small stylistic changes or more profound editorial excisions, and they change the overall sense of many of these speeches. Second, the minutes of entire meetings have been censored, either officially in the mainland or in the Red Guard material smuggled out of China during the Cultural Revolution. And third, while historians have given much weight to meetings on which leading party members have later commented, crucial events and decisions have simply been ignored or censored, even in the otherwise very reliable official biographies of leaders published by party historians with access to the Central Archives in Beijing. This is the case, as we have seen, with the meeting at the Jinjiang Hotel in Shanghai on 25 March 1959 at which Mao suggested that a third of all grain should be procured to meet foreign commitments.

In short, the entire record of the Maoist era, as reflected in official and internally published sources, is a skilful exercise in obfuscation and, as such, an inadequate basis for historical research. This rather sceptical view is confirmed by a recent biography of Zhou Enlai by Gao Wenqian. Gao, a party historian who worked in the Central Archives in Beijing for many years, smuggled out his notes before absconding to the United States. The premier described in Gao's groundbreaking biography is substantially different from the iconic figure most of us are used to (Gao Wenqian, *Zhou Enlai: The Last Perfect Revolutionary*, New York: PublicAffairs, 2007). However, while bearing these shortcomings in mind, anything published by the Central Documents Research Office (Zhongyang wenxian yanjiu shi), including their voluminous and carefully referenced biographies of leaders, is invaluable. The problem with these publications is the vast amount of crucial information that has been deliberately excluded, and the same can be said of the post-1949 manuscripts of Mao published in a dozen volumes as Mao Zedong, *Jianguo yilai Mao Zedong wengao* (Mao Zedong's manuscripts since the founding of the People's Republic), Beijing: Zhongyang wenxian chubanshe, 1987–96.

China, like all communist states, has a sprawling bureaucracy in which obsessive attention to the most minute details – even in the midst of widespread want – can reach absurd dimensions, but not every scrap of paper ends up carefully preserved in an archive. Factories, government units, even the courts and the police sometimes dispose of their files, for instance when they move to new quarters. Some of these documents – confessions, reports, directives, permits and certificates of every sort – end up in the delightfully chaotic flea markets of Guangzhou, Shanghai or Beijing. Over many a weekend, as the archives are closed, I have sifted through dusty papers: some of these were in bundles spread on a blanket, with the owner squatting on a pile of old newspapers; others were displayed on makeshift tables among memorabilia, postcards, magazines and stamps. I have built up a small collection of documents (as well as a pile of ration coupons of every shade and colour, since they are one of the very few artefacts of bureaucracy to have survived the famine), but have quoted very few of them, and then only when no equivalent exists in the official party archives.

A small proportion of the evidence comes from foreign archives, in particular Russian and East German, the two countries that were most closely involved with China at the time. All in all, they are helpful in reconstructing the foreign trade and policy aspects of the era, although they are much more limited when it comes to observations about every-day life. Most advisers were confined to the cities, and by 1960 even the East Germans – who remained sympathetic to the Great Leap Forward for much longer than other Eastern Europeans – were leaving in droves. A few snippets can be gleaned from reports to London, although overall the fabled sinologists in the British embassy were pretty clueless – and poorly prepared too, without any apparent knowledge of collectivisation and its effects. A low-ranking scribbler with experience of the Soviet Union would have done a better job. Very much the opposite could be said of the staff of the secret services in Taiwan, who compiled extremely detailed and insightful reports about every aspect of the famine for Chiang Kai-shek and a select few of his acolytes in regular intelligence bulletins, which can be found in the Bureau of Investigation in Hsin-tien, on the outskirts of Taipei. The United States refused to believe Chiang Kai-shek (as CIA reports show), no doubt fearing that the Generalissimo might drag them into an invasion of the mainland. However, since the party archives in China are much more reliable, I have not used this material at all.

Several times a week the official press agency Xinhua compiled a report three to ten pages long called *Internal Reference* (*Neibu cankao*) which was distributed to officials at the ministerial level and higher. This source pales in comparison with the archival material, as it was heavily censored, but nonetheless contains interesting snippets of information. Finally, some of the memoirs and personal recollections of party members, interpreters, secretaries and diplomats can be useful, although many suffer from self-censorship and lack of concrete detail. Pride of place should be given to Mao's personal physician Li Zhisui. Much maligned by some sinologists for being too 'sensational', he is a very reliable guide whose recollections can be verified, sometimes almost verbatim, in the party archives (an observation also confirmed by Lorenz Lüthi, who worked extensively with Soviet documents; see Lorenz M. Lüthi, *The Sino-Soviet Split: Cold War in the Communist World*, Princeton: Princeton University Press, 2008, p. 354).

I have used a small number of interviews to give a voice occasionally to ordinary people – although, of course, they speak loudly and volubly in many a party document, from opinion surveys to police reports. About a hundred interviews were conducted by researchers specifically trained for this project by me over several years, often in the format of what specialists refer to as 'insider interviewing', meaning that interviewers spoke with people from the same social background in their own dialect, sometimes from the same village or even family, cutting out both the presence of an alien interviewer (foreign or urban Chinese) and a translator. All these interviews have been transcribed and deposited with the Universities Service Centre for China Studies at the Chinese University of Hong Kong. All the names of the interviewees, as well as those of a very small number of people who may still be alive, have been anonymised.

Finally, a short word about secondary sources. While for many decades the best specialists on the Maoist era were to be found in Europe, the United States and Japan, the centre of gravity has decidedly moved back to China. A small but growing body of work has been published on the famine by historians who have spent time in very different archival collections. Their publications are not always welcome in China, and more often than not appear in Hong Kong – a city which is rapidly emerging, once again, as the key interface between the mainland and the rest of the world. Yu Xiguang is the historian with by far the most experience in teasing out vital information from the archives, as is made clear by his superb anthology (Yu Xiguang, *Dayuejin ku rizi: Shangshuji* [The Great Leap Forward and the years of bitterness: A collection of memorials], Hong Kong: Shidai chaoliu chubanshe, 2005). Special mention must be made of Yang Jisheng, a retired journalist who was one of the first to use archival collections from the provinces (Yang Jisheng, *Mubei: Zhongguo liushi niandai dajihuang jishi* [Wooden gravestone: A true history of the Great Famine in China in the 1960s], Hong Kong: Tiandi tushu youxian gongsi, 2008). His work remains important, in particular in so far as few other historians have been able to research and publish on the famine in Henan province. But his two volumes do suffer from a number of serious shortcomings. Those familiar with the material will see that the book is more of a compilation of notes from different sources than a carefully constructed text. At times it looks like a hotchpotch which simply strings together large chunks of text, some lifted from the Web, a few from published sources, and others transcribed from archival material. Invaluable documents are thrown together with irrelevant anecdotes, making it difficult for the reader to see the wood for the trees. In some cases the author spent only a day or two in the archives, missing the most vital, and openly available, documents. This is the case for the chapter on Guangdong, which relies on a single file for the entire famine. But most of all there is no time line: by dispensing with a meaningful historical narrative and focusing heavily on grain shortages, the author misses an important dimension of the disaster. More solid is Lin Yunhui's magisterial book, essential in tracing the development of the Great Leap Forward. While it relies for the greatest part on published sources and is concerned solely with court politics, its sheer scope and breadth of analysis supersede all other books in political science on the topic (Lin Yunhui, *Wutuobang yundong: Cong dayuejin dao dajihuang, 1958–1961* [Utopian movement: From the Great Leap Forward to the Great Famine, 1958–61], Hong Kong: Xianggang zhongwen daxue dangdai Zhongguo wenhua yanjiu zhongxin, 2008). Last but not least, Gao Wangling's work on peasant forms of resistance during the famine is a model of originality and insight, and it has been a major inspiration for this book (Gao Wangling, *Renmin gongshe shiqi Zhongguo nongmin 'fanxingwei' diaocha* [Acts of peasant resistance in China during the people's communes], Beijing: Zhonggong dangshi chubanshe, 2006).

In English much of the literature on the famine now looks rather dated, but readers interested in elite politics will still enjoy reading Roderick MacFarquhar, *The Origins of the Cultural Revolution: The Great Leap Forward, 1958–1960*, New York: Columbia University Press, 1983. More recent is Alfred Chan, whose analysis of how Mao's vision was actually implemented in Guangdong remains unsurpassed (Alfred L. Chan, *Mao's Crusade: Politics and Policy Implementation in China's Great Leap Forward*, Oxford: Oxford University Press, 2001). There are some good village studies based on interviews, although of course they tend to rely on the words of those who survived, leaving the dead without a voice. A recent example is Ralph A. Thaxton, *Catastrophe and Contention in Rural China: Mao's Great Leap Forward, Famine and the Origins of Righteous Resistance in Da Fo Village*, New York: Cambridge University Press, 2008. Jasper Becker's account of the famine remains very readable (Jasper Becker, *Hungry Ghosts: Mao's Secret Famine*, New York: Henry Holt, 1996). Other authors whose work has touched on the famine include David Bachman, *Bureaucracy, Economy, and Leadership in China: The Institutional Origins of the Great Leap Forward*, Cambridge: Cambridge University Press, 1991; Thomas P. Bernstein, 'Mao Zedong and the Famine of 1959–1960: A Study in Wilfulness', *China Quarterly*, no. 186 (June 2006), pp. 421–45 and 'Stalinism, Famine and Chinese Peasants: Grain Procurements during the Great Leap Forward', *Theory and Society*, vol. 13 (May 1984), pp. 339–77; Edward Friedman, Paul G. Pickowicz and Mark Selden with Kay Ann Johnson, *Chinese Village, Socialist State*, New Haven: Yale University Press, 1991; Jean-Luc Domenach, *The Origins of the Great Leap Forward: The Case of One Chinese Province*, Boulder: Westview Press, 1995; Penny Kane, *Famine in China, 1959–61: Demographic and Social Implications*, Basingstoke: Macmillan, 1988; Roderick MacFarquhar, *The Origins of the Cultural Revolution*, vol. 3: *The Coming of the Cataclysm, 1961–1966*, New York: Columbia University Press, 1999; Frederick C. Teiwes and Warren Sun, *China's Road to Disaster: Mao, Central Politicians, and Provincial Leaders in the Unfolding of the Great Leap Forward, 1955–1959*, Armonk, NY: M. E. Sharpe, 1999; Dali L. Yang, *Calamity and Reform in China: State, Rural Society, and Institutional Change since the Great Leap Famine*, Stanford: Stanford University Press, 1996. Other helpful studies are listed in the Select Bibliography.

Select Bibliography

Archives

Non-Chinese Archives

AVPRF – Arkhiv Vneshnei Politiki Rossiiskoi Federatsii, Moscow, Russia
BArch – Bundesarchiv, Berlin, Germany
ICRC – International Committee of the Red Cross, Geneva, Switzerland
MfAA – Politische Archiv des Auswärtigen Amts, Berlin, Germany
PRO – National Archives, London, United Kingdom
PRO, Hong Kong – Public Record Office, Hong Kong
RGAE – Rossiiskii Gosudarstvennyi Arkhiv Ekonomiki, Moscow, Russia
RGANI – Rossiiskii Gosudarstvennyi Arkhiv Noveishei Istorii, Moscow, Russia

Central Archives

Ministry of Foreign Affairs – Waijiaobu Dang'anguan, Beijing

Provincial Archives

Gansu – Gansu sheng dang'anguan, Lanzhou
91 Zhonggong Gansu shengwei (Gansu Provincial Party Committee)
96 Zhonggong Gansu shengwei nongcun gongzuobu (Gansu Provincial Party Committee Department for Rural Work)

Guangdong – Guangdong sheng dang'anguan, Guangzhou
216 Guangdong shengwei tongzhanbu (Guangdong Provincial Party Committee Office for the United Front)
217 Guangdong sheng nongcunbu (Guangdong Provincial Bureau for Rural Affairs)
218 Guangdong sheng gongyebu (Guangdong Province Bureau for Industry)
231 Guangdong sheng zonggonghui (Guangdong Province Federation of Trade Unions)
235 Guangdong sheng renmin weiyuanhui (Guangdong Provincial People's Congress)

253　Guangdong sheng jihua weiyuanhui (Guangdong Province Planning Committee)

262　Guangdong sheng yinglinbu (Guangdong Province Bureau for Forestry)

266　Guangdong sheng shuidianbu (Guangdong Province Bureau for Water Conservancy and Hydroelectricity)

300　Guangdong sheng tongjiju (Guangdong Province Office for Statistics)

307　Guangdong sheng wenhuaju (Guangdong Province Office for Culture)

314　Guangdong sheng jiaoyuting (Guangdong Province Bureau for Education)

317　Guangdong sheng weishengting (Guangdong Province Bureau for Health and Hygiene)

Guangxi – Guangxi sheng dang'anguan, Nanning

X1　Zhonggong Guangxi shengwei (Guangxi Provincial Party Committee)

Guizhou – Guizhou sheng dang'anguan, Guiyang

90　Zhonggong Guizhou sheng nongyeting (Guizhou Province Agricultural Bureau)

Hebei – Hebei sheng dang'anguan, Shijiazhuang

855　Zhonggong Hebei shengwei (Hebei Provincial Party Committee)

856　Zhonggong Hebei shengjiwei (Hebei Provincial Committee for Inspecting Discipline)

878　Shengwei shenghuo bangongshi (Hebei Provincial Party Committee Office for Daily Life)

879　Zhonggong Hebei shengwei nongcun gongzuobu (Hebei Provincial Party Committee Department for Rural Work)

880　Zhonggong Hebei shengwei nongcun zhengfeng zhengshe bangongshi (Hebei Provincial Party Committee Office for Rectification in the Countryside)

884　Zhonggong Hebei shengwei zhengfa weiyuanhui (Hebei Provincial Party Committee Commission on Political and Legal Affairs)

979　Hebei sheng nongyeting (Hebei Province Agricultural Bureau)

Hubei – Hubei sheng dang'anguan, Wuhan

SZ1　Zhonggong Hubei sheng weiyuanhui (Hubei Provincial Party Committee)

SZ18　Zhonggong Hubei sheng weiyuanhui nongcun zhengzhibu (Hubei Provincial Party Committee Department for Rural Politics)

SZ29　Hubei sheng zonggonghui (Hubei Province Federation of Trade Unions)

SZ34　Hubei sheng renmin weiyuanhui (Hubei Provincial People's Congress)

SZ113　Hubei sheng shuiliting (Hubei Province Bureau for Water Conservancy)

SZ115　Hubei sheng weishengting (Hubei Province Bureau for Health and Hygiene)

Hunan – Hunan sheng dang'anguan, Changsha

141　Zhonggong Hunan sheng weiyuanhui (Hunan Provincial Party Committee)

146 Zhonggong Hunan shengwei nongcun gongzuobu (Hunan Provincial Party Committee Department for Rural Work)

151 Zhonggong Hunan shengwei zhengce yanjiushi (Hunan Provincial Party Committee Office for Policy Research)

163 Hunan sheng renmin weiyuanhui (Hunan Provincial People's Congress)

186 Hunan sheng jihua weiyuanhui (Hunan Province Planning Committee)

187 Hunan sheng tongjiju (Hunan Province Statistics Office)

207 Hunan sheng shuili shuidianting (Hunan Province Bureau for Water Conservancy and Hydroelectricity)

265 Hunan sheng weisheng fangyiting (Hunan Province Bureau for Health and Epidemic Prevention)

Shandong – Shandong sheng dang'anguan, Jinan

A1 Zhonggong Shandong shengwei (Shandong Provincial Party Committee)

Sichuan – Sichuan sheng dang'anguan, Chengdu

JC1 Shengwei bangongting (Office of the Provincial Party Committee)

JC12 Sichuan shengwei mingongwei (Sichuan Provincial Party Committee on Ethnic Affairs)

JC44 Sichuan sheng minzhengting (Sichuan Province Bureau for Civil Affairs)

JC50 Sichuan sheng renwei zongjiao shiwuchu (Office for Religious Affairs of the Sichuan Provincial People's Congress)

JC67 Sichuan shengwei tongjiju (Sichuan Province Statistics Office)

JC133 Sichuan sheng weishengting (Sichuan Province Bureau for Health and Hygiene)

Yunnan – Yunnan sheng dang'anguan, Kunming

2 Zhonggong Yunnan shengwei (Yunnan Provincial Party Committee)

11 Zhonggong Yunnan shengwei nongcun gongzuobu (Yunnan Provincial Party Committee Department for Rural Work)

81 Yunnan sheng tongjiju (Yunnan Province Statistics Office)

105 Yunnan sheng shuili shuidianting (Yunnan Province Bureau for Water Conservancy and Hydroelectricity)

120 Yunnan sheng liangshiting (Yunnan Province Bureau for Grain)

Zhejiang – Zhejiang sheng dang'anguan, Hangzhou

J002 Zhonggong Zhejiang shengwei (Zhejiang Provincial Party Committee)

J007 Zhejiang shengwei nongcun gongzuobu (Zhejiang Provincial Party Committee's Department for Rural Work)

J116 Zhejiang sheng nongyeting (Zhejiang Province Bureau for Agriculture)

J132 Zhejiang sheng liangshiting (Zhejiang Province Bureau for Grain)

J165 Zhejiang sheng weishengting (Zhejiang Province Bureau for Health and Hygiene)

County and City Archives

Beijing – Beijing shi dang'anguan, Beijing

1 Beijing shi weiyuanhui (Beijing Municipal Party Committee)
2 Beijing shi renmin weiyuanhui (Beijing Municipal People's Congress)
84 Beijing shi funü lianhehui (Beijing Municipal Women's Federation)
92 Beijing shi nonglinju (Beijing Municipal Bureau of Agriculture and Forestry)
96 Beijing shi shuili qixiangju (Beijing Municipal Bureau for Water Conservancy and Meteorology)
101 Beijing shi zonggonghui (Beijing Municipal Federation of Trade Unions)

Chishui – Chishui shi dang'anguan, Chishui, Guizhou

1 Chishui shiwei (Chishui Municipal Party Committee)

Fuyang – Fuyang shi dang'anguan, Fuyang, Anhui

J3 Fuyang shiwei (Fuyang Municipal Party Committee)

Guangzhou – Guangzhou shi dang'anguan, Guangzhou, Guangdong

6 Guangzhou shiwei xuanchuanbu (Guangzhou Municipal Party Committee's Bureau for Propaganda)
13 Guangzhou shi nongcun gongzuobu (Guangzhou Municipal Party Committee's Department for Rural Work)
16 Guangzhou shiwei jiedao gongzuobu (Guangzhou Municipal Party Committee's Task Unit on Neighbourhoods)
69 Guangzhou shiwei gangtie shengchan zhihuibu bangongshi (Bureau of the Municipal Party Committee's Headquarters for Steel Production)
92 Guangzhou shi zonggonghui (Guangzhou Municipal Federation of Trade Unions)
94 Guangzhou shi funü lianhehui (Guangzhou Municipal Women's Federation)
97 Guangzhou shi renmin weiyuanhui bangongting (Office of the Guangzhou Municipal People's Congress)
176 Guangzhou shi weishengju (Guangzhou Municipal Bureau for Health and Hygiene)

Guiyang – Guiyang shi dang'anguan, Guiyang, Guizhou

61 Zhonggong Guiyang shiwei (Guiyang Municipal Party Committee)

Kaiping – Kaiping shi dang'anguan, Kaiping, Guangdong

3 Kaiping shiwei (Kaiping Municipal Party Committee)

Macheng – Macheng shi dang'anguan, Macheng, Hubei

1 Macheng xianwei (Macheng County Party Committee)

Nanjing – Nanjing shi dang'anguan, Nanjing, Jiangsu

4003   Nanjing shiwei (Nanjing Municipal Party Committee)

4053   Nanjing shiwei chengshi renmin gongshe lingdao xiaozu bangongshi (Nanjing Municipal Party Committee Office of the Group Leading the Urban Communes)

5003   Nanjing shi renmin zhengfu (Nanjing Municipal People's Government)

5012   Nanjing shi minzhengju (Nanjing Municipal Bureau for Civil Affairs)

5035   Nanjing shi zhonggongyeju (Nanjing Municipal Bureau for Heavy Industry)

5040   Nanjing shi shougongyeju (Nanjing Municipal Bureau for Handicraft Industry)

5065   Nanjing shi weishengju (Nanjing Municipal Bureau for Health and Hygiene)

6001   Nanjing shi zonggonghui (Nanjing Municipal Federation of Trade Unions)

Shanghai – Shanghai shi dang'anguan, Shanghai

A2   Shanghai shiwei bangongting (Office of the Shanghai Municipal Party Committee)

A20   Shanghai shiwei linong gongzuo weiyuanhui (Shanghai Municipal Party Committee's Committee on Neighbourhood Work)

A23   Shanghai shiwei jiaoyu weishengbu (Shanghai Municipal Party Committee's Bureau for Education and Health)

A36   Shanghai shiwei gongye zhengzhibu (Shanghai Municipal Party Committee's Bureau for Industry and Politics)

A70   Shanghai shiwei nongcun gongzuobu (Shanghai Municipal Party Committee's Department for Rural Work)

A72   Shanghai shiwei nongcun gongzuo weiyuanhui (Committee for Rural Work of the Shanghai Municipal Party Committee)

B29   Shanghai shi jingji jihua weiyuanhui (Shanghai Municipal Committee for Economic Planning)

B31   Shanghai shi tongjiju (Shanghai Municipal Bureau for Statistics)

B112   Shanghai shi yejin gongyeju (Shanghai Municipal Bureau for Metallurgy)

B123   Shanghai shi diyi shangyeju (Shanghai Municipal First Commercial Bureau)

B242   Shanghai shi weishengju (Shanghai Municipal Bureau for Health)

Suiping – Suiping shi dang'anguan, Suiping, Henan

1   Suiping xianwei (Suiping County Party Committee)

Wuhan – Wuhan shi dang'anguan, Wuhan, Hubei

13   Wuhan shi renmin zhengfu (Wuhan Municipal People's Government)

28   Wuhan shi Jiang'anqu weiyuanhui (Wuhan Committee on Jiang'an District)

30   Wuhan shi Jianghanqu weiyuanhui (Wuhan Committee on Jianghan District)

70   Wuhan shi jiaoyuting (Wuhan Municipal Bureau for Education)

71 Wuhan shi weishengju (Wuhan Municipal Bureau for Health and Hygiene)
76 Wuhan shi gongshang guanliju (Wuhan Municipal Bureau for the Administration of Industry and Commerce)
83 Wuhan shi minzhengju (Wuhan Municipal Bureau for Civil Affairs)

Wujiang – Wujiang xian dang'anguan, Wujiang, Jiangsu
1001 Wujiang xianwei bangongshi (Office of the Wujiang County Party Committee)

Wuxi – Wuxi shi dang'anguan, Wuxi, Jiangsu
B1 Wuxi xianwei bangongshi (Office of the Wuxi County Party Committee)

Wuxian – Wuxian xian dang'anguan, Wuxian, Jiangsu
300 Wuxian xianwei bangongshi (Office of the Wuxian County Party Committee)

Xinyang – Xinyang xian dang'anguan, Xinyang, Henan
229 and 304 Xinyang xianwei (Xinyang County Party Committee)

Xuancheng – Xuancheng xian dang'anguan, Xuancheng, Anhui
3 Xuancheng xianwei bangongshi (Office of the Xuancheng County Party Committee)

Published Works

Arnold, David, *Famine: Social Crisis and Historical Change*, Oxford: Blackwell, 1988.
Ashton, Basil, Kenneth Hill, Alan Piazza and Robin Zeitz, 'Famine in China, 1958–61', *Population and Development Review*, vol. 10, no. 4 (Dec. 1984), pp. 613–45.
Bachman, David, *Bureaucracy, Economy, and Leadership in China: The Institutional Origins of the Great Leap Forward*, Cambridge: Cambridge University Press, 1991.
Banister, Judith, 'An Analysis of Recent Data on the Population of China', *Population and Development Review*, vol. 10, no. 2 (June 1984), pp. 241–71.
Banister, Judith, *China's Changing Population*, Stanford: Stanford University Press, 1987.
Becker, Jasper, *Hungry Ghosts: Mao's Secret Famine*, New York: Henry Holt, 1996.
Belasco, Warren, 'Algae Burgers for a Hungry World? The Rise and Fall of Chlorella Cuisine', *Technology and Culture*, vol. 38, no. 3 (July 1997), pp. 608–34.
Berlin, Isaiah, *The Crooked Timber of Humanity: Chapters in the History of Ideas*, Vintage Books, 1992.
Bernstein, Thomas P., 'Mao Zedong and the Famine of 1959–1960: A Study in Wilfulness', *China Quarterly*, no. 186 (June 2006), pp. 421–45.

Bernstein, Thomas P., 'Stalinism, Famine and Chinese Peasants: Grain Procurements During the Great Leap Forward', *Theory and Society*, vol. 13 (May 1984), pp. 339–77.

Birch, Cyril, 'Literature under Communism', in Roderick MacFarquhar, John King Fairbank and Denis Twitchett (eds), *The Cambridge History of China*, vol. 15: *Revolutions within the Chinese Revolution, 1966–1982*, Cambridge: Cambridge University Press, 1991, pp. 743–812.

Bo Yibo, *Ruogan zhongda shijian yu juece de huigu* (Recollections of several important decisions and events), Beijing: Zhonggong zhongyang dangxiao chubanshe, 1991–3.

Boone, A., 'The Foreign Trade of China', *China Quarterly*, no. 11 (Sept. 1962), pp. 169–83.

Brown, Jeremy, 'Great Leap City: Surviving the Famine in Tianjin', in Kimberley E. Manning and Felix Wemheuer (eds), *New Perspectives on China's Great Leap Forward and Great Famine*, Vancouver: University of British Columbia Press, 2010.

Cao Shuji, *Da jihuang: 1959–1961 nian de Zhongguo renkou* (The Great Famine: China's population in 1959–1961), Hong Kong: Shidai guoji chuban youxian gongsi, 2005.

The Case of Peng Teh-huai, 1959–1968, Hong Kong: Union Research Institute, 1968.

Chan, Alfred L., *Mao's Crusade: Politics and Policy Implementation in China's Great Leap Forward*, Oxford: Oxford University Press, 2001.

Chang, G. H. and G. J. Wen, 'Communal Dining and the Chinese Famine of 1958–1961', *Economic Development and Cultural Change*, no. 46 (1997), pp. 1–34.

Chang, Jung, *Wild Swans: Three daughters of China*, Clearwater, FL: Touchstone, 2003.

Chang, Jung and Jon Halliday, *Mao: The Unknown Story*, London: Jonathan Cape, 2005.

Chao, Kang, *Agricultural Production in Communist China, 1949–1965*, Madison: University of Wisconsin Press, 1970.

Cheek, Timothy, *Propaganda and Culture in Mao's China: Deng Tuo and the Intelligentsia*, Oxford: Oxford University Press, 1997.

Chen Jian, *Mao's China and the Cold War*, Chapel Hill: University of North Carolina Press, 2001.

Cheng, Tiejun and Mark Selden, 'The Construction of Spatial Hierarchies: China's *hukou* and *danwei* Systems', in Timothy Cheek and Tony Saich (eds), *New Perspectives on State Socialism in China*, Armonk, NY: M. E. Sharpe, 1997, pp. 23–50.

Chinn, Dennis L., 'Basic Commodity Distribution in the People's Republic of China', *China Quarterly*, no. 84 (Dec. 1980), pp. 744–54.

Conquest, Robert, *The Harvest of Sorrow: Soviet Collectivization and the Terror-Famine*, New York: Oxford University Press, 1986.

Dai Qing (ed.), *The River Dragon has Come! The Three Gorges Dam and the Fate of China's Yangtze River and its People*, Armonk, NY: M. E. Sharpe, 1998.

Davis-Friedmann, Deborah, *Long Lives: Chinese Elderly and the Communist Revolution*, Stanford: Stanford University Press, 1991.

Dikötter, Frank, *China before Mao: The Age of Openness*, Berkeley: University of California Press, 2008.

Dikötter, Frank, 'Crime and Punishment in Post-Liberation China: The Prisoners of a Beijing Gaol in the 1950s', *China Quarterly*, no. 149 (March 1997), pp. 147–59.

Dikötter, Frank, *Exotic Commodities: Modern Objects and Everyday Life in China*, New York: Columbia University Press, 2006.

Ding Shu, *Renhuo: Dayuejin yu dajihuang* (A man-made catastrophe: The Great Leap Forward and the Great Famine), Hong Kong: Jiushi niandai zazhi, 1996.

Dirks, Robert, 'Social Responses during Severe Food Shortages and Famine', *Current Anthropology*, vol. 21, no. 1 (Feb. 1981), pp. 21–32.

Domenach, Jean-Luc, *L'Archipel oublié*, Paris: Fayard, 1992.

Domenach, Jean-Luc, *The Origins of the Great Leap Forward: The Case of One Chinese Province*, Boulder: Westview Press, 1995.

Domes, Jurgen, *Peng Te-huai: The Man and the Image*, Stanford: Stanford University Press, 1985.

Donnithorne, Audrey, *China's Economic System*, London: Allen & Unwin, 1967.

Fang Weizhong, Jin Chongji et al. (eds), *Li Fuchun zhuan* (A biography of Li Fuchun), Beijing: Zhongyang wenxian chubanshe, 2001.

Fitzpatrick, Sheila, *Everyday Stalinism: Ordinary Life in Extraordinary Times: Soviet Russia in the 1930s*, New York: Oxford University Press, 1999.

Fitzpatrick, Sheila, 'Signals from Below: Soviet Letters of Denunciation of the 1930s', *Journal of Modern History*, vol. 68, no. 4 (Dec. 1996), pp. 831–66.

Friedman, Edward, Paul G. Pickowicz and Mark Selden with Kay Ann Johnson, *Chinese Village, Socialist State*, New Haven: Yale University Press, 1991.

Fu Zhengyuan, *Autocratic Tradition and Chinese Politics*, Cambridge: Cambridge University Press, 1993.

Fuyang shiwei dangshi yanjiushi (eds), *Zhengtu: Fuyang shehuizhuyi shiqi dangshi zhuanti huibian* (Compendium of special topics on the party history of Fuyang during the socialist era), Fuyang: Anhui jingshi wenhua chuanbo youxian zeren gongsi, 2007.

Gao Wangling, *Renmin gongshe shiqi Zhongguo nongmin 'fanxingwei' diaocha* (Acts of peasant resistance in China during the people's communes), Beijing: Zhonggong dangshi chubanshe, 2006.

Gao Wenqian, *Zhou Enlai: The Last Perfect Revolutionary*, New York: PublicAffairs, 2007.

Gao Xiaoxian, ' "The Silver Flower Contest": Rural Women in 1950s China and the Gendered Division of Labour', *Gender and History*, vol. 18, no. 3 (Nov. 2006), pp. 594–612.

Ginsburgs, George, 'Trade with the Soviet Union', in Victor H. Li, *Law and Politics in China's Foreign Trade*, Seattle: University of Washington Press, 1977, pp. 70–120.

Greenough, Paul R., *Prosperity and Misery in Modern Bengal: The Famine of 1943–44*, New York: Oxford University Press, 1983.

Gu Shiming, Li Qiangui and Sun Jianping, *Li Fuchun jingji sixiang yanjiu*

(Research on Li Fuchun's economic thought), Xining: Qinghai renmin chubanshe, 1992.

Hayek, Friedrich A., *The Road to Serfdom: Text and Documents*, Chicago: University of Chicago Press, 2007.

Huang Kecheng, *Huang Kecheng zishu* (The autobiography of Huang Kecheng), Beijing: Renmin chubanshe, 1994.

Huang Zheng, *Liu Shaoqi yisheng* (Liu Shaoqi: A life), Beijing: Zhongyang wenxian chubanshe, 2003.

Huang Zheng, *Liu Shaoqi zhuan* (A biography of Liu Shaoqi), Beijing: Zhongyang wenxian chubanshe, 1998.

Huang Zheng, *Wang Guangmei fangtan lu* (A record of conversations with Wang Guangmei), Beijing: Zhongyang wenxian chubanshe, 2006.

Ji Fengyuan, *Linguistic Engineering: Language and Politics in Mao's China*, Honolulu: University of Hawai'i Press, 2004.

Jiang Weiqing, *Qishi nian zhengcheng: Jiang Weiqing huiyilu* (A seventy-year journey: The memoirs of Jiang Weiqing), Nanjing: Jiangsu renmin chubanshe, 1996.

Jin Chongji (ed.), *Zhou Enlai zhuan, 1898–1949* (A biography of Zhou Enlai, 1898–1949), Beijing: Zhongyang wenxian chubanshe, 1989.

Jin Chongji and Chen Qun (eds), *Chen Yun*, Beijing: Zhongyang wenxian chubanshe, 2005.

Jin Chongji and Huang Zheng (eds), *Liu Shaoqi zhuan* (A biography of Liu Shaoqi), Beijing: Zhongyang wenxian chubanshe, 1998.

Kane, Penny, *Famine in China, 1959–61: Demographic and Social Implications*, Basingstoke: Macmillan, 1988.

Kapitsa, Mikhael, *Na raznykh parallelakh: Zapiski diplomata*, Moscow: Kniga i biznes, 1996.

Khrushchev, Nikita, *Vremia, liudi, vlast'*, Moscow: Moskovskiye Novosti, 1999.

Kiernan, Ben, *The Pol Pot Regime: Race, Power, and Genocide in Cambodia under the Khmer Rouge, 1975–79*, New Haven: Yale University Press, 1996.

King, Richard, *Heroes of China's Great Leap Forward: Two Stories*, Honolulu: University Press of Hawaii, 2010.

Kitchen, Martin, *A History of Modern Germany, 1800–2000*, New York: Wiley-Blackwell, 2006.

Klochko, M. A., *Soviet Scientist in China*, London: Hollis & Carter, 1964.

Krutikov, K. A., *Na Kitaiskom napravlenii: Iz vospominanii diplomata*, Moscow: Institut Dal'nego Vostoka, 2003.

Kueh, Y. Y., *Agricultural Instability in China, 1931–1991*, Oxford: Clarendon Press, 1995.

Kung, James Kai-sing and Justin Yifu Lin, 'The Causes of China's Great Leap Famine, 1959–1961', *Economic Development and Cultural Change*, vol. 52, no. 1 (2003), pp. 51–73.

Li Huaiyin, 'Everyday Strategies for Team Farming in Collective-Era China: Evidence from Qin Village', *China Journal*, no. 54 (July 2005), pp. 79–98.

Li, Lilian M., *Fighting Famine in North China: State, Market, and Environmental Decline, 1690s–1990s*, Stanford: Stanford University Press, 2007.

Li Rui, *Dayuejin qin liji* (A witness account of the Great Leap Forward), Haikou: Nanfang chubanshe, 1999.

Li Rui, *Lushan huiyi shilu* (A true record of the Lushan plenum), Zhengzhou: Henan renmin chubanshe, 1999.

Li, Wei and Dennis Yang, 'The Great Leap Forward: Anatomy of a Central Planning Disaster', *Journal of Political Economy*, vol. 113, no. 4 (2005), pp. 840–77.

Li Yueran, *Waijiao wutaishang de xin Zhongguo lingxiu* (The leaders of new China on the diplomatic scene), Beijing: Waiyu jiaoxue yu yanjiu chubanshe, 1994.

Li Zhisui, *The Private Life of Chairman Mao: The Memoirs of Mao's Personal Physician*, New York: Random House, 1994.

Lin, Justin Yifu, and Dennis Tao Yang, 'On the Causes of China's Agricultural Crisis and the Great Leap Famine', *China Economic Review*, vol. 9, no. 2 (1998), pp. 125–40.

Lin Yunhui, *Wutuobang yundong: Cong dayuejin dao dajihuang, 1958–1961* (Utopian movement: From the Great Leap Forward to the Great Famine, 1958–1961), Hong Kong: Xianggang zhongwen daxue dangdai Zhongguo wenhua yanjiu zhongxin, 2008.

Liu Chongwen, Chen Shaochou et al. (eds), *Liu Shaoqi nianpu, 1898–1969* (A chronicle of Liu Shaoqi's life), Beijing: Zhongyang wenxian chubanshe, 1996.

Lu Xiaobo, *Cadres and Corruption: The Organizational Involution of the Chinese Communist Party*, Stanford: Stanford University Press, 2000.

Lüthi, Lorenz M., *The Sino-Soviet Split: Cold War in the Communist World*, Princeton: Princeton University Press, 2008.

MacFarquhar, Roderick, *The Origins of the Cultural Revolution*, vol. 1: *Contradictions among the People, 1956–1957*, London: Oxford University Press, 1974.

MacFarquhar, Roderick, *The Origins of the Cultural Revolution*, vol. 2: *The Great Leap Forward, 1958–1960*, New York: Columbia University Press, 1983.

MacFarquhar, Roderick, *The Origins of the Cultural Revolution*, vol. 3: *The Coming of the Cataclysm, 1961–1966*, New York: Columbia University Press, 1999.

MacFarquhar, Roderick, Timothy Cheek and Eugene Wu (eds), *The Secret Speeches of Chairman Mao: From the Hundred Flowers to the Great Leap Forward*, Cambridge, MA: Harvard University Press, 1989.

Manning, Kimberley E., 'Marxist Maternalism, Memory, and the Mobilization of Women during the Great Leap Forward', *China Review*, vol. 5, no. 1 (Spring 2005), pp. 83–110.

Mao Zedong, *Jianguo yilai Mao Zedong wengao* (Mao Zedong's manuscripts since the founding of the People's Republic), Beijing: Zhongyang wenxian chubanshe, 1987–96.

Mao Zedong, *Mao Zedong waijiao wenxuan* (Selection of writings on foreign affairs by Mao Zedong), Beijing: Zhongyang wenxian chubanshe, 1994.

Mićunović, Veljko, *Moscow Diary*, New York: Doubleday, 1980.

Mueggler, Erik, *The Age of Wild Ghosts: Memory, Violence, and Place in Southwest China*, Berkeley: University of California Press, 2001.

Näth, Marie-Luise (ed.), *Communist China in Retrospect: East European Sinologists Remember the First Fifteen Years of the PRC*, Frankfurt: P. Lang, 1995.

Ó Gráda, Cormac, *The Great Irish Famine*, Basingstoke: Macmillan, 1989.

Oi, Jean C., *State and Peasant in Contemporary China: The Political Economy of Village Government*, Berkeley: University of California Press, 1989.

Osokina, Elena, *Our Daily Bread: Socialist Distribution and the Art of Survival in Stalin's Russia, 1927–1941*, Armonk, NY: M. E. Sharpe, 2001.

Pang Xianzhi, Guo Chaoren and Jin Chongji (eds), *Liu Shaoqi*, Beijing: Xinhua chubanshe, 1998.

Pang Xianzhi and Jin Chongji (eds), *Mao Zedong zhuan, 1949–1976* (A biography of Mao Zedong, 1949–1976), Beijing: Zhongyang wenxian chubanshe, 2003.

Pasqualini, Jean, *Prisoner of Mao*, Harmondsworth: Penguin, 1973.

Patenaude, Bertrand M., *The Big Show in Bololand: The American Relief Expedition to Soviet Russia in the Famine of 1921*, Stanford: Stanford University Press, 2002.

Peng Dehuai, *Peng Dehuai zishu* (The autobiography of Peng Dehuai), Beijing: Renmin chubanshe, 1981.

Peng Dehuai zhuan (A biography of Peng Dehuai), Beijing: Dangdai Zhongguo chubanshe, 1993.

Peng Xizhe, 'Demographic Consequences of the Great Leap Forward in China's Provinces', *Population and Development Review*, vol. 13, no. 4 (Dec. 1987), pp. 639–70.

Pepper, Suzanne, *Radicalism and Education Reform in 20th-Century China: The Search for an Ideal Development Model*, Cambridge: Cambridge University Press, 1996.

Reardon, Lawrence C., *The Reluctant Dragon: Crisis Cycles in Chinese Foreign Economic Policy*, Hong Kong: Hong Kong University Press, 2002.

Russell, Sharman Apt, *Hunger: An Unnatural History*, New York: Basic Books, 2005.

Salisbury, Harrison E., *The New Emperors: China in the Era of Mao and Deng*, Boston: Little, Brown, 1992.

Service, Robert, *Comrades: A History of World Communism*, Cambridge, MA: Harvard University Press, 2007.

Shapiro, Judith, *Mao's War against Nature: Politics and the Environment in Revolutionary China*, New York: Cambridge University Press, 2001.

Shen Zhihua, *Sikao yu xuanze: Cong zhishifenzi huiyi dao fanyoupai yundong (1956–1957)* (Reflections and choices: The consciousness of intellectuals and the anti-rightist campaign, 1956–1957), Hong Kong: Xianggang zhongwen daxue dangdai Zhongguo wenhua yanjiu zhongxin, 2008.

Shevchenko, Arkady N., *Breaking with Moscow*, New York: Alfred Knopf, 1985.

Short, Philip, *Pol Pot: The History of a Nightmare*, London: John Murray, 2004.

Smil, Vaclav, *The Bad Earth: Environmental Degradation in China*, Armonk, NY: M. E. Sharpe, 1984.

Tao Lujia, *Mao zhuxi jiao women dang shengwei shuji* (Chairman Mao taught us how to be a provincial party secretary), Beijing: Zhongyang wenxian chubanshe, 1996.

Taubman, William, *Khrushchev: The Man and his Era*, London: The Free Press, 2003.

Teiwes, Frederick C., *Politics and Purges in China: Rectification and the Decline of Party Norms*, Armonk, NY: M. E. Sharpe, 1993.

Teiwes, Frederick C. and Warren Sun, *China's Road to Disaster: Mao, Central*

Politicians, and Provincial Leaders in the Unfolding of the Great Leap Forward, 1955–1959, Armonk, NY: M. E. Sharpe, 1999.

Thaxton, Ralph A., *Catastrophe and Contention in Rural China: Mao's Great Leap Forward Famine and the Origins of Righteous Resistance in Da Fo Village*, New York: Cambridge University Press, 2008.

Tooze, Adam, *The Wages of Destruction: The Making and Breaking of the Nazi Economy*, New York: Allen Lane, 2006.

Townsend, James R. and Brantly Womack, *Politics in China*, Boston: Little, Brown, 1986.

Viola, Lynn, *Peasant Rebels under Stalin: Collectivization and the Culture of Peasant Resistance*, New York: Oxford University Press, 1996.

Walker, Kenneth R., *Food Grain Procurement and Consumption in China*, Cambridge: Cambridge University Press, 1984.

Wang Yan et al. (eds), *Peng Dehuai nianpu* (A chronicle of Peng Dehuai's life), Beijing: Renmin chubanshe, 1998.

Watson, James L. and Evelyn S. Rawski (eds), *Death Ritual in Late Imperial and Modern China*, Berkeley: University of California Press, 1988.

Wu Hung, *Remaking Beijing: Tiananmen Square and the Creation of a Political Space*, London: Reaktion Books, 2005.

Wu Lengxi, *Shinian lunzhan: 1956–1966 Zhong Su guanxi huiyilu* (Ten years of theoretical disputes: My recollection of Sino-Soviet relationships), Beijing: Zhongyang wenxian chubanshe, 1999.

Wu Lengxi, *Yi Mao zhuxi: Wo qinshen jingli de ruogan zhongda lishi shijian pianduan* (Remembering Chairman Mao: Fragments of my personal experience of certain important historical events), Beijing: Xinhua chubanshe, 1995.

Wu Ningkun and Li Yikai, *A Single Tear: A Family's Persecution, Love, and Endurance in Communist China*, New York: Back Bay Books, 1994.

Xiong Huayuan and Liao Xinwen, *Zhou Enlai zongli shengya* (The life of Zhou Enlai), Beijing: Renmin chubanshe, 1997.

Yan Mingfu, 'Huiyi liangci Mosike huiyi he Hu Qiaomu' (Recollecting Hu Qiaomu attending two Moscow conferences), *Dangdai Zhongguo shi yanjiu*, no. 19 (May 1997), pp. 6–21.

Yang, Dali L., *Calamity and Reform in China: State, Rural Society, and Institutional Change since the Great Leap Famine*, Stanford: Stanford University Press, 1996.

Yang Jisheng, *Mubei: Zhongguo liushi niandai dajihuang jishi* (Wooden gravestone: A true history of the Great Famine in China in the 1960s), Hong Kong: Tiandi tushu youxian gongsi, 2008.

Yang Xianhui, *Jiabiangou jishi: Yang Xianhui zhongduan pian xiaoshuo jingxuan* (A record of Jiabian Valley: A selection of stories by Yang Xianhui), Tianjin: Tianjin guji chubanshe, 2002.

——*Woman From Shanghai: Tales of Survival From a Chinese Labor Camp*, New York: Pantheon, 2009.

Yu Xiguang, *Dayuejin ku rizi: Shangshuji* (The Great Leap Forward and the years of bitterness: A collection of memorials), Hong Kong: Shidai chaoliu chubanshe, 2005.

Zazerskaya, T. G., *Sovetskie spetsialisty i formirovanie voenno-promyshlennogo kompleksa Kitaya (1949–1960 gg.)*, St Petersburg: Sankt Peterburg Gosudarstvennyi Universitet, 2000.

Zhang Letian, *Gaobie lixiang: Renmin gongshe zhidu yanjiu* (Farewell to idealism: Studies on the People's Communes), Shanghai: Shanghai renmin chubanshe, 2005.

Zhang Shu Guang, *Economic Cold War: America's Embargo against China and the Sino-Soviet Alliance, 1949–1963*, Stanford: Stanford University Press, 2001.

Zubok, Vladislav and Constantine Pleshakov, *Inside the Kremlin's Cold War: From Stalin to Khrushchev*, Cambridge, MA: Harvard University Press, 1996.

Notes

Preface

1 This has been known for some time thanks to the work of Alfred L. Chan, *Mao's Crusade: Politics and Policy Implementation in China's Great Leap Forward*, Oxford: Oxford University Press, 2001; see also Frederick C. Teiwes and Warren Sun, *China's Road to Disaster: Mao, Central Politicians, and Provincial Leaders in the Unfolding of the Great Leap Forward, 1955–1959*, Armonk, NY: M. E. Sharpe, 1999.

2 The most recent village study is Ralph A. Thaxton, *Catastrophe and Contention in Rural China: Mao's Great Leap Forward Famine and the Origins of Righteous Resistance in Da Fo Village*, New York: Cambridge University Press, 2008; a classic study is Edward Friedman, Paul G. Pickowicz and Mark Selden with Kay Ann Johnson, *Chinese Village, Socialist State*, New Haven: Yale University Press, 1991.

3 Robert Service, *Comrades: A History of World Communism*, Cambridge, MA: Harvard University Press, 2007, p. 6.

Chapter 1: Two Rivals

1 William Taubman, *Khrushchev: The Man and his Era*, London: The Free Press, 2003, p. 230.

2 Pang Xianzhi and Jin Chongji (eds), *Mao Zedong zhuan, 1949–1976* (A biography of Mao Zedong, 1949–1976), Beijing: Zhongyang wenxian chubanshe, 2003, p. 534.

3 Li Zhisui, *The Private Life of Chairman Mao: The Memoirs of Mao's Personal Physician*, New York: Random House, 1994, pp. 182–4.

4 A helpful overview of the Socialist High Tide appears in Chan, *Mao's Crusade*, pp. 17–24.

5 Wu Lengxi, *Yi Mao zhuxi: Wo qinshen jingli de ruogan zhongda lishi shijian pianduan* (Remembering Chairman Mao: Fragments of my personal experience of certain important historical events), Beijing: Xinhua chubanshe, 1995, p. 57.

6 Lorenz M. Lüthi, *The Sino-Soviet Split: Cold War in the Communist World*, Princeton: Princeton University Press, 2008, pp. 71–2.

7 Roderick MacFarquhar, *The Origins of the Cultural Revolution*, vol. 1: *Contradictions among the People, 1956–1957*, London: Oxford University Press, 1974, pp. 313–15.

Chapter 2: The Bidding Starts

1 Wu Lengxi, *Shinian lunzhan: 1956–1966 Zhong Su guanxi huiyilu* (Ten years of theoretical disputes: My recollection of Sino-Soviet relationships), Beijing: Zhongyang wenxian chubanshe, 1999, pp. 205–6; see also Lüthi, *Sino-Soviet Split*, p. 74.
2 Li, *Private Life of Chairman Mao*, pp. 220–1.
3 Ibid., p. 221.
4 Mao Zedong, *Jianguo yilai Mao Zedong wengao* (Mao Zedong's manuscripts since the founding of the People's Republic), Beijing: Zhongyang wenxian chubanshe, 1987–96, vol. 6, pp. 625–6.
5 See the reminiscences of one of Mao's translators, Li Yueran, *Waijiao wutaishang de xin Zhongguo lingxiu* (The leaders of new China on the diplomatic scene), Beijing: Waiyu jiaoxue yu yanjiu chubanshe, 1994, p. 137; see also Yan Mingfu, 'Huiyi liangci Mosike huiyi he Hu Qiaomu' (Recollecting Hu Qiaomu attending two Moscow conferences), *Dangdai Zhongguo shi yanjiu*, no. 19 (May 1997), pp. 6–21.
6 Nikita Khrushchev, *Vremia, liudi, vlast'*, Moscow: Moskovskiye Novosti, 1999, vol. 3, p. 55.
7 Veljko Mićunović, *Moscow Diary*, New York: Doubleday, 1980, p. 322.
8 Mao, *Jianguo yilai*, vol. 6, pp. 640–3.
9 Mikhael Kapitsa, *Na raznykh parallelakh: Zapiski diplomata*, Moscow: Kniga i biznes, 1996, p. 60.
10 Mao, *Jianguo yilai*, vol. 6, p. 635.
11 '1957: Nikita Khrushchev', *Time*, 6 Jan. 1958.
12 'Bark on the wind', *Time*, 3 June 1957.
13 Taubman, *Khrushchev*, pp. 305 and 374–5.
14 'N. S. Khrushchov's report to anniversary session of USSR Supreme Soviet', Moscow: Soviet News, 7 Nov. 1957, p. 90.
15 Mao, *Jianguo yilai*, vol. 6, p. 635.

Chapter 3: Purging the Ranks

1 MacFarquhar, *Origins*, vol. 1, p. 312.
2 Huang Zheng, *Liu Shaoqi yisheng* (Liu Shaoqi: A life), Beijing: Zhongyang wenxian chubanshe, 2003, p. 322.
3 *Renmin ribao*, 1 Jan. 1958, p. 1; Wu, *Yi Mao zhuxi*, p. 47.
4 *Renmin ribao*, 8 Dec. 1957, p. 1.
5 *Renmin ribao*, 25 Jan. 1958, p. 2.
6 Jin Chongji (ed.), *Zhou Enlai zhuan, 1898–1949* (A biography of Zhou Enlai, 1898–1949), Beijing: Zhongyang wenxian chubanshe, 1989, p. 1234.

7 Minutes of Nanning meeting, Gansu, 28 Jan. 1958, 91-4-107, p. 1.

8 Li Rui, *Dayuejin qin liji* (A witness account of the Great Leap Forward), Haikou: Nanfang chubanshe, 1999, vol. 2, pp. 68–9.

9 At the time the editorial was published in June 1956, Deng Tuo was the editor of the *People's Daily*; he was replaced by Wu Lengxi in July 1957 and dismissed in November 1958, although he continued to write in support of the Great Leap Forward for several years; Wu, *Yi Mao zhuxi*, pp. 47–9; on Deng Tuo see Timothy Cheek, *Propaganda and Culture in Mao's China: Deng Tuo and the Intelligentsia*, Oxford: Oxford University Press, 1997.

10 Li, *Private Life of Chairman Mao*, p. 230.

11 Bo Yibo, *Ruogan zhongda shijian yu juece de huigu* (Recollections of several important decisions and events), Beijing: Zhonggong zhongyang dangxiao chubanshe, 1991–3, p. 639.

12 Xiong Huayuan and Liao Xinwen, *Zhou Enlai zongli shengya* (The life of Zhou Enlai), Beijing: Renmin chubanshe, 1997, p. 241.

13 Minutes of Nanning meeting, Gansu, 28 Jan. 1958, 91-4-107, pp. 9–10; also in Mao, *Jianguo yilai*, vol. 7, p. 59.

14 'Rubber communist', *Time*, 18 June 1951.

15 Gao Wenqian, *Zhou Enlai: The Last Perfect Revolutionary*, New York: PublicAffairs, 2007, p. 88.

16 Mao's speech on 15 Nov. 1956, Gansu, 91-18-480, p. 74.

17 Mao's speech on 10 March 1958 at Chengdu, Gansu, 91-18-495, p. 211.

18 Li, *Dayuejin*, vol. 2, p. 288.

19 See also Roderick MacFarquhar, *The Origins of the Cultural Revolution*, vol. 2: *The Great Leap Forward, 1958–1960*, New York: Columbia University Press, 1983, p. 57.

20 Teiwes, *China's Road to Disaster*, p. 246, quoting from a record of Liu's statement; see also Jin Chongji and Huang Zheng (eds), *Liu Shaoqi zhuan* (A biography of Liu Shaoqi), Beijing: Zhongyang wenxian chubanshe, 1998, pp. 828–9.

21 Memoirs of the secretary Fan Ruoyu as quoted in Jin, *Zhou Enlai zhuan*, pp. 1259–60.

22 Nathan, 'Introduction', Gao, *Zhou Enlai*, p. xiii.

23 Teiwes, *China's Road to Disaster*, p. 85.

24 Tao Lujia, *Mao zhuxi jiao women dang shengwei shuji* (Chairman Mao taught us how to be a provincial party secretary), Beijing: Zhongyang wenxian chubanshe, 1996, pp. 77–8.

25 Mao's speech on 28 Jan. 1958, Gansu, 91-18-495, p. 200.

26 Deng's speech on 15 Jan. 1958, Gansu, 91-4-107, pp. 73 and 94.

27 Gansu, 9 Feb. 1958, 91-4-104, pp. 1–10.

28 Gansu, 12 Jan. 1961, 91-4-735, pp. 75–6.

29 Gansu, 12 Jan. 1961, 91-18-200, p. 35.

30 Gansu, 3 Dec. 1962, 91-4-1028, p. 8.

31 Yunnan, 20 April 1958, 2-1-3059, pp. 57–62; see also *Renmin ribao*, 26 May 1958, p. 4.

32 Yunnan, 25 Sept. 1958, 2-1-3059, pp. 2–3.

33 Mao's speech on 10 March 1958 at Chengdu, Gansu, 91-18-495, p. 211.

34 On these purges see Frederick C. Teiwes, *Politics and Purges in China: Rectification and the Decline of Party Norms*, Armonk, NY: M. E. Sharpe, 1993.

35 Ibid., p. 276; see also Zhang Linnan, 'Guanyu fan Pan, Yang, Wang shijian' (The anti-Pan, Yang and Wang incident), in Zhonggong Henan shengwei dangshi gongzuo weiyuanhui (eds), *Fengyu chunqiu: Pan Fusheng shiwen jihianji*, Zhengzhou: Henan renmin chubanshe, 1993.

36 Thaxton, *Catastrophe and Contention in Rural China*, p. 116.

37 Jiang Weiqing, *Qishi nian zhengcheng: Weiqing huiyilu* (A seventy-year journey: The memoirs of Jiang Weiqing), Nanjing: Jiangsu renmin chubanshe, 1996, pp. 415–16.

38 Yunnan, 22 May 1959, 2-1-3700, pp. 93–8.

39 Chen's speech on 19 Dec. 1957 in Beijing, Gansu, 91-8-79, p. 179.

Chapter 4: Bugle Call

1 Judith Shapiro, *Mao's War against Nature: Politics and the Environment in Revolutionary China*, New York: Cambridge University Press, 2001, p. 49.

2 The story is told by Shang Wei, 'A Lamentation for the Yellow River: The Three Gate Gorge Dam (Sanmenxia)', in Dai Qing (ed.), *The River Dragon has Come! The Three Gorges Dam and the Fate of China's Yangtze River and its People*, Armonk, NY: M. E. Sharpe, 1998, pp. 143–59.

3 Shapiro, *Mao's War against Nature*, pp. 53–4.

4 Zhou's speech on 19 Sept. 1961, Gansu, 91-18-561, p. 31.

5 Ministry of Foreign Affairs, Beijing, 23 July 1964, 117-1170-5, pp. 45–7.

6 *Renmin ribao*, 1 Feb. 1958, p. 11; Shui Fu, 'A Profile of Dams in China', in Dai, *The River Dragon has come!*, p. 22.

7 Yi Si, 'The World's Most Catastrophic Dam Failures: The August 1975 Collapse of the Banqiao and Shimantan Dams', in Dai, *The River Dragon has Come!*, p. 30.

8 Gansu, 29 Jan. 1958, 91-4-138, pp. 135–7.

9 Gansu, 20 Oct. 1958, 91-4-263, pp. 29–30.

10 Gansu, 9 Sept. 1958, 229-1-118.

11 Gansu, 26 April 1959, 91-4-348, pp. 30–5.

12 ' "Yin Tao shangshan" de huiyi' (Recollections of the 'Raising the Tao River up the Mountains' campaign), in Qiu Shi (ed.), *Gongheguo zhongda juece chutai qianhou* (How important decisions of the People's Republic were made), Beijing: Jingji ribao chubanshe, 1997–8, vol. 3, p. 226.

13 Gansu, 18 April 1962, 91-4-1091, pp. 1–8.

14 Shui, 'A Profile of Dams in China', p. 22.

15 Beijing, 1959, 96-1-14, pp. 38–44.

16 Jan Rowinski, 'China and the Crisis of Marxism-Leninism', in Marie-Luise Näth (ed.), *Communist China in Retrospect: East European Sinologists Remember the First Fifteen Years of the PRC*, Frankfurt: P. Lang, 1995, pp. 85–7.

17 M. A. Klochko, *Soviet Scientist in China*, London: Hollis & Carter, 1964, pp. 51–2.

18 Rowinski, 'China and the Crisis of Marxism-Leninism', pp. 85–7; Klochko, *Soviet Scientist*, pp. 51–2.
19 Li, *Private Life of Chairman Mao*, pp. 247–8.
20 Ibid., pp. 249–51.
21 Yunnan, 9 Jan. 1958, 2-1-3227, p. 5.
22 *Renmin ribao*, 15 Jan. 1958, p. 1.
23 Yunnan, 5 Oct. 1958, 2-1-3227, pp. 109–23.
24 *Renmin ribao*, 19 Jan. 1958, p. 1.
25 *Renmin ribao*, 18 Feb. 1958, p. 2.
26 Yunnan, 21 April 1958, 2-1-3260, p. 117.
27 Li, *Dayuejin*, vol. 2, p. 363.
28 Yunnan, 23 June 1958, 2-1-3274, pp. 37–9.
29 Yunnan, 20 Nov. 1958, 2-1-3078, pp. 116–23; 22 Aug. 1958, 2-1-3078, pp. 1–16.
30 Jiang, *Qishi nian zhengcheng*, p. 421.
31 Gansu, 14 Feb. 1961, 91-18-205, p. 58.

Chapter 5: Launching Sputniks

1 Li, *Private Life of Chairman Mao*, pp. 226–7.
2 Hunan, July 1958, 186-1-190, pp. 1–2; also July 1958, 141-2-62, pp. 1–2.
3 William W. Whitson, *The Chinese High Command: A History of Communist Military Politics, 1927–71*, New York: Praeger, 1973, p. 204, quoted in MacFarquhar, *Origins*, vol. 2, p. 83.
4 Hunan, 11 May 1959, 141-1-1066, pp. 80–3.
5 Hunan, Sept. 1959, 141-1-1117, pp. 1–4; 18 Sept. 1959, 141-1-1066, pp. 5–13.
6 As he later admitted; see minutes of the Lushan meeting, Gansu, Aug. 1959, 91-18-96, p. 570.
7 Yunnan, 29 July 1958, 2-1-3102, p. 20.
8 Yunnan, 4 Sept. 1958, 2-1-3101, pp. 1–35.
9 Yunnan, Sept. 1958, 2-1-3101, pp. 36–9, 48–65, 66–84, 94–104, 105–23.
10 Guangdong, 20 Jan. 1961, 217-1-645, pp. 15–19.
11 Teiwes, *China's Road to Disaster*, p. 85.
12 Bo, *Ruogan zhongda shijian*, p. 682; the system is described by MacFarquhar, *Origins*, vol. 2, p. 31.
13 Record of the Nanning meeting, Gansu, 28 Jan. 1958, 91-4-107, p. 2.
14 Interview in Lu Xiaobo, *Cadres and Corruption: The Organizational Involution of the Chinese Communist Party*, Stanford: Stanford University Press, 2000, p. 84.
15 Suiping, 13 Feb. 1958, 1-201-7, pp. 8 and 32; 29 Oct. 1958, 1-221-8.
16 For an example from Chuxiong county, Yunnan, see Erik Mueggler, *The Age of Wild Ghosts: Memory, Violence, and Place in Southwest China*, Berkeley: University of California Press, 2001, p. 176.
17 Guangdong, 1961, 217-1-618, p. 36.
18 *Renmin ribao*, 26 Nov. 1957, p. 2; 29 Dec. 1957, p. 2; 21 Jan. 1958, p. 4; 16 Aug. 1958, p. 8.

19 Macheng, 15 July 1958, 1-1-331; 13 April 1959, 1-1-370, p. 37.

20 Guangdong, 31 Dec. 1960, 217-1-576, pp. 54–68.

21 Jiang, *Qishi nian zhengcheng*, p. 431.

22 Bo, *Ruogan zhongda shijian*, p. 683; the practice came from a collective farm in Shandong.

23 Report from the Centre, Yunnan, 3 Sept. 1958, 120-1-84, pp. 52–67.

24 Guangdong, 31 Dec. 1961, 217-1-642, pp. 11–12.

25 Guangdong, 7 Jan. 1961, 217-1-643, pp. 120–2.

26 Roderick MacFarquhar, Timothy Cheek and Eugene Wu (eds), *The Secret Speeches of Chairman Mao: From the Hundred Flowers to the Great Leap Forward*, Cambridge, MA: Harvard University Press, 1989, p. 450.

27 Macheng, 15 Jan. 1959, 1-1-443, p. 10.

28 Interview with Liu Shu, born 1946, Renshou county, Sichuan, April 2006.

29 Interview with Luo Bai, born 1930s, Hongya county, Sichuan, April 2006.

30 Zhejiang, 4 May 1961, J007-13-48, pp. 1–8.

31 Macheng, 20 Jan. 1959, 1-1-378, p. 22.

32 Hebei, 16 April 1961, 884-1-202, pp. 35–47.

33 Guangdong, 5 Jan. 1961, 217-1-643, pp. 50–60.

34 Li, *Private Life of Chairman Mao*, p. 278.

35 Minutes of conversation, Hebei, 4–5 Aug. 1958, 855-4-1271, pp. 6–7 and 13–14; see also *Renmin ribao*, 4 Aug. 1958, p. 1, 11 Aug. 1958, pp. 1 and 4.

36 Hunan, 19 Oct. 1958, 141-2-64, pp. 78–82; Hunan, 18 Sept. 1958, 141-1-1066, pp. 7–8.

37 Hunan, 19 Oct. 1958, 141-2-64, pp. 78–82.

38 Hunan, 5 Nov. 1958, 141-1-1051, p. 124.

39 Directive from the State Council, Gansu, 7 Jan. 1959, 91-8-360, pp. 5–6.

Chapter 6: Let the Shelling Begin

1 Zhonggong zhongyang wenxian yanjiushi (eds), *Mao Zedong waijiao wenxuan* (Selection of writings on foreign affairs by Mao Zedong), Beijing: Zhongyang wenxian chubanshe, 1994, pp. 323–4.

2 Lüthi, *Sino-Soviet Split*, pp. 92–3.

3 Li, *Waijiao wutaishang*, p. 149.

4 Harrison E. Salisbury, *The New Emperors: China in the Era of Mao and Deng*, Boston: Little, Brown, 1992, pp. 155–6.

5 Li, *Waijiao wutaishang*, p. 151.

6 Russian minutes in 'Peregovory S. Khrushcheva s Mao Tszedunom 31 iiulia–3 avgusta 1958 g. i 2 oktiabria 1959 g.', *Novaia i Noveishaia Istoria*, no. 1 (2001), pp. 100–8; reference on page 117.

7 Khrushchev, *Vremia, liudi, vlast'*, vol. 3, pp. 76–7.

8 Li, *Private Life of Chairman Mao*, p. 261.

9 Li, *Waijiao wutaishang*, pp. 149–50.

10 As he recollected while addressing a plenum a few years later; see RGANI, Moscow, 18 Jan. 1961, 2-1-535, pp. 143–6; see also RGANI, Moscow, 14 Feb. 1964, 2-1-720, p. 137.

11 Vladislav Zubok and Constantine Pleshakov, *Inside the Kremlin's Cold War: From Stalin to Khrushchev*, Cambridge, MA: Harvard University Press, 1996, pp. 225–6.
12 Li, *Private Life of Chairman Mao*, p. 270.
13 Mao, *Mao Zedong waijiao wenxuan*, pp. 344 and 347.
14 Roland Felber, 'China and the Claim for Democracy', in Näth, *Communist China in Retrospect*, p. 117; more recently Lorenz Lüthi, an expert on Sino-Soviet relations, has also underlined how domestic developments alone determined the timing of the shelling of Quemoy; Lüthi, *Sino-Soviet Split*, p. 99.

Chapter 7: The People's Communes

1 Li, *Private Life of Chairman Mao*, p. 263.
2 Hebei, Sept. 1957, 855-4-1271, pp. 1–5.
3 Hebei, 13 Feb. and 30 April 1958, 855-18-541, pp. 13–20 and 67–81.
4 Mao, *Jianguo yilai*, vol. 7, p. 143.
5 *Renmin ribao*, 17 April 1958, p. 2.
6 Chen Boda, 'Zai Mao Zedong tongzhi de qizhi xia', *Hongqi*, 16 July 1958, no. 4, pp. 1–12.
7 Speech on 19 and 21 Aug. 1958, Gansu, 91-18-495, pp. 316 and 321.
8 Li, *Dayuejin*, vol. 2, p. 31.
9 *Renmin ribao*, 1 Sept. 1958, p. 3.
10 Jin and Huang, *Liu Shaoqi zhuan*, pp. 832–3.
11 *Renmin ribao*, 18 Sept. 1958, p. 2; 24 Sept. 1958, p. 1.
12 Mao, *Jianguo yilai*, vol. 7, p. 494.
13 Ji Fengyuan, *Linguistic Engineering: Language and Politics in Mao's China*, Honolulu: University of Hawai'i Press, 2004, p. 88.
14 Speech on 21 and 24 Aug. 1958; Hunan, 141-1-1036, pp. 24–5 and 31.
15 *Renmin ribao*, 3 Oct. 1958, p. 2.
16 *Renmin ribao*, 6 Oct. 1958, p. 6; 13 Oct. 1958, p. 1.
17 Hunan, 18 Sept. 1958, 141-1-1066, p. 5.
18 John Gittings, 'China's Militia', *China Quarterly*, no. 18 (June 1964), p. 111.
19 Macheng, 15 Jan. 1959, 1-1-443, pp. 9 and 24.
20 Nanjing, 10 April 1961, 4003-2-481, pp. 75–83.
21 Hunan, 4 Feb. 1961, 151-1-20, pp. 8–9.
22 Guangdong, 10 Dec. 1960, 217-1-643, p. 44.
23 Interview with Li Yeye, born 1935, Langzhong county, Sichuan, April 2007.
24 Interview with Feng Dabai, born 1930s, Langzhong county, Sichuan, Sept. 2006.
25 Sichuan, 26 Feb. 1960, JC1-1846, p. 22.
26 Guangdong, 10 Dec. 1960, 217-1-643, p. 45.
27 Guangdong, 12 Feb. 1959, 217-1-69, pp. 25–33.
28 Guangdong, 7 Jan. 1961, 217-1-643, p. 111.
29 Guangzhou, 27 Oct. 1958, 16-1-1, p. 76.
30 Wuhan, 3 Nov. 1958, 83-1-523, p. 126.
31 Wuhan, 19 Sept. and 3 Nov. 1958, 83-1-523, pp. 21–5 and 126–32.

32 Guangzhou, 27 Oct. 1958, 16-1-1, p. 76.

33 Wuhan, 1958, 83-1-523, p. 87.

34 Macheng, 20 Jan. 1959, 1-1-378, p. 24; 11 Dec. 1960, 1-1-502, pp. 207 and 213; 16 April 1959, 1-1-383, p. 1.

35 Sichuan, 1961, JC1-2606, pp. 18–19.

36 Gansu, 16 Jan. 1961, 91-18-200, p. 94.

37 Hunan, 2–4 Sept. 1959, 141-1-1116, p. 11.

38 Macheng, 13 May 1961, 1-1-556, pp. 2–3; also 20 Jan. 1959, 1-1-378, p. 23.

39 Macheng, 18 April 1959, 1-1-406, p. 1.

40 Macheng, 29 Jan. and 2 Feb. 1959, 1-1-416, pp. 36 and 49; 26 April 1958, 1-1-431, p. 37.

41 Nanjing, 4003-1-150, 30 Dec. 1958, p. 89.

Chapter 8: Steel Fever

1   Yunnan, 8 Nov. 1958, 105-9-1, pp. 11–14; 11 March 1958, 105-9-6, pp. 71–4.

2   Mao, *Jianguo yilai*, vol. 7, p. 236.

3   Informal talks after main speeches by Mao Zedong as reported by Xie Fuzhi to the top leadership in Yunnan and Guizhou, Guiyang, 61-8-84, 28 May 1958, p. 2.

4   Lin Keng, 'Home-Grown Technical Revolution', *China Reconstructs*, Sept. 1958, p. 12.

5   Lin Yunhui, *Wutuobang yundong: Cong dayuejin dao dajihuang, 1958–1961* (Utopian movement: From the Great Leap Forward to the Great Famine, 1958–1961), Hong Kong: Xianggang zhongwen daxue dangdai Zhongguo wenhua yanjiu zhongxin, 2008, p. 132.

6   Guangdong, 31 Dec. 1960, 217-1-642, pp. 10–16.

7   These different figures are all discussed in MacFarquhar, *Origins*, vol. 2, pp. 88–90.

8   Gu Shiming, Li Qiangui and Sun Jianping, *Li Fuchun jingji sixiang yanjiu* (Research on Li Fuchun's economic thought), Xining: Qinghai renmin chubanshe, 1992, p. 115.

9   The conversation was witnessed by Chen Yun; see Pang and Jin, *Mao Zedong zhuan*, pp. 824–5; see also Yunnan, 23 June 1958, 2-1-3276, pp. 1–9; Mao, *Jianguo yilai*, vol. 7, pp. 281–2.

10 Report from the Ministry of Metallurgy, Yunnan, 23 June 1958, 2-1-3276, pp. 1–9; see also Bo, *Ruogan zhongda shijian*, pp. 700–1.

11 Jin Chongji and Chen Qun (eds), *Chen Yun*, Beijing: Zhongyang wenxian chubanshe, 2005, p. 1143; see also Chan, *Mao's Crusade*, pp. 73–4.

12 Yunnan, 10 Sept. 1958, 2-1-3276, pp. 99–100.

13 Yunnan, 16 Sept. 1958, 2-1-3101, pp. 105–23.

14 Yunnan, 17 Sept. 1958, 2-1-3102, pp. 58–78.

15 Yunnan, 20 Sept. 1958 and 5 Jan. 1959, 2-1-3318, pp. 1–5 and 10–19.

16 Yunnan, 23 Sept. 1958, 2-1-3102, pp. 147–9.

17 Yunnan, 25 Sept. 1958, 2-1-3101, p. 185.

18 Yunnan, 18 Oct. 1958, 2-1-3102, pp. 160 and 230; Oct. 1958, 2-1-3102, pp. 235–73.
19 Yunnan, 14 Dec. 1958, 2-1-3259, pp. 165–72.
20 Yunnan, 5 Jan. 1959, 2-1-3318, p. 18.
21 Macheng, 20 Jan. 1959, 1-1-378, p. 23.
22 Macheng, 15 Jan. 1959, 1-1-443, p. 10.
23 Interview with Zhang Aihua, born 1941, Dingyuan county, Anhui, Sept. 2006.
24 Nanjing, 1958, 4003-4-292, pp. 16 and 48–52.
25 Gansu, 20 May 1959, 91-18-114, p. 209.
26 Guojia tongjiju guomin jingji zonghe tongjisi (eds), *Xin Zhongguo wushi nian tongji ziliao huibian* (Compendium of statistical material on the new China's first fifty years), Beijing: Zhongguo tongji chubanshe, 1999, p. 3, quoted in Lin, *Wutuobang yundong*, p. 205.
27 Klochko, *Soviet Scientist*, p. 82.
28 Shanghai, 12 March 1959, B98-1-439, pp. 9–13.
29 Yunnan, 16 May 1959, 81-4-25, p. 2.
30 Yunnan, 8 Nov. 1958, 105-9-1, p. 15; also 105-9-3, pp. 9–16.
31 Yunnan, 29 July 1958, 2-1-3102, p. 19.
32 Yunnan, 21 April 1958, 2-1-3260, p. 116.
33 These can only be very rough approximations, and they varied from place to place: in Hunan the number of people who did not engage in agricultural tasks increased by 40 per cent after 1958; Hunan, 4 June 1959, 146-1-483, p. 116; in Shandong only 50 per cent of the workforce worked in the fields: talk by Tan Zhenlin, Gansu, 26 June 1959, 91-18-513, p. 16.
34 Yunnan, 29 July 1958, 2-1-3102, p. 21.
35 Guangdong, 5 Jan. 1961, 217-1-643, pp. 50–60.
36 Speech by Tan Zhenlin, Oct. 1958, Hunan, 141-2-62, p. 148.

Chapter 9: Warning Signs

1 Yunnan, 12 April 1958, zhongfa (58) 295, 120-1-75, pp. 2–4.
2 Hunan, 25 April 1958, 141-1-1055, pp. 66–7.
3 Yunnan, 20 Nov. 1958, 2-1-3078, pp. 116–23; 22 Aug. 1958, 2-1-3078, pp. 1–16.
4 Yunnan, 20 Nov. 1958, 2-1-3078, pp. 116–23.
5 Yunnan, 12 Sept. 1958, 2-1-3077, pp. 55–77; 12 Sept. 1958, 2-1-3076, pp. 97–105; Sept. 1958, 2-1-3075, pp. 104–22.
6 Yunnan, 28 Feb. 1959, 2-1-3700, pp. 93–8.
7 Yunnan, 16 May 1959, 81-4-25, p. 17; for the average death rate in 1957 see *Zhongguo tongji nianjian, 1984*, Beijing: Zhongguo tongji chubanshe, 1984, p. 83.
8 Mao, *Jianguo yilai*, vol. 7, pp. 584–5; the original is in Yunnan, 25 Nov. 1958, 120-1-84, p. 68; see also documents from the Zhengzhou conference, 25 Nov. 1958, Hunan, 141-2-76, pp. 99–103.
9 Hebei, 16 April 1961, 884-1-202, pp. 35–47.
10 Hebei, 19 Feb. 1961, 856-1-227, p. 3.

11 Hebei, 25 Dec. 1958, 855-4-1271, pp. 58–65.

12 Hebei, 18 Oct. 1958, 855-4-1270, pp. 1–7.

13 Hebei, 23 Oct. 1958, 855-4-1271, pp. 25–6.

14 Hebei, 24 Oct. 1958, 855-4-1271, pp. 42–3.

15 Hunan, 5 Nov. 1958, 141-1-1051, p. 123.

16 Li Jingquan at provincial party committee, Sichuan, 17 March 1959, JC1-1533, pp. 154–5.

17 Gansu, 25 Jan. 1959, 91-18-114, p. 113.

18 For instance an extra 600,000 tonnes was shipped to Beijing and 800,000 to Shanghai; see Shanghai, 12 March 1959, B98-1-439, pp. 9–13.

19 Yunnan, 18 Dec. 1958, 2-1-3101, pp. 301, 305–12.

Chapter 10: Shopping Spree

1 Ministry of Foreign Affairs, Beijing, 6 Sept. 1963, 109-3321-2, pp. 82–5.

2 K. A. Krutikov, *Na Kitaiskom napravlenii: Iz vospominanii diplomata*, Moscow: Institut Dal'nego Vostoka, 2003, p. 253; see also T. G. Zazerskaya, *Sovetskie spetsialisty i formirovanie voenno-promyshlennogo kompleksa Kitaya (1949–1960 gg.)*, St Petersburg: Sankt Peterburg Gosudarstvennyi Universitet, 2000.

3 AVPRF, Moscow, 9 March 1958, 0100-51-6, papka 432, p. 102.

4 Ministry of Foreign Affairs, Beijing, 10 June 1958, 109-828-30, pp. 176–7.

5 George Ginsburgs, 'Trade with the Soviet Union', in Victor H. Li, *Law and Politics in China's Foreign Trade*, Seattle: University of Washington Press, 1977, p. 100.

6 BArch, Berlin, 2 Dec. 1958, DL2-4037, pp. 31–9.

7 *Jahrbuch 1962*, Berlin, 1962, p. 548, and MfAA, Berlin, 25 Nov. 1963, C572-77-2, p. 191.

8 BArch, Berlin, 7 Jan. 1961, DL2-4039, p. 7; 1959, DL2-VAN-172.

9 See *Zhou Enlai nianpu*, vol. 2, pp. 149, 165, 231, 256, quoted in Zhang Shu Guang, *Economic Cold War: America's Embargo against China and the Sino-Soviet Alliance, 1949–1963*, Stanford: Stanford University Press, 2001, pp. 212–13.

10 See p. 105.

11 A. Boone, 'The Foreign Trade of China', *China Quarterly*, no. 11 (Sept. 1962), p. 176.

12 BArch, Berlin, 6 Oct. 1957, DL2-1932, pp. 331–2.

13 Lawrence C. Reardon, *The Reluctant Dragon: Crisis Cycles in Chinese Foreign Economic Policy*, Hong Kong: Hong Kong University Press, 2002, pp. 91–2.

14 Martin Kitchen, *A History of Modern Germany, 1800–2000*, New York: Wiley-Blackwell, 2006, p. 336.

15 MfAA, Berlin, 27 Sept. 1958, A6861, p. 145.

16 Ibid., pp. 151–2.

17 BArch, Berlin, 24 June 1959, DL2-1937, p. 231.

18 'Russia's trade war', *Time*, 5 May 1958; see also see Boone, 'Foreign Trade of China'.

19 'Squeeze from Peking', *Time*, 21 July 1958.
20 'Made well in Japan', *Time*, 1 Sept. 1958.
21 Ministry of Foreign Affairs, Beijing, 8 Nov. 1958, 109-1907-4, p. 49.
22 Ministry of Foreign Affairs, Beijing, Jan. 1959, 109-1907-3, pp. 24–5.
23 Ministry of Foreign Affairs, Beijing, 8 Nov. 1958, 109-1907-4, pp. 46–50.
24 Ministry of Foreign Affairs, Beijing, 23 Dec. 1958, 109-1907-2, pp. 12–13; for Germany see MfAA, Berlin, 21 Sept. 1959, A9960-2, pp. 183–4.
25 Ministry of Foreign Affairs, Beijing, 8 Nov. 1958, 109-1907-4, pp. 44–5.
26 Ministry of Foreign Affairs, Beijing, 23 Nov. 1958, 109-1907-5, p. 56.
27 Hunan, 22 Jan. 1959, 163-1-1052, p. 237.
28 Hunan, Jan. 1959, 141-2-104, pp. 10–12.
29 Gansu, 25 Jan. 1959, 91-18-114, p. 119; Ministry of Foreign Affairs, Beijing, 23 Dec. 1958, 109-1907-2, pp. 12–13.
30 Ministry of Foreign Trade, Shanghai, 31 Oct. 1958, B29-2-97, p. 23.
31 Guangdong, 10 Aug. 1961, 219-2-318, p. 14.
32 Hunan, 7 Feb. 1959, 163-1-1052, p. 11.
33 Ibid., p. 12.
34 Ibid., p. 11.
35 Ministry of Foreign Affairs, Beijing, 10 April 1959, 109-1907-8, p. 100; also speech on 25 March 1959, Gansu, 19-18-494, p. 46.
36 For statements of Peng and Zhou, see minutes in Ministry of Foreign Affairs, Beijing, 10 April 1959, 109-1907-8, p. 101.
37 The order came by telephone; Hunan, 26 May 1959, 141-1-1252, pp. 39–40.
38 Hunan, 20 Nov. 1959, 163-1-1052, pp. 25–9.
39 Hunan, 6 June 1959, 163-1-1052, pp. 119–24.
40 Gansu, zhongfa (60) 98, 6 Jan. 1960, 91-18-160, pp. 187–90.
41 Hunan, 6 Jan. 1960, 141-2-126, pp. 14–15.
42 Gansu, zhongfa (60) 98, 6 Jan. 1960, 91-18-160, pp. 187–90.
43 Hunan, 24 Nov. 1959, 163-1-1052, pp. 21–4.
44 Shanghai, 20 Feb. 1960, B29-2-112, pp. 2–5.
45 Shanghai, 1 Dec. 1959, B29-2-112, pp. 2–5.

Chapter 11: Dizzy with Success

1 Lin, *Wutuobang yundong*, pp. 371–2; Wu, *Yi Mao zhuxi*, pp. 105–6.
2 Zhao Ziyang's report on Leinan county, Kaiping, 27 Jan. 1959, 3-A9-78, pp. 17–20.
3 *Neibu cankao*, 5 Feb. 1959, pp. 3–14.
4 Mao, *Jianguo yilai*, vol. 8, pp. 52–4.
5 Ibid., pp. 80–1.
6 Ibid., pp. 52–4.
7 Mao's speech at Zhengzhou on 18 March 1959, Gansu, 91-18-494, pp. 19–20 and 22.
8 Mao's speech on 5 March 1959, quoted in Pang and Jin, *Mao Zedong zhuan*, p. 922.
9 Mao's speech on 2 Feb. 1959, Gansu, 91-18-494, pp. 10–11.

10 Mao's instructions to Wang Renzhong, Hunan, 13 April 1959, 141-1-1310, p. 75.

11 Bo, *Ruogan zhongda shijian*, p. 830.

12 Mao's speech in sixteen points on the morning of 5 April 1959, Hunan, 141-2-98, pp. 1–12; see also Lin, *Wutuobang yundong*, pp. 413–17.

13 Mao, *Jianguo yilai*, vol. 8, p. 33.

14 Minutes of Mao's talk, Gansu, 18 March 1959, 91-18-494, p. 19.

15 As quoted by Wu Jinnan, regional party secretary in Guangxi on 14 Feb. 1959; see minutes, Guangxi, X1-25-316, pp. 8–9.

16 Minutes of Mao's talk, Gansu, 25 March 1959, 19-18-494, pp. 44–8.

17 Telephone conference, Gansu, 20 June 1959, 91-18-539, p. 41.

18 Li, *Dayuejin*, vol. 2, p. 393.

19 Telephone conference on 20 Jan. 1959, Gansu, 91-18-513, p. 59.

20 Telegram from Mao, Gansu, 26 April 1959, 91-8-276, pp. 90–2.

Chapter 12: The End of Truth

1 Speech by Mao on 11 Aug. 1959, Gansu, 91-18-494, p. 81.

2 Li, *Private Life of Chairman Mao*, pp. 310–11.

3 Wang Yan et al. (eds), *Peng Dehuai nianpu* (A chronicle of Peng Dehuai's life), Beijing: Renmin chubanshe, 1998, p. 738.

4 Jin, *Zhou Enlai zhuan*, p. 1326.

5 Hunan, 31 Aug. 1959, 141-1-1115, pp. 107–9 and 111–13.

6 Peng Dehuai, *Peng Dehuai zishu* (The autobiography of Peng Dehuai), Beijing: Renmin chubanshe, 1981, p. 275.

7 See Peng Dehuai's conversation with Zhou Xiaozhou, Gansu, 13 Aug. 1959, 91-18-96, p. 518.

8 The description comes from Kung Chu, an early comrade in arms, in *The Case of Peng Teh-huai, 1959–1968*, Hong Kong: Union Research Institute, 1968, p. i.

9 Gansu, 14 July 1959, 91-18-96, pp. 579–84.

10 Li, *Private Life of Chairman Mao*, p. 314.

11 Mao, *Jianguo yilai*, vol. 8, p. 356.

12 Li Rui, *Lushan huiyi shilu* (A true record of the Lushan plenum), Zhengzhou: Henan renmin chubanshe, 1999, pp. 111–15.

13 Huang Kecheng's confession, Gansu, Aug. 1959, 91-18-96, p. 491.

14 Huang Kecheng, *Huang Kecheng zishu* (The autobiography of Huang Kecheng), Beijing: Renmin chubanshe, 1994, p. 250.

15 Mao's speech on 11 Aug. 1959, Gansu, 91-18-494, p. 78.

16 Gansu, 21 July 1959, 91-18-96, pp. 532–47.

17 Peng Dehuai's confession about his links with Zhang Wentian, Gansu, Aug. 1959, 91-18-96, p. 568.

18 Gansu, 91-18-488, 15 July 1959, pp. 106–8.

19 Letter by Zhou Xiaozhou to Mao Zedong, Gansu, 13 Aug. 1959, 91-18-96, p. 518.

20 *Neibu cankao*, 26 July 1959, pp. 19–20.

21 Mao, *Jianguo yilai*, vol. 8, p. 367; the report is in Ministry of Foreign Affairs, Beijing, 2 July 1959, 109-870-8, pp. 81–3.

22 Wu Lengxi's unpublished memoirs as quoted in Pang and Jin, *Mao Zedong zhuan*, p. 983.
23 Gansu, 11 Aug. 1959, 91-18-494, p. 84.
24 Gansu, 23 July 1959, 91-18-494, pp. 50–66.
25 Li, *Private Life of Chairman Mao*, p. 317.
26 Gansu, 2 Aug. 1959, 91-18-494, pp. 67–70.
27 Li, *Lushan huiyi*, pp. 206–7.
28 Huang Zheng, *Wang Guangmei fangtan lu* (A record of conversations with Wang Guangmei), Beijing: Zhongyang wenxian chubanshe, 2006, p. 199.
29 Li, *Lushan huiyi*, pp. 359–60.
30 Huang Kecheng's self-criticism, Gansu, Aug. 1959, 91-18-96, p. 495.
31 Gansu, Aug. 1959, 91-18-96, p. 559.
32 Gansu, 11 Aug. 1959, 91-18-494, pp. 82–3.
33 Gansu, 16 Aug. 1959, 91-18-96, p. 485.

Chapter 13: Repression

1 Gao, *Zhou Enlai*, pp. 187–8.
2 Gansu, 19 Sept. 1959, 91-18-561, p. 28.
3 Gansu, zhongfa (60) 28, 8 Jan. 1960, 91-18-164, pp. 109–14.
4 Gansu, 3 Dec. 1962, 91-4-1028, pp. 8–9.
5 Mao, *Jianguo yilai*, vol. 8, p. 529.
6 Gansu, 1 July 1960, 91-4-705, pp. 1–5.
7 Yunnan, 28 Oct. 1959, 2-1-3639, pp. 23–31.
8 Hebei, 1960, 879-1-116, p. 43.
9 Hebei, 9 Nov. 1959, 855-5-1788, pp. 3–6.
10 Mao, *Jianguo yilai*, vol. 8, p. 431.
11 Hunan, 2–4 Sept. 1959, 141-1-1116, pp. 40–3, 49–50 and 121.
12 Li, *Private Life of Chairman Mao*, pp. 299–300; an almost identical conversation took place earlier over the phone, as Zhou ridiculed Wang's sputnik fields and challenged him to come to Changsha to find out about the local supplies of grain; see Hunan, 1 Sept. 1959, 141-1-1115, pp. 235–7.
13 Roderick MacFarquhar, *The Origins of the Cultural Revolution*, vol. 3: *The Coming of the Cataclysm, 1961–1966*, New York: Columbia University Press, 1999, pp. 61, 179 and 206–7; Lu, *Cadres and Corruption*, p. 86, quoting from figures provided at the time in the *People's Daily*; speaking in September 1959, Peng Zhen put the party membership at 13,900,000 and the number of cadres purged over the two preceeding years at 700,000; see Gansu, 19 Sept. 1959, 91-18-561, p. 28.

Chapter 14: The Sino-Soviet Rift

1 Instructions from State Council, Ministry of Foreign Affairs, Beijing, 1 Aug. 1960, 109-927-1, pp. 1–5.
2 Klochko, *Soviet Scientist*, p. 171.

3 Several diplomats see this as the main reason for the rift; see Kapitsa, *Na raznykh parallelakh*, pp. 61–3; Arkady N. Shevchenko, *Breaking with Moscow*, New York: Alfred Knopf, 1985, p. 122.

4 Zubok and Pleshakov, *Inside the Kremlin's Cold War*, p. 232.

5 The original letter of recall, in Russian and Chinese, can be found in the Ministry of Foreign Affairs, Beijing, 16 July 1960, 109-924-1, pp. 4–8.

6 Jung Chang and Jon Halliday, *Mao: The Unknown Story*, London: Jonathan Cape, 2005, p. 465.

7 Wu, *Shinian lunzhan*, p. 337.

8 Gansu, 5 Aug. 1960, 91-9-91, pp. 7–11.

9 Ministry of Foreign Affairs, Beijing, 1960–1, 109-2248-1, p. 38.

10 Ministry of Foreign Affairs, Beijing, 20 Aug. 1963, 109-2541-1, pp. 12–13.

11 Ministry of Foreign Affairs, Beijing, 28 March 1960, 109-2061-1, p. 3; Ministry of Foreign Affairs, Beijing, 1962, 109-3191-6, p. 5.

12 Ministry of Foreign Affairs, Beijing, 109-2541-1, pp. 12–13.

13 Report from the Bank for Foreign Trade, RGANI, Moscow, 2 June 1961, 5-20-210, p. 34; for the deal see *Sbornik osnovnykh deistvuiushchikh dogovorokh i sogloshenii mezhdu SSSR i KNR, 1949–1961*, Moscow: Ministerstvo Inostrannykh Del, no date, p. 198.

14 Ginsburgs, 'Trade with the Soviet Union', pp. 100 and 106.

15 BArch, Berlin, 12 Nov. 1960, DL2-1870, p. 34.

16 RGANI, Moscow, 14 Feb. 1964, 2-1-720, p. 75.

17 Interview with Mr Chan, born 1946, Hong Kong, July 2006.

18 Taubman, *Khrushchev*, p. 471.

19 Li, *Private Life of Chairman Mao*, p. 339.

Chapter 15: Capitalist Grain

1 Jin, *Zhou Enlai zhuan*, p. 1398.

2 Ministry of Foreign Affairs, Beijing, 20 Aug. 1960, 118-1378-13, pp. 32–3.

3 Oleg Hoeffding, 'Sino-Soviet Economic Relations, 1959–1962', *Annals of the American Academy of Political and Social Science*, vol. 349 (Sept. 1963), p. 95.

4 Ministry of Foreign Affairs, Beijing, 31 Dec. 1960, 110-1316-11, pp. 1–5.

5 Ministry of Foreign Affairs, Beijing, 18 Jan. 1961, 109-3004-2, p. 8.

6 Ministry of Foreign Affairs, Beijing, 31 Dec. 1960, 110-1316-11, pp. 1–5.

7 BArch, Berlin, 12 Nov. 1960, DL2-1870, p. 34.

8 'Famine and bankruptcy', *Time*, 2 June 1961.

9 Jin, *Zhou Enlai zhuan*, pp. 1414–15.

10 Colin Garratt, 'How to Pay for the Grain', *Far Eastern Economic Review*, vol. 33, no. 13 (28 Sept. 1961), p. 644.

11 Jin, *Zhou Enlai zhuan*, p. 1413.

12 Report by Zhou Enlai, Hunan, 4 Dec. 1961, 141-1-1931, p. 54.

13 MfAA, Berlin, 1962, A6792, p. 137.

14 Report by Zhou Enlai, Hunan, 4 Dec. 1961, 141-1-1931, p. 54.

15 Boone, 'Foreign Trade of China'.

16 Report by Zhou Enlai, Hunan, 4 Dec. 1961, 141-1-1931, pp. 52–3.

17 'Famine and bankruptcy', *Time*, 2 June 1961.

18 Ministry of Foreign Affairs, Beijing, 8 March 1961, 109-3746-1, pp. 17–18.

19 RGANI, Moscow, 14 Feb. 1964, 2-1-720, pp. 81–2; the contract for the delivery of sugar is in *Sbornik osnovnykh deistvuiushchikh dogovorokh i sogloshenii mezhdu SSSR i KNR, 1949–1961*, Moscow: Ministerstvo Inostrannykh Del, no date, pp. 196–7.

20 Ministry of Foreign Affairs, Beijing, 4 April 1961, 109-2264-1, pp. 1–8.

21 Ministry of Foreign Affairs, Beijing, 22 Aug. 1961, 109-2264-2, p. 38.

22 Ministry of Foreign Affairs, Beijing, 6 April 1962, 109-2410-3, p. 53.

23 Ibid.

24 Ministry of Foreign Affairs, Beijing, 15 Aug. 1962, 109-2410-1, pp. 62–3.

25 BArch, Berlin, 1962, DL2-VAN-175, p. 15.

26 Chang and Halliday, *Mao*, p. 462.

27 MfAA, Berlin, 11 July 1962, A17334, p. 92.

28 Ministry of Foreign Affairs, Beijing, 1 July 1960, 102-15-1, pp. 26–39; see also MfAA, Berlin, 11 July 1962, A17334, pp. 89–94.

29 Shanghai, 1 Dec. 1959, B29-2-112, p. 3.

30 Report from the Ministry of Finance, Gansu, 1 July 1961, 91-18-211, p. 25.

31 MfAA, Berlin, 4 Jan. 1962, A6836, p. 33; see also the analysis of the East Germans of the policy of foreign aid, which they identified as one of the main reasons for the famine; MfAA, Berlin, 4 Jan. 1962, A6836, p. 16.

32 Report from the Ministry of Finance, Gansu, 1 July 1961, 91-18-211, pp. 22–5.

33 Hunan, 29 March 1960, 163-1-1083, pp. 119–22; by the end of the year, following a resolution at Beidaihe in September 1960, this was lowered to 310 million, with rice halved to some 144,000 tonnes; see Hunan, 22 Oct. 1960, 163-1-1083, pp. 130–4.

34 Guangdong, 29 Sept. 1960, 300-1-195, p. 158.

35 Guangzhou, 5 April 1961, 92-1-275, p. 105.

36 Gansu, 16 Jan. 1961, 91-18-200, p. 72.

37 Shanghai, 21 Oct. 1960, B29-2-112, pp. 2–5.

38 'Back to the farm', *Time*, 3 Feb. 1961.

39 ICRC, Geneva, telegrams of 18, 28 and 30 Jan. and 6 Feb. 1961, BAG 209-048-2.

40 ICRC, Geneva, discussions on 1 and 14 March 1961, BAG 209-048-2.

41 Ministry of Foreign Affairs, Beijing, 27 Jan. 1959, 109-1952-3, p. 13.

Chapter 16: Finding a Way Out

1 Bo, *Ruogan zhongda shijian*, p. 892.

2 Mao, *Jianguo yilai*, vol. 9, p. 326; Lin, *Wutuobang yundong*, p. 607.

3 Zhang Zhong, 'Xinyang shijian jiemi' (Revealing the Xinyang incident), *Dangshi tiandi*, 2004, no. 4, pp. 40–1.

4 Yang Zhengang, Zhang Jiansheng and Liu Shikai, 'Guanyu huaifenzi Ma Longshan da gao fanmanchan jiqi houguo deng youguan cailiao de diaocha baogao', 9 Nov. 1960, p. 7.

5 Li Zhenhai, Liu Zhengrong and Zhang Chunyuan, 'Guanyu Xinyang diqu

Xincai qu dong jin chun fasheng zhongbing siren he ganbu yanzhong weifa luanji wenti de diaocha baogao', 30 Nov. 1960, p. 1.

6 Xinyang diwei zuzhi chuli bangongshi, 'Guanyu diwei changwu shuji Wang Dafu tongzhifan suo fan cuowu ji shishi cailiao', 5 Jan. 1962, pp. 1–2.

7 Zhang, 'Xinyang shijian jiemi', p. 42; see also Qiao Peihua, *Xinyang shijian* (The Xinyang incident), Hong Kong: Kaifang chubanshe, 2009.

8 Mao, *Jianguo yilai*, vol. 9, p. 349.

9 *Nongye jitihua zhongyao wenjian huibian (1958–1981)* (A compendium of important documents on agricultural collectivisation [1958–1981]), Beijing: Zhongyang dangxiao chubanshe, 1981, vol. 2, pp. 419–30.

10 Chester J. Cheng (ed.), *The Politics of the Chinese Red Army*, Stanford: Hoover Institution Publications, 1966, pp. 117–23.

11 Zhonggong zhongyang wenxian yanjiushi (eds), *Jianguo yilai zhongyao wenxian xuanbian*, Beijing: Zhongyang wenxian chubanshe, 1992, vol. 13, pp. 660–76.

12 Bo, *Ruogan zhongda shijian*, pp. 893–6.

13 Li, *Private Life of Chairman Mao*, p. 339.

14 Speech by Liu Shaoqi, Gansu, 20 Jan. 1961, 91-6-79, pp. 46–51 and 103–7.

15 Speech by Mao Zedong, Gansu, 18 Jan. 1961, 91-6-79, p. 4.

16 Huang, *Liu Shaoqi yisheng*, pp. 346–8; Huang, *Wang Guangmei fangtan lu*, pp. 225–6 and 240.

17 Liu Shaoqi conversations on 25, 28 and 30 April 1961, Hunan, 141-1-1873, pp. 106–50; see also Huang, *Wang Guangmei fangtan lu*, pp. 238–40; Jin and Huang, *Liu Shaoqi zhuan*, pp. 865–6.

18 Jin and Huang, *Liu Shaoqi zhuan*, p. 874.

19 Letter by Liu Shaoqi, Gansu, April–May 1961, 91-4-889, pp. 2–4.

20 Liu Shaoqi, 31 May 1961, Gansu, 91-6-81, pp. 69–73.

21 Jin, *Zhou Enlai zhuan*, pp. 1441–2.

22 Speech by Li Fuchun at the Ninth Plenum of the Eighth Central Committee, Hunan, 14 Jan. 1961, zhongfa (61) 52, 186-1-505, pp. 1–28.

23 Speech by Li Fuchun, Hunan, 17 July 1961, 186-1-584, pp. 7 and 13.

24 Documents from Beidaihe conference, Hunan, 11 Aug. 1961, 186-1-584, pp. 38–48, 125, 134 and 152.

25 Li, *Private Life of Chairman Mao*, p. 380.

Chapter 17: Agriculture

1 Jean C. Oi, *State and Peasant in Contemporary China: The Political Economy of Village Government*, Berkeley: University of California Press, 1989, pp. 48–9.

2 Hebei, 11 April 1961, 878-1-14, pp. 56–8.

3 Yunnan, 29 July 1958, 2-1-3102, pp. 16–22.

4 Kenneth R. Walker, *Food Grain Procurement and Consumption in China*, Cambridge: Cambridge University Press, 1984.

5 The plan for 1959–60 with the procurement figures broken down by province are in Gansu, 31 July 1959, zhongfa (59) 645, 91-18-117, p. 105.

6 Zhejiang, 16 July 1961, J132-13-7, pp. 22–8, quoted in Yang Jisheng, *Mubei:*

Zhongguo liushi niandai dajihuang jishi (Wooden gravestone: A true history of the great famine in China in the 1960s), Hong Kong: Tiandi tushu youxian gongsi, 2008, p. 418; compare this with Yang's statistics on p. 417.

7 Guizhou, 1962, 90-1-2706, printed page 3; rough equivalents of these percentages are also found in more detailed estimates at the county level, for instance in the case of Zunyi county (26.5 per cent in 1957, 46.3 per cent in 1958, 47 per cent in 1959 and 54.7 per cent in 1960), Guizhou, 1962, 90-1-2708, printed page 7; the same file contains many other similar examples, some with procurement rates up to 80 per cent; for the Bureau of Grain, see Yang, *Mubei*, p. 540.

8 Speech on 25 March 1959, Gansu, 19-18-494, pp. 44–6.

9 Zhejiang, 16 July 1961, J132-13-7, pp. 22–8; compare with Yang, *Mubei*, p. 540.

10 Report from the State Council, Gansu, 15 June 1960, zhongfa (60) 547, 91-18-160, pp. 208–12.

11 Guangdong, 10 Aug. 1961, 219-2-318, pp. 9–16.

12 Deng Xiaoping speech on 11 Dec. 1961, Hunan, 141-2-138, p. 43.

13 Speech on 25 March 1959, Gansu, 19-18-494, p. 48.

14 Shanghai, 4 April 1961, B6-2-392, pp. 20 ff.

15 Shanghai, 8 July 1958, B29-2-97, p. 17.

16 Oi, *State and Peasant in Contemporary China*, pp. 53–5.

17 For the policy document and for an example from Hunan, see Hunan, 3 Nov. and 1 Dec. 1959, 146-1-483, pp. 9, 18–20 and 86.

18 Zhejiang, Jan. 1961, J116-15-10, pp. 1–14.

19 Guangdong, 7 Jan. 1961, 217-1-643, pp. 120–2.

20 Guangdong, 2 Jan. 1961, 217-1-643, pp. 61–6.

21 Speech on 30 Aug. 1958, Hunan, 141-1-1036, p. 38. A *mu* is equivalent to 0.0667 of a hectare.

22 Hunan, 1964, 187-1-1355, p. 64.

23 Zhejiang, 1961, J116-15-139, p. 1; 29 Jan. 1961, J116-15-115, p. 29.

24 Hubei, 13 Jan. 1961, SZ18-2-200, p. 27.

25 Gansu, 20 June 1959, 91-18-539, p. 35.

26 Gansu, 12 Feb. 1961, 91-18-209, p. 246; Walker estimated the sown area for 1958 at 130 million hectares, Walker, *Food Grain Procurement*, p. 147.

27 Walker, *Food Grain Procurement*, pp. 21–2.

28 Guangdong, 1 March 1961, 235-1-259, pp. 23–5.

29 Yunnan, 20 Sept. 1961, 120-1-193, pp. 85–92.

30 Gansu, 20 Feb. 1961, zhongfa (61) 145, 91-18-211, p. 91.

31 Guangdong, 1 March 1961, 235-1-259, pp. 23–5.

32 Hunan, 15 Nov. 1960, 163-1-1082, p. 106.

33 Yunnan, 6 Feb. 1961, 120-1-193, pp. 108–9.

34 Beijing, 29 Nov. and 10 Dec. 1960, 2-12-262, pp. 21–3.

35 Yunnan, 14 Dec. 1960 and 20 Sept. 1961, 120-1-193, pp. 85–92 and 112–15.

36 Gansu, 20 Feb. 1961, zhongfa (61) 145, 91-18-211, p. 92.

37 Yunnan, 14 Dec. 1960, 120-1-193, pp. 112–15.

38 Hunan, 20 Aug. 1959, 141-1-1259, pp. 51–2.

39 MfAA, Berlin, 1962, A6860, p. 100.

40 Zhejiang, 29 Jan. 1961, J116-15-115, p. 12.
41 Guangdong, 15 March 1961, 217-1-119, p. 78.
42 MfAA, Berlin, 1962, A6792, p. 136.
43 Hunan, 6 Nov. 1961, 141-1-1914, pp. 48–52.
44 Yunnan, 1962, 81-7-86, p. 13.
45 Hunan, 19 Feb. 1959, 163-1-1052, pp. 82–7.
46 Report by Qian Zhiguang, minister for the textile industry, Hunan, 11 Aug. 1961, 186-1-584, p. 107.
47 Guangzhou, 28 Feb. 1961, 6-1-103, pp. 3–4.
48 Beijing, 8 Jan. 1962, 2-13-138, pp. 1–3.
49 Report by Hu Yaobang on 1 Oct. 1961, Hunan, 141-2-138, p. 197.
50 Hebei, 1962, 979-3-870, pp. 1–30.
51 Hunan, 15 March 1959, 141-1-1158, p. 140.
52 Guangdong, 3 July 1959, 217-1-69, pp. 74–5.
53 Guangdong, 12 Oct. 1961, 235-1-259, p. 13.
54 Zhejiang, 29 Jan. 1961, J116-15-115, pp. 16–21.
55 Hunan, 15 Jan. 1961, 146-1-580, p. 13.
56 Guangdong, 20 May 1961, 217-1-210, pp. 82–7.
57 Zhejiang, 29 Jan. 1961, J116-15-115, pp. 16–21.
58 Conversation between Li Jingquan and Zhou Enlai in the premier's office on 1 April 1962, Sichuan, JC1-3198, p. 33.
59 Shanghai, 1961, B181-1-510, pp. 17–20.
60 Beijing, 31 July 1962, 1-9-439, pp. 1–4.
61 Report from Moscow embassy, Ministry of Foreign Affairs, Beijing, 18 Sept. 1958, 109-1213-14, p. 142.
62 Zhejiang, 21 March 1960, J002-3-3, p. 34.
63 Shanghai, 1961, B181-1-510, p. 7.
64 Ministry of Foreign Affairs, Beijing, 10 April 1959, 109-1907-8, p. 100; also speech on 25 March 1959, Gansu, 19-18-494, p. 46.
65 Shanghai, 1961, B29-2-980, p. 143.
66 Guangdong, 16 Sept. 1961, 235-1-259, p. 71.
67 Zhejiang, 29 Jan. 1961, J116-15-115, pp. 5 and 16.
68 Xuancheng, 17 May 1961, 3-1-257, pp. 127–31.
69 Shanghai, 1961, B181-1-511, p. 25.
70 Hunan, 11 Aug. 1961, 186-1-584, p. 134.
71 Hunan, 15 March 1959, 141-1-1158, p. 152.
72 Guangdong, 25 Feb. 1961, 217-1-119, p. 57.
73 Hebei, 1962, 979-3-870, pp. 1–30.
74 Zhejiang, 29 Jan. 1961, J116-15-115, pp. 15 and 29.
75 Ibid., p. 52.
76 Guangdong, 25 Feb. 1961, 217-1-119, p. 58.

Chapter 18: Industry

1 Klochko, *Soviet Scientist*, pp. 85–6.
2 Guangdong, 1961, 218-2-320, pp. 26–31.

3 MfAA, Berlin, 7 June 1961, A6807, pp. 20–4.
4 MfAA, Berlin, 14 Nov. 1962, A6860, pp. 142–5.
5 Beijing, 31 July 1961, 1-5-371, pp. 5–10.
6 Guangdong, 1961, 218-2-320, pp. 26–31.
7 Klochko, *Soviet Scientist*, p. 91.
8 *Neibu cankao*, 25 Nov. 1960, p. 7.
9 Hunan, 21 Sept. 1961, 186-1-525, pp. 2–6.
10 Ibid.
11 Shanghai, 28 March 1959, B29-1-34, pp. 16–21.
12 Hunan, 5 May 1961, 141-1-1939, pp. 33–4.
13 Beijing, 26 June 1961, 2-13-89, pp. 14–15.
14 Hunan, 26 Dec. 1959 and 16 Jan. 1960, 163-1-1087, pp. 70–2 and 91–5.
15 Speech on 25 March 1959, Gansu, 19-18-494, p. 46.
16 Reports by He Long and Nie Rongzhen, Gansu, 13 Sept. 1960, 91-6-26, pp. 69–75.
17 *Neibu cankao*, 25 Nov. 1960, p. 9.
18 Nanjing, 2 Sept. 1960, 6001-1-73, pp. 12–15.
19 Guangzhou, 1960, 19-1-255, pp. 39–41; 11 Sept. 1961, 19-1-525, pp. 94–100.
20 Guangdong, 7 Aug. 1961, 219-2-319, pp. 17–31.
21 Beijing, 17 Jan. and 31 March 1959, 101-1-132, pp. 14–18 and 26–40.
22 Beijing, 29 March 1960, 101-1-138, p. 3.
23 Beijing, 24 March 1961, 1-28-28, p. 6.
24 Beijing, 28 Sept. 1961, 2-13-138, pp. 25–9.
25 Nanjing, 13 July and 22 Nov. 1960, 5065-3-395, pp. 7–19 and 35–52.
26 Nanjing, 13 July 1960, 5065-3-395, pp. 7–19.
27 Nanjing, 1961, 5065-3-443, pp. 51, 60 and 66.
28 Beijing, 31 July 1961, 1-5-371, pp. 5–10.
29 Nanjing, 15 Sept. 1961, 6001-3-328, pp. 25–8.
30 Nanjing, 1960, 4053-2-4, p. 98. These salaries were generally fixed; only in the winter of 1961–2 were fixed salaries replaced for a variety of compensation schemes, including pay by piece or a share of the profits; see Nanjing, 4 Dec. 1961, 4053-2-5, p. 1.
31 Nanjing, 15 Sept. 1961, 6001-2-329, pp. 30–1.
32 Beijing, 29 March 1960, 101-1-138, p. 4.
33 Nanjing, 1960, 4053-2-4, p. 93.
34 Hunan, 3 Sept. 1959, 141-1-1259, pp. 69–70.
35 Beijing, 30 July 1961, 1-5-371, p. 8.
36 Report from Ministry of Coal, Gansu, 91-18-193, 11 Sept. 1961, p. 71.
37 These were Quren, Nanling, Luojiadu and Lianyang; Guangdong, June 1960, 253-1-99, pp. 17–20.
38 Gansu, Feb. 1961, 91-18-200, p. 245.
39 Shanghai, Jan. 1961, A36-1-246, pp. 2–3.
40 Shanghai, Aug. 1961, B29-2-655, p. 92.
41 Guangdong, Aug. 1961, 219-2-319, pp. 31–56.

Chapter 19: Trade

1 Hunan, 13 Sept. and 7 Nov. 1960, 163-1-1083, pp. 83–5 and 95–7.
2 Shanghai, 11 Aug. 1960, B123-4-782, pp. 26–9.
3 Yunnan, 23 Oct. 1958, zhongfa (58) 1060, 2-1-3276, pp. 131–5.
4 Yunnan, 15 Oct. 1960, zhongfa (60) 841, 2-1-4246, pp. 103–8.
5 Shanghai, Aug. 1961, B29-2-655, p. 160; 20 April 1961, B29-2-980, p. 248.
6 Yunnan, 15 Oct. 1960, zhongfa (60) 841, 2-1-4246, pp. 103–8.
7 Yunnan, 3 Dec. 1960, zhongfa (60) 1109, 2-1-4246, pp. 117–19.
8 Ministry of Foreign Affairs, Beijing, 1 Jan. 1960, 118-1378-13, p. 82.
9 Yunnan, 25 Oct. 1961, 2-1-4654, pp. 44–6.
10 Yunnan, 22 Sept. 1960, 2-1-4269, pp. 36–9.
11 Hunan, 3 Aug. 1959, 141-1-1259, p. 148.
12 MfAA, Berlin, 11 Dec. 1961, A6807, pp. 347–51.
13 Guangdong, Aug. 1961, 219-2-319, pp. 31–56.
14 Shanghai, May 1961, B29-2-940, p. 161.
15 On retailing and the material culture of pre-revolutionary China, see Frank Dikötter, *Exotic Commodities: Modern Objects and Everyday Life in China*, New York: Columbia University Press, 2006.
16 Klochko, *Soviet Scientist*, p. 53.
17 Nanjing, Nov. 1961, 5040-1-18, pp. 14–19 and 20–6.
18 Nanjing, 12 Jan. and 26 April 1959, 4003-1-167, pp. 22–4 and 36–8.
19 J. Dyer Ball, *The Chinese at Home*, London: Religious Tract Society, 1911, p. 240, quoted in Dikötter, *Exotic Commodities*, p. 63.
20 Guangzhou, 22 Aug. 1959, 16-1-13, pp. 56–7; Guangzhou, 20 July 1961, 97-8-173, p. 18.
21 Nanjing, 1 July 1959, 4003-1-167, pp. 39–46.
22 *Neibu cankao*, 2 Dec. 1960, p. 11.
23 Shanghai, 7 May 1961, A20-1-60, pp. 64–6.
24 Nanjing, 4 June 1959, 5003-3-722, pp. 77–81.
25 *Neibu cankao*, 23 Nov. 1960, pp. 15–16.
26 *Neibu cankao*, 5 May 1961, pp. 14–16.
27 Guangzhou, 27 March, 1 June and 6 July 1961, 97-8-173, pp. 45–6 and 52–3; 60-1-1, pp. 80 and 105–11.
28 Wuhan, 29 July 1959, 76-1-1210, p. 68.
29 Speech at Beidaihe, Gansu, 11 Aug. 1961, 91-18-561, p. 51.
30 Beijing, 26 June 1961, 2-13-89, pp. 2–3.
31 Beijing, 31 July 1961, 2-13-100, pp. 1–6.
32 Nanjing, Nov. 1961, 5040-1-18, pp. 14–19 and 20–6.
33 *Neibu cankao*, 10 Aug. 1960, pp. 13–15.
34 Beijing, 28 March 1961, 1-28-28, pp. 9–11.
35 Shanghai, 31 July 1961, A20-1-55, pp. 23–9.
36 Interview with Lao Tian, born 1930s, Xushui, Hebei, Sept. 2006.

Chapter 20: Housing

1 Shen Bo, 'Huiyi Peng Zhen tongzhi guanyu renmin dahuitang deng "shida jianzhu" de sheji de jiaodao' (Remembering comrade Peng Zhen's directions concerning the design of the Great Hall of the People and the ten great edifices), *Chengjian dang'an*, no. 4 (2005), pp. 10–11.

2 Wu Hung, *Remaking Beijing: Tiananmen Square and the Creation of a Political Space*, London: Reaktion Books, 2005, p. 24.

3 'Ten red years', *Time*, 5 Oct. 1959.

4 Xie Yinming and Qu Wanlin, 'Shei baohule gugong' (Who protected the Imperial Palace), *Dang de wenxian*, no. 5 (2006), pp. 70–5.

5 PRO, London, 15 Nov. 1959, FO371-133462.

6 PRO, London, 23 July 1959, FO371-141276.

7 Beijing, 27 Dec. 1958 and 2 Feb. 1959, 2-11-128, pp. 1–3 and 8–14.

8 Hunan, 21 Jan. 1959, 141-2-104.

9 Gansu, 9 Jan. 1961, 91-18-200, pp. 18–19.

10 Gansu, 22 Feb. 1961, 91-18-200, pp. 256–8.

11 Hunan, 3 and 14 April 1961, 151-1-24, pp. 1–13 and 59–68.

12 Guangdong, 20 Jan. 1961, 217-1-645, pp. 15–19.

13 Report at the Lushan conference, Gansu, Sept. 1961, 91-18-193, p. 82.

14 Gansu, 24 Oct. 1960, zhongfa (60) 865, 91-18-164, pp. 169–72.

15 Speech by Li Fuchun, Hunan, 20 Dec. 1961, 141-1-1931, pp. 154–5.

16 Shanghai, 28 July 1959, B258-1-431, pp. 4–5.

17 Wuhan, 15 May and 23 June 1959, 13-1-765, pp. 44–5 and 56.

18 Hunan, April 1960, 141-2-164, p. 82.

19 Guangdong, 5 July 1961, 307-1-186, pp. 47–52.

20 Sichuan, 22 and 24 March 1960, JC50-315.

21 Sichuan, Dec. 1961, JC50-325.

22 Beijing, 4 March and 7 Aug. 1959, 2-11-146, pp. 1–23.

23 Nanjing, 16 April 1959, 4003-1-279, p. 153.

24 Guangdong, 7 Jan. 1961, 217-1-643, pp. 110–15.

25 Sichuan, Feb. 1961, JC1-2576, pp. 41–2.

26 Guangdong, 10 Dec. 1960, 217-1-643, pp. 44–9.

27 Guangdong, 12 Dec. 1960, 217-1-643, pp. 33–43.

28 Hunan, 11 May 1961, 141-2-139, p. 61.

29 Hunan, 17 May 1961, 146-1-584, p. 26.

30 Sichuan, Aug. 1961, JC1-2584, p. 14.

31 Sichuan, 1962, JC44-1440, pp. 127–8.

32 Hubei, 18 Nov. 1960, SZ18-2-198, pp. 69–71.

33 Hunan, 4 Aug. 1962, 207-1-744, p. 9.

34 Li Heming, Paul Waley and Phil Rees, 'Reservoir Resettlement in China: Past Experience and the Three Gorges Dam', *Geographical Journal*, vol. 167, no. 3 (Sept. 2001), p. 197.

35 Guangdong, Oct. 1961, 217-1-113, pp. 58–61.

36 Hunan, 15 Dec. 1961 and 21 March 1962, 207-1-753, pp. 103–5 and 106–9.

37 Beijing, 25 April 1961, 2-13-39, pp. 1–14.

38 James L. Watson, 'The Structure of Chinese Funerary Rites', in James L. Watson and Evelyn S. Rawski (eds), *Death Ritual in Late Imperial and Modern China*, Berkeley: University of California Press, 1988.

39 *Neibu cankao*, 7 Dec. 1960, pp. 12–13.

40 Hunan, 14 Feb. 1958, 141-1-969, p. 19.

41 Interview with Wei Shu, born 1920s, Langzhong county, Sichuan, April 2006.

42 Beijing, 18 April 1959, 2-11-36, pp. 7–8 and 17–18.

43 Beijing, 14 Nov. 1958, 2-11-33, p. 3.

44 The report was sent to the provincial party committee in Hunan; Hunan, March 1959, 141-1-1322, pp. 108–10.

Chapter 21: Nature

1 Ferdinand P. W. von Richthofen, *Baron Richthofen's Letters, 1870–1872*, Shanghai: North-China Herald Office, 1903, p. 55, quoted in Dikötter, *Exotic Commodities*, p. 177.

2 I. T. Headland, *Home Life in China*, London: Methuen, 1914, p. 232, quoted in Dikötter, *Exotic Commodities*, p. 177.

3 Shapiro, *Mao's War against Nature*, pp. 3–4.

4 Mao's speech at Supreme State Conference on 28–30 Jan. 1958, Gansu, 91-18-495, p. 202.

5 Hunan, 13 April 1962, 207-1-750, pp. 1–10.

6 Hunan, 6 Oct. 1962, 207-1-750, pp. 44–9.

7 RGAE, Moscow, 7 Aug. 1959, 9493-1-1098, p. 29.

8 Hunan, 13 April 1962, 207-1-750, pp. 1–10.

9 Gansu, 17 Aug. 1962, zhongfa (62) 430, 91-18-250, p. 66.

10 Beijing, 3 March 1961, 2-13-51, pp. 7–8.

11 Beijing, 26 May 1961, 92-1-143, pp. 11–14.

12 Ibid.

13 Beijing, 3 March 1961, 2-13-51, pp. 7–8.

14 Hubei, SZ113-2-195, 12 Feb. and 1 Nov. 1961, pp. 8–10 and 28–31.

15 Gansu, 23 Oct. 1962, 91-18-250, p. 72.

16 Gansu, 31 Oct. 1962, 91-18-250, p. 83.

17 Guangdong, 10 May 1961, 217-1-210, pp. 88–9.

18 Nanjing, 25 Dec. 1958, 4003-1-150, p. 73.

19 Beijing, 26 May 1961, 92-1-143, pp. 11–14.

20 Gansu, 17 Aug. 1962, zhongfa (62) 430, 91-18-250, p. 69.

21 Hubei, 10 March 1961, SZ113-2-195, pp. 2–3.

22 Hunan, 28 Nov. 1961, 163-1-1109, pp. 138–47.

23 Gansu, 31 Oct. 1962, 91-18-250, p. 83.

24 Hunan, 18 Nov. 1961, 163-1-1109, p. 60.

25 Gansu, 17 Aug. 1962, 91-18-250, p. 65.

26 For estimates based on published sources, see Shapiro, *Mao's War against Nature*, p. 82.

27 Gansu, 17 Aug. 1962, 91-18-250, p. 68.

28 Gansu, 31 Oct. 1962, 91-18-250, p. 82.

29 Hunan, 6 Oct. 1962, 207-1-750, pp. 44–9.

30 Guangdong report on forests, 21 Sept. 1962, Hunan, 141-2-163, p. 50.

31 Yu Xiguang, *Dayuejin ku rizi: Shangshuji* (The Great Leap Forward and the years of bitterness: A collection of memorials), Hong Kong: Shidai chaoliu chubanshe, 2005, p. 8; to give a sense of proportion, by some estimates the forest cover stood at 83 million hectares in 1949; see Vaclav Smil, *The Bad Earth: Environmental Degradation in China*, Armonk, NY: M. E. Sharpe, 1984, p. 23.

32 Beijing, 15 Sept. 1959, 2-11-63, pp. 31–6 and 48–52.

33 One of the earliest descriptions is by Tan Zhenlin in a telephone conference on the summer crop; see Gansu, 26 June 1959, 92-28-513, pp. 14–15.

34 Y. Y. Kueh, *Agricultural Instability in China, 1931–1991*, Oxford: Clarendon Press, 1995, examined metereological data and concluded that bad weather did contribute to a reduction in crop production but that similar weather conditions in the past did not have the same effect.

35 Beijing, 7 May 1960, 2-12-25, pp. 3–6.

36 Beijing, 8 Sept. 1962, 96-2-22, pp. 15–18.

37 Hebei, 15 Aug. 1961, 878-1-6, pp. 31–44.

38 Report by Hu Yaobang on 1 Oct. 1961, Hunan, 141-2-138, pp. 186–9.

39 Hunan, 13 April 1962, 207-1-750, pp. 1–10.

40 Hunan, 6 Oct. 1962, 207-1-750, pp. 44–9.

41 Hunan, 4 Aug. 1962, 207-1-744, pp. 1–12.

42 Hunan, 6 Oct. 1962, 207-1-750, pp. 44–9.

43 Hunan, 13 and 15 May 1961, 146-1-584, pp. 13 and 18.

44 Hunan, 24 April 1961, 146-1-583, p. 108; large reservoirs were defined by Beijing as having a capacity of over 100 million cubic metres, medium ones ranging from 10 to 100 million cubic metres and small ones having less than 10 million cubic metres.

45 Hunan, 4 Aug. 1962, 207-1-744, pp. 1–12.

46 Hunan, 7 Jan. 1962, 207-1-743, pp. 85–105.

47 Hunan, 1 Dec. 1961, 163-1-1109, p. 101.

48 Hubei, 12 Sept. 1959, SZ18-2-197, pp. 39–43.

49 Hubei, 1 Aug. 1959, SZ113-1-209, p. 3.

50 Hubei, 27 March 1961, SZ18-2-201.

51 Hubei, 18 March and 9 June 1961, SZ113-1-26, pp. 1–3 and 12–14.

52 Hubei, 14 April 1962, SZ113-2-213, p. 25.

53 Hunan, 1964, 187-1-1355, p. 64.

54 Guangdong, Dec. 1960, 266-1-74, pp. 105–18.

55 Report by Ministry of Water Conservancy and Hydraulic Electricity, 27 July 1960, Hunan, 141-1-1709, p. 277.

56 Guangdong, Dec. 1960, 266-1-74, p. 117.

57 Yi, 'World's Most Catastrophic Dam Failures', pp. 25–38.

58 Shui, 'Profile of Dams in China', p. 23.

59 As reported by the secretary of the south-central region Li Yiqing; Hunan, 11 Aug. 1961, 186-1-584, p. 134.

60 Beijing, 17 April 1962, 96-2-22, p. 6.

61 Hebei, 1 July 1961, 979-3-864, pp. 4–5.
62 Hebei, 1962, 979-3-870, p. 7; see also Hebei, 13 July 1962, 979-3-871, pp. 1–22, for a much lower figure for the increase in alkaline land.
63 Report by Liu Jianxun, 24 Dec. 1961, Hunan, 141-2-142, p. 225.
64 Report by Hu Yaobang, 1 Oct. 1961, Hunan, 141-2-138, pp. 186–7.
65 Report by Hua Shan, 9 May 1962, Shandong, A1-2-1125, pp. 5–7.
66 Gansu, 9 March 1960, zhongfa (60) 258, 91-18-154, pp. 254–5.
67 Beijing, 17 Sept. 1959, 2-11-145, pp. 3–6.
68 Gansu, 9 March 1960, zhongfa (60) 258, 91-18-154, pp. 254–5.
69 Gansu, 24 Feb. 1960, 91-18-177, pp. 14–17.
70 Gansu, 9 March 1960, zhongfa (60) 258, 91-18-154, pp. 254–5.
71 Nanjing, 22 Nov. 1960, 5065-3-395, pp. 35–52.
72 Report by Mao Qihua, Gansu, 4 Sept. 1960, zhongfa (60) 825, 91-18-154, p. 104.
73 Shanghai, Oct. 1961, B29-2-954, p. 57.
74 Ibid.
75 Ibid., p. 76.
76 Hubei, 10 Jan. 1961, SZ34-5-45, pp. 22–4; 23 Jan. 1961, SZ1-2-906, p. 17.
77 Klochko, *Soviet Scientist*, pp. 71–3.
78 Nanjing, 18 March 1959, 5065-3-367, pp. 20–2; 25 March 1959, 5003-3-721, pp. 8–9.
79 Shanghai, 1959, A70-1-82, p. 9.
80 Shapiro, *Mao's War on Nature*, p. 88.
81 Hubei, 8 and 25 July 1961, SZ18-2-202, pp. 78 and 101.
82 Nanjing, 24 Oct. 1960, 4003-1-203, pp. 20–1.
83 Zhejiang, 29 Jan. 1961, J116-15-115, p. 11.

Chapter 22: Feasting through Famine

1 James R. Townsend and Brantly Womack, *Politics in China*, Boston: Little, Brown, 1986, p. 86.
2 Tiejun Cheng and Mark Selden, 'The Construction of Spatial Hierarchies: China's *hukou* and *danwei* Systems', in Timothy Cheek and Tony Saich (eds), *New Perspectives on State Socialism in China*, Armonk, NY: M. E. Sharpe, 1997, pp. 23–50.
3 Guangdong, 15 March 1962, 300-1-215, pp. 205–7.
4 Li, *Private Life of Chairman Mao*, pp. 78–9.
5 Fu Zhengyuan, *Autocratic Tradition and Chinese Politics*, Cambridge: Cambridge University Press, 1993, p. 238.
6 Lu, *Cadres and Corruption*, p. 86.
7 Shanghai, 1961, B50-2-324, pp. 15–24.
8 *Neibu cankao*, 25 Nov. 1960, pp. 11–12.
9 *Neibu cankao*, 6 March 1961, p. 5.
10 *Neibu cankao*, 22 Feb. 1961, pp. 13–14.
11 Guangdong, 5 Sept. 1960, 231-1-242, pp. 72–7.
12 Guangdong, 18 June 1960, 231-1-242, pp. 63–5.

13　Guangdong, 10 Dec. 1960, 217-1-643, pp. 44–9.
14　Ibid., p. 45.
15　Guangdong, 24 July 1959, 217-1-497, pp. 61–3.
16　Guangdong, 1961, 217-1-116, p. 48.
17　Guangdong, 26 June 1959, 217-1-69, pp. 33–8.
18　PRO, London, 15 Nov. 1959, FO371-133462.
19　Shanghai, 8 Oct. 1960, A20-1-10, pp. 19 ff.
20　Hebei, 8 May 1959, 855-5-1758, pp. 97–8.
21　Beijing, 14 Feb. 1959, 1-14-573, p. 65.
22　Shanghai, 27 Jan. 1961, A36-1-246, pp. 9–17.

Chapter 23: Wheeling and Dealing

1　Shanghai, 20 Dec. 1960, A36-2-447, pp. 64–5.
2　*Neibu cankao*, 2 June 1960, pp. 14–15.
3　*Neibu cankao*, 16 Nov. 1960, pp. 11–13.
4　Shanghai, Feb. 1961, A36-2-447, p. 22.
5　Guangdong, Nov. 1960, 288-1-115, p. 1.
6　*Neibu cankao*, 16 Nov. 1960, pp. 11–13.
7　Guangdong, 9 Feb. 1961, 235-1-255, pp. 39–40.
8　Guangdong, 5 Dec. 1961, 235-1-259, p. 75.
9　Nanjing, 27 May 1959, 4003-1-279, p. 242.
10　*Neibu cankao*, 25 Nov. 1960, pp. 13–15.
11　Gansu, 24 Oct. 1960, zhongfa (60) 865, 91-18-164, pp. 169–72.
12　Report from Ministry of Finance, Gansu, 5 Nov. 1960, zhongfa (60) 993, 91-18-160, pp. 275–80.
13　*Neibu cankao*, 7 Dec. 1960, pp. 14–15.
14　Speech at Beidaihe, Gansu, 11 Aug. 1961, 91-18-561, pp. 51 and 55.
15　Report from Ministry of Finance, Gansu, 5 Nov. 1960, zhongfa (60) 993, 91-18-160, pp. 275–80.
16　*Neibu cankao*, 8 Aug. 1960, pp. 5–7.
17　Hebei, 19 April 1959, 855-5-1758, pp. 105–6.
18　Beijing, 23 June 1961, 1-5-376, pp. 4–10.
19　Nanjing, Aug. 1960, 4003-1-199, p. 19.
20　Nanjing, 14 Aug. 1960, 4003-1-199, pp. 1–4.
21　*Neibu cankao*, 25 Nov. 1960, pp. 12–13; 30 Dec. 1960, pp. 10–11.
22　Beijing, 27 April 1961, 1-28-30, pp. 1–4.
23　Shanghai, 7 Aug. 1961, A20-1-60, pp. 181–5.
24　Beijing, 28 Nov. 1960, 101-1-138, pp. 13–29.
25　Shanghai, 28 March 1959, B29-1-34, pp. 48–9.
26　*Neibu cankao*, 26 Dec. 1960, pp. 10–11.
27　*Neibu cankao*, 17 May 1961, p. 22.
28　Guangdong, 23 Jan. 1961, 217-1-644, pp. 10–12.
29　Guangzhou, 24 Feb. 1961, 92-1-275, p. 74.
30　Nanjing, 1 Sept. 1959, 5003-3-722, p. 89.
31　Hunan, 15 Jan. 1961, 146-1-580, p. 15.

32 For a description see Dennis L. Chinn, 'Basic Commodity Distribution in the People's Republic of China', *China Quarterly*, no. 84 (Dec. 1980), pp. 744–54.

33 *Neibu cankao*, 18 Aug. 1960, p. 16.

34 Guangdong, 9 Feb. 1961, 235-1-259, pp. 39–40.

35 *Neibu cankao*, 7 Dec. 1960, p. 24.

36 Guangdong, 9 Feb. 1961, 235-1-259, pp. 39–40.

37 Beijing, 29 Dec. 1960, 2-12-262, pp. 18–20.

38 Hunan, 13 June 1961, 163-1-1109, pp. 21–2.

39 MfAA, Berlin, March–April 1961, A17009, pp. 3–4.

40 *Neibu cankao*, 23 Jan. 1961, pp. 10–11; 6 Feb. 1962, pp. 5–6.

41 See also Jeremy Brown, 'Great Leap City: Surviving the Famine in Tianjin', in Kimberley E. Manning and Felix Wemheuer (eds), *New Perspectives on China's Great Leap Forward and Great Famine*, Vancouver: University of British Columbia Press, 2010.

42 MfAA, Berlin, 6 Sept. 1962, A6862, p. 8.

43 Hubei, 7 Aug. 1961 and July 1962, SZ29-1-13, pp. 73–4 and 76–7.

44 Sichuan, 16 Aug. and 12 Sept. 1962, JC44-3918, pp. 105–7 and 117–19.

45 Hubei, 18 Sept. 1961, SZ18-2-199, pp. 6–7.

46 Hebei, 6 May 1959, 855-5-1744, pp. 101–3.

47 Sichuan, 1962, JC1-3047, pp. 1–2.

48 Shandong, 10 Aug. 1959, A1-2-776, p. 72.

Chapter 24: On the Sly

1 Hunan, 12 Feb. 1961, 151-1-20, pp. 32–3.

2 Beijing, 24 March 1961, 1-28-28, pp. 2–6.

3 Shanghai, 25 Oct. 1961, B123-5-144, p. 176.

4 Shanghai, Aug. 1961, B29-2-655, p. 82.

5 Sichuan, 1959, JC9-249, p. 160.

6 Sichuan, 1959, JC9-250, pp. 14 and 46.

7 Interview with Ding Qiao'er, born 1951, Huangxian county, Shandong, Dec. 2006.

8 *Neibu cankao*, 2 June 1960, pp. 14–15.

9 *Neibu cankao*, 19 Dec. 1960, p. 21.

10 Ibid., pp. 23–4.

11 *Neibu cankao*, 7 Dec. 1960, pp. 21–4.

12 Nanjing, 26 Feb. 1959, 4003-1-171, p. 62.

13 Shanghai, 31 March 1960, B123-4-588, p. 3; 22 May 1961, B112-4-478, pp. 1–2.

14 Thaxton, *Catastrophe and Contention in Rural China*, p. 201.

15 *Neibu cankao*, 2 Sept. 1960, pp. 5–7.

16 Xuancheng, 3 May 1961, 3-1-259, pp. 75–6.

17 Interview with Zeng Mu, born 1931, Pengzhou, Sichuan, May 2006.

18 Guangdong, 1 March 1961, 235-1-259, pp. 23–5.

19 Guangdong, 1 and 27 March 1961, 235-1-259, pp. 23–5 and 32–4.

20 *Neibu cankao*, 26 April 1961, p. 20.
21 Hebei, 27 Sept. 1960, 855-5-1996, pp. 52-4.
22 Wuxian, 15 May 1961, 300-2-212, p. 243.
23 Guangdong, 21 Jan. 1961, 235-1-259, pp. 16-17.
24 Hubei, 22 Feb. 1959, SZ18-2-197, pp. 19-21.
25 Hebei, 2 June 1959, 855-5-1758, pp. 46-7.
26 Hubei, 22-23 Feb. 1959, SZ18-2-197, pp. 6-8 and 12-14.
27 Hebei, 13 Dec. 1960, 855-18-777, pp. 40-1.
28 Hebei, 1 June 1959, 855-5-1758, pp. 126-7.
29 Hunan, 10 and 18 Dec. 1959, 146-1-507, pp. 81 and 90-3.
30 Hunan, 31 Dec. 1959, 146-1-507, pp. 120-1.
31 Hebei, 1 June 1959, 855-5-1758, pp. 126-7.
32 Nanjing, 4 June 1959, 5003-3-722, pp. 77-81.
33 Nanjing, 26 Jan. 1960, 5012-3-556, p. 60.
34 Hunan, 13 Feb. 1961, 151-1-18, pp. 24-5.
35 Interview with Li Erjie, born 1922, Chengdu, Sichuan, April 2006.
36 Hubei, 11 May 1961, SZ18-2-202, pp. 25-6.
37 Guangdong, 1961, 235-1-256, p. 73.
38 Hubei, 18 Sept. 1961, SZ18-2-199, p. 7.
39 Yunnan, 30 Dec. 1958, 2-1-3442, pp. 11-16.

Chapter 25: 'Dear Chairman Mao'

1 Hebei, 4 Jan. 1961, 880-1-11, p. 30.
2 I resist the temptation to provide more than a few examples, although interested readers can turn to a remarkable chapter in Jasper Becker, *Hungry Ghosts: Mao's Secret Famine*, New York: Henry Holt, 1996, pp. 287-306.
3 François Mitterrand, *La Chine au défi*, Paris: Julliard, 1961, pp. 30 and 123.
4 PRO, London, Nov. 1960, PREM11-3055.
5 Nanjing, 17 March 1959, 4003-1-279, pp. 101-2.
6 *Neibu cankao*, 7 Dec. 1960, pp. 21-4.
7 Shanghai, 7 May 1961, A20-1-60, pp. 60-2.
8 Hubei, 14 Oct. 1961, SZ29-2-89, pp. 1-8.
9 Guangdong, 1962, 217-1-123, pp. 123-7.
10 Guangzhou, 24 Feb. 1961, 92-1-275, p. 75.
11 Guangdong, 1962, 217-1-123, pp. 123-7.
12 Guangdong, 1961, 217-1-644, p. 20.
13 Nanjing, 16 July 1959, 5003-3-721, pp. 26-7.
14 Gansu, 5 Sept. 1962, 91-18-279, p. 7.
15 Hebei, June 1959, 884-1-183, p. 39.
16 Gansu, 5 Sept. 1962, 91-18-279, p. 7.
17 Ministry of Public Security report, Gansu, 8 Feb. 1961, 91-4-889, pp. 25-30.
18 Nanjing, 16 July 1959, 5003-3-721, pp. 26-7.
19 Hebei, 27 June 1959, 884-1-183, pp. 136 and 140.
20 Hubei, 5 Sept. 1959, SZ18-2-197, p. 34.
21 Sichuan, 25 May 1959, JC1-1721, p. 3.

22 Cyril Birch, 'Literature under Communism', in Roderick MacFarquhar, John King Fairbank and Denis Twitchett (eds), *The Cambridge History of China*, vol. 15: *Revolutions within the Chinese Revolution, 1966–1982*, Cambridge: Cambridge University Press, 1991, p. 768.

23 Shanghai, 7 May 1961, A20-1-60, p. 62.

24 Guangdong, 3 Jan. 1961, 217-1-643, p. 102.

25 Interview with Yang Huafeng, born 1946, Qianjiang county, Hubei, Aug. 2006.

26 Guangdong, 2 Jan. 1961, 217-1-643, pp. 61–6.

27 Sichuan, 1961, JC9-464, p. 70.

28 Some very inspiring pages on rumours during collectivisation have been written by Lynn Viola, *Peasant Rebels under Stalin: Collectivization and the Culture of Peasant Resistance*, New York: Oxford University Press, 1996, pp. 45–7.

29 Wuhan, 3 Nov. 1958, 83-1-523, p. 134.

30 Guangdong, 23 Jan. 1961, 217-1-644, pp. 10–12.

31 Hubei, 4 Jan. 1961, SZ18-2-200, p. 11.

32 Hubei, 5 May 1961, SZ18-2-201, p. 95.

33 Sichuan, 1961, JC1-2614, p. 14.

34 *Neibu cankao*, 9 June 1960, pp. 7–8.

35 Guangdong, 5 Feb. 1961, 217-1-119, p. 45.

36 Guangdong, 23 Jan. 1961, 217-1-644, pp. 10–12 and 20.

37 Hunan, 23 Jan. 1961, 146-1-580, p. 54.

38 Gansu, 5 Sept. 1962, 91-18-279, p. 7.

39 Nanjing, 19 March 1959, 5003-3-722, pp. 68–9.

40 Hebei, June 1959, 884-1-183, pp. 84–92 and 128.

41 On denunciations in the Soviet Union, one reads with pleasure Sheila Fitzpatrick, 'Signals from Below: Soviet Letters of Denunciation of the 1930s', *Journal of Modern History*, vol. 68, no. 4 (Dec. 1996), pp. 831–66.

42 Hunan, 1959–61, 163-2-232, entire file.

43 Nanjing, 7 March and 13 May 1961, 5003-3-843, pp. 1–4 and 101.

44 Shanghai, 30 Nov. 1959, A2-2-16, p. 75.

45 Guangdong, 1961, 235-1-256, p. 90.

46 *Neibu cankao*, 31 May 1960, pp. 18–19.

47 *Neibu cankao*, 19 Dec. 1960, pp. 15–17.

48 Hunan, 31 Dec. 1961, 141-1-1941, p. 5.

49 Guangdong, 24 Feb. 1961, 235-1-256, pp. 40–2.

50 *Neibu cankao*, 12 June 1961, p. 23.

51 Gansu, 14 Jan. 1961, 91-18-200, p. 50.

52 Report by provincial party committee work team, Sichuan, 1961, JC1-2616, p. 111.

Chapter 26: Robbers and Rebels

1 Hebei, 15 Aug. 1961, 878-1-6, p. 38.

2 *Neibu cankao*, 16 Dec. 1960, p. 9.

3 For instance Hebei, 27 June 1959, 884-1-183, p. 135.

4 Hubei, 6 Jan. 1961, SZ18-2-200, p. 22.
5 Hunan, 17 Jan. 1961, 146-1-580, p. 29.
6 Gansu, 24 Jan. 1961, 91-9-215, pp. 117–20.
7 Ibid.
8 *Neibu cankao*, 20 June 1960, pp. 11–12.
9 Report from the Ministry of Railways, Gansu, 20 Jan. 1961, 91-4-889, pp. 19–21.
10 Hunan, 22 Nov. 1959, 146-1-507, pp. 44–6.
11 Sichuan, 26 May 1959, JC1-1721, p. 37.
12 Sichuan, 8 June 1959, JC1-1721, p. 153.
13 Hunan, 9 March 1959, 163-1-1046, p. 24.
14 Hebei, June 1959, 884-1-183, p. 40; 25 April 1960, 884-1-184, p. 20.
15 Nanjing, 30 Jan. 1959, 4003-1-171, p. 35.
16 Nanjing, 19 March 1959, 5003-3-722, pp. 68–9.
17 Hubei, 4 Jan. 1961, SZ18-2-200, p. 11.
18 Hubei, 22 Feb. 1959, SZ18-2-197, pp. 6–8.
19 Sichuan, 2–4 Nov. 1959, JC1-1808, p. 137.
20 Guangdong, 3 Feb. 1961, 262-1-115, pp. 86–7.
21 Kaiping, 29 Dec. 1960, 3-A10-81, p. 2.
22 Hunan, 17 Jan. 1961, 146-1-580, p. 29.
23 Gansu, 18 June 1958, zhongfa (58) 496, 91-18-88, pp. 29–34.
24 Yunnan, 30 Nov. 1960, 2-1-4108, pp. 72–5; 2 Dec. 1960, 2-1-4108, pp. 1–2; see also 8 Nov. and 9 Dec. 1960, 2-1-4432, pp. 1–10 and 50–7.
25 Ministry of Public Security report, Gansu, 8 Feb. 1961, 91-4-889, pp. 25–30.
26 Hebei, June 1959, 884-1-183, pp. 39–40 and 132.
27 Hebei, 26 April 1960, 884-1-184, p. 36.
28 Guangdong, 1961, 216-1-257, pp. 64–5.

Chapter 27: Exodus

1 Shanghai, 12 March 1959, B98-1-439, pp. 9–13.
2 Zhang Qingwu, 'Kongzhi chengshi renkou de zengzhang', *Renmin ribao*, 21 Aug. 1979, p. 3, quoted in Judith Banister, *China's Changing Population*, Stanford: Stanford University Press, 1987, p. 330.
3 Yunnan, 18 Dec. 1958, 2-1-3101, p. 301.
4 Shanghai, 20 April 1959, A11-1-34, pp. 1–3.
5 Shanghai, 12 and 17 March 1959, B98-1-439, pp. 12 and 25.
6 Shanghai, 20 April 1959, A11-1-34, pp. 4–14.
7 Xinyang, 4 Aug. 1960, 304-37-7, p. 68.
8 Hebei, 28 Feb., 11 March and 15 April 1959, 855-5-1750, pp. 74–5, 91–4 and 132–4.
9 Zhejiang, 3 March 1959, J007-11-112, pp. 1–6.
10 Guangdong, 23 Jan. 1961, 217-1-644, pp. 10–12.
11 Hebei, 15 April 1959, 855-5-1750, pp. 132–4.
12 Wuhan, 14 April 1959, 76-1-1210, pp. 87–8.
13 *Neibu cankao*, 20 June 1960, pp. 11–12.

14 Hebei, 11 March 1959, 855-5-1750, pp. 91–4.

15 Beijing, 23 Jan. and 31 Aug. 1959, 2-11-58, pp. 3–4 and 8–10.

16 Nanjing, 14 March 1959, 4003-1-168, pp. 39–49; 14 Aug. 1960, 4003-1-199, p. 2.

17 Nanjing, 23 Dec. 1959, 5003-3-721, p. 115; 21 July 1959, 4003-2-315, pp. 11–18.

18 Nanjing, 21 July 1959, 4003-2-315, pp. 11–18.

19 Ibid.

20 Yunnan, 29 Nov. 1958, zhongfa (58) 1035, 2-1-3276, pp. 250–3.

21 Nanjing, 14 Aug. 1960, 4003-1-199, p. 2.

22 Nanjing, 21 Nov. 1959, 4003-2-315, p. 32.

23 Gansu, 14 Jan. 1961, 91-18-200, pp. 47–8.

24 Guangdong, 5 Jan. 1961, 217-1-643, p. 63.

25 Hebei, 15 Aug. 1961, 878-1-6, pp. 31–44.

26 Yunnan, 29 Nov. 1958, zhongfa (58) 1035, 2-1-3276, pp. 250–3.

27 Hebei, 15 April 1959, 855-5-1750, p. 133.

28 Hubei, 25 Feb. 1958, SZ34-4-295, p. 7.

29 Hubei, Sept. 1958, SZ34-4-295, pp. 38–42.

30 Hebei, 17 Dec. 1960, 878-2-8, pp. 8–10.

31 Reports from the State Council and the Ministry of Public Security, Hubei, 6 Feb., 5 June and 10 Nov. 1961, SZ34-5-15, pp. 7–8 and 58–61.

32 Sichuan, Nov.–Dec. 1961, JC1-2756, pp. 84–5.

33 *Neibu cankao*, 1 May 1960, p. 30.

34 Gansu, 31 Aug. 1960, 91-9-58, pp. 32–7.

35 Hubei, 18 April 1961, SZ34-5-15, p. 9.

36 Hubei, 1961, SZ34-5-15, pp. 9–10.

37 Gansu, 16 June 1961, zhong (61) 420, 91-18-211, pp. 116–19.

38 Yunnan, Aug. 1960, 2-1-4245, p. 55; Yunnan, 10 July 1961, 2-1-4587, p. 83.

39 Yunnan, 10 and 22 July 1961, 2-1-4587, pp. 82 and 112–14.

40 Guangdong, 20 July, 2 Aug. and 23 Nov. 1961, 253-1-11, pp. 44, 51 and 53.

41 Xuancheng, 25 June 1961, 3-1-257, p. 32.

42 Hunan, 12 Dec. 1961, 186-1-587, p. 5.

43 Ministry of Foreign Affairs, Beijing, 12 June 1958 and 14 Jan. 1959, 105-604-1, pp. 21 and 24–30.

44 PRO, London, 28 Feb. 1959, FO371-143870.

45 Ministry of Foreign Affairs, Beijing, 23 Aug. 1961, 106-999-3, pp. 40–55.

46 RGANI, Moscow, 22 May 1962, 5-30-401, p. 39.

47 Ministry of Foreign Affairs, Beijing, 10 May 1962, 118-1100-9, pp. 71–9.

48 RGANI, Moscow, 28 April 1962, 3-18-53, pp. 2–3 and 8–12.

49 RGANI, Moscow, May 1962, 3-16-89, pp. 63–7.

50 Ministry of Foreign Affairs, Beijing, 30 June 1962, 118-1758-1, pp. 1–8.

51 RGANI, Moscow, 6 Nov. 1964, 5-49-722, pp. 194–7.

52 *Hong Kong Annual Report*, Hong Kong: Government Printer, 1959, p. 23.

53 ICRC, Geneva, report from J. Duncan Wood, Sept. 1963, BAG 234 048-008.03.

54 *Hong Kong Standard*, 11 May 1962.

55 According to a defector interviewed by the CIA; see CIA, Washington, 27 July 1962, OCI 2712-62, p. 4; a similar report was carried by the *South China Morning Post*, 6 June 1962.

56 ICRC, Geneva, report from Paul Calderara, 5 June 1962, BAG 234 048-008.03.

57 Ibid.; see also PRO, Hong Kong, 1958–60, HKRS 518-1-5.

58 Hansard, 'Hong Kong (Chinese Refugees)', HC Deb, 28 May 1962, vol. 660, cols 974–7; ICRC, Geneva, report from J. Duncan Wood, Sept. 1963, BAG 234 048-008.03.

59 Aristide R. Zolberg, Astri Suhrke and Sergio Aguayo, *Escape from Violence: Conflict and the Refugee Crisis in the Developing World*, Oxford: Oxford University Press, 1989, p. 160.

60 'Refugee dilemma', *Time*, 27 April 1962.

Chapter 28: Children

1 Wujiang, 13 April 1959, 1001-3-92, pp. 63–9.

2 Beijing, 4 and 18 Aug. 1960, 84-1-167, pp. 1–9 and 43–52.

3 Beijing, 31 March 1959, 101-1-132, pp. 26–40.

4 Guangzhou, 9 Jan., 7 March, 29 April, 18 May and 14 Dec. 1959, 16-1-19, pp. 19–24, 51–5, 57–61, 64–6 and 70; on the use of physical punishment in Shanghai see Shanghai, 24 Aug. 1961, A20-1-54, p. 18.

5 Shanghai, 7 May 1961, A20-1-60, p. 64; 24 Aug. 1961, A20-1-54, pp. 16–24.

6 Beijing, 4 Aug. 1960, 84-1-167, pp. 43–52.

7 Beijing, 18 Aug. 1960, 84-1-167, pp. 1–9.

8 Nanjing, 14 Nov. 1961, 5012-3-584, p. 79.

9 Guangzhou, 18 May 1959, 16-1-19, pp. 51–5.

10 Nanjing, 21 April 1960, 4003-2-347, pp. 22–6.

11 Hubei, 25 Dec. 1960, SZ34-5-16, pp. 2–3.

12 Guangdong, 1961, 314-1-208, p. 16.

13 For the rules and regulations in the secondary school system, see Suzanne Pepper, *Radicalism and Education Reform in 20th-Century China: The Search for an Ideal Development Model*, Cambridge: Cambridge University Press, 1996, pp. 293 ff.

14 Wuhan, 9 April and 26 Dec. 1958, 70-1-767, pp. 33–45.

15 Wuhan, 6 Jan. 1959, 70-1-68, pp. 19–24.

16 Nanjing, 28 Dec. 1958, 4003-1-150, p. 81.

17 Hunan, 2 June 1960, 163-1-1087, pp. 43–5.

18 Sichuan, May 1961, JC1-2346, p. 15.

19 Guangdong, 25 Jan. 1961, 217-1-645, pp. 11–14.

20 Guangdong, 1961, 217-1-646, pp. 10–11.

21 Hunan, 8 April 1961, 146-1-583, p. 96.

22 Ibid.

23 Guangdong, 31 Dec. 1960, 217-1-576, pp. 54–68.

24 Hunan, 13 Feb. 1961, 151-1-18, pp. 24–5.

25 Guangdong, 1960, 217-1-645, pp. 60–4.

26 *Neibu cankao*, 30 Nov. 1960, p. 16.
27 Yunnan, 22 May 1959, 2-1-3700, pp. 93–8.
28 Interview with Ding Qiao'er, born 1951, Huangxian county, Shandong, Dec. 2006.
29 Interview with Liu Shu, born 1946, Renshou county, Sichuan, April 2006.
30 Interview with Li Erjie, born 1922, Chengdu, Sichuan, April 2006.
31 On this phenomenon one should read Robert Dirks, 'Social Responses during Severe Food Shortages and Famine', *Current Anthropology*, vol. 21, no. 1 (Feb. 1981), p. 31.
32 Nanjing, 10 May 1960, 5003-3-722, pp. 27–31.
33 Hebei, 10 Feb. 1960, 855-18-778, p. 36.
34 Interview with Li Erjie, born 1922, Chengdu, Sichuan, April 2006.
35 Nanjing, 4 Jan. 1960, 4003-1-202, p. 1; 21 July, 30 Sept. and 15 Dec. 1959, 4003-2-315, pp. 17, 20, 27 and 36.
36 Nanjing, 4 Jan. 1960, 4003-1-202, p. 1; 21 July, 30 Sept. and 15 Dec. 1959, 4003-2-315, pp. 17, 27 and 36.
37 Nanjing, 20 May 1959, 4003-2-315, pp. 12–14.
38 Wuhan, 20 July 1959, 13-1-765, pp. 72–3; Hubei, 30 Aug. 1961, SZ34-5-16, pp. 35–6.
39 Hubei, 18 Sept. 1961, SZ34-5-16, pp. 41–2.
40 Hebei, 17 Aug. 1961, 878-2-17, pp. 142–5.
41 Hebei, 24 Jan. 1961, 878-2-17, pp. 1–5.
42 Guangdong, 10 Feb. 1961, 217-1-640, pp. 18–28.
43 Sichuan, 1 Oct. 1961, JC44-1432, pp. 89–90; a September 1962 report mentions 200,000 orphans; see JC44-1442, p. 34.
44 Sichuan, 1962, JC44-1440, pp. 46 and 118–19.
45 Sichuan, 1962, JC44-1441, p. 35.
46 Interview with Zhao Xiaobai, born 1948, Lushan county, Henan, May and Dec. 2006.
47 Sichuan, 1961, JC1-2768, pp. 27–9.
48 Hubei, 24 April, 30 Aug. and 18 Sept. 1961, SZ34-5-16, pp. 19, 35–6 and 41–2.
49 Yunnan, 16 May 1959, 81-4-25, p. 17.
50 Hunan, 30 June 1964, 187-1-1332, p. 14.

Chapter 29: Women

1 See Dikötter, *Exotic Commodities*.
2 On this one should read Gao Xiaoxian, '"The Silver Flower Contest": Rural Women in 1950s China and the Gendered Division of Labour', *Gender and History*, vol. 18, no. 3 (Nov. 2006), pp. 594–612.
3 Hunan, 13 March 1961, 146-1-582, pp. 80–1.
4 Sichuan, 1961, JC1-2611, p. 3.
5 Hunan, 13 March 1961, 146-1-582, pp. 80–1.
6 Guangdong, 23 March 1961, 217-1-643, pp. 10–13.
7 Guangdong, 1961, 217-1-618, pp. 18–41.

8 Guangdong, 2 Jan. 1961, 217-1-643, pp. 61–6.

9 Beijing, 15 March 1961, 1-28-29, pp. 1–2.

10 Beijing, 10 Feb. 1961, 84-1-180, pp. 1–9.

11 The figure for Hunan was an estimate of 'gynaecological problems', defined as prolapse of the uterus or lack of menstrual periods for a duration of at least half a year in working women, excluding those who were too sick actually to work; Shanghai, 1 Feb. 1961, B242-1-1319-15, p. 1; Hunan, 8 Dec. 1960, 212-1-508, p. 90; see also Hebei, 19 Jan. 1961, 878-1-7, pp. 1–4.

12 Hubei, 23 Feb. 1961, SZ1-2-898, pp. 12–17.

13 Guangdong, 6 April 1961, 217-1-643, pp. 1–9.

14 Hebei, 27 June 1961, 880-1-7, pp. 53 and 59.

15 Hebei, 27 April 1961, 880-1-7, p. 88.

16 Hebei, 2 June 1960, 855-9-4006, p. 150.

17 Hunan, 21 Jan. 1961, 146-1-580, p. 45.

18 Hunan, 24 Feb. 1961, 146-1-588, p. 9.

19 Hunan, 1959, 141-1-1322, pp. 2–5 and 14.

20 *Neibu cankao*, 30 Nov. 1960, p. 17.

21 Kaiping, 24 Sept. 1960, 3-A10-76, p. 19.

22 Kaiping, 6 June 1959, 3-A9-80, p. 6.

23 Sichuan, 18 Aug. 1962, JC44-3927, pp. 2–6.

24 Nanjing, 20 May 1959, 4003-2-315, p. 12.

25 *Neibu cankao*, 13 Feb. 1961, pp. 14–15.

26 *Neibu cankao*, 12 June 1961, pp. 9–10.

27 Guangdong, 1961, 217-1-618, pp. 18–41.

28 David Arnold, *Famine: Social Crisis and Historical Change*, Oxford: Blackwell, 1988, p. 89.

Chapter 30: The Elderly

1 Charlotte Ikels, *Aging and Adaptation: Chinese in Hong Kong and the United States*, Hamden: Archon Books, 1983, p. 17.

2 Macheng, 15 Jan. 1959, 1-1-443, p. 28.

3 Deborah Davis-Friedmann, *Long Lives: Chinese Elderly and the Communist Revolution*, Stanford: Stanford University Press, 1991, p. 87, quoting the *People's Daily* dated 15 Jan. 1959.

4 Beijing, May 1961, 1-14-666, p. 25.

5 Guangdong, 10 Feb. 1961, 217-1-640, pp. 18–28.

6 Sichuan, 29 Nov. and 24 Dec. 1958, JC1-1294, pp. 71 and 129.

7 Sichuan, 1959, JC44-2786, p. 55.

8 Hunan, 1961, 167-1-1016, pp. 1 and 144.

9 Hunan, 1960, 146-1-520, p. 102.

10 Interview with Jiang Guihua, born 1940, Zhaojue county, Sichuan, April 2007.

11 Hubei, 3 July 1961, SZ18-2-202, p. 70.

Chapter 31: Accidents

1 Hunan, 5 Nov. 1958, 141-1-1051, p. 123.
2 Hunan, 9 March 1959, 163-1-1046, p. 24.
3 Nanjing, 16 April 1959, 4003-1-279, pp. 151–2.
4 Nanjing, 31 Oct. 1959, 5003-3-711, p. 33.
5 Hubei, 5 Jan. 1960, SZ34-4-477, p. 34.
6 Hunan, 16 Jan. and 12 Feb. 1960, 141-1-1655, pp. 54–5 and 66–7.
7 Report from the State Council, Hubei, 3 March 1960, SZ34-4-477, p. 29.
8 Hunan, July 1959, 141-1-1224, pp. 13–14.
9 Chishui, 27 Feb. 1959, 1-A10-25, p. 2.
10 Li, *Dayuejin*, vol. 2, p. 233.
11 Report by Mao Qihua to the centre, Gansu, 4 Sept. 1960, zhongfa (60) 825, 91-18-154, pp. 99–106; the report estimated that, out of 13,000 casualties, about 5,000 happened in the mining industry.
12 Sichuan, 15 June to 19 Nov. 1962, JC1-3174, pp. 4–6.
13 Hunan, 4 Oct. 1959, 141-1-1258, pp. 12–13; July 1959, 141-1-1224, pp. 13–14.
14 Nanjing, Sept.–Oct. 1959, 5035-2-5, pp. 15–21; 3 Aug. 1961, 9046-1-4, pp. 47–54.
15 Nanjing, 12 Jan. 1959, 5003-3-721, pp. 1–7.
16 Nanjing, 9 Jan. 1959, 4003-1-171, p. 17.
17 Hunan, May 1959, 141-1-1258, pp. 63–4.
18 Hubei, 12 Sept. 1960, SZ34-4-477, pp. 70–81.
19 Gansu, 1 Nov. 1961, 91-9-215, p. 72.
20 Guangdong, 7 Aug. 1961, 219-2-319, pp. 56–68.
21 Gansu, 12 and 16 Jan. 1961, 91-18-200, pp. 32 and 84.

Chapter 32: Disease

1 Li, *Private Life of Chairman Mao*, pp. 339–40.
2 Nanjing, 7–10 Oct. 1961, 5065-3-467, pp. 33–7 and 58–61.
3 Wuhan, 11 Sept. 1959, 30-1-124, pp. 40–2; 22 June 1959, 28-1-650, pp. 27–8.
4 Sichuan, 18 Jan. 1961, JC1-2418, p. 2; also JC1-2419, p. 43.
5 Sichuan, 1961, JC1-2419, p. 46.
6 Sichuan, 1960, JC133-220, p. 137.
7 Guangdong, 30 Oct. 1961, 235-1-255, pp. 170 and 179; Shanghai, 28 July and 24 Aug. 1961, B242-1-1285, pp. 28–37 and 46–9.
8 Sichuan, 1960, JC1-2007, pp. 38–9.
9 A systematic analysis of all county gazetteers appears in Cao Shuji, *Da jihuang: 1959–1961 nian de Zhongguo renkou* (The Great Famine: China's population in 1959–1961), Hong Kong: Shidai guoji chuban youxian gongsi, 2005, and a good example is p. 128.
10 Hunan, 5 Jan. 1959, 141-1-1220, pp. 2–3; 1962, 265-1-309, pp. 4–5.

11 Nanjing, 6 April 1959, 4003-1-171, p. 138.
12 Nanjing, 25 Oct. 1959, 5003-3-727, pp. 19–21.
13 Hubei, 1961, SZ1-2-898, pp. 18–45.
14 Shanghai, 18 Oct. 1959, B242-1-1157, pp. 23–6.
15 Wuxi, 1961, B1-2-164, pp. 58–66.
16 Hubei, 25 Feb. and 7 July 1961, SZ1-2-898, pp. 7–11 and 45–9.
17 Hunan, 25 Nov. 1960, 265-1-260, p. 85; 8 Dec. 1960, 212-1-508, p. 163.
18 Nanjing, 27 Aug. 1959, 5003-3-727, p. 88.
19 Hubei, 6 June 1961, SZ1-2-906, p. 29; 21 July 1961, SZ1-2-898, pp. 49–52.
20 Nanjing, 3 April 1959, 5003-3-727, p. 67.
21 Wuhan, 19 Feb. 1962, 71-1-1400, pp. 18–21.
22 Guangdong, 1960, 217-1-645, pp. 60–4.
23 Guangdong, 1959, 217-1-69, pp. 95–100.
24 Zhejiang, 10 May 1960, J165-10-66, pp. 1–5.
25 Sichuan, 9 July 1960, JC133-219, p. 106.
26 Wuhan, 16 Aug. 1961, 71-1-1400, pp. 9–10.
27 Interview with Li Dajun, born 1947, Xixian county, Henan, Oct. 2006.
28 Nanjing, 1961, 5065-3-381, pp. 53–4.
29 Shanghai, 11 May 1961, B242-1-1285, pp. 1–3.
30 Wuhan, 30 June 1959, 30-1-124, pp. 31–3.
31 Wuhan, 1 July 1960, 28-1-650, p. 31.
32 Wuhan, 30 June 1959, 30-1-124, pp. 31–3.
33 Sichuan, 16 May 1960, JC1-2115, pp. 57–8.
34 Sichuan, 1960, JC1-2114, p. 8.
35 Sichuan, 1959, JC9-448, pp. 46–7.
36 Sichuan, 1959, all of JC44-2786.
37 Report from the Ministry of Health, Hubei, 24 April 1960, SZ115-2-355, pp. 10–13.
38 Hunan, 11 May 1960, 163-1-1082, pp. 26–8.
39 A good description appears in Jung Chang, *Wild Swans: Three Daughters of China*, Clearwater, FL: Touchstone, 2003, p. 232.
40 Warren Belasco, 'Algae Burgers for a Hungry World? The Rise and Fall of Chlorella Cuisine', *Technology and Culture*, vol. 38, no. 3 (July 1997), pp. 608–34.
41 Jean Pasqualini, *Prisoner of Mao*, Harmondsworth: Penguin, 1973, pp. 216–19.
42 Beijing, 1 Feb. 1961, 1-14-790, p. 109.
43 Barna Talás, 'China in the Early 1950s', in Näth, *Communist China in Retrospect*, pp. 58–9.
44 Interview with Yan Shifu, born 1948, Zhiyang, Sichuan, April 2007.
45 Interview with Zhu Erge, born 1950, Jianyang, Sichuan, April 2007.
46 Hebei, 30 April and Aug. 1960, 855-18-777, pp. 167–8; 855-18-778, pp. 124–5.
47 Reports from the Ministry of Health, Hubei, March and Dec. 1960, SZ115-2-355, pp. 12–15.
48 Beijing, 14 April 1961, 2-13-135, pp. 5–6.
49 Interview with Meng Xiaoli, born 1943, Qianjiang county, Hubei, Aug. 2006.

50 Interview with Zhao Xiaobai, born 1948, Lushan county, Henan, May and Dec. 2006.

51 Interview with Zhu Erge, born 1950, Jianyang, Sichuan, April 2007.

52 Beijing, 3 July 1961, 2-1-136, pp. 23–4.

53 Sichuan, 1960, JC133-219, p. 154.

54 Sichuan, Oct. 1961, JC1-2418, p. 168; 1962, JC44-1441, p. 27.

55 Sichuan, 31 Aug. 1961, JC1-2620, pp. 177–8.

56 Interview with He Guanghua, born 1940, Pingdingshan, Henan, Oct. 2006.

57 How hunger works is ably analysed in Sharman Apt Russell, *Hunger: An Unnatural History*, New York: Basic Books, 2005.

58 Wu Ningkun and Li Yikai, *A Single Tear: A Family's Persecution, Love, and Endurance in Communist China*, New York: Back Bay Books, 1994, p. 130.

59 Guangdong, 23 March 1961, 217-1-643, pp. 10–13.

60 Shanghai, Jan.–Feb. 1961, B242-1-1285, pp. 1–3 and 17–27.

61 Hebei, 1961, 878-1-7, pp. 12–14.

62 Hebei, 21 Jan. 1961, 855-19-855, p. 103.

Chapter 33: The Gulag

1 'Shanghai shi dongjiaoqu renmin fayuan xingshi panjueshu: 983 hao', private collection, Frank Dikötter.

2 Forty per cent were sentenced to a term of one to five years, 25 per cent were put under supervision; Nanjing, 8 June 1959, 5003-3-722, p. 83.

3 See Frank Dikötter, 'Crime and Punishment in Post-Liberation China: The Prisoners of a Beijing Gaol in the 1950s', *China Quarterly*, no. 149 (March 1997), pp. 147–59.

4 Papers from the tenth national conference on national security, Gansu, 8 April 1960, zhongfa (60) 318, 91-18-179, pp. 11–12.

5 Hebei, 1962, 884-1-223, p. 149.

6 Hebei, 23 Oct. 1960, 884-1-183, p. 4.

7 Guangdong, 1961, 216-1-252, pp. 5–7 and 20.

8 Gansu, 3 Feb. 1961, 91-18-200, pp. 291–2; the novelist Yang Xianhui vividly described the conditions in the camp on the basis of interviews with survivors, and estimated that 1,300 out of 2,400 prisoners perished, which is confirmed by the Gansu archives; Yang Xianhui, *Jiabiangou jishi: Yang Xianhui zhong-duan pian xiaoshuo jingxuan* (A record of Jiabian Valley: A selection of stories by Yang Xianhui), Tianjin: Tianjin guji chubanshe, 2002, p. 356.

9 Report from the provincial Public Security Bureau, Gansu, 26 June 1960, 91-9-63, pp. 1–4.

10 Gansu, 15 Jan. 1961, 91-18-200, p. 62.

11 Hebei, 1962, 884-1-223, p. 150.

12 Papers from the tenth national conference on national security, Gansu, 8 April 1960, zhongfa (60) 318, 91-18-179, p. 26.

13 Ibid.

14 Ibid., pp. 11–12.

15 Speech on 21 Aug. 1958, Hunan, 141-1-1036, p. 29.

16 Hebei, 27 June 1959, 884-1-183, p. 128.

17 Papers from the tenth national conference on national security, Gansu, 8 April 1960, zhongfa (60) 318, 91-18-179, p. 26.

18 Hebei, 16 April 1961, 884-1-202, pp. 35–47.

19 Yunnan, 22 May 1959, 2-1-3700, pp. 93–8.

20 Guangdong, 2 Jan. 1961, 217-1-643, pp. 61–6.

21 Kaiping, 22 Sept. 1960, 3-A10-31, p. 10.

22 *Neibu cankao*, 30 Nov. 1960, p. 16.

23 Guangdong, 15 Aug. 1961, 219-2-318, p. 120.

24 Beijing, 11 Jan. 1961, 1-14-790, p. 17.

25 This is also the estimate of Jean-Luc Domenach, who has written what remains the most detailed and reliable history of the camp system in China; Jean-Luc Domenach, *L'Archipel oublié*, Paris: Fayard, 1992, p. 242.

Chapter 34: Violence

1 Beijing, 13 May 1959, 1-14-574, pp. 38–40.

2 Interview with Li Popo, born 1938, Langzhong county, Sichuan, April 2007.

3 *Neibu cankao*, 27 June 1960, pp. 11–12.

4 Guangdong, 25 Jan. 1961, 217-1-645, p. 13.

5 Guangdong, 30 Dec. 1960, 217-1-576, p. 78.

6 Guangdong, 5 Feb. 1961, 217-1-645, pp. 35–49.

7 Hunan, 3 April 1961, 151-1-24, p. 6.

8 Hunan, 1960, 146-1-520, pp. 97–106.

9 Hunan, 8 April 1961, 146-1-583, p. 96.

10 Guangdong, 1960, 217-1-645, pp. 25–8.

11 Hebei, 4 Jan. 1961, 880-1-11, p. 30.

12 Hunan, 1960, 146-1-520, pp. 97–106.

13 Guangdong, 16 April 1961, 217-1-643, pp. 123–31; 25 Jan. 1961, 217-1-646, pp. 15–17.

14 Xinyang diwei zuzhi chuli bangongshi, 'Guanyu diwei changwu shuji Wang Dafu tongzhifan suo fan cuowu ji shishi cailiao', 5 Jan. 1962, pp. 1–2.

15 Guangdong, 16 April 1961, 217-1-643, pp. 123–31.

16 This happened in Rongxian; Sichuan, 1962, JC1-3047, pp. 37–8.

17 Guangdong, 16 April 1961, 217-1-643, pp. 123–31; 25 Jan. 1961, 217-1-646, pp. 15–17.

18 Guangdong, 23 March 1961, 217-1-643, pp. 10–13.

19 Hunan, 15 Nov. 1960, 141-1-1672, pp. 32–3.

20 *Neibu cankao*, 21 Oct. 1960, p. 12; Sichuan, 25 May 1959, JC1-1721, p. 3.

21 Guangdong, 23 March 1961, 217-1-643, pp. 10–13.

22 Guangdong, 1960, 217-1-645, pp. 60–4.

23 Hebei, 27 June 1961, 880-1-7, p. 55.

24 Sichuan, 27 Jan. 1961, JC1-2606, p. 65; 1960, JC1-2116, p. 105.

25 Guangdong, 12 Dec. 1960, 217-1-643, pp. 33–43.

26 Guangdong, 23 March 1961, 217-1-642, p. 33.

27 Guangdong, 1961, 217-1-644, pp. 32–8.

28 Guangdong, 29 Jan. 1961, 217-1-618, pp. 42–6; also Hebei, 27 June 1961, 880-1-7, p. 55.

29 Hunan, 3 and 14 April 1961, 151-1-24, pp. 1–13 and 59–68; also 3 Feb. 1961, 146-1-582, p. 22.

30 *Neibu cankao*, 21 Oct. 1960, p. 12.

31 Guangdong, 1960, 217-1-645, pp. 60–4.

32 *Neibu cankao*, 30 Nov. 1960, p. 17.

33 Hunan, 3 Feb. 1961, 146-1-582, p. 22.

34 Hunan, 10 Aug. 1961, 146-1-579, pp. 32–3.

35 Sichuan, 1960, JC1-2112, p. 4.

36 Guangdong, 16 April 1961, 217-1-643, pp. 123–31; 25 Jan. 1961, 217-1-646, pp. 15–17.

37 Guangdong, 1961, 217-1-644, pp. 32–8; 1961, 217-1-618, pp. 18–41, in particular pp. 21 and 35.

38 Hunan, 1961, 151-1-20, pp. 34–5.

39 Interview with Mr Leung, born 1949, Zhongshan county, Guangdong, 13 July 2006.

40 Guangdong, 1960, 217-1-645, pp. 60–4.

41 Hunan, 8 April 1961, 146-1-583, p. 96; also 12 May 1960, 146-1-520, pp. 69–75.

42 Hunan, Sept. 1959, 141-1-1117, pp. 1–4.

43 Macheng, 20 Jan. 1959, 1-1-378, p. 24; Guangdong, 1960, 217-1-645, pp. 60–4; *Neibu cankao*, 30 Nov. 1960, p. 17.

44 Beijing, 7 Jan. 1961, 1-14-790, p. 10.

45 Hunan, 1961, 151-1-20, pp. 34–5.

46 Guangdong, 1961, 217-1-644, pp. 32–8.

47 Report by Xu Qiwen, Hunan, 12 March 1961, 141-1-1899, pp. 216–22.

48 Yunnan, 9 Dec. 1960, 2-1-4157, p. 171.

49 Report by provincial party committee work team, Sichuan, 1961, JC1-2616, pp. 110–11.

50 Hunan, 15 Nov. 1960, 141-2-125, p. 1.

51 Hunan, 8 April 1961, 146-1-583, p. 95.

52 Report by Xu Qiwen, Hunan, 12 March 1961, 141-1-1899, p. 222.

53 Xinyang diwei zuzhi chuli bangongshi, 'Guanyu diwei changwu shuji Wang Dafu tongzhifan suo fan cuowu ji shishi cailiao', 5 Jan. 1962, pp. 1–2.

54 Sichuan, 5 Jan. 1961, JC1-2604, p. 35.

55 Speeches on 21 and 24 Aug. 1958, Hunan, 141-1-1036, pp. 24–5 and 31.

56 Speech by Li Jingquan on 5 April 1962, Sichuan, JC1-2809, p. 11.

57 Hunan, 4 Feb. 1961, 151-1-20, p. 14.

58 Hunan, 1961, 151-1-20, pp. 34–5.

59 Report from central inspection committee, Hunan, 15 Nov. 1960, 141-2-125, p. 3.

60 Sichuan, 29 Nov. 1960, JC1-2109, p. 118.

61 Hunan, 4 Feb. 1961, 151-1-20, p. 14.

62 Ibid., pp. 12–13.

63 Yunnan, 9 Dec. 1960, 2-1-4157, p. 170.

64 Guangdong, 1961, 217-1-644, pp. 32–8.

65 Sichuan, 2 May 1960, JC1-2109, pp. 10 and 51.

66 Sichuan, 1961, JC1-2610, p. 4.

67 Interview with Wei Shu, born 1920s, Langzhong county, Sichuan, April 2006.

68 Sichuan, 1960, JC133-219, pp. 49 and 131.

69 Adam Tooze, *The Wages of Destruction: The Making and Breaking of the Nazi Economy*, New York: Allen Lane, 2006, pp. 530–1.

70 Guangdong, 8 May 1960, 217-1-575, pp. 26–8.

71 Sichuan, 3 May 1959, JC1-1686, p. 43.

72 Yunnan, 22 May 1959, 2-1-3700, pp. 93–4.

73 Guangdong, 5 Feb. 1961, 217-1-119, p. 44.

74 Guangdong, 2 Jan. 1961, 217-1-643, pp. 61–6.

75 Kaiping, 6 June 1959, 3-A9-80, p. 6.

76 Nanjing, 15 Sept. 1959, 5003-3-721, p. 70.

77 Nanjing, 8 May 1959, 5003-3-721, p. 12.

Chapter 35: Sites of Horror

1   Hunan, 6 Aug. 1961, 146-1-579, pp. 5–6.

2   Material quoted in Yang, *Mubei*, pp. 901–3.

3   Gansu, 5 July 1965, 91-5-501, pp. 4–5.

4   Ibid., p. 24.

5   Ibid., pp. 5–7.

6   Ibid., p. 7.

7   Gansu, 12 Jan. 1961, 91-4-735, p. 79.

8   Gansu, 10 Feb. 1960, 91-4-648, entire file; 24 March 1960, 91-4-647, entire file.

9   Gansu, 21 April 1960, 91-18-164, pp. 153–60.

10 Sichuan, 1961, JC1-2608, pp. 1–3 and 21–2; 1961, JC1-2605, pp. 147–55.

11 Sichuan, 1961, JC1-2605, p. 171.

12 Sichuan, 1961, JC1-2606, pp. 2–3.

13 Reports by Yang Wanxuan, Sichuan, 22 and 27 Jan. 1961, JC1-2606, pp. 48–9 and 63–4; also 25 and 27 Jan. 1961, JC1-2608, pp. 83–8 and 89–90.

14 Sichuan, 8 Dec. 1958, JC1-1804, pp. 35–7.

15 Sichuan, 4 April 1961, JC12-1247, pp. 7–14.

16 Report from the supervisory committee, Chishui, 1961, 2-A6-2, pp. 25–6.

17 Chishui, 30 Sept. 1958, 1-A9-4, pp. 30–1; 14 Jan. 1961, 1-A12-1, pp. 83–7; Dec. 1960, 1-A11-30, pp. 67–71; also 25 April 1960, 1-A11-39, pp. 11–15.

18 Chishui, 9 May 1960, 1-A11-9, pp. 5–9.

19 Guizhou, 1960, 90-1-2234, p. 24.

20 Guizhou, 1962, 90-1-2708, printed pages 1–6.

21 Chishui, 9 May 1960, 1-A11-9, pp. 5–9.

22 Letter from Nie Rongzhen to Mao Zedong sent from Chengdu, Gansu, 16 March 1960, 91-9-134, p. 2.

23 Shandong, 1962, A1-2-1130, pp. 39–44.

24 Shandong, 1962, A1-2-1127, pp. 7–11.

25 Report by Tan Qilong to Shu Tong and Mao Zedong, Shandong, 11 April 1959, A1-1-465, p. 25.

26 Confession by Shu Tong, Shandong, 10 Dec. 1960, A1-1-634, p. 23.

27 Ibid., p. 9.

28 Letter by Yang Xuanwu on Shu Tong to the provincial party committee, Shandong, 9 April 1961, A1-2-980, p. 15; see also 1961, A1-2-1025, pp. 9–10.

29 This is the estimate of a group of official party historians from Fuyang: Fuyang shiwei dangshi yanjiushi (eds), *Zhengtu: Fuyang shehuizhuyi shiqi dangshi zhuanti huibian* (Compendium of special topics on the party history of Fuyang during the socialist era), Fuyang: Anhui jingshi wenhua chuanbo youxian zeren gongsi, 2007, p. 155.

30 Fuyang, 17 Aug. 1961, J3-2-280, p. 114.

31 Fuyang, 12 March 1961, J3-1-228, p. 20; 18 Aug. 1961, J3-2-280, p. 126.

32 Fuyang, 10 Jan. 1961, J3-2-278, p. 85.

33 Ibid., p. 86.

34 Fuyang, 12 Aug. 1961, J3-1-228, p. 96b.

35 Fuyang, 17 Aug. 1961, J3-2-280, p. 115.

36 Fuyang, 10 Jan. 1961, J3-2-278, p. 86.

37 Fuyang, 30 Jan. 1961, J3-2-278, pp. 2–9.

38 Confession by Hao Ruyi, leader of Jieshou, Fuyang, 10 Jan. 1961, J3-2-280, p. 48.

39 Ibid.

40 Confession by Zhao Song, leader of Linquan, 15 Feb. 1961, Fuyang, J3-2-280, p. 91.

41 Fuyang, 6 Jan. 1961, J3-1-227, pp. 54–5.

42 Fuyang, 12 June 1961, J3-2-279, p. 15.

43 Fuyang, 20 March 1961, J3-2-278, pp. 67 and 69.

44 Ibid.

45 Fuyang, 29 Feb. 1961, J3-2-278, p. 64.

46 Report from party secretary Liu Daoqian to the regional party committee, Fuyang, 6 Jan. 1961, J3-1-227, pp. 54–5.

Chapter 36: Cannibalism

1 Yunnan, 28 Feb. 1959, 2-1-3700, p. 103.

2 Guangdong, 1961, 217-1-646, pp. 25–30.

3 Xili county was a combination, at the time, of Lixian county and Xihe county; police report to the Ministry of Public Security, Gansu, 13 April 1961, 91-9-215, p. 94.

4 Ibid.

5 Report by work group sent by the provincial party committee, Shandong, 1961, A1-2-1025, p. 7.

6 Confession by Zhang Zhongliang, Gansu, 3 Dec. 1960, 91-18-140, p. 19.

7 Confession by Shu Tong, Shandong, 10 Dec. 1960, A1-1-634, p. 10.

8 Minutes of county party committee meeting, Chishui, 9 Dec. 1960, 1-A11-34, pp. 83 and 96.

9 *Neibu cankao*, 14 April 1960, pp. 25–6.

10 Gansu, Jan.–Feb. 1961, 91-18-200, p. 271.

11 Gansu, 3 March 1961, 91-4-898, pp. 82–7.

12 Sichuan, 1961, JC1-2608, pp. 93 and 96–7.

13 Very much the same happened in the Soviet Union; see Bertrand M. Patenaude, *The Big Show in Bololand: The American Relief Expedition to Soviet Russia in the Famine of 1921*, Stanford: Stanford University Press, 2002, p. 262.

Chapter 37: The Final Tally

1 Basil Ashton, Kenneth Hill, Alan Piazza and Robin Zeitz, 'Famine in China, 1958–61', *Population and Development Review*, vol. 10, no. 4 (Dec. 1984), pp. 613–45.

2 Judith Banister, 'An Analysis of Recent Data on the Population of China', *Population and Development Review*, vol. 10, no. 2 (June 1984), pp. 241–71.

3 Peng Xizhe, 'Demographic Consequences of the Great Leap Forward in China's Provinces', *Population and Development Review*, vol. 13, no. 4 (Dec. 1987), pp. 639–70; Chang and Holliday, *Mao*, p. 438.

4 Yang, *Mubei*, p. 904.

5 Cao, *Da jihuang*, p. 281.

6 Becker, *Hungry Ghosts*, pp. 271–2.

7 Hubei, 1962, SZ34-5-143, entire file.

8 Hubei, March 1962, SZ34-5-16, p. 43.

9 Gansu, 16 March 1962, 91-9-274, p. 1; followed by a reminder sent on 24 May 1962 on p. 5.

10 Fuyang, 1961, J3-1-235, p. 34.

11 Sichuan, Nov.–Dec. 1961, JC1-2756, p. 54.

12 Sichuan, Oct. 1961, JC1-2418, p. 106.

13 Sichuan, 2 Nov. 1959, JC1-1808, p. 166.

14 Hebei, 10 Jan. 1961, 856-1-221, pp. 31–2; 17 Dec. 1960, 858-18-777, pp. 96–7.

15 Hebei, 29 Dec. 1960, 855-18-777, pp. 126–7.

16 Sichuan, May–June 1962, JC67-4; also in JC67-1003, p. 3.

17 Sichuan, 23 Feb. 1963, JC67-112, pp. 9–12.

18 Yunnan, 16 May 1959, 81-4-25, p. 17; for the average death rate in 1957 see *Zhongguo tongji nianjian, 1984*, Beijing: Zhongguo tongji chubanshe, 1984, p. 83; Cao, *Da jihuang*, p. 191.

19 Speech by Liu Shaoqi, May 1961, Hunan, 141-1-1901, p. 120.

20 Hebei, 21 Jan. 1961, 855-19-855, pp. 100–4; on Hu Kaiming, see Yu, *Dayuejin ku rizi*, pp. 451–75.

21 Cao, *Da jihuang*, p. 234.

22 Hebei, 19 Jan. 1961, 878-1-7, pp. 1–4; Cao, *Da jihuang*, p. 246.

23 Hebei, 19 Jan. 1961, 878-1-7, pp. 1–4; Cao, *Da jihuang*, pp. 240 and 246.

24 Gansu, Jan.–Feb. 1961, 91-18-200, p. 57; Cao, *Da jihuang*, pp. 271 and 465.

25 Gansu, Jan.–Feb. 1961, 91-18-200, p. 94; Cao, *Da jihuang*, p. 273.

26 Gansu, Jan.–Feb. 1961, 91-18-200, p. 107; Cao, *Da jihuang*, p. 275.

27 Gansu, Jan.–Feb. 1961, 91-18-200, p. 45; Cao, *Da jihuang*, p. 275.

28 Guizhou, 1962, 90-1-2706, printed page 19.

29 Chishui, 14 Jan. 1961, 1-A12-1, pp. 83–7; Dec. 1960, 1-A11-30, pp. 67–71; Cao, *Da jihuang*, p. 158.

30 Chishui, 9 May 1960, 1-A11-9, pp. 5–9; Cao, *Da jihuang*, p. 164.

31 Report on Yanhe county, Guizhou, 1961, 90-1-2270, printed page 1; Cao mentions 24,000 premature deaths for the Tongren region as a whole; Cao, *Da jihuang*, p. 166.

32 Shandong, 1962, A1-2-1127, p. 46; Cao, *Da jihuang*, p. 219.

33 Shandong, 1962, A1-2-1130, p. 42.

34 Shandong, 7 June 1961, A1-2-1209, p. 110; Cao, *Da jihuang*, p. 231.

35 Guangdong, 1961, 217-1-644, p. 72; Cao, *Da jihuang*, p. 129.

36 Guangdong, 20 Jan. 1961, 217-1-644, p. 61; Cao, *Da jihuang*, pp. 126–8.

37 Hunan, June and 28 Aug. 1964, 141-1-2494, pp. 74 and 81–2.

38 Ministry of Public Security report on population statistics, 16 Nov. 1963, Chishui, 1-A14-15, pp. 2–3.

39 Report by Central Census Office, 26 May 1964, Chishui, 1-A15-15, pp. 6–7.

40 Becker, *Hungry Ghosts*, p. 272.

41 Yu, *Dayuejin ku rizi*, p. 8.

Epilogue

1 Liu's speech on 27 Jan. 1962, Gansu, 91-18-493, pp. 58–60 and 62.

2 Li, *Private Life of Chairman Mao*, p. 386.

3 Lin Biao speech, Gansu, 29 Jan. 1962, 91-18-493, pp. 163–4.

4 Zhou Enlai speech, Gansu, 7 Feb. 1962, 91-18-493, p. 87.

5 Liu Yuan, 'Mao Zedong wei shenma yao dadao Liu Shaoqi', quoted in Gao, *Zhou Enlai*, pp. 97–8. For a slightly different version from Liu's wife, see Huang, *Wang Guangmei fangtan lu*, p. 288.

Index

A NOTE ON THE TYPE

The text of this book is set in Adobe Garamond. It is one of several versions of Garamond based on the designs of Claude Garamond. It is thought that Garamond based his font on Bembo, cut in 1495 by Francesco Griffo in collaboration with the Italian printer Aldus Manutius. Garamond types were first used in books printed in Paris around 1532. Many of the present-day versions of this type are based on the *Typi Academiae* of Jean Jannon cut in Sedan in 1615.

Claude Garamond was born in Paris in 1480. He learned how to cut type from his father and by the age of fifteen he was able to fashion steel punches the size of a pica with great precision. At the age of sixty he was commissioned by King Francis I to design a Greek alphabet; for this he was given the honourable title of royal type founder. He died in 1561.